PRAISE FOR
GRAYSTON L. LYNCH'S
SHOCKING EYEWITNESS ACCOUNT
OF THE BAY OF PIGS INVASION

DECISION FOR DISASTER

"Grabs and retains the reader's attention with fast-paced action, convincing tactical commentary, tales of bravery, a few accounts of cowardice, and the story of a brutal, tragic end to the enterprise. . . . Thought provoking [and] highly recommended."

—*Military History Quarterly*

"Lynch was there at the Bay of Pigs and was in perfect position to write the definitive ground-level account of what went right and what went wrong. . . . This is not a book for those who love [Kennedy's] Camelot."

—Seymour M. Hersh,
author of *The Dark Side of Camelot*

"A welcome addition to the literature on the subject."   —*Military Intelligence*

"Excellent."   —Latin American News Syndicate

"Devastating."   —*The American Spectator*

DECISION FOR DISASTER

THE BATTLE OF THE BAY OF PIGS

GRAYSTON L. LYNCH

POCKET BOOKS
New York   London   Toronto   Sydney   Singapore

POCKET BOOKS, a division of Simon & Schuster, Inc.
1230 Avenue of the Americas, New York, NY 10020

ISBN: 0-7434-7428-7

First Pocket Books paperback edition December 2003

10 9 8 7 6 5 4 3 2 1

POCKET and colophon are registered trademarks of Simon & Schuster, Inc.

Cover design by Rod Hernandez
Front cover photo © Bettmann/Corbis

Manufactured in the United States of America

For information regarding special discounts for bulk purchases, please contact Simon & Schuster Special Sales at 1-800-456-6798 or business@simonandschuster.com

This book is dedicated to William "Rip" Robertson. He served his country well. A most extraordinary man, the likes of whom we shall not see again. For he was the last of the "old breed."

To

The men of the 2506 Assault Brigade. They fought like tigers in a battle they did not realize was lost before it began—but a battle fought for a cause they knew could never be lost.

And, finally, to the memory of

LEO F. BAKER
WADE C. GRAY
THOMAS W. RAY
and
RILEY W. SHAMBURGER

Four gallant Americans who found a cause worth dying for, and because they believed in that cause, they did not die in vain.

Acknowledgments

IT HAS TAKEN ME OVER THIRTY-FIVE YEARS TO WRITE THIS book. Not only were some of the facts classified, but the events that took place that April of 1961 have also been a heavy emotional burden for me, making writing about them extremely difficult. In fact, without the understanding of my wife, Karen, and her constant encouragement and invaluable assistance throughout the writing process, this book would never have gone on to completion. It was her skill as a writer that turned my words into the finished product you see before you.

I would also like to thank two people who were invaluable in editing this manuscript: Jerry Gross of Gross Associate, Inc., my personal editor, my severest critic, and my friend; and John Piesen, a successful writer in his own right and a friend, who did the grammatical editing.

I would also like to thank the many people who

lent me their knowledge of situations I was not privy to, especially Richard M. Bissell, Jr., the late Admiral Arleigh R. Burke, Marine Colonel Jack Hawkins, and the men of the 2506 Assault Brigade for their open and candid descriptions of what they saw and what they did.

"FOR THE GREATEST ENEMY OF THE TRUTH
IS VERY OFTEN NOT THE LIE,
DELIBERATE, CONTRIVED AND DISHONEST,
BUT THE *MYTH*,
PERSISTENT, PERVASIVE AND UNREALISTIC."

John F. Kennedy
Yale University
June 11, 1962

Contents

Contents

List of Maps

Preface

MANY YEARS HAVE PASSED SINCE THAT NIGHT IN APRIL 1961 when a brigade of brave and determined Cubans stormed ashore in Cochinos Bay in the midnight darkness in a desperate bid to rid their country of Fidel Castro and Soviet Communism.

This event has become known as the Bay of Pigs Invasion. Much has been written about it, enough to ensure its proper niche in history had it been told correctly, but it was not. The true story has never been told, and history does not easily accept half-truths and incomplete accounts in its final recording of human events.

Because after the invasion I was deeply involved in the effort to oust Castro, I had hoped that eventually someone else would break the silence and erase the misconceptions that have obscured the facts. This has not been done, and I feel I can wait no longer, for I am the sole surviving American who both knows the story and lived it. It is for that reason that I feel I must now record as well as I can the complete and factual account of how this event occurred and why the United States found itself, on that April night, involved in the full support of a clandestine effort to remove Fidel Castro's Communist government from Cuba by force of arms.

There were two Americans in Cochinos Bay on that night, agents of the Central Intelligence Agency, whose mission was to act as American representatives to the 2506 Assault Brigade and as insurance against any mishap that might endanger the effort. These two agents were William "Rip" Robertson, a tall, rugged Texan who was to become a legend in the clandestine services, and me. Our role in this event would not have been of any great significance had the operation been conducted as planned. But when the invasion began to run into trouble, our roles were suddenly changed and we were thrust directly into the center of the action.

These actions at Cochinos Bay culminated several days later in complete disaster—a disaster that would have grave consequences for the 2506 Assault Brigade, for the United States, and for the people of Cuba. This failure reverberated around the world, and the Bay of Pigs Invasion has since become a symbol of failure—the failure not just of a band of gallant, freedom-loving Cubans but also of the will and determination of the United States of America.

The 2506 Assault Brigade fought hard to prevent

this disaster, but, as we were to discover later, no amount of effort on its part could have prevented it, for this invasion was doomed long before the men of the brigade first sighted the dim outlines of Cochinos Bay.

This disaster raised many questions, questions that until now have never been answered to the full satisfaction of most Americans. In this book I have attempted to answer them: to explain how it happened, why it happened, and, most important, why it failed. There are those who, for various reasons, will not accept my answers, but they are, nevertheless, the true facts of the case, and no amount of challenge or denial can change them.

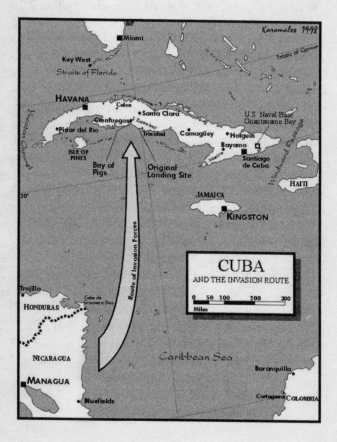

Karamales 1998

Miami

Key West
Straits of Florida

HAVANA

Colon
• Santa Clara
Cienfuegos•   Escambray

•Pinar del Rio   Trinidad   • Camagüey

U.S. Naval Base
Guantanamo Bay

• Holguin
Bayamo

ISLE OF
PINES

Bay of
Pigs

Maestre

Santiago
de Cuba

Original
Landing Site

HAITI

Windward Passage

Yucatan Channel

JAMAICA

KINGSTON

Tropic of Cancer

20°

Route of Invasion Forces

CUBA
AND THE INVASION ROUTE

0   50 100   200   300

Miles

Trujillo

HONDURAS

Cabo de
Gracias a Dios

Caribbean Sea

NICARAGUA

MANAGUA

• Bluefields

Baranquilla

Cartagena COLOMBIA

of lights on the far horizon that marked their landing point, Blue Beach, Playa Girón. The appearance of these men and their dress might have seemed outlandish in a different setting, but their dark green combat clothing and the array of deadly weapons and knives each carried were completely appropriate to the task that lay ahead of them, for these men were the spearhead of the invasion by the 2506 Assault Brigade. They were set to go ashore a half hour ahead of the first wave of landing craft to scout and mark with signal lights the portion of the coast designated on the charts as Blue Beach.

Strung out in a column behind the *Blagar* were the other five ships and seven assault landing craft carrying the remaining fifteen hundred Cuban exiles who made up the 2506 Assault Brigade—a brigade that had been formed, trained, and equipped for this invasion by the Central Intelligence Agency, acting under direct orders of the president of the United States, John F. Kennedy.

We were now less than two hours from a landing that would begin an effort, over a year in the making, to overthrow the Communist-dominated government of Fidel Castro. This effort, if it succeeded, would mean for the men of this "light brigade" the liberation of their homeland and an opportunity to establish a truly free, democratic form of government in Cuba. For the United States, it would mean this and more. Our interest went deeper than just the return of freedom to Cuba. It concerned the freedom of the entire Western Hemisphere and our national security.

This security was threatened by the now obvious fact that the revolutionary government of Fidel Castro was rapidly being converted into a Communist dictatorship. The Soviet Union was at the point of gaining the strategic foothold in the Western Hemisphere that it had sought for so long, a foothold that the United States had warned it would not tolerate.

The opportunity for this foothold, ninety miles off the coast of the United States, was the result of an effort similar to ours that had been staged four years earlier. On December 2, 1956, Castro and a small group of followers landed in Oriente Province. His invasion could in no way compare in power and potential to the 2506 Brigade's effort, for Castro could not even pinpoint his landing beach on radar, because he had none. His force had not been in a convoy over a mile in length, as was ours. The old, leaky, sixty-two-foot yacht *Granma* was his convoy, and his force totaled eighty-three men.

Their voyage from Mexico to Cuba, which was plagued by seasickness, had taken over a week. On their arrival, another three hours of searching up and down the coast of Oriente was necessary before their navigator could locate their landing point. He further complicated the problem by falling overboard.

After losing another hour locating and pulling this latter-day Magellan back aboard, the captain settled the selection of their landing site by running the old yacht hard aground on a mudbank directly in front of a mangrove swamp. Since daylight was near, Castro's band had no choice but to disembark and plow their way through the swamps to terra firma. True to his run of luck, Castro and his men arrived on this firm ground just as one of Cuban President Fulgencio Batista's patrolling B-26 bombers arrived on the scene. It proceeded to shoot up the *Granma* and the invading force. It was joined by several other B-26s, and the aircraft prevented the invaders from unloading any of their supplies.

The arrival of a large force of Batista's men soon had Castro's men on the run, and they stayed on the run until late in the afternoon, when Batista's troops surrounded them in a canefield. When the battle was over, only twelve of Castro's eighty-three men remained. The others were dead or captured.

As darkness fell, the survivors—including Castro and his younger brother, Raúl, and Ché Guevera and Camilo Cienfuegos—slipped through the encircling troops and escaped into the nearby Sierra Maestra. They had no food or supplies, and their only weapons were those that each man had carried during the day-long running fight with Batista's troops. It was not a very good start for an effort ballyhooed by Castro as an invasion of a liberating army of the masses.

During its first month of wandering through the Sierra Maestra, the Rebel Army was reduced from twelve to nine men, and most of their efforts were directed toward obtaining enough food to stay alive until they could get around to the task of liberating Cuba. Three months after the near disaster

4

of their landing, Castro's band had, as a result of a vigorous recruiting campaign, been able to double its strength. It now numbered a formidable eighteen.

Castro did have a few contacts in Santiago and Havana. He instructed these outside supporters to bring to his camp in the mountains the most gullible American news reporter they could find. This was a fairly easy task, for the Havana contacts had the perfect man already spotted. His name was Herbert Matthews, of the prestigious *New York Times.*

They brought Matthews to Oriente Province in late February 1957, after first exposing him to some razzle-dazzle spook maneuvers of mysterious contacts in the night and whispered code words. By the time Matthews reached the Sierra Maestra, he was thoroughly convinced that he was in the hands of a veritable network of James Bonds and that if he made a sound above a whisper, Batista's entire forty-thousand-man army would jump out of the nearest bush and fill him full of bullet holes for consorting with their "Enemy Número Uno," the mighty Castro.

This strain on Matthews's nerves could have been avoided if he had bothered to check with Batista's army prior to his danger-fraught journey to the mountains. Not only were Batista's men not looking for Castro, they didn't even know he existed. After the battle of the canefield, the Havana headquarters for Batista's army had announced that

Castro had been killed and his entire band wiped out.

Matthews quickly brought Castro back to life, in a big way. Matthews wrote a series of editions, based on his interview with Castro, and the *Times* gave them top billing in its Sunday edition. They were quickly picked up by news services around the world. This brought instant fame to the Robin Hood of the Sierra Maestra, as Matthews described Castro. The contents of the interview made Castro look ten feet tall.

Matthews described, in the best manner of a Broadway public relations firm, an army and a war that did not exist. He wrote of the forty men Castro had in his camp, and of bands of similar size that he "knew were close by." In addition, he described a network of guerrillas, spread throughout the mountains, that enabled Castro to maintain "complete mastery of the Sierra Maestra." This would have been rather difficult for Castro, since at the time, as he later admitted, he had only eighteen men under his command. He may not have had complete mastery over the Sierra Maestra, but he did over Herbert Matthews, and this was worth more than ten thousand men.

The publicity generated by Matthews's articles focused world attention on "El Barbudo," the bearded one, as Castro was known. Soon a parade of newsmen began to trudge up the slopes of Pico Turquino, the site of Castro's press camp. At times the interviewers even outnumbered the interviewees. By the time the stories appeared in print, the Rebel Army of Fidel Castro, as it was called, not only controlled the Sierra Maestra but was defeating Batista's army in great battles that threatened all of Cuba.

These accounts of "great battles" had, of course, come straight out of Castro's own communiqués. If they had been reduced to their proper proportion, they would have ranked somewhere just below a quiet Sunday in Chicago during the Al Capone era. Real or imgined, they went down in history books as Castro victories.

A little more than a year after Matthews's first article appeared, Castro started to believe his own press releases. He declared "total war" on Batista. He called for general strikes, supported by military actions, to take place on April 9, 1958. The Cuban people, who presumably had not read the *Times*, generally ignored the call to arms. There was a small, limited strike that was suppressed by Batista, but no general strike, no military actions. Castro was hardly in a position to begin military actions. In the sixteen months he had been waging the "Great War," his forces had reached a grand total of 180 men, hardly what one would have gathered from Matthews.

But Matthews's articles touting Castro's fame and high ideals had been believed by many Americans. They had made him better known in the United States than he was in Cuba. Among the Americans who were taking an interest in Castro were two men who could do him more good than even the faithful Matthews, they were high and influential officials of the U.S. State Department—Roy Rubottom, assistant secretary of state for Latin American affairs, and his assistant William Wieland, director of the Office of Middle American Affairs, the section of the State Department that was directly responsible for the relations between the United States and Cuba. Rubottom and Wieland did more to bring Castro from his mountain hideout to the Presidential Palace in Havana than the Rebel Army could have hoped to accomplish.

Rubottom and Wieland, impatient with Castro's lack of success, decided that if he could not generate enough support inside Cuba to overthrow Batista, they would simply force the dictator out. And they did. In less than one year, their concentrated efforts against Batista did the job. They distorted or blocked reports that did not support their position and started such a campaign of unfounded charges against Batista that they made him seem something of a combination of Hitler, Attila the Hun, and Ivan the Terrible.

Castro, on the other hand, received nothing but praise. Grossly inflated reports of his strength and support convinced the U.S. government that it might be better for all concerned if Batista went into quiet exile somewhere. The State Department communicated this opinion to Batista in late December 1958. He took the advice, packing his bags with all the loot they could hold. Then, just after dark on New Year's Day 1959, Batista departed Havana for the Dominican Republic with several planeloads of his close associates. He continued on to Spain to "suffer" his exile.

Rubottom and Wieland had done their work with such speed that Castro was caught flat-footed when the news of Batista's sudden departure reached him. Castro was totally unprepared to take over Oriente Province, let alone all of Cuba. He was also uncertain of the reception he would receive in Havana if he rushed in to claim the empty office of the president. After thinking this possibly dangerous maneuver over, he decided to play it safe.

On the day following Batista's departure, Castro led his men down out of the Sierra Maestra and captured unresisting Santiago, which he promptly proclaimed the new capital of Cuba. This move did not go over well in the rest of the country, so Castro's followers quickly headed him toward the proper capital, Havana. But because of his great fear of being rejected there, his march of triumph was deliberately slowed to a snail's pace. It took him a full week to complete the six-hundred-mile journey.

Castro's fears of not being well received in Havana were, as it turned out, completely unfounded, for upon his arrival the people of Cuba went wild with joy, as only uninhibited Cubans can. They greeted him as though he were indeed the great savior of Cuba that Matthews, Rubottom, and Wieland had claimed he was. In fact, the people of Cuba were so happy to see Batista leave that they took the *Times* at its word, accepting Castro and his scruffy army of *barbudos* as the answer to all their prayers, the salvation of Cuba.

They remembered his ringing manifesto of the Sierra Maestra and the democratic ideals that he embraced. In this manifesto, broadcast over his rebel radio, Castro had promised free elections, a free press, freedom of speech, a fair and impartial system of justice, a fair land reform program. He also promised a return to Cuba's Constitution of 1940, which contained all the guarantees of freedom and true democracy in government that had been so sadly lacking in this troubled land. All these things and more Castro promised.

Castro accepted the accolades of a people caught in heady, uninhibited celebration of their new freedom. Responding in the same jubilant and impassioned spirit, he told the people of Cuba what they wanted to hear. His speeches were filled with promises of a new and shining era. He spoke of a new Cuba, a free, democratic nation, dedicated to the dignity of man, founded on the principles of the nineteenth-century Cuban patriot José Martí.

The Cubans loved it, and they loved their new Maximum Leader, Fidel Castro. He exuded charm and charisma. The people were fascinated by him. They quickly discovered that he was an accomplished speaker, a superb orator. What they were yet to discover was that he was also an accomplished liar and superb con artist.

Castro was withholding some very important facts

from the people of Cuba. He had no intention of carrying out his promise of establishing a free, democratic Cuba. He did not believe in the principles of democracy. Instead, he was a follower of the teachings and beliefs of Karl Marx. In other words, Castro was a Communist. He intended to make Cuba an enemy of the United States and an ally of the Soviet Union. Cuba was to become a Soviet satellite.

It was not until December 2, 1961, that Castro, on both Cuban radio and TV, would finally reveal his political philosophy to the people of Cuba. In a speech celebrating his "glorious landing" at Oriente, he stated for the first time, "I am a Marxist-Leninist, and I will be a Marxist-Leninist to the last day of my life. Did I believe in Marxism on the first of January, 1959 [when he came to power]? I did believe on the first of January. Did I believe on the twenty-sixth of July [when he attacked the Moncada barracks in Santiago in 1953]? I did believe on the twenty-sixth of July. Do I have any doubts about Marxism? I have not the least doubt."

This statement left no doubt in the minds of the Cuban people that what the swell of opposition to Castro had been claiming was all too true. He was indeed a Communist.

Castro went on to explain why he had not revealed his true beliefs before coming to power. He said, "If we had paused to tell the people we were Marxist-Leninists while we were on Pico Turquino, and not yet strong, it is possible that we would never have been able to descend to the plains."

These were the beliefs of Castro, but, in 1959, they had not as yet been revealed. His opponents saw many indications of his true intentions and tried to warn the Cuban people of the danger that his power posed for the future. They were not successful. It was too early. The people of Cuba could not believe that they had fought and sacrificed for so long only to exchange one dictator for another.

Castro's critics, in those first months of his regime, were branded as traitors to the revolution and *batistianos*. They were neither. Many had been ardent supporters of Castro and had fought Batista longer and harder than Castro ever had. Their opposition to Castro brought down on them the full fury of the mighty pen of Matthews, and the scorn of Rubottom and Wieland in the State Department in Washington. How dare they attack the Savior of Cuba, whom they had labored so hard to build up and install as the Maximum Leader in Havana?

Many influential Americans were also taken in by Castro's promises. Among them was Senator John F. Kennedy. Kennedy described Castro in his book *The Strategy of Peace* as "part of the legacy of Simón Bólivar."

Some looked upon Castro as the great liberator. But many considered him the most brutal and dangerous of a long line of dictators to plague Cuba since its beginning. To these men, the replacement of a corrupt dictator such as Batista, who had no outside support and very little support inside Cuba, with another dictator, who had a large and vocal following and the full support of the Soviet Union, was no gain for anyone. What the Castro apologists had pointedly overlooked was that there had been other alternatives. There were several Cubans who could have taken over the country. But they had been warned that if they attempted such a move, they could not expect support from the U.S. State Department. None of them had tried, since they were well aware that without U.S. backing, no one could hope to retain power for long in Cuba.

Castro was also aware that he must not alienate the State Department until he was firmly in control of the sources of the power in Cuba. He gave them all the required lip service. He did not, however, fare as well with the American public. This group of former supporters was not blinded by his famous charisma, as were Matthews, Rubottom, and Wieland. They were quick to note that there was a large gap between Castro's public statements and his actions. They were especially revolted by his "revolutionary justice."

Although his "two-year war" with Batista had been relatively bloodless, only 867 persons having lost their lives on both sides, Castro, it appeared, was determined to make up for it. He did so by executing as many "enemies of the revolution" as his firing squads could handle. In the first three months of his regime, Castro topped the 867 figure with room to spare. He was given yeoman support in this effort by his younger brother, Raúl, who executed more than 250 "enemies" in Santiago in the first week of his brother's "New Order" in Cuba.

It was not just the executions themselves that the American public objected to, but also the manner in which his so-called Tribunals of Revolutionary Justice were conducting their trials. The most notable of the many "enemies" he brought to his tribunal were accorded public trials in the Havana Sports Arena. These public trials were held under conditions comparable to those experienced by the persecuted Christians in the Roman Colosseum.

In addition, private property was being seized without due process of law, and foreign-owned companies were expropriated without compensation.

A small group of spokesmen for Castro now emerged. They were his admirers and supporters. Although many of them were good and sincere men, puzzled by the events taking place in Cuba, their belief in Castro was so strong that they searched for ways to justify these brutal and fearful events. They tried to explain that all of Castro's actions were necessary in order to rid Cuba of the Batista criminals and to return the wealth and commerce of Cuba to the Cuban people.

These apologists for Castro slowly dwindled in number until only a small group of diehard supporters remained. The most vocal of these continued to be Matthews.

He wrote in a *New York Times* article, "Fidel knows exactly what he is doing, just be patient because soon the unpleasant, but necessary part of the Revolution will be over. He can then begin to do those things that mean the most to him. He can then begin the building of a new Cuba. Fidel does not yet have control of the situation that he knows he must have. Some of his men have done things they should not have done, but he is taking steps to put a stop to that. Be patient and you will see this will come to pass."

The world waited patiently, and sure enough, what Matthews had said all came true. Castro did tighten his control and he did build a new Cuba. The only problem was that under the new tight control, Castro alone made the decisions—decisions that were not questioned. And the new Cuba that he built was so rigidly Communist and so oppressive that in comparison the citizens of Moscow could have been envied as free men.

Castro's rebuilding of Cuba resulted in Cuba's descent from its position as number three in economic power among all Latin American countries to just above the bottom country, Haiti.

More than five thousand Cubans would meet their death at the *paredón*, the firing wall. Another fifty thousand would jam to overflowing the old Spanish prisons, considered to be among the most archaic and brutal in the world. Yet another eight hundred thousand would flee the new paradise in any manner they could. A lucky few secured commercial airline tickets, but many were forced to make the ninety-mile journey to their new home in the United States across the treacherous Florida straits on rafts constructed of little more than inner tubes.

All of these, the executed, the imprisoned, and the refugees, were labeled by Castro as *gusanos*, worms, and enemies of the revolution.

As the numbers swelled to a full eighth of the country's population, a high-ranking officer of Castro's Revolutionary Army (who was later to die at the *paredón*) commented, "If all these people he calls enemies had truly been enemies of ours when we were in the mountains, we could never have won. With this number, they could have been armed only with broomsticks, and could have beaten us to death."

2

The Charade

THE UNITED STATES HAD BEEN AMONG THE FIRST NA-
tions to recognize the new Castro regime. It maintained a large, imposing embassy on the Malecón,
Havana's beautiful waterfront drive. From this embassy, U.S. State Department Foreign Service officers and the Central Intelligence Agency were
issuing countless messages to Washington concerning the deteriorating state of affairs within Cuba.
While the Foreign Service officers and the CIA were
in substantial agreement in their judgment and
evaluation of the Castro regime, the men in Washington to whom the messages were sent were not.

The CIA, very early in the game, reported on
Castro's Communist leanings and the Communist
backgrounds of some of his advisers, but the State
Department, led by the chief of Latin American affairs, Roy Rubottom, presented only glowing reports on the new Cuban premier. In fact, Rubottom

was emphatic in his support of Castro. Because of this slanted evaluation, the State Department forged a foreign policy program that, in essence, extended the hand of friendship to Castro. While not condoning or ignoring his excesses, the State Department welcomed him as a full member in the family of American states and as a friend of the United States.

Although the State Department was sincere in its effort and did everything to make it succeed, in the end it failed. It failed not because, as some would like to believe, we turned our backs on Castro and this drove him into the arms of Communism, but because Castro had, as most students of Cuban affairs now agree, made two decisions long before the success of the revolution brought him to Havana.

These decisions were, first, he wanted to become Maximum Leader of Cuba, a role equivalent to dictator. Second, he wanted to completely change the economic and social structure of Cuba along socialist lines and make it a Communist state. He hated the United States and wanted an anti-U.S. revolution.

While keeping these aspirations to himself, Castro played a waiting game. He needed time to consolidate his hold on Cuba, time to weed out from his followers those who truly believed in the new Cuban revolution and those who would not support a Communist dictatorship in Cuba regardless of who headed it.

He also needed time to firm up support from the only country in the world that could, and would, give him the aid he needed to impose a socialist system on Cuba, the Soviet Union. Castro offered the Soviets something they had been yearning for for many years, a foothold in the Western Hemisphere. The cost of maintaining it would be minimal, and the advantages it offered were significant. It was not a difficult sale.

While Castro negotiated with his soon-to-be-allies in the Soviet Union, he played a cat-and-mouse game with the United States. He visited New York, rubbed shoulders with world leaders, played the game of "hug the Russian bear" with Khrushchev. He even addressed the United Nations General Assembly in his familiar fatigues.

Castro was having a ball. He was thoroughly enjoying the fruits of his victory, while his subordinates were completing plans and negotiations to make his stay in office secure. He presented himself as the idol of the people, without a worry in the world.

In 1976, in an interview in Havana with Bill Moyers of CBS News, which later appeared in the CBS Reports program "The CIA's Secret Army," Castro related to Moyers his memories of this visit to the United States and his meeting with Vice President Nixon. Castro stated that Nixon "appeared very young" to him and that Nixon "listened to me with intent, and with some indulgence." He indicated that they'd had a pleasant meeting, then shook hands and departed. Later, he learned that Nixon had sent a memo of their meeting to Eisenhower in which Nixon said that Castro was a Communist.

At this point, Moyers asked Castro, "Well, were you a Communist?"

Castro listened to the interpreter translate the question, paused, looked puzzled for a moment, then answered, "Yes, I was a Communist at that time."

It would appear to anyone who saw this program that Castro had slipped up. He had meant to show that the United States were prejudiced against him—the boyish Nixon had had the gall to call him a Communist. Then he had admitted that he was a "Marxist-Leninist."

There were those who observed these events who had reason to worry. Castro's dealings with the Soviets had not gone unnoticed by the CIA. As disturbing reports provided by the CIA reached the top members of the Eisenhower administration, reports of Soviet advisers and weapons pouring into Cuba, including the prospect of Soviet MiGs, ninety miles from our borders, the picture became alarmingly clear. Cuba was well on its way to becoming a Soviet satellite.

The word was passed to the CIA to intensify its surveillance and monitoring of the rapidly changing situation. High-level meetings of top U.S. government officials were held to evaluate the situation and to assess its effect on the United States. It rapidly became evident that Cuba presented a clear and potential danger to U.S. security.

Up until now, our efforts had been to seal off the Communist threat posed by the Soviet Union and its satellites by keeping them contained within their

Iron Curtain. Suddenly, in one tremendous leap, the Communists had landed on our doorstep.

The ninety miles separating Cuba and the United States might have been sufficient in years past, but in the nuclear age of supersonic jets and missiles, it was only a whisper away. It was pointed out at the time that Cuban aircraft were so close they would have to put on their brakes to keep from overshooting us. They were looking right down our throats.

The administration's options? It could ignore the threat, do nothing. But that was inconceivable. The administration at that time had been seriously concerned about Khrushchev's boastful threat "We will bury you." It could not sit idly by, watching Castro and the Soviets extend the Iron Curtain to our backyard. At the opposite end of the scale, sending in the Marines was equally unthinkable. We were living in a new and dangerous age. A nuclear cloud hung over the Cold War conflict. It was uppermost in everyone's mind.

A middle-of-the-road solution was sought. A way had to be found to stop the Soviets that would not involve a direct clash, something neither side wanted.

The United States and the Soviet Union had been involved in the Cold War for fifteen years. There had been, without direct consultation, an unwritten agreement that both sides would try to avoid a direct clash, but that "covert actions," not openly admitted to by either side, would not be a basis for confrontation.

President Eisenhower once stated, "There has to be an option left open to a president to counter Communist aggression short of declaring war." The option he was referring to was the CIA, whose charter read that "in addition to the primary function of collecting and evaluating foreign intelligence, it will perform certain other functions as directed by the National Security Council." Eisenhower set his administration's goals in reference to Cuba in a speech he gave on March 4, 1960, in Groton, Connecticut. He said, "This nation cannot and will not tolerate the establishment of a Soviet satellite ninety miles off our shores."

It was decided that covert action would be taken to keep Castro and the Soviets from establishing a Soviet foothold in the Western Hemisphere. The CIA was instructed to prepare itself to overthrow the government of Castro and to enable a democratic government, friendly to the United States, to be put in its place.

To carry out these instructions, the CIA, in July 1960, formed a separate and special Cuban Task Force in the Western Hemisphere Division of its Clandestine Services. It was to be headed by Jake Esterline, an old hand in the field of covert actions. He was a former OSS officer, as were most of the top officials of the CIA, and had helped to oust the Communist regime of Jacobo Arbenz in Guatemala in 1954. He was well versed in Cuban and Latin American affairs.

Assigned to oversee the entire effort was Richard

Bissell, chief of Clandestine Services. A former Harvard professor of economics, Bissell was the father of the daring and astonishingly successful U-2 spy plane project, which even the Soviets recognized as the single greatest breakthrough in the history of intelligence collection.

As the Cuban Task Force was assembling, the CIA stepped up its intelligence collection efforts in Cuba. It renewed contact with anti-Castro elements both inside Cuba and within the exile groups in Florida.

The CIA contingent in Havana was enlarged, and a branch station was established in Miami, where many of the torrent of refugees pouring out of Cuba were settling. There was no shortage of ready and willing agents inside Cuba. The underground organizations that had carried the brunt of the fight against Batista, while Castro and his band sat it out in the Sierra Maestra, were now reforming for another struggle. It was painfully clear to them that they had only exchanged one dictator for another, and a much more brutal and dangerous one at that. Arms, ammunition, and any other assistance necessary to mount an underground war were to be provided them.

While the Cuban underground looked like the method of choice to rid Cuba of Castro, it proved to be one of the most frustrating and impossible tasks ever handed to the CIA. To most people, the Cuban underground appeared to be a large, well-organized fighting organization, but it was not.

True, it was large, but it was not organized. And instead of a fighting force, it was a hodgepodge of political organizations that not only would not organize as a single force but distrusted each other and went their separate ways.

Although all the groups were anti-Communist and anti-Castro, they were organized primarily as political groups. Each was striving to become the largest and most politically powerful in the struggle against Castro. The reason was simple. If and when Castro was defeated, the most powerful group would form the new government of Cuba.

In the fight against Batista, the major underground organizations numbered a half-dozen or so. They were all, with the exception of Castro's own 26th of July Movement, now back in business. However, the situation was different this time, for no longer were they engaged in a fight against a universally hated dictator with a small, dispirited, and inefficient armed force and intelligence service. Instead, now they were up against Castro, who still had the of approval of most of the Cuban people, along with the support of the Soviet Union, which was supplying him with Soviet-made small arms. His forces grew in strength daily, and in addition to his regular Rebel Army, he was organizing and training worker militia units.

Yet to come from his Soviet benefactors were jet fighters (sixty MiG-21s) and their latest, most powerful tanks, artillery, antiaircraft weapons, and heavy mortars. Intelligence information revealed that the first shipload of heavy weapons would arrive in Havana on March 15, 1961, followed by one or two ships per day thereafter. Thus the crucial target date for whatever action was to be taken was set at March 10, 1961. Time was running out. If Castro was to be overthrown, it would have to be done before his forces were fully equipped and trained by the Soviets.

The most disturbing factor was the effectiveness of Castro's intelligence service. Known as the G-2 and trained by the KGB, it had become a first-rate service—almost a Caribbean branch of the KGB. From the onset, the agents of the CIA found that all of the underground organizations had been penetrated to some extent by the G-2. Some of them were so riddled by G-2 agents that their value to the effort was considered practically nil.

To understand the ease with which the G-2 was able to accomplish the undermining of these organizations one must understand the Cuban makeup. The average Cuban is a highly emotional, vocal, and thoroughly likable individual. Consequently, as an intelligence operative, he is his own worst enemy. He cannot keep a secret. When entrusted with a most secret matter, he will solemnly agree never to tell a living soul, even under the pain of death, and he truly means it. But all too soon, he discovers, he will have to tell someone or he will explode from the effort of holding the secret in. He will tell you that you must keep in mind that he has told only one person, and that was his best and lifelong friend. If one cannot trust such a friend, it is a sad world indeed. This would probably not have posed much of a problem if it ended there. Of course, his best friend was obliged to inform his best friend, and so forth down the line until one of the best friends turns out to be a G-2 agent.

The Cuban underground fighter in the early days was a trusting and, at times, naive individual. For this most human and understandable trait he was to pay a terrible price.

Many men were taken into these organizations with their sole qualification being that they were anti-Castro. No amount of warning or prodding by the CIA agents in contact with these groups could move them to clean out their organizations and set up at least basic security systems. Since the groups were originally political organizations and were still highly political in nature, they tended to count their strength by the number of men on their roster instead of the quality of the members and above all their ability to perform the many hard and dangerous tasks of a guerrilla unit.

Although the CIA agents worked long and hard with the Cuban underground groups, it was soon apparent that more than mere support and advice was needed if a successful campaign was to be launched against Castro in the short time remaining. It was decided that some of the best of the refugees in Miami would be recruited and given extensive training in the highly complex skills of guerrilla warfare.

The first fifty of these agents were sent out of Miami in September 1960 to a training camp in the jungles of the Panama Canal Zone. This group was followed in short order by other groups. A new, larger camp was built to accommodate them in the high mountains on the Pacific coast of Guatemala, near Retalhuleu. The Panama camp was closed, and all training was done in a complex of camps in Guatemala. An airfield was built near Retalhuleu to supply these camps and also to train pilots to be used to drop arms and supplies to the Cuban underground.

Another base was set up in the Florida Keys to service the growing fleet of boats being utilized to move supplies in to the coast of Cuba. These craft were also used to bring out certain selected underground figures for training by the CIA in the South Florida area.

The reappraisal of the Cuban underground and the decision to begin a major training program for them was seen in Washington as a necessary step. Still, there was more to do, and it had to be done quickly.

When the two hundred Cuban aviation cadets who had been sent to Prague, Czechoslovakia, to train as pilots of the Soviet MiG jets returned, it would signal the end of the supply program to the underground, as well as of the movement of agents into and out of Cuba. The slow-moving transport planes and the small boats used in the surface supply activities would become sitting ducks for the MiGs. This was a race against time, a time when Castro with the help of the Soviets would become too strong to knock out. Soviet weapons, Soviet advisers, and something completely new to Cuba, Communist discipline, were rapidly changing the situation.

The United States had entered the race at a very late date. It had a lot of catching up to do. The disadvantages it faced were many and varied, and some were, by the very nature of the struggle, inherent to it. While Castro and the Soviets could work openly, the United States could not. Because of the clandestine nature of the effort, a heavy burden was imposed on all activities. All movement of men and supplies, training, and operations were done at night, in remote and difficult areas.

If given sufficient time, the CIA could have conducted these activities in complete secrecy, but time was one thing it did not have. Therefore, compromises had to be made. Security had to give way to necessity. Consequently, many activities of the agency were observed or known of by the people in South Florida and Latin America. They saw, they knew, but since they approved of the effort being made, they kept their knowledge to themselves.

3

The Light Brigade

AMONG THE FIRST RECRUITS SELECTED WERE MANUEL Artime, the National Agrarian Reform Institute (INRA) chief of Oriente Province, and former Cuban army officers José "Pepe" and Roberto San Román, who were brothers, and Erneido Oliva and Alejandro del Valle.

This group was processed through a CIA center on Useppa Island near Fort Myers, Florida, during May 1960. Twenty-eight of them under Pepe San Román were flown to the CIA training base in the Panama Canal Zone. After eight weeks of vigorous guerrilla training, they were flown in July to Retalhuleu, on the Pacific coast of Guatemala, to join those men who had been flown directly from Miami to this area. The group now totaled 160 men. Their first task was to construct a training camp high in the mountains above Retalhuleu on a coffee plantation owned by Roberto Alejos, a well-known wealthy Guatemalan.

The Retalhuleu camp was to become the central training facility for the guerrilla warfare teams, officially called infiltration teams and patterned on the concept of the Special Forces A-Teams. The teams' composition and size varied according to mission and area of operation, but were usually from five to nine men. The majority of the teams were meant to work as unilateral assets, to bypass the mishmash of internal resistance units in Cuba, many of whom were known to be riddled by G-2 agents, and to recruit and form their own independent guerilla units.

In the beginning, living conditions at the base camp were not good. The weather was bad, the food terrible, and the work hard. All the barracks and training facilities had to be built by the men before the real job of organizing and training the teams could begin. There were shortages of everything from weapons to building supplies. In a different setting, with different men, these obstacles could have shattered morale and seriously affected the effort, but these men believed that under the Americans things would improve and they could get on with the goal of all Cuban exiles—the overthrow of Castro and the liberation of their homeland.

Early in July 1960, while the presidential election campaign was in full swing, the Eisenhower administration ordered the CIA to bring the leaders of the different Cuban factions based in Miami into a coalition movement under one central governing committee. This was accomplished after a great deal of patient negotiating and some plain old-fashioned butt-kicking.

The group adopted the name Frente Revolucionario Democratico (Democratic Revolutionary Front). It became known as the FRD or Frente. The selection of Frente's top five men was made by the Eisenhower administration from lists submitted by the State Department and the CIA. The mission of the FRD was to act as government in arms when Castro fell and until a regular election could be held in Cuba.

The Frente held many a stormy session. The differences among the many resistance movements became clear at these meetings. Eventually a chairman was elected. He was Manuel Antonio de Varona, a former prime minister of Cuba and president of the Senate. Early in July, Artime, head of the Movement for the Recovery of the Revolution (MRR), the largest of the underground groups, left the training camps and returned to Miami to serve as a board member of Frente.

In early June 1960, a U.S. civilian construction company, contracted by the CIA through the Guatemalan air force, began construction of an airfield on a plateau overlooking the Pacific at Retalhuleu. The training camp for the infiltration teams would eventually be located about twenty-five miles north of this airfield, high in the mountains. In need of a cover or this airfield, the CIA arranged for the Guatemalan air force to keep some of its planes there and practice landings during the day, so as to make it appear that its aircraft were based there. The CIA also arranged to have a detachment of the Guatemalan army guard the airfield.

The construction of the airfield was to take thirty days, but bad weather delayed completion for another sixty days. Upon its completion, a small group of Cuban transport pilots who had been recruited from among the exiles in Miami were assembled there to begin training in a program designed to give them the necessary proficiency to make night parachute drops of arms and supplies to the guerrilla bands inside Cuba. Unlike the camp for the infiltration teams, this was a first-class facility with regular U.S. Air Force–type barracks, a mess hall, and all the comforts of home.

The CIA had determined that airlifting supplies was necessary, because of the slowness and unreliability of the over-water route from Florida. The small craft used were restricted in range to the western part of the north coast of Cuba. Their size limited them to approximately a thousand pounds of supplies and arms per trip. The underground now required equipment and arms calculated by tons. Another drawback to the overwater method of delivery was that the trip itself was hazardous. Often the small boats were turned back by the capricious, violent weather of the Florida Straits, necessitating repeat trips for the same load of supplies.

The resistance movement had been heavily penetrated by Castro's G-2, whose ability to pinpoint the time and place of deliveries caused many to fall into the G-2's hands. The G-2 also ambushed reception parties on the beaches, or en route to the sanctuaries where the weapons were to be cached.

Since the resistance movement had moved into the mountains of Cuba, it was hoped that the airdrops would provide quick, direct delivery with pinpoint accuracy of large amounts of supplies. The techniques used for this type of aerial delivery had been worked out and perfected by our military since World War II, but it still requires a skilled pilot and navigator with special training. It is considered to be one of the most difficult feats of flying that any pilot can be called upon to perform.

Since most of the guerrilla units were headquartered in the high mountains of the Sierra Maestra and Escambray ranges, making the drops required the pilots, barreling their four-engine transports through pitch-dark mountain valleys, to hit, with split-second timing, a drop zone marked only by flashlights, at the exact time specified in the flight plan. A difficult assignment, to say the least. The transport crews, a mix of Cuban air force and commercial aviation pilots, had flown the four-engine DC-4s used to make the drops thousands of hours, but not in the manner now required. The job was to become more than they could perform.

The area around Retalhuleu was mostly mountains. Its close resemblance to the eastern portion of Cuba with its Sierra Maestra and Sierra Cristal ranges and the central Cuban Escambray range provided the pilots and PDOs (parachute dispatch operators) with an excellent training area. While this training was underway, the Miami CIA station sent shipments of arms and equipment for the Cuban underground to Retalhuleu Airfield, along with a drop schedule for the units inside Cuba.

The planes flew daily, the pilots perfecting their navigation and timing and the PDOs their drop skills, until their daylight drop performance was such that the American instructors felt they were ready to advance to the more difficult night drops. At first, the practice night drops were all misses, but gradually the Cubans raised their hit average to where the Americans felt they were competent enough to handle some of the easier combat missions into Cuba. But there were still more misses and aborted missions than successes, so the pilots returned for further training.

Unfortunately, the situation did not improve. Out of a total of sixty-eight supply missions flown into Cuba by the Cuban Transport Group, only three were successful. This lack of success should not be construed as a reflection on the willingness of these men to succeed in their mission, or on their capabilities as pilots. The real culprit in this failure was that the time allotted for learning this specialized skill was simply too short.

By the end of September the infiltration teams had completed the initial construction of their training camp above Retalhuleu, and they began a training program to prepare themselves for their mission inside Cuba. Construction continued throughout the training period, since each new shipment of men, now constantly arriving at the camp, meant more barracks were required. By mid-October, the camp contained more than three hundred men. The weather at this altitude of seven thousand feet was cold and often rainy; since Cubans are used to a balmy climate, they found life at these camps often miserable.

The long-planned infiltration of the teams was far behind schedule. Many teams had already gone into Cuba, but more would be required, and soon. The delay was caused by the inability of the small craft, operating from Florida, to deliver men and supplies at the same time, and of the transport pilots' inability to deliver the arms, which would have left the boats free to deliver the infiltration teams.

There was growing concern in Washington over this bottleneck. Plans were underway to land a large force of the infiltration teams at one time into the mountains of Cuba, where they would set up a new, unilaterally controlled guerrilla organization, and thus break away from the bickering and internecine politicking of the older organizations.

The atmosphere in Washington was also heating up as the presidential campaigns of Kennedy and Nixon were getting into full swing. The question of Cuba was raised time and again by Kennedy. He attacked the Eisenhower administration for its lack of support of the exiles, calling for armed overthrow of Castro and pledging, if elected, his full support.

Nixon, as vice president, was the Eisenhower administration's chief project officer for the Cuban effort. This placed him in a difficult position. Nixon unsuccessfully attempted to ward off the charges of inaction by Kennedy, yet still maintain the secrecy cover on the entire operation. It may have cost him the election. Nixon was defeated by only a hundred thousand votes, and the polls showed that more than this number had decided in favor of Kennedy at the last minute because of his hard stand on Cuba. He'd taunted Nixon, saying, "If you can't stand up to Castro, how can you stand up to Khrushchev?"

Kennedy's New Frontier administration would take control of the government on January 20, 1961. It had openly pledged its support to the exiles, bringing new life to the struggle. The men of the infiltration teams were jubilant, but they, like many others in the Miami area, were a little too confident in their eventual success. They believed that with the president of the United States behind them they couldn't lose.

The election results and a new directive from Washington reached Guatemala at the same time. The directive, a result of several months of discussion and planning, indicated the underground effort would be scrapped, and that a decision had been made to go for the quick solution to the problem—an armed invasion. It was the opinion of the Special Group in Washington, a group composed of representatives of the CIA, the Defense Department, the National Security Council, and the State Department, that the underground could not be expected to expel Castro before he had his Soviet MiGs flying on May 1, 1961.

The Special Group could not approve a plan that was to be carried out by the next administration, however. It ordered the CIA to continue its plans, but to await formal approval by the president-elect. One of the many myths that exist about this operation is that the invasion was approved by President Eisenhower. It was not. The approval came from John F. Kennedy.

The early-November order called for the formation of a force of several companies of infantry and supporting weapons, with a target date of combat readiness to be achieved by March 1, 1961.

The training camps now contained approximately 470 men. Some had completed their guerrilla training as infiltration teams and were awaiting infiltration orders. Sixty of them were selected to continue the guerrilla effort and were sent back to the United States.

To further support this invasion, a new air arm in addition to the transport planes was forged at Retalhuleu Airfield. Another group of Cuban pilots were formed into a B-26 squadron. This post-world War II fighter-bomber was chosen because it was what the Cuban air force was flying and the pilots were already familiar with it, and it had the "plausible denial" aspect built in; with Cuban air force markings painted on the planes, they could be passed off as Castro's.

A new concept had been ordered, an invasion

force was forming in Guatemala, the mists were lifting over the Cuban situation, and the road to Cochinos Bay now was clearly visible.

That November, there came to Retalhuleu a sudden shift in both the concept by which Castro was to be overthrown and the quality and intensity of the training. Indications of the importance of the force being formed appeared as new equipment and weapons began pouring into the camp, along with a different type of adviser-instructor. These Americans wore casual civilian clothes, but their bearing and professionalism marked them as military men. They were members of the U.S. Army's Special Forces. The Green Berets had entered the Cuban effort, and they quickly transformed the camp, now called TRAX, into a disciplined military installation.

They were friendly to the Cubans and extremely patient in coaching them in their new military subjects, but they were no-nonsense individuals who took their work seriously. This attitude quickly earned the respect of the Cuban Brigade.

The brigade, which began with four hundred men, grew to fifteen hundred by the time it set out for Cochinos Bay. Its name, 2506, was selected in honor of the first man of the brigade to die. 2506 was the serial number of Carlos Rafael Santana, who was killed in a training operation at TRAX when he slipped and fell from a high mountain cliff.

The concept of this brigade was one of a cadre or skeleton force. It could be quickly expanded to its full strength of five thousand men when it arrived in Cuba and began to pick up recruits. It was composed of six infantry battalions, a heavy weapons battalion, an armored truck battalion, and a tank company. In number of men the battalions were equal to regular companies, and their companies were the size of platoons. They were the leaders, a hard core around which a much larger force could be built. It was envisioned that new recruits would be derived from two sources—the residents of the beachhead area and the Cuban exiles in Miami. The latter were to be flown directly from Miami onto the beachhead after it had been secured.

The men now training in Guatemala would be required to train and lead the new men, while simultaneously engaged in battle. To accomplish this, they needed hard and intensive training, as it would be necessary for them to be familiar with all the weapons and tactics of the entire brigade.

To command them, the brigade selected José "Pepe" San Román. Pepe was a product of the Cuban Military Academy. He had fought against Batista, was imprisoned by him and released only when Castro took over, then was imprisoned again when he was charged with counterrevolutionary activities after he became disillusioned by the Communist influence he saw beginning to take control. He had defected to the United States and was among the first members of the infiltration teams.

After completing the weapons training program in the mountains, the brigade was moved south to the coastal plains above San José. This was a welcome change for the Cubans, because these plains seemed more like their Cuban shores.

The move also brought the brigade together with its 1st Battalion, which had been trained as paratroopers at a different camp and sent to San José earlier. This airborne battalion was an elite unit with a high degree of proficiency and esprit de corps. Its members had made their training jumps from the brigade's C-46s, and they were extremely proud of the shiny new paratrooper's wings that adorned their uniforms. Their commander, the young and handsome Alejandro del Valle, kept his men training and preparing for their special task, which was to be the first men of the brigade into Cuba.

The 2nd Infantry Battalion, also an elite unit, was commanded by Hugo Sueiro, a tough little fighter, as Castro was soon to find out.

The 3rd Infantry Battalion, was commanded by Noelio Montero, a former officer in the Cuban army.

The 4th Infantry Battalion a motorized unit with armor-plated two-and-a-half-ton trucks, was commanded by Valentine Baccallo.

To head the 6th Battalion, the CIA, in August 1960, recruited and brought from Mexico City Francisco Montiel, a former Rebel Army captain with Raúl Castro's column in the Sierra Cristal mountains, and eleven of his men, also former Rebel Army soldiers.

Montiel's battalion was the last to be formed. Because of the limited time available before the invasion, this battalion received the least training. They were forced to complete their weapons training while en route to the invasion. They used oil drums, either tossed overboard or towed on a long cable behind the ship, for target practice. Despite its late start and short training period, the 6th Battalion did well in combat, thanks principally to Montiel's combat experience and that of the other battalion leaders who had fought in Cuba.

The heavy weapons battalion commander was Roberto San Román, Pepe's brother. This battalion was the brigade's big punch. It contained a company of 4.2-inch mortars that could rain shells on Castro's army at six thousand yards, along with a company of 75mm recoilless rifles. These light artillery pieces could be handled by a few men, but had the power to stop a tank at two thousand yards. A company of smaller 57mm recoilless rifles and one of 50-caliber machine guns completed the heavy weapons battalion. While this battalion was to support the entire brigade, each of the infantry battalions had a heavy weapons platoon made up of 81mm mortars and 57mm recoilless rifles for its own direct support.

The tank company was actually a platoon of five U.S.-made M-41 tanks. The M-41 was a new tank, and it was entering its first battle. It carried as its main armament a high-velocity 76mm gun that could fire an armor-piercing round at forty-two hundred feet per second. This was four hundred feet per second faster than the dreaded German 88mm tank of World War II fame. The M-41s would be faced with opposition from the heavier

Soviet tanks. They passed the test, as time and again during the battle they proved their superiority. The crews of the M-41s were trained at Fort Knox, Kentucky, the home of the U.S. Army Armor School and Center.

The CIA had felt that the Cuban brigade should have a strength of at least three thousand men, but the recruiting and processing of new recruits by the Frente was slowed to an agonizing pace, mainly because of squabbling and infighting by members of the Frente and among the Cuban exiles. Some of the problems were normal, caused by rivalry between different revolutionary organizations that were attempting to send their own men to the training camps but at the same time objecting to the inclusion of men of rival groups in the same shipment.

There was another more serious problem that almost brought the recruiting of the brigade to a halt. This was the inability of the majority of the exiles to reconcile themselves to serving alongside those Cubans who had been members of the Rebel Army of Castro, or, in fact, any other Cubans who had at one time been active Castro supporters. By this time, of course, there were thousands of these former Castro supporters who had quickly become disillusioned by the repressive actions of the new government. In many cases they were even more militant in their efforts to overthrow Castro than were the earlier exiles to reach Miami. Since Cubans in this category were the fastest-growing group in the exile community, they could not be ignored, especially since many had received some type of military training and had combat experience.

In an attempt to solve the recruiting slowdown, the CIA dispatched Pepe and a group of brigade officers to Miami to straighten out this impasse. The solution they mediated was that the former Rebel Army members were to be put in a separate unit under Nino Diaz, a former major in Castro's Rebel Army, that was being formed in Louisiana. Their objective was to land in the mountains of Oriente Province to divert forces from the main landing. To balance this, the 5th Battalion was formed, composed mainly of former Cuban army members and to be commanded by a former Cuban army officer, Ricardo Montero Duque.

This realignment of the brigade was successful to a point. It did increase the flow of recruits to the brigade, though not to the degree hoped for. When the brigade was ready to leave the camps in Guatemala for the invasion, it numbered just under fifteen hundred men, half the number the CIA had aimed for.

Although the 2506 Brigade was not as large as it could have been, it was determined by those sent from Washington to view and evaluate it that it was well trained and led—a potent force that could be expected to more than hold its own in any encounter with Castro's Rebel Army and militia.

In Cuba, the 2506 Brigade more than lived up to these expectations.

4

The Trinidad Plan

WHILE THE CUBAN BRIGADE WAS BEING FORMED IN Guatemala, the paramilitary staff of the Cuban Task Force, at CIA headquarters, was beginning preparation of plans for an invasion of Cuba. The site selected for the landings was near the town of Trinidad, on the south coast. Other possible landing points had been examined, but each had been lacking in some vital requirement. Trinidad had everything the planners were looking for in the selection of a "defensible beachhead," and it contained an airfield that could, with a slight extension to the runways, enable the brigade's B-26s to operate from Cuban soil.

The invasion envisioned was not one in which a brigade of fifteen hundred men would capture all of Cuba and overthrow the Fidel Castro government in one quick movement. Instead, the brigade was to seize and hold the beachhead, while the brigade air force's B-26s struck the main blows against Castro's Rebel Army and attacked his supply depots and other means of waging war. It was believed that if the B-26s could operate unopposed for two to three weeks, the majority of the Cuban citizens would be convinced that Castro must, in the end, lose. Many of these Cubans were sitting on the fence. They were opposed to Castro, but would enter an open effort to oust him only when they believed that their effort would succeed.

When the beachhead was established and secured, the United States planned to fly in the Frente, the political coalition group from Miami, and set up a provisional government. This new government of Cuba would be immediately recognized by the U.S. government. Many other countries of Latin America would be expected to follow suit. Once this was accomplished, the CIA would be replaced by the Department of Defense. This would allow the United States to aid the new government openly through the National Defense Assistance Program and to furnish the brigade with whatever was needed to finish the effort, including more and better aircraft, additional tanks, and even heavy artillery. The brigade would be built up, during this holding period on the beachhead, to a strength of ten to fifteen thousand men. This would be accomplished by recruiting men from within the beachhead area itself, and from among the exiled Cubans in Miami.

The Rebel Army would be faced with a force that

it could not dislodge, a force that also ruled the skies over Cuba. This, together with open support of the provisional government from the United States and most of the Latin American countries, was considered sufficient to convince Castro's supporters that eventually they must lose. When this realization began to sink in, they could be expected to throw in the towel. The brigade could move at a time of its own choosing, against little or no opposition.

The area that the CIA selected was ideal for this purpose. The city of Trinidad, with a population of twenty-six thousand, was a hotbed of anti-Castro opponents. The brigade could expect to pick up more than two thousand men from its inhabitants. Besides an airfield, the area also contained a deep-water port, at Casilda, six miles to the southeast. The landings were to be made on sand beaches, three miles west of Trinidad. Directly behind the beaches was a good paved road that led directly to the town. The ease with which this beachhead could be defended against Castro's forces was its outstanding feature.

The west flank of the beachhead would be anchored in the Escambray mountain range. This high, rugged mass would effectively block any attack from that direction. The north portion of the beachhead defense line was to be along the Marati River, which comes out of the Escambray and curves in an arc around Trinidad, finally ending in a large swamp where it meets the sea. The swamp would be the eastern anchor of the beachhead, and would also prevent any attacking force coming from that direction.

The only portion of the beachhead that could be attacked by Castro forces was the six-mile-long defense line dug in behind the Marati River. To breach this river line, Castro would be compelled to mass a large amount of his troops in a very small area. With the brigade air force based only miles away, any massing of troops would be suicidal.

The brigade's B-26s were twin-engine propeller planes. An early version of the B-26 was first used by the United States in Korea. Our later-model B-26s were armed with eight .50-caliber machine guns and eight 5-inch rockets and had the capability to carry bombs and napalm. Although they were slower than jet aircraft, they still packed quite a punch.

To allow these planes to attack Castro's forces at will, it would first be necessary to destroy his small force of fighter aircraft on the ground. These included a small number of T-33 jets and British Sea Fury fighters, which, if allowed to become airborne, could easily outfly and shoot down the slower B-26s.

To avoid this, the CIA planners proposed to strike Castro's airfields at dawn, on the morning of the invasion, with twenty-two B-26s. This raid was to be carried out from the Puerto Cabezas airfield in Nicaragua and was scheduled to strike the Cuban airfields simultaneously.

In addition to the airfields, several of the planes

were targeted to strike the mass of tanks, trucks, and artillery that Castro had parked in long parallel lines, bumper to bumper, on the parade ground at Campo Libertad, on the outskirts of Havana. Dropping a heavy load of bombs and napalm on this tempting target could wipe out a sizable portion of Castro's armor in one strike.

After these attacks, the B-26s would return to Puerto Cabezas, would be rearmed and refueled, and return to Cuba, striking these same targets again, along with any of Castro's forces moving toward the Trinidad beachhead. After the second raid, instead of returning to Puerto Cabezas, the B-26s would land at the airfield on the beachhead at Trinidad.

While the runway of this airfield was considered slightly short of the length required for B-26s, by late afternoon of D-day the brigade would have lengthened it by the installation of prefabricated pierced-steel planking. This task was expected to be completed early on the afternoon of D-day, in plenty of time to receive the B-26s. The Trinidad field, by this time, would be fully supplied with both fuel and armaments for the planes, and would now become the primary base of operations.

The brigade air force would return to the attack on the following morning, D+1. In addition to striking Castro's forces around the beachhead and on the highways of Cuba, they would begin an interdiction campaign against key bridges and highway choke points. As soon as the opportunity presented itself, the B-26s would strike the electric power plants at Havana, Matanzas, and Santiago; the refineries; and the fifteen fuel storage areas located throughout the island. Without fuel and power, the Cuban economy would quickly grind to a halt. The psychological effect of this upon the Cuban population would be immense.

Although the brigade's force of planes was small, they could inflict a terrific amount of damage. Castro's Rebel Army and its support facilities would have felt their full force.

The tactical plan for seizing the area called for a parachute drop of the 1st Battalion, to open the attack at H-hour, which was set for first light. They were to seize the two bridges over the Marati River and the Trinidad airfield and to block all roads leading to the beaches.

At the same time, two of the brigade's infantry battalions would land on the beaches, west of Trinidad. One battalion would block the road along the coast that led to Cienfuegos and the mountain roads into the Escambray. The other battalion would move east to link up with the paratroopers and encircle the town of Trinidad.

Two more of the brigade's infantry battalions would follow quickly behind the first wave. These two battalions would seize the town of Trinidad and then move to the Marati River line, eleven miles north of Trinidad. The last battalion to land would take over the landing beaches and begin unloading the supplies for the brigade.

Later in the day, the brigade would seize the port of Casilda and use its docks for unloading supplies directly from the cargo ships to trucks. This port was used primarily to receive oil shipments, and a large oil storage tank farm was located at the docks. These tanks contained enough fuel to supply the brigade for months.

One other feature of this area of Trinidad that was very much in our favor was that the Escambray mountains at that time contained a large and active force of anti-Castro guerrillas. This force could assist the brigade in blocking these mountains against Castro's forces.

A two-phase plan to draw Castro's forces away from the Trinidad area was prepared. The first phase was to take place two nights prior to the invasion, in western Cuba in Pinar del Río Province. This was to appear to be a landing of a large body of troops, from an appropriately large number of landing crafts. They would seem to be supported by an entire fleet of ships, some of them to considerable size. In reality, there were no troops, no landing craft, and no large ships, but a clever illusion created electronically by CIA craft to give Cuban radar and any observers a completely false picture of what was actually happening.

This electronic illusion would be convincing enough to cause Castro to send Ché Guevara with a column of several thousand troops racing to the far western end of Pinar del Río to combat an invasion fleet that never was.

The following night, the second phase of the plan would be carried out. This was not a deception, but rather a diversion, since it would not be done "with mirrors," like the supposed landing in Pinar del Río, but with actual troops. This was to be the landing of a force of approximately 175 men in far eastern Cuba at Río Mocambo, a small inlet halfway between Baracoa and Guantánamo, in Oriente.

This landing force was to be led by Nino Diaz. As a major in Castro's Rebel Army, Diaz had led a force of Castro's troops in this very area, the Sierra Purial mountains, which came directly down to the sea at this landing point. The plan called for Diaz and his men to move into these high mountains and immediately begin actions, so as to draw attention away from the main invasion at Trinidad. Since this force had a large area in which to operate, and to withdraw if necessary, it was certain that it would not be overwhelmed in the short time before the Trinidad landing drew the Rebel Army forces away.

In all the planning for this invasion, there was one element of the Cuban effort that was to play no part in the invasion. That was the so-called underground movement. It was not, under any circumstances, to be forewarned of the date of the landings. The reason for this was that Castro had been preparing long lists of the underground members to be arrested the moment this organization was notified of the coming invasion. The CIA knew that the G-2 was closely watching the underground for the sign that the invasion was imminent. It also knew that if this message was sent to the underground it would be on Castro's desk within hours. It would be the signal for the G-2 security forces to begin its planned roundup of the underground members and its move to smash the groups, resulting in a bloodbath that would be of little aid to the Trinidad landings.

The branch of Castro's armed forces that the CIA felt sure would play little or no part in opposing the invasion was his navy. Like his air force, it had been inherited from the Batista government, and it was considered totally unreliable by Castro. Reports from agents in contact with the navy indicated that most ships would never leave port if an invasion occurred.

Though the Cuban navy was in no way considered modern, it did have some surplus U.S. Navy frigates, and some patrol craft. These ships mounted 3-inch and 4-inch guns and could wreak havoc on any unarmed invasion convoy. The closest Cuban navy vessel to Trinidad was a frigate based at Cienfuegos, forty-five miles to the west, but agents reported that this ship would not leave the harbor to interfere with a landing against Castro.

To transport the 2506 Brigade and its supplies to the beaches of Trinidad, the CIA procured six cargo ships from the Cuban-owned García Line, whose owners were active in the anti-Castro underground. The procurement was made necessary by the State Department's request that only Cuban-owned and -registered ships be used in the invasion. The ships were the *Caribe, Atlantico, Houston, Río Escondido,* and

Lake Charles. The invasion convoy also included two converted LCIs (Landing Craft Infantry), outfitted as command ships, that were owned by the CIA and were exempt from this State Department request.

Four of the García ships, the *Caribe*, *Atlantico*, *Houston*, and *Río Escondido*, would be loaded with ammunition and supplies required to support a force of fifteen thousand men for thirty days. These ships were to be involved in the first landings at Trinidad. The remaining García ship, the *Lake Charles*, was to be loaded with fifteen days' worth of supplies and would unload on D+5. It would also transport the men of the Operation 40 Group. Trained in Florida, these men would act as the staff of a military government and would administer the beachhead and all liberated areas in Cuba.

A sixth ship, to be leased from a U.S. commercial shipping line, would land on D+10, with arms for ten thousand men and supplies for thirty days.

The brigade landing craft, the four LCVPs (Landing Craft Vehicle Personnel) and three LCUs (Landing Craft Utility), would be combat-loaded with five M-41 tanks, ten two-and-a-half-ton trucks with trailers, a three-quarter-ton truck with a water trailer, a bulldozer with a crane attachment, six jeeps, and a seven-thousand-gallon fuel tanker truck, filled with aviation fuel for the brigade planes. The trucks and trailers would all be loaded with ammunition and immediate supplies for the first days of combat. The loaded landing craft would be transported to a point fifteen miles off the

Trinidad area by a U.S. Navy LSD (Landing Ship Dock), where the landing craft would be launched and turned over to their Cuban crews.

The date set for the Cuban invasion was March 10, 1961. This date was of great significance to the plan, because behind its selection was a second, and to many, more important, reason for the invasion—a Soviet arms buildup on the island. Intelligence information had revealed that the first shipload of Soviet weapons for Castro's army was scheduled to arrive in Cuba on March 15. This ship was to be followed by many others scheduled to deliver, among other things, Soviet tanks and artillery. These deliveries were scheduled to extend into early April 1961.

The CIA planning staff realized that if the invasion took place in early March, the brigade's air force would, according to the "Trinidad plan," have wiped out Castro's small force of planes on the ground. Having accomplished this before March 15, it would have gained full control of the air over Cuba. With the brigade air force controlling the air over Cuba, none of the Soviet ships would have dared enter Cuban ports. The Soviets would realize that if they tried to sneak into the Cuban ports at night, the planes would find them the next morning and sink them. They would also be faced with a time problem. To avoid the patrolling B-26s that would be on the lookout for them, the Soviet freighters would be forced to stay well out to sea until sunset. Only then could they begin to approach the ports. It would be early morning before they made the docks. Picket boats equipped with radar would be stationed off each Cuban port to spot the Soviet ships as they came in and alert the B-26s. The Soviet ships would be attacked at first light, before they had a chance to unload their cargo. It would also be possible for the B-26s to hit them during the night by using illumination flares to expose them in the darkness.

If the Soviet ships could be prevented from delivering their cargo, Castro would be left to fight against the invasion force with only the weapons and ammunition that he had inherited from Batista's army. This was considered to be inadequate, especially the ammunition supply, which would be unable to sustain any prolonged major engagement with a force with the firepower and strength of the 2506 Brigade.

Castro knew that he needed a cushion of at least two weeks, more if he could get it, between the time the Soviet ships arrived and any combat action, in order to train his army to use the new weapons. Training tank companies and artillery and heavy mortar battalions requires time, lots of it, even to cover the basic rudimentary skills.

The CIA staff recognized this. Thus, March 10 was selected as the last date available for us to launch an invasion that would deny Castro the Soviet weapons he needed to turn the military balance of power to his advantage. To ignore this March 10 deadline was, to the Joint Chiefs of Staff and the CIA, unthinkable.

5

Change of Plans

THE FIRST OFFICIAL BRIEFING ON THE PLAN TO INVADE
Cuba was given President Kennedy by Allen
Dulles, head of the CIA, on November 29, 1960,
twenty-one days after Kennedy's election and
twenty-five days after the formation of the 2506
Brigade. After hearing the detailed briefing,
Kennedy instructed Dulles "to carry the work forward," but he made clear that he reserved the right
to cancel the operation at any time. The response
was sufficiently affirmative that Dulles took it as an
instruction to expedite the project. The Trinidad
plan was prepared, and was tentatively scheduled
to be put into operation on March 10. Kennedy received five more briefings by Dulles before he took
office.

The Trinidad plan was presented to the president
by the CIA on January 28, 1961. Kennedy again instructed the CIA to continue with its preparations,

but asked the Joint Chiefs of Staff (JCS) to conduct a formal evaluation of the plan and to report back to him on its chances of success. One week later, the JCS reported to the president that the Trinidad Plan stood a "fair" chance of success.

The March 10 date for the invasion was scrapped by the CIA in February when it became apparent that the Kennedy administration was in no hurry to approve the plan. In fact, it was not until March 11 that Kennedy called the formal approval meeting.

Present at this meeting were General Lyman Lemnitzer and Admiral Arleigh Burke of the JCS; Allen Dulles, director of central intelligence; General Charles Cabell, deputy director of central intelligence; and Richard Bissell, chief of CIA Operations, the man directly responsible for the Cuban operation. From the State Department came Secretary of State Dean Rusk and Under Secretary for Latin Affairs Thomas Mann. Also present were Assistant Secretary of Defense Paul Nitze; Senator William J. Fulbright, chairman of the Senate Foreign Relations Committee; Treasury Secretary Douglas Dillon; McGeorge Bundy, head of the National Security Council; and presidential assistants Arthur Schlesinger, Richard Goodwin, and Adolf Berle.

This was the New Frontier's first look at the plans for the Trinidad landings. Kennedy, on Rusk's advice, rejected the plan entirely, not because it would not succeed, but because the State Department would take some political heat when the actions took place. State's position on the matter was that in size and scope the Trinidad plan was too much like a World War II invasion, and this would indicate U.S. involvement. The fact that State would take the heat on any plan of this nature, especially one it intended to support only halfheartedly, dooming it to failure, somehow eluded State.

Another of State's objections to the Trinidad plan was the time of the landing. State preferred a night landing. Some members of this group even spoke of "sneaking them in during the night." The U.S. armed forces had conducted more invasions than all the other armed forces combined, but never had they conducted one at night. It is a most difficult military maneuver under the best of conditions. To attempt it in darkness is to invite dangerous complications.

The possibility of anyone seeing the invasion fleet as it approached Cuba, and immediately broadcasting its presence to the world, was rather farfetched, as there was to be no press coverage. Anyone able to view the landings could do so only from within the beachheads, which would already have been sealed off by the paratroopers before the landings took place.

Another point of contention was the size of the Trinidad airfield, which State claimed was too small. It was, in fact, able to handle the B-26s. However, in the interest of safety, the brigade was carrying enough pierced-steel planking in with it to extend it by three hundred feet. This extension could be in place in little more than an hour, allowing the B-26s that were due to hit Castro's airfields at first light to land there.

Despite this contingency, State remained firm. The reason for this was that State intended to announce to the world that the attacks on Castro's airfields had been made by Castro's own defecting pilots. These attacks were supposed to have originated from Cuban soil. Since State allegedly does not deal in lies, if the Trinidad airfield was known to be too short for the B-26s, State would certainly be branded as a liar and suffer untold tortures in the press. (It makes one wonder about State's selective morality. It was perfectly willing to lie about the fact that the B-26s belonged to Castro, but not about the airfield.)

One participant in that meeting, who shall remain nameless, suggested, facetiously, of course, that we could have the planes fly to Trinidad on the way to their attacks and simply touch their wheels down onto that runway for a split second before flying on to their targets. That way, State could honestly say that the planes had taken off from Cuba.

Incredibly, State thought this was a good idea—until someone pointed out that if the B-26s were to hit their targets at first light, this little touch-and-go exercise would have to occur around four in the morning. This was an hour and a half before the brigade was due to hit the beaches. By that time, the Cuban authorities in Trinidad would have alerted Havana to this crazy stunt, questioning why sixteen B-26s were practicing these unorthodox touch-and-go landings in the middle of the night.

State let the matter drop.

Still another objection was that since the city of Trinidad contained over twenty-six thousand people, this plan would "involve citizens," and there might be casualties. The CIA pointed out that the landing beaches were three miles west of Casilda and backed by the Escambray mountains. They were considered undefended, and thus, no fighting was expected at the beaches. Even if there was fighting, because of the distance it would not involve the civilian population of the town. The CIA also pointed out that the brigade was depending upon this civilian population to obtain badly needed reinforcements.

The objections stood. The Trinidad plan was rejected.

The paramilitary (PM) staff, led by Marine Colonel Jack Hawkins and made up of representatives of the air, ground, and maritime sections, who had worked so long and hard to prepare this plan, were dejected. Since the council had not stated that it was interested in any further efforts against Cuba, it was believed that the entire project was to be abandoned. The PM staff decided that since there was nothing else to do, this would be a good time to take the evening off. Several of them went out to dinner. Then the White House called that evening, after normal working hours, and wanted a new plan, for a new area, immediately. It was two in the morning before the last of the PM planners were rounded up.

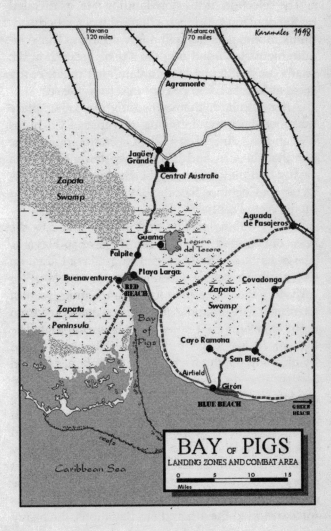

Havana
120 miles

Matanzas
70 miles

Karamales 1998

Agramonte

Jagüey
Grande

Central Australia

Zapata
Swamp

Aguada
de Pasajeros

Guama

Laguna
del Tesoro

Falpite

Buenaventura

Playa Larga

Covadonga

RED
BEACH

Zapata
Swamp

Zapata
Peninsula

Bay
of
Pigs

Cayo Ramona

San Blas

Airfield

Girón

BLUE BEACH

GREEN
BEACH

Caribbean Sea

BAY OF PIGS
LANDING ZONES AND COMBAT AREA

0   5   10   15
Miles

The selection of the new landing site, as dictated by the demands and restrictions of the Kennedy administration, was done in a few minutes. Those requirements included that the site be located on the south coast of Cuba and contain an airfield, easily accessible, that could be captured from the sea.

After Trinidad, there was only one other place that met these requirements, the area of Cochinos Bay and the airfield at Playa Girón. In spite of the fact that the CIA and JCS had written memoranda saying that they preferred the Trinidad plan, the selection of Cochinos Bay, the Bay of Pigs, was upheld by the New Frontier.

The new landing site was ninety miles to the west of Trinidad, and 120 miles closer to Havana. The beachhead would extend from Playa Larga, on the northern tip of Cochinos Bay, eastward for forty-two miles to a road junction ten miles west of Cienfuegos. Its inland dimensions would vary from eight to twenty-five miles at its deepest point. The beachhead was large, but could easily be defended by blocking the three exit roads. It contained a good airstrip that did not require lengthening to accommodate the brigade's B-26s.

Three landing points were selected. The west end of the beachhead at Playa Larga, to be called Red Beach, would be where the 2nd and 5th Infantry Battalions would go ashore. The center landing, at Playa Girón, designated as Blue Beach, would be composed of the main body of the brigade. This force included the 4th and 6th Battalions, the heavy weapons battalion, the armored truck battalion, the tank company, and brigade headquarters. The last landing, Green Beach, would be the smallest, and would involve only the 3rd Battalion.

The 1st Battalion, the paratroopers, would be dropped into three drop zones to block the three exit roads from the beachhead. They included the road from Red Beach at Playa Larga to Jagüey Grande, a distance of seventeen miles. Five miles of this road ran through the Zapata Swamp, and this stretch was dubbed "shooting gallery number one" by the brigade air force. The second road ran from Blue Beach at Playa Girón to San Blas, eight miles from which the road forked. The left fork ran twelve miles to Covadonga. Seven miles of it ran through the Zapata Swamp, and this shelter thus became shooting gallery number two. The right fork ran from San Blas to Yaguaramas, a distance of twenty-two miles, nine miles of it running through the swamp. It was designated shooting gallery number three.

The only other road was a good all-weather road that ran along the coast, the full length of the beachhead. It connected Playa Larga and Playa Girón and ended at Green Beach, twenty-one miles east of Playa Girón. At this point, the good road turned sharply inland, connecting with exit three, the road to Yaguaramas, but on the beachhead side of the Zapata Swamp. Down the coast, past Green Beach, the road became nothing more than a trail, dead-ending short of Cienfuegos Bay.

To block and hold the three exit roads, the

brigade planned to place the 2nd and the 5th Battalions and part of the 1st Battalion (paratroopers), along with two tanks, 75mm recoilless rifles, and mortars, at exit one; the 4th Battalion, a company of the 1st Battalion, a platoon of 4.2-inch mortars, and one of the M-41 tanks at exit two; the 3rd Battalion minus one company, a company of the 1st Battalion, one M-41 tank, and a company of 4.2-inch mortars at exit three.

At the road junction on the coast at Green Beach would be one company of the 3rd Battalion, reinforced with 75mm recoilless rifles and 81mm mortars, dug in behind a minefield.

Brigade headquarters at Playa Girón would hold the 6th Battalion and one M-41 tank in reserve, as a fire brigade force, ready to be sent to any of the exits that was seriously threatened. While in this reserve position, the 6th Battalion was to be kept busy as stevedores on the beach, unloading the cargo ships and setting up the brigade supply depot in the many empty resort houses. These numerous motel-type structures, in various stages of completion, would also house the brigade hospital and the POW enclosure.

To control the far-flung units of the brigade, the brigade commander would have as his headquarters a special radio communications center, built into a trailer.

The brigade air force was to be stationed at the airfield, outside Playa Girón. To enable the B-26s to begin operations immediately on D-day, sixteen ground crewmen, a seven-thousand-gallon fuel tanker truck, and sufficient bombs, rockets, napalm, and .50 caliber machine gun ammunition were to land with the brigade.

When the Kennedy administration rejected the Trinidad plan, the mass air strike of twenty-two B-26s on Castro's airfields also was scrapped, because of objections from the State Department that a strike of this size would indicate U.S. backing and was "politically unsafe." In its place, a compromise plan was worked out.

The State Department insisted that a "cover story" be inserted into the plan. It would place the blame for the air attacks on Cuban pilots as they defected to the United States. To separate this cover-story attack from the invasion, the "defecting pilots" raid would have to occur on D-2, two days before the landings.

This attacking force was also to be reduced from twenty-two to sixteen planes, since the State Department felt twenty-two was too large a number to fit the cover story. There would be five raids on Castro's airfields, each consisting of sixteen planes. The first was scheduled for first light on D-2, and the second for last light that same day. Raids three and four were scheduled for first and last light on D-1. The fifth raid would strike at first light on D-day, six hours after the brigade was ashore. These planes would not return to Puerto Cabezas but would land at the Girón airfield, where the waiting ground crews would rearm and refuel them for continued attacks throughout the day.

After the three exit roads were blocked, any attempt by Castro's forces to use them would give the B-26s a turkey shoot. Less than five minutes' flying time from Girón, these roads were built-up causeways, forty feet wide, with deep swamps on both sides. There was nowhere for the Rebel Army to get off or hide. The carnage the B-26s could bring about on these death traps was terrible even to imagine. No tanks, trucks, or troops could survive a napalm attack. After a few columns had been turned into charred and stinking rubble, Castro would have difficulty finding troops willing to try to force these exits.

The plan did have disadvantages. First, the entire coast was coral rock. There were no sandy landing beaches such as those at Trinidad. It did not have a deepwater port such as the one at Casilda. The ships would have to unload off the beaches, by landing craft, in water too deep (about nine hundred feet) for them to anchor. Nor did it have a city of twenty-six thousand from which the brigade could draw support. The population of the entire beachhead did not exceed one thousand. Most of these were construction workers, building resort housing at Playa Larga, Playa Girón, and Playa Buena Vista, which was less than a mile to the west of Playa Larga.

The most serious disadvantage of the Cochinos beachhead was that, unlike the Trinidad area, it had no escape hatch if things went wrong. The only way out, besides the three exit roads, was the sea. There were no convenient mountains like the Escambray range at Trinidad to fade into, and the beachhead was surrounded by swamps. The Escambray was sixty-one miles from Cochinos Bay. In the end, this proved to be a disadvantage that was to have grave results for the 2506 Brigade.

This was the Cochinos plan. It was submitted to the JCS for evaluation. The response of the JCS was that it was a weaker plan than the one for Trinidad, and that they still preferred the Trinidad area, but, the JCS concluded, *"if carried out as planned,"* the Cochinos plan stood a chance of success.

On April 4, the president called a meeting to examine this plan. The meeting, held at the State Department, was well attended. Present besides Kennedy were Rusk, McNamara, Lemnitzer, Dillon, Thomas Mann, Fulbright, Nitze, Dulles, and Bissell. The plan was presented, and *approved as written,* with *no objections* from members present, except Fulbright, who opposed it on "moral grounds." The invasion was set for midnight, April 17, 1961. At no time was there a request made by anyone for the use of U.S. military forces in this operation, and the brigade understood this.

A misunderstanding occurred at this meeting that the Kennedy administration later tried to use to lay the blame for the failure of the invasion on the CIA.

The Trinidad plan had contained, almost as an afterthought, an alternate plan. If the brigade was forced back from its defense line around Trinidad, it could simply withdraw into the high, rugged Escambray range and continue the effort as guerrillas. The Trinidad area itself suggested this escape hatch. The escape plan should have died with the Trinidad plan, for the Cochinos area did not have a natural escape hatch.

The escape plan should have died, but it didn't, and the subject of it was never even brought up at the meeting. However, some administration officials claimed they believed that the possibility of the brigade's escaping into the Escambray range still existed with the Cochinos plan, even though a glance at the map provided them would have shown them that under the Cochinos plan, the brigade was sixty-one miles from the Escambray range and would have had to pass through the encircling Rebel Army to reach it. Yet after the failure of the invasion, these same administration officials claimed that the only reason they voted for approval of the Cochinos plan was that they believed the Trinidad escape plan still existed.

The first I heard of this Trinidad escape plan was when Haynes Johnson made such a furor over it in his book *The Bay of Pigs.* He claimed it was one of the reasons the invasion failed. Much had been made of this alternate escape-hatch plan by the apologists of the New Frontier, but none of them ever explained why, if this part of the plan was so important, they had rejected the Trinidad plan, into which it fit so perfectly.

After the final approval of the Cochinos plan, the

State Department started to have second thoughts. On April 14, the day before the first strikes were to take place, State persuaded the president to reduce the number of preinvasion air strikes against Castro's airfields. State wanted the first raid, which already had been reduced from twenty-two to sixteen planes, further reduced to six. Even worse, it requested that the second strike, of sixteen planes, set for April 15, D-2, be canceled, along with both strikes scheduled for April 16, D-1. These cuts were necessitated, according to the State Department, to preserve the "noninvolvement image" of the United States. Kennedy approved these cuts routinely, without consulting the CIA or the JCS.

Now only one full-strength strike remained. Any further cuts and the State Department wouldn't have to worry about our "involvement image," for there wouldn't be anything left for us to be found involved in.

Another restriction, imposed by the State Department, was that the brigade air force was prohibited from using napalm in its raids. This too might indicate U.S. involvement. This reduction in the number of planes and the elimination of the napalm would leave untouched the huge motor park, packed with tanks and guns, that Castro had so conveniently left sitting out, like sitting ducks, at Campo Libertad.

Previous to the State Department's success in getting the prelanding air strikes cut down, it had received additional reinforcement. To its aid came

Arthur Schlesinger, who convinced Kennedy, on April 10, that he should make a public announcement pledging that under no circumstances would the U.S. armed forces be committed in any manner in Cuba. Kennedy made this commitment by a statement in a press conference on April 12. He did it without any prior notice to or consultation with either the CIA or the JCS.

Kennedy's willingness to make this kind of commitment showed the difference between his philosophy on covert operations and Eisenhower's. Eisenhower was confronted with a similar situation in the case of Jacobo Arbenz's Communist-leaning regime in Guatemala in 1954. In that case, as in this one, the CIA had been told to present a plan to overthrow the regime. When the plan was presented to him, Eisenhower asked the CIA if it thought it had sufficient manpower and supplies for the operation. It replied that it was confident that it did. Eisenhower then assured the CIA that whatever assistance it needed would be made available. He reminded the CIA that he considered any covert action as "committing the flag of the United States," that he would accept nothing less than a completely successful operation, and that the CIA would be held accountable to that end. The result of Eisenhower and his administration's complete support of the Arbenz operation was that it was a success.

One must remember that CIA covert operations began just prior to Eisenhower's taking office. So, essentially, almost all of the CIA's covert operations had been conducted for one president. Therefore, the top CIA officials were confident that any covert actions ordered and approved by the president of the United States would be fully supported by his administration, as they had been in the past. The halfhearted support the Bay of Pigs operation received from the Kennedy administration was well noted by these CIA officials, but they were powerless to do anything about the situation. President Kennedy had ordered the Cochinos plan carried out, and there was no higher authority to appeal to on the matter but God.

When the men of the CIA and JCS heard this "statement of commitment," they were concerned not because they expected any U.S. involvement, but because the statement could only serve to assure Castro and the Soviet Union that they need have no fear that the United States would come to the brigade's aid. It was a totally useless gesture on America's part, but for the purposes of the State Department and for the New Frontier liberals it was perfect. In one move, they had tied the hands of the president, who now could not use his armed forces even if he wished to.

6

Trampoline

I ENTERED THE PICTURE IN DECEMBER 1960. BOB MOORE, a close friend who had been the CIA's liaison man at Fort Bragg, was the catalyst for my joining the Agency.

I was retiring from the United States Army on November 30, 1960, after twenty-one years of military service, beginning in 1938 with the 5th Cavalry (Horse), Fort Clark, Texas, and culminating with five years as a captain of a U.S. Army Special Forces A-Team. In January 1960, Moore had set up a meeting for me with Desmond Fitzgerald, then head of the Far East Division of the CIA. Fitzgerald was aware that my final assignment with the Special Forces was to be in Laos. He assured me that he would have a job for me upon my retirement. At that meeting, Fitzgerald had me fill out a long questionnaire, which was an application, and which authorized the CIA to do an extensive background check. It was the first step in signing on with the Agency.

Fitzgerald indicated that he would send a cable to the chief of station in Vientiane, Laos, and that while I was there someone from the station would contact me and conduct an interview. When that was completed, they would make arrangements to pick me up sixty days before my retirement date.

Once in Laos, I worked on Operation Hotfoot, late known as White Star, with CIA personnel on a daily basis. No one from the station ever contacted me, so when I returned to Washington in December, I thought my deal with Fitzgerald had fallen through. Since I knew I would just be reassigned to Laos by the Agency, since Fitzgerald was chief of the Far East Division, and that possibility did not really thrill me, I was not entirely disappointed.

Still, I dropped in to see Moore. I asked him if he had anything for me. He said he did, and to come back and see him in a couple of weeks. I decided to take a vacation before rejoining the workforce, so I postponed my return until early January 1961.

When I called him on my return, he was frantic. "Where have you been?" he asked. "I've been trying to find you for weeks. I want you here this afternoon."

When I arrived at his headquarters in Quarters Eye (the old home of the covert operations division of the CIA before the Langley complex was built; during World War II, it housed the U.S. Navy's WAVE officer's quarters), I was immediately ushered into a small office and instructed to fill out a ream of forms. Somewhere in the midst of the stack, Moore showed up and ended the ordeal.

"I was going to set up your background investigation," he said, "when I checked the files and found the one Fitzgerald had done on you was completed. You already are cleared. We can get this thing done in a hurry. All you have to do is report for processing to Building A at the Old Brewery on E Street"—then CIA headquarters.

I reported at eight o'clock the next morning. The process began with a complete physical examination, followed by a three-hour psychological evaluation, which consisted of a two-and-a-half-hour written test and a half hour with the resident psychiatrist. He pronounced all my marbles to be perfectly round and arranged in the proper order.

We finished at one-thirty. I reported back to the chief processor and asked, "Mind if I get some lunch?"

He said, "Sure."

But as I started for the door he yelled, "Hold it—there's a red priority tag on your papers. You're going to have to forget about lunch, because we have to finish this today."

I spent from one-thirty to four filling out more papers and undergoing more tests. At four, I reported back to him.

He said, "You have one thing left. Report to Building 7." And he headed me in that direction.

Building 7 turned out to be a small innocent-looking structure behind headquarters. It had no identification other than the number on it. Upon entering it, you realized you had entered the dreaded chamber of horrors, the Polygraph Room.

Inquisition time!

The man in charge reassured me, as I shook in my shoes, that there was no reason to be nervous—that he realized most new recruits feared him, since he was that last thing that stood between them and employment.

He interviewed me briefly, then said, "I'm going to ask you a lot of questions. Simply answer them yes or no."

I wasn't worried. I was a good guy, white hat and all.

Before he actually started, he read me a series of questions he would ask on the test. Then he strapped me into the "electric chair" and fired away. At the completion of this, he took a look at the chart and said, "It looks good to me. I'll be right back."

When he returned, he said, "Everything checks out except one question. A minor one, but we have to go through it again. Don't worry—almost no one goes through clear on the first try."

God, I was nervous. What was the question?

It turned out to be "Have you ever used, or been known by, another name?"

"Let's talk it over," he said. We went through all the possibilities, nicknames, etc. Then he ran me through the polygraph test again.

He said. "You're through. You're clean."

I never really got an explanation of why I'd failed the first test, but if I had to guess I'd say it was because my friends had called me Gray instead of Grayston all of my life and I hadn't mentioned it, thinking it didn't matter.

I left the building with an immense sense of relief, took a cab back to Quarters Eye, and reported to Moore. He told me to be back at eight the following morning to finish my processing.

I said, "But I'm finished."

He was amazed. "You mean you completed everything in one day?"

He immediately took me down to security, where my picture was taken and I was provided with a set of credentials.

Now some people may wonder how a person could come into the Agency, be run through this paperwork, and then, without any special training, be sent out on a mission of the magnitude of the Bay of Pigs.

Well, first of all, since the CIA's Cuban Task Force did not have time to train people, it was taking only people already trained. Since I had learned the CIA's methods of operating while working with it in Laos and already had an extensive background in paramilitary warfare, the CIA did not need to put me through any further training.

I spent the next two days being briefed on the Cuban operation. It was apparent from this briefing that there was a large group of Cubans being trained in Guatemala, but at this point there was no mention of any plans for an invasion.

The following day I met William Robertson, better known as "Rip" to everyone in the paramilitary section to which we were both assigned. Rip and I hit it off immediately. We had many things in common. We were fellow Texans, in the midst of a large group of Yankee Ivy Leaguers, or, as Rip referred to them, "feather merchants." We both were former military officers with combat experience in World War II and in Korea. Rip had been a Marine captain in the Pacific in World War II and a paramilitary case officer with the CIA in Korea.

The Cuban operation was Rip's second tour with the CIA. He had been brought into the Agency originally in 1950, at the beginning of the Korean War, by his former regimental commander, General Robert Cushman. At that time, Cushman was with the Far East Division of the CIA. He needed to come up with some ex-military types for Korea and remembered Rip, who he felt was well suited to the position. After Korea, Rip played a major and decisive role in the CIA's direct overthrow of the left-wing government of Jacobo Arbenz in Guatemala in 1954.

His actions and accomplishments in the success of the Guatemalan operation, however, were marred by one small mistake, a mistake that in truth was not directly his fault.

The task force for the Guatemalan operation had been warned to be on the lookout for a ship, carrying a load of Soviet-supplied arms, headed for Guatemala to arm Arbenz's military forces. It was instructed to prevent this ship from reaching port by any means possible.

The ship was tracked on its long voyage into the

Caribbean, but for some reason, its exact location at this critical point was lost. Finally, a ship fitting its description was reported in a Guatemala port, in the process of discharging its cargo. Rip had a small group of fighter planes under his control, and he dispatched a P-38 Lightning to hit the ship.

The pilot of the P-38 did a beautiful job. He made a couple of low passes over the ship, firing a few warning bursts into the water. The crew got the message and quickly scurried ashore. When the pilot was sure the ship was unmanned, he made another pass and put two five-hundred-pound bombs squarely into the open forward hold. The ship sank.

There was only one small problem. It was the wrong ship. It turned out to be a British ship carrying a cargo of grain, and the biggest problem was that it was insured by Lloyd's of London. Even the CIA doesn't mess with Lloyd's of London.

When J. C. King, the CIA's Western Hemisphere chief, learned of the mistake, he hit the roof. When he later learned that Lloyd's of London, finding out through its vast intelligence network that the ship it had insured had been sunk in a CIA operation, had diplomatically but firmly requested the CIA pay for the ship, he really blew up. Lloyd's was paid. The Agency knew, as did most government agencies around the world, that there was no point in arguing with Lloyd's over such matters. Covert actions might be successfully hidden from the press and even the KGB, but Lloyd's of London could always find the means to keep informed about all activities that might endanger its vast and varied interests. The CIA also knew from experience that when something of this nature occurred, it was better to pay up fast, for Lloyd's was very persistent.

As a result of this episode, Rip had been put so deep in King's doghouse that he finally resigned from the Agency. He reentered the picture when the CIA's Cuban Task Force began setting up training bases for our assets in Guatemala and Nicaragua to support their efforts to oust Castro.

Rip was in Nicaragua, engaged in water-well drilling and gold mining. To be able to operate in Central America he had, of necessity, made a lot of friends in high government positions, including President Luis Somoza. The CIA station in Nicaragua had called on Rip to use his influence with these government officials and secure their cooperation in obtaining the bases the CIA needed to operate from. The CIA men were so impressed by Rip's ability to get things done, his knowledge of how to deal with the Latin Americans, and his fluency in Spanish that they called up headquarters and suggested that he might be the perfect case officer for the Cuban Task Force. Headquarters agreed and brought him to Washington as a contract employee, since this category did not require King's approval.

Rip and I were introduced to our new boss, the chief of the paramilitary section, Colonel Jack Hawkins, who was on loan from the U.S. Marine Corps. Hawkins had a distinguished record with the Corps. He had been a captain in the 4th Marines on

Corrigidor in the Philippines at the beginning of World War II, and he became a prisoner of the Japanese when Corrigidor fell. Hawkins was a fighter; he did not make a very good prisoner. He escaped and made his way to Australia, where he requested to be returned to combat duty. His last action of the war was the invasion of Okinawa. In Korea, Hawkins commanded a Marine battalion, one of the first Marine units to land in the Inchon invasion.

I felt very confident working for Hawkins, for he was a man who had seen and done it all. Amphibious invasions were his specialty, and he had not gained his knowledge just from books. If anyone wanted to plan an invasion of Cuba, Hawkins was the man to see.

The next day Rip and I got our assignments. He was assigned to the Key West, Florida, base of the CIA, as case officer of the LCI (Landing Craft Infantry) *Barbara J.* I was to proceed to Louisiana, where the CIA was in the process of opening a temporary training base in an old World War II naval ammunition depot, on the west bank of the Mississippi River, twenty miles below New Orleans.

My orders were to assist in the opening of the base and to give commando training to a team of eleven Cuban frogmen who were being flown in from Vieques Island, Puerto Rico. These frogmen had been training on the U.S. Marine reservation on Vieques for two months in swimming and underwater demolition techniques. Now they were to be trained in small arms, demolition, and commando tactics. They were accompanied by "Steve," a chief instructor and chief petty officer, and Underwater Demolition Team (UDT) specialist called "Bob," who was on loan from the Navy. (This is a good place to stop and explain that if I first identify someone simply by a first name in quotation marks, you are to understand that this name is an alias. Save for CIA officials and Rip Robertson and myself, all CIA agents are referred to by aliases.)

It took several days of hard work just to get our training areas in usable condition, because the base had been inactive for many years and had not been maintained. The base swimming pool, which was needed for continued underwater training, had several years' growth of algae and grime, which needed to be cleaned out. The area to be used for demolition training and small-arms firing was overgrown with bushes and even some fair-sized trees.

The old ammo bunkers, huge concrete structures buried under mounds of earth, were able to hold two hundred men with space left over. They were in good condition. We cleaned them out and used them as quarters for the troops. Nino Diaz's group, along with several infiltration teams and their case officers, were housed there.

After a week of housekeeping and brush-cleaning chores, the Underwater Demolition Team men got down to some serious training. They fired and became familiar with most of the small arms being used by the Cuban Task Force—submachine guns, handguns, Browning Automatic Rifles (BARs), and the .30- and .50-caliber machine guns.

I needed a few girders and plates to use on the demo range. I asked "Gil," the base chief, for some, or for anything he could find that I could use as demolition targets. He contacted a nearby Navy base and requested something of this description from its salvage yard.

Gil called me the following day to tell me the Navy was sending the steel over by truck. He wanted me to meet the truck at the front gate and direct it to where I wanted the steel dumped. I went to the gate and was surprised to see a Navy lowboy truck drive up with a god-awful load of steel items stacked ten feet high. I led the truck to the demo range, where the frogmen were waiting to unload the steel. We got it all off, and I thanked the driver for the excellent training aids. Then we just stood back, shook our heads, and wondered how we could ever blow all this stuff up.

The Navy must have sent us half the salvage yard. There were 3-inch guns and mounts, and 20mm antiaircraft guns and mounts, enough demo material to train the whole U.S. Army. So we blew and blew, charge after charge, until finally we made a dent in the pile.

The next day Gil told me to take the frogmen to an island six miles out in the Gulf, about forty miles east of New Orleans, for weapons firing and field demolition work and to practice some landings. This island was under the control of some military command.

About three miles long and a mile wide, it was uninhabited and was used as a live firing range.

We traveled to a point opposite the island in two station wagons and two cars. An LCM (Landing Craft Medium) was waiting for us. Once ashore, we found the place was covered by small pine trees and large areas of three-foot-high brown sea grass and sea oats. The men had a good day firing, but the demo work was hampered by the certainty that we would set the surrounding area on fire with each charge we blew. That meant we had to beat each fire out with pine branches before we could continue.

Just before dark, the LCM showed up to take us back. We were engaged at the time in trying to put out another blaze. The man in charge of the LCM was unconcerned by the fire, and he told us to let it burn—they needed the island cleared of weeds for a training exercise. So we boarded the landing craft and headed for shore. It was dark, and as we looked back, we could see that the fire had spread across the entire island. The whole thing was on fire. We had certainly solved the weed problem!

By this time, it was the end of February, and the ammo base was humming with activity. Diaz had 150 men in training. Another 150 men had arrived. They were later to become part of the 5th Battalion of the brigade that now was being trained in Guatemala.

At about this time, I received orders from Washington to proceed to Key West, where I was to take over as the case officer of the LCI (Landing Craft Infantry) *Blagar*. I arrived in Key West and was met by "Billy," the security chief of the base, and driven out to Stock Island, just north of Key West. The CIA base there was an excellent one, and in a perfect location for maritime operations. They had secured the site of the Key West terminal of the former Havana–Key West ferry. This property had a deepwater channel out to the Atlantic and lots of dock space. The depot, a large metal building located on the dock, contained tons of weapons and supplies. Ammunition was stored in dug-in bunkers outside the main building. It was the main shipping point for supplying the underground in Cuba.

There were two LCIs docked there, the *Blagar* and the *Barbara J*. Next door to the base was a marina and several docks where five or six of the black "ghost boats" were docked. These boats ranged in size from thirty-five feet up to a 110-foot former submarine chaser. They were the supply boats for the underground and the CIA's own infiltration teams. They were called "ghost boats" by the residents of Key West because of their appearance, solid black or gray, and the stealth of their night movements; they would leave quietly one night to return just as quietly a few nights later.

The base was isolated on a tip of land on the seaward end of the channel. It was closed off by a chain-link fence and a locked gate. But the large boat basin also contained a portion of the Key West shrimp fleet, a ship repair yard, and a couple of private marinas. It was in plain sight of these and visible to anyone driving around on Stock Island. Most Key West residents were aware of what it was, but with their close proximity to Cuba and knowing the threat Castro's regime posed to them, they approved of its presence. They even provided unsolicited "cover stories" to visitors who inquired about the ghost boats. They considered themselves partners in the effort, and were always ready to offer any assistance they could.

The Key West Police Department, the Monroe County Sheriff's Department, U.S. Customs, the Border Patrol, and the Navy command all had been briefed on the base, and their assistance was always available. Without this type of official and nonofficial support, the base could never have operated in the highly efficient manner that it did. Its cover would have been blown in a matter of days. These people were all patriotic, anti-Castro Americans who approved of their country's plans to knock Castro out of Cuba. I was very impressed with them, and I have included this episode to show what can be accomplished, and in secrecy, when you have the American public united on your side. This situation brought back memories of how it had been in America during World War II. If the American people understand and approve of their government's foreign policies, anything and everything is possible. But without this support, we are very likely to fall on our faces, no matter how hard we try and how much money is poured in.

We Americans are a unique breed, a mystery to

many in the world, but I suppose that is why our age-old slogan is so true and important: "United we stand, divided we fall."

At the Key West base I rejoined Rip, who had just returned on the *Barbara J* from making some supply drops to the teams inside Cuba and conducting a commando raid on the Texaco refinery in Santiago. The *Blagar* also had just returned from making a series of arms and supply drops along the south coast of Cuba. Since each LCI had lost a landing boat to the rocks and coral reefs on its mission, we ordered two twenty-foot catamarans from a factory in my hometown of Victoria, Texas, to replace them.

The two LCIs were former World War II infantry landing craft. Each was 159 feet long and had a large hold that ran almost the full length and could carry several tons of cargo. The hold was served by two large hatches, one in the mid-stern section, the other in the forward well deck. This well deck was a cutaway section between the bridge and the forward crew compartment in the bow. It had cradles for the two twenty-foot boats used to run supplies to shore. There was a large gasoline-powered crane mounted in front of the bridge, used to load and unload the two boats and the cargo from the forward hatch.

The ships were powered by twin banks of four General Motors diesel engines that ran a single-shaft propeller with electric reduction gears. This allowed the ship to run on all or some of its eight diesel engines.

Each ship carried a crew of thirty men. The officers, engineers, radio operators, and mates were all Americans whom the Agency had on loan from the MSTS (Military Sea Transportation Service). They were well qualified and experienced, but they were civilian merchant marine sailors, not U.S. Navy combat men. They were not trained for combat. Their service had all been on merchant ships that sailed charted sea-lanes, and in their minds the safety of the ship always came first.

My captain on the *Blagar* was a middle-aged man of Scandinavian background named Sven Ryberg. I liked him from the start. He was an able and experienced captain, well liked by his crew. I wondered whether he and his crew really knew what they were about to get into. At the time, I did not know the details of our upcoming mission, but I was sure it would take us into what is known to sailors as "harm's way" and could well be a shooting operation.

In the next few days, a small army of technicians and headquarters people descended on Key West. First came a team of RCA electronic technicians, who installed a large and varied array of radios and electronic gear on the LCIs, including a new radar with a thirty-mile range. Next came a team of General Motors reps, who made an extensive overhaul of the engines, particularly the clutch systems, which had been giving us a lot of trouble. They brought with them a supply of spare parts from God knows where, since all the components of these engines had been out of production since 1945.

After the work on the radios and engines was

complete, we were visited by the Navy commander, our maritime chief from Quarters Eye, and the chief of the Cuban Task Force, Jake Esterline, who worked directly under Bissell. After inspecting the ships and approving what had been done, they ordered the *Blagar* to load a thousand-man pack aboard from the warehouse, and the *Barbara J* a five-hundred-man pack. The packs, which are in sets of one hundred, include all the weapons, ammunition, and radio and other equipment needed to arm one hundred men. For each group of one hundred there is an additional pack of light machine guns and 57mm recoilless rifles and a pack of ammo resupply and medical and food supplies. For each set of five hundred there is an extra, rather large pack that contains more machine guns and mortars.

One night after the ships had been loaded, Esterline took Rip and me out into the parking lot and briefed us on our mission.

Esterline told us for the first time of the 2506 Brigade, which was training in Guatemala and was to be landed in Cuba in an amphibious invasion. He told us that our jobs as case officers of the LCIs were to sail them as soon as possible to Puerto Cabezas, Nicaragua, where the brigade air force had its base, and from where the brigade would be launched on the invasion.

We were told that our UDT frogmen would join us there and that we were to use them to recon and mark the landing beaches. We also were told that we would sail in the invasion aboard our respective ships, and that, in addition to marking the beaches, it would be our job to stand by as troubleshooters if anything came up that the Cubans couldn't handle. Esterline made it clear that he wanted people of our background and experience on the scene to represent the United States in the operation. (Later Esterline denied to Bissell having ordered us on the ships. This information was revealed to me in an interview with Bissell.)

At this time we were not told anything of the plan for the invasion, not even when or where it would take place. We were told that at Puerto Cabezas we would receive detailed instructions before taking the 2506 Brigade to Cuba.

The two ships' captains were briefed separately by the chief of maritime. I was not there, but I learned later that they were told only to take their ships to Puerto Cabezas, where they would receive further orders.

Well, now at least Rip and I knew that we were indeed sailing into "harm's way." At the time we had no idea how harmful that way was to become.

The only thing that was holding up our departure was the arrival of the two catamarans. We had arranged for the marina next door to install two seventy-horsepower Mercury outboards on each boat and to fabricate steel plates and mounts for a .50-caliber machine gun in the bow and a .30-caliber in the stern. All this material was ready to install when at four in the afternoon on March 28, the trailer carrying the boats arrived. The marina went to work, and by midnight both boats were ready. We gave them a short shakedown run out into the ocean, loaded them aboard, and at one in the morning of the 29th, we made sail for Puerto Cabezas.

The *Blagar* had only four .50-calibers mounted on the four corners of the bridge, for antiaircraft protection. I did not consider this nearly enough. After our briefing with Esterline, I went to the warehouse and got twelve more. The next morning, I informed Ryberg that I wanted as many of these mounted on the ship as he could find room for. He didn't like the idea very much, because, as he said, it made the crew nervous. Since I knew what we were going to face in Cuba, it was not the nerves of the crew that concerned me. It was the protection of the ship. So we mounted eight more of the .50-calibers, and I began gunnery training for the crew.

I had put aboard the *Blagar* a number of old rusty fifty-five-gallon drums from the Key West base. While en route to Puerto Cabezas, we tossed these overboard one at a time and shot them up with the .50s. When all the guns cut loose there was a thunderous roar and the steel plates of the little ship vibrated like a harp. The blasts from the guns also caused the chimney pipes of the oil-fired stoves in the galley to spout large black plumes of soot that had been collecting there for years. The cooks would come charging out of the galley, yelling that we were blowing the place apart. We paid them no mind. After three days the crew had become, to some degree, proficient, and the *Blagar* had very clean stove chimneys.

During the voyage I had been sleeping in a bunk in the forward well deck hold. I preferred this spot. It was cooler and roomier than the crowded, hot cabins on the main deck occupied by the ship's officers. Everything was fine in my hold except for an odor I could not locate. It smelled as though something had crawled into the hold and died.

We hit some rough seas on the last night of our voyage, and the *Blagar* started into a rock-and-roll routine that caused me to hang on to the sides of the bunk with both hands just to stay in it. After one particularly wild roll, some loose cargo in the hold started sliding around, and a wooden crate slid out from under my bunk. I had found the source of the odor. It turned out to be a case of Captain Ryberg's favorite food, smoked Norwegian herring.

I put the case back under the bunk, but next morning I moved it to the mid-stern section of the hold. Ryberg was informed that his herring was safe and the forward hold smelled fresh and clean, but the stern hold now smelled like there was something rotten in Norway. He laughed and said he had made bets with the officers as to how long it would take me to locate his hidden cache.

We arrived at the anchorage at Puerto Cabezas on the morning of April 1. A delegation from the CIA air base, representatives of Nicaraguan customs, and the Guardia Nacional (the Nicaraguan army) met us.

The *Barbara J* had arrived the night before. I found Rip and we went into town to find a hotel room. Since we would be doing most of our business ashore, we had to stay in town. Selecting a hotel was not a big problem, since there turned out to be only one. We nicknamed it the Puerto Cabezas Hilton, though it bore little resemblance to any Hilton either of us had ever known.

The hotel was run by a huge black woman everyone called Big Mama, who took us under her wing and gave us two of her best rooms. These turned out to be small cubicles furnished with an army-style steel cot and a washstand. There was only a curtain for a door. The walls of the cubicle were eight feet high in a building that had a twelve-foot ceiling, so, it was definitely not soundproof. At night you could hear an assortment of snores, snorts, and other strange noises from the other cubicles. Despite these minor inconveniences, it was better than staying on the ship. Spartan, but very interesting.

The town of Puerto Cabezas, really a village, was only a few blocks wide and about ten or twelve blocks long. Its main street, on which this "Hilton" was located, was unpaved and was lined with uneven wooden sidewalks and stores with high false fronts on them that reminded us of the set of the then popular TV series *Gunsmoke*.

The town looked exactly like an old Wild West town. It was shabby and down at the heels and looked as though a good wind would blow it away. It was Dodge City, even down to the hitching rails for horses in front of some of the stores. Rip and I agreed that if Marshal Matt Dillon and Chester were to come riding down the main street, they would not have received a second look.

The town's one and only industry was a large American-operated sawmill, which was quite busy. There were several large areas in front of it with huge stocks of milled and drying lumber. We found out this backlog was the result of a tight security block that Somoza's government had placed on the entire area.

While the brigade was assembling there for the invasion, Puerto Cabezas was quietly and secretly sealed off from the outside world. No ships came into port. All radio transmitters in the area had been seized by the Guardia Nacional, and the telephone and telegraph offices were taken over. No outgoing calls or messages were allowed, and the Guardia handled all incoming calls and cables. Managua had been told that Puerto Cabezas was having technical difficulties with its communications systems and that repairs would require a week or more. All persons in the town suspected of being Castro sympathizers (I believe there were four) had been placed in the Guardia lockup for the duration.

Later that day, Rip and I looked around town for a vehicle. We found a man who had a jeep. It was in such good shape it looked like a Cadillac compared to the rest of the vehicles in town. He agreed to rent it to us for ten dollars a day. We paid the week's rent in advance and drove out to the air base.

The airfield was located about a mile north of town and had a long, wide concrete runway that ended at the edge of the bluffs overlooking the

Caribbean. It had been built by the United States in World War II as an antisubmarine patrol base. Although the structures of the base had been dismantled long ago, the runway had been maintained and was in excellent condition. It also served as the civilian airport for Puerto Cabezas' only commercial airline, Lanica. Three of Somoza's air force planes were based there. They were World War II–vintage F-51 Mustang fighters.

We drove to the main CIA and brigade air force facility at the far end of the runway. A large tent city had been erected under the high trees of the jungle, where it was almost invisible from the air. The tents were standard Army-issue twelve-man squad tents, some with wooden floors and screen sides. One area was set aside for the pilots and maintenance crews of the brigade air force, and there was a separate section for the American personnel—the instructors and logistics people, Rip's "feather merchants." There was a large tent complex for the mess, one for the aircraft parts and supplies, and one each for the base commander and the security and intelligence sections. Alongside the north side of the strip were some large tents for the storage of supplies, weapons, and ammunition. Next to it was a large earth-bank-enclosed bomb and rocket storage site that looked as though it contained enough aviation ordnance to sink the island of Cuba.

We were duly impressed, but what impressed us the most was the lineup of what appeared to be at least twenty B-26s, six C-46 cargo planes, three or four C-54 cargo planes, and an old Catalina amphibious patrol plane.

The place was a beehive of activity. Planes were taking off and landing every few minutes. The B-26s took off in pairs to go out to a gunnery target area, where they engaged in air-to-ground strafing practice with their eight .50-caliber nose-mounted guns and eight wing-mounted rockets. They also practiced bomb runs in another area.

We met with the CIA chief of the base, named "Gar," and a pilot named Reid, who we later discovered was Major General Reid Doster of the Alabama Air National Guard. We also learned that most of the American B-26 civilian instructors were members of his Air Guard group from Birmingham. They had been selected for this job because they were the last Air Guard unit in the United States that had flown the B-26 and was familiar was it.

Gar informed us that a transport plane was due in the next day with a cargo of some thirty-odd metal and fiberglass boats and outboard engines. These were to go on the brigade ships as additional landing craft. He wanted us and as many of the crew of the *Blagar* and *Barbara J* as could be spared to come to the airfield the next day to assemble these boats, rig them out, and test the engines. A military officer in civilian dress was to accompany them. This man was a logistics expert sent by the JCS and would be in charge of assembling the boats.

We returned to our ships and passed the word to

the captains of our task. Then we arranged for some trucks to pick us up early the next morning.

Rip and I went to bed early, as we planned to get started at six-thirty. We found out we didn't need an alarm clock or a wakeup call from the "Hilton" desk, for as dawn was breaking over the sleeping village, two of Somoza's F-51s came in from the sea and roared over the rooftops, including, of course, our hotel. They cleared it by a good safe margin of about a hundred feet, but the roar of those powerful engines at maximum RPM was enough to send us to the top of our cubicles.

We were definitely awake. Not only awake, but wondering if the air base was still in friendly hands. Later that morning we learned that these two F-51s went out every morning to search the sea out to a distance of fifty miles for any signs of Castro's ships or "hostile activity." Maybe they thought they could spot Castro's "7th Fleet" on its way to invade Puerto Cabezas.

The early-morning reveille woke us each day; once we knew to expect it, we accepted it. We never really got used to it. We just learned to live with it.

When Rip, the ships' crews, and I got to the airbase, we found that the boats had arrived during the night and had been stacked in what appeared to be an old gravel pit, on the south side of the field. This pit was hotter than the hinges of hell. We stripped down to shorts, tied sweat bands around our heads, and began to assemble the boats.

They were a mixed lot of aluminum and fiberglass models, fifteen or sixteen feet in length, just the bare hulls with the components separate. The outboard motors were seventy-five-horsepower Evinrudes, at that time the most powerful and heaviest outboard in production.

We installed the steering cables and wheels, then set to work on the big seventy-fives, equipped with electric starters and batteries. The manuals that came with the motors indicated these were the first of a new family of Evinrudes and the fuel mixture used in the old motors had been changed. Instead of the usual one quart of oil to six gallons of gas, this mixture called for one pint. We filled the fuel tanks with this mixture, then hoisted the heavy Evinrudes into fifty-five-gallon drums of water and fired them up with the electric starters. They purred like cats. The motors were started and restarted until we were satisfied there were no bugs in them. Then we mounted them on the boats.

We had test-run only three or four motors when the JCS logistical expert arrived on the scene. When he saw the completed boats, he blew his top.

"That is not what I wanted done," he yelled. "Take out those steering cables and steering wheels."

We were aghast. Who the hell was this character?

He informed us that he was an expert in boats and motors and that he wanted the boats steered from the stern.

When we pointed out to him that these huge engines did not come equipped with the traditional steering handle of smaller outboards, he replied, "What do you think these handles on the front of the motors are for?"

The handles he was referring to were the two four-inch-long lifting lugs that were used to hoist the heavy engines around. We had to show him the manual before he would believe us. We also pointed out to him that if the boat operator had to steer from the stern of the boat, he would be unable to see over the heads of the troops he was carrying to shore.

The "expert" relented and told us to leave the steering cables and steering wheels in the boats.

This great victory of logic over expertise was shattered by his next pronouncement. "If you people will look at these motors," he said, "you will see that I had the manufacturer install a pull start on each engine. I don't want the troops to have to depend on the electric starters. The batteries or the electric wiring could fail. I want to use only the pull starts, so take those batteries and cases out of the boats."

We were so shocked by this order that we were speechless. He wanted us to rip out the ignition system the Evinrude Company had built into its motors. We all started to laugh. We all knew that pull starters were not standard equipment on these motors for the simple reason that the compression was so high that only King Kong could start them by hand.

The "expert" turned so red in the face at our insubordination that he looked like a stoplight. He wheeled on the nearest man to him and screamed, "You may think you're funny, but you won't be laughing when I get through reporting you to the captain of your ship."

At this statement, we laughed even harder.

"What's your name, mister?" the expert asked. "And who is the captain of your ship?"

The man stopped his laughing and in a calm voice said, "My name is 'George,' my ship is the *Barbara J*, and for your information, buster, *I am the captain!* I want to tell you right now, Mr. Expert, you don't know a damn thing about boats or engines."

The man's face turned a deep shade of purple. He wheeled about, jumped in his jeep, and roared away in the direction of base headquarters.

Later a jeep drove up with two of Gar's command staff. They told us, "You guys are in deep shit. That expert from the JCS is at headquarters raising all kinds of hell."

We explained what had happened and our reasons for objecting to his orders. They were on our side. They said, "We may not be experts, but you're right. This guy must be stupid. The only problem is, Gar can't help you. I'm sure he would agree with you too, but the expert answers only to the JCS, or maybe only to God. He may be wrong, but he has the authority to do as he pleases."

We thanked them for their information and support, and they drove back to headquarters.

After we'd discussed the matter among us, we

came to the conclusion that the only thing we could do was to finish the job and hope for the best.

We saw the "expert" again for the last time when he returned with a detail of men and began filling the fifty-five-gallon drums with gasoline that was to go to the brigade ships as fuel for the landing boats.

He ignored us. This was just dandy, because we wanted no more dealings with the man. It was only when we heard him giving orders to the men to add the oil to the drums for the mix that we spoke up. He was giving them the wrong formula, one quart per six gallons.

This was wrong, and we pointed it out to him. We even showed him the manual that clearly spelled out the proper mix. He ignored this advice and continued filling the drums with the double oil formula. We tried to explain to him that with this oil-gasoline mix, the engines would be very hard to start, would smoke like hell, and could never attain their full power.

He told us to mind our own business!

We did, but we knew for sure that this fool's mistake would cost us somewhere down the line. We finished the assembly task in two days, sweating like hell in the quarry, and sick of the whole thing.

One by one, the ships for the invasion began arriving at Puerto Cabezas. The *Río Escondido* came in bringing our eleven frogmen, and I held a happy reunion with them. Rip had never met them, so we all got together for a couple of beers at the biggest and loudest bar in town, the Estrella, located next door to our "Hilton."

The next ships in, the *Houston*, *Caribe*, and *Atlantico*, completed our little invasion fleet. I looked them over and just shook my head. They were a scruffy-looking lot, rusty, in need of a good cleaning and a paint job. I suppose I was expecting something in the way of U.S. troop transports.

Unfortunately, this was the best the CIA could do, since the State Department had Cubanized the equipment for the invasion, requiring the Agency to use only Cuban-registered ships and Cuban crews. All of these ships, and the *Lake Charles*, which was yet to arrive, were from the García Line in Havana. Eduardo García, one of the owners of the line, was very anti-Castro. He had been approached by the CIA about the use of his ships. A deal was made to lease his entire fleet, and an elaborate schedule had been worked out so that all his ships would be in U.S. ports at the same time. There they would be taken over by García, and all pro-Castro crewmen would be removed and held in detention by the U.S. Emigration Service.

The ships had been sent to New Orleans, where they were loaded with 1,630 tons of weapons, ammunition, vehicles, and other military equipment and supplies for the invasion. The crews were told that this cargo was to be carried to several Latin American countries as U.S.-supplied aid under the MDAP (Military Defense Assistance Program). The first stop would be Nicaragua.

García arrived in Puerto Cabezas at the same time as the ships. He visited each one in turn and informed the crews, without going into detail, that they would be involved in an action in Cuba against Castro. García gave them all an opportunity to decline the voyage if they felt that it would endanger their families in Cuba. One ship's captain and five crewmen chose not to go. They were detained by the Guardia Nacional, and replacements for them were flown in from Miami.

A few days later, all ships were ordered out to sea for a thirty-six-hour period, because an Esso tanker had to be brought into the dock at Puerto Cabezas to refill the fuel storage tanks. The harbor was cleared and all planes grounded.

The pier at Puerto Cabezas extended five hundred yards from shore. The tanker was brought in at the far end—from there it could observe nothing unusual. It came, was unloaded, and went without incident.

The next day our ships returned. Two by two they came into the pier, refueled, and took on fresh supplies. That night most of the ships' crewmen were given shore leave. Every bar and saloon in town was packed with drunken sailors. They were still celebrating at two the next morning.

Suddenly the whooping and yelling coming from the Estrella, next door to our hotel, grew deafening. Since Rip and I couldn't sleep with such a racket going on, we decided to walk over and see what the noise was all about.

When we arrived, we found all the sailors in a

large semicircle at one end of the bar. As we moved through the crowd we could see one of the sailors and a barmaid from the Estrella standing in front of the bar, holding hands. Behind the bar was the mayor of Puerto Cabezas, resplendent in a white suit, and with his impressive badge of office and multicolored sash across his chest. He had a large leather-bound book opened in front of him on the bar. To our amazement, we heard him reading off the marriage vows to the couple. It was a wedding ceremony, and an official one at that.

We just shook our heads. Now we had seen everything. We sat down at an empty table and watched as the tipsy seamen ushered the bride and groom out the front door and, with loud cheers, sent them off on their honeymoon.

A bar girl came up to take our order. We both asked for beer.

She asked if we wanted local beer or imported.

Well, I thought, why not go first class. So I told her, "Imported, of course."

A few minutes later, she set a rusty can of Schlitz in front of me. So much for class!

Early the next morning, Rip and I drove out to the pier. As we made our way to our ships, we came upon a group of four people engaged in a heated discussion. It was Gar, his chief of security, the captain in command of the Guardia Nacional, and the barmaid we had seen being married in the Estrella.

As we walked past them, the barmaid was pointing to a ship out in the anchorage. We heard her say,

"He told me he was captain of that ship, and now he has deserted me."

Gar turned to the security man and the Guardia commander and told them, "That's it—no more shore leave. This town is off-limits to all ship personnel."

Rip chuckled knowingly and said, "Well, that was a short honeymoon. But that marriage was probably only good for the duration of the shore leave anyway!"

To enforce this off-limits, the Guardia Nacional posted two men at the end of the long pier to prevent any of the crewmen from leaving the dock, and maybe marrying all the eligible maidens in Puerto Cabezas. But the Guardia did not prove much of an obstacle to the frogmen. The next night, half of them put their civilian attire in a rubber raft and swam, towing the raft until they were right behind our hotel. There they made their way ashore.

Rip and I learned of their presence when at about midnight we heard the Estrella bar going full blast. We walked over, expecting to find some of the ship's crew. Instead there were our UDT men, tanked up and having a grand old time. We were about to warn them to get out of there before the Guardia patrol came by when we spotted the sergeant major of the Guardia command seated in their midst, drinking right along with them.

The frogmen told us they had met him earlier, when he'd stopped them and informed them that the town was off limits to the ships' crews. They had convinced him that they were not crewmen but *hombre ranas* (frogmen) and had nothing to do with the ships and, in fact, were based at the airport.

The old sergeant had thought this one over, then swallowed their story, hook, line, and sinker. "Go live it up," he said, and when they invited him along, he joined in the partying with them.

We cautioned them to go easy on the booze, because they had to swim back to the boat that night. They told us not to worry, that they planned to sleep on the beach under the dock and go back to the ship the next morning. They did, and as far as we knew, no one ever discovered this last night on the town.

The next day the brigade transport planes all took off for Retalhuleu Airfield in Guatemala to pick up the 2506 Assault Brigade. This shuttle airlift continued day and night for three days, until the entire 1,474 men of the brigade were all assembled in the jungle area around the airfield.

In the middle of this movement of troops, a plane arrived from Washington with the planners and briefers for the Cuban Task Force. They were in three groups: a maritime group for the ships, another group for the brigade air force, and the largest group to brief the brigade. They had with them a set of plans for the invasion that was at least an inch thick. It covered the tactical phase, the maritime movement to the invasion site, and logistical and communication annexes. The sets were in both English and Spanish. They came with map sets for the brigade and maritime charts for the ships.

Colonel Hawkins was in charge of the groups and supervised the ground and maritime briefings. The brigade air force was handled separately. We were not informed of just what the planes were to do, except that the briefers assured us "the sky will be ours. No Castro planes will get off the ground."

Rip and I were briefed by the maritime chief and Hawkins. We were told Puerto Cabezas had been rechristened Trampoline base, since it was the launching site for the invasion. Each of us was given a set of the English plans to study. Now for the first time we knew our destination, Bahía de Cochinos, the Bay of Pigs, and April 17 was D-day.

Our objective was located on the south coast of Cuba, thirty-five miles west of Cienfuegos. There were to be three landing beaches. Red Beach at Playa Larga, located at the far north end of the bay, was assigned to Rip and the *Barbara J.* Blue Beach, the main invasion site, at Playa Girón, just inside the entrance to the bay on the east side, and Green Beach, sixteen miles east of Playa Girón, were assigned to me and the *Blagar.*

The *Blagar* was designated as the command ship, and Captain Ryberg was named as the naval commander for the movement of the ships and for the landing itself.

Rip was assigned three of the UDT frogmen for Red Beach, and I was given the other eight men, five for Red Beach, three for Green Beach.

The Blue Beach landing would be the first at 0015 on April 17. Red Beach was set for 0300, since the invaders would have to move eighteen miles past Blue Beach to reach it. The last one, Green Beach, was set for 0630.

The 2nd and 5th Battalions were to land on Red Beach, and the 4th and 6th Battalions, the tank company, most of the heavy weapons battalion, and brigade headquarters were to land at Blue Beach. The 3rd Battalion was to be taken aboard the *Blagar* after the troops at Blue Beach were ashore and landed at Green Beach.

The 1st Battalion, the paratroopers, were to jump at first light in two zones—one company to the north of Red Beach, and the remainder of the battalion at San Blas, eight miles inland from Playa Girón to the northeast.

Sixteen ground crewmen of the brigade air force were to land at Blue Beach along with a six-thousand-gallon tanker truck of aviation fuel. They were to go to the airstrip at Playa Girón to service the brigade planes that would be landing after they knocked out Castro's air force on the ground in a dawn attack.

The first ship to unload cargo was to be the *Río Escondido*, which would send, in its first load, enough rockets, .50-caliber ammo, and bombs to rearm the planes as soon as they came in.

The plan called for all ships to sail separate routes to a rendezvous point eighteen miles southeast of Cayo Largo, twenty-seven miles from the entrance to the bay. The rendezvous time was set for 1800 hours on April 16. At this point, the ships would form a single column and, with the *Blagar* in the lead, head for the Bay of Pigs. Midway to the mouth of the bay's entrance, we would be met by the U.S. Navy LSD *San Marcos*, carrying all our landing craft.

When we met the *San Marcos*, the column of ships was to stop while the landing craft were brought out and transferred to the brigade crews. The *San Marcos* would then depart, and the convoy would continue into the bay at eight knots.

After the briefing was over, Rip brought up the question of just what our positions were in this command setup. He pointed out that we were case officers for the ships, but nowhere in the plan were we even mentioned, and Ryberg had been named naval commander.

We were told not to worry about this. It was only a formality. Captains of command ships were traditionally named commander of all the ships. We would be in charge of our UDTs for the beach-marking task, and if everything went smoothly, our position in the effort need not be spelled out. The maritime chief also informed us that as soon as the brigade was firmly emplaced in Cuba, our two ships would be ordered out. He expected that would be on the third or fourth day.

Rip pointed out that we were to play the role of "troubleshooters," as they had called it, but how were we to do this if we had no formal authority over the ships' captains?

The maritime chief's answer was vague and ambiguous. He said, "I don't think you will have any authority problem if anything goes wrong. No one is going to want to question your orders, and you always have your frogmen to back you up."

We were still dissatisfied with the setup, but there seemed to be no concern on their part, so we let it go at that and left for our ships.

After the invasion was over and we were back in Washington, we found out why we had been left out of the plan. No one in the upper echelons above Western Hemisphere 4 (WH-4), whose area of operation included the Caribbean and all of Central America down to Panama, had been informed of our task, or even that we were aboard the ships.

That night, April 13, Rip and I checked out of the "Hilton" and boarded our respective ships. We were due to sail just after midnight.

After I was settled in on the *Blagar,* I gathered my eight frogmen, Octavio Soto, Blas Casares, and Amado Cantillo, their leader, who were scheduled to land at Green Beach, and Eduardo Zayas-Bazan, Filipe Silva, Jorge Silva, Jésus Llamas, and their leader, José Enrique Lamar, who were scheduled to land at Blue Beach, and gave them the essentials of the invasion plan. I also gave Lamar, who was also the chief of the entire eleven-man group, a copy of the plan in Spanish and the U-2 photographs of the Playa Girón area. The remaining three frogmen, Carlos Betancourt, Carlos Font, and their leader, Andres Pruna, were to land with Rip at Red Beach.

José came to see me later, saying he was worried about the dark shadows under the water in front of Blue Beach. He said, "Gray, that stuff is black coral, and it's nasty. We will never get landing craft over that. It extends out for a hundred yards from the beach and across the entire area."

I indicated to him that I was also concerned about this, and had, in fact, seen this as coral when I was first handed the U-2 photos at the briefing. I had mentioned it to the maritime chief, who told me to take it over to the air base photo-intelligence section and have the analysts take a look at it under the glasses. I was told it was probably seaweed.

I told José that whatever it was, we were going to have to go through or around it, because at this stage of the game, it was too late to persuade anyone to hold up or change the plans.

José was still worried. So was I. But we knew we could not change the landing site. After talking the plan over until the *Blagar* was well out to sea, we finally called it a night.

I was uneasy with the coral, and also with the entire plan, because as I saw it, everything was so dependent on the preinvasion air strikes to take out Castro's planes. If the strikes did not get them all, we were going to be in a world of trouble! Yet, I mentioned nothing, other than my concern about the coral reefs, to anyone. My faith in my government was complete. It was inconceivable to me that it had not considered all the angles.

The die had been cast. It was D-3 and counting. The 2506 Assault Brigade was on its way for a rendezvous with destiny.

7

En Route to Cochinos

ON THE NIGHT OF APRIL 14, THE 2506 BRIGADE, ABOARD its small fleet of ships, slipped quietly out of Puerto Cabezas anchorage and set course for Cochinos Bay.

No chance was to be taken that the ships would be spotted, allowing Castro to set a trap for them. Each ship followed a different course so that they were spread out over a hundred miles of the Caribbean. The individual courses would converge to a central rendezvous point, eighteen miles east of the first Cuban landfall, Cayo Largo. This point was twenty-seven miles southeast of Cochinos Bay.

The ships were to reach this point at six in the evening on April 16 and converge on the *Río Escondido*, which was carrying the 6th Battalion. It had been sent out from Puerto Cabezas on April 12, because in leaving New Orleans, its propellers had struck a log in the Mississippi River, damaging the blades. Although the ship was in good condition otherwise, it could be safely run at only six knots.

The brigade did not enjoy the voyage. The ships of the García Line were not cruise ships. They were rusty, dirty cargo ships. The troops slept on the open decks. The food was cold, because the ships' cargo of gasoline and ammunition made them floating bombs. No cooking or smoking was permitted.

The troops boarded the ships in khaki uniforms. By April 16, when they changed into their camouflage combat uniforms, the original khakis had turned fire-engine red, from the rusty decks. The voyage was uncomfortable, but thankfully short.

My ship, the *Blagar*, was the command ship. It carried the brigade headquarters group and Pepe San Román, its commander. Pepe kept his staff closeted in the ship's tiny wardroom from morning to late at night, poring over the maps and plans of the invasion.

Pepe's staff, like him, were young, but fiercely dedicated. They had trained long and hard for this moment. They knew the task ahead of them would not be an easy one. Their confidence in their men, in each other, and especially in the United States left no doubt in their minds that although the coming battle might be long and bloody, its outcome was certain. They would win. Of this they were absolutely sure. Even if all other factors might be questioned, the one factor that would never be in doubt was that the United States never backed a loser. Until April 1961, the United States had never lost a war, and above all had never deserted a friend. They would win, and when they'd won, they would always be grateful to the United States for its backing, though they understood this did not include the use of U.S. military forces, for without U.S. support no overthrow of Castro was possible.

On Saturday morning, the radios of the ships came alive with news of the brigade air force attack on the Cuban airfields. When I passed this news to the brigade staff, there was wild cheering. The first blow had been struck against Castro, and another attack was to come on Sunday morning. The Brigade would strike the third blow at 11:57 p.m. on Sunday.

Late that Saturday night, I stopped by the ship's wardroom on my way to bed. Pepe was still sitting at the map-littered table, a copy of the invasion plans in his hand. He was fast asleep. I turned out the lights and left him there. He would sleep better in the wardroom than in the small, stuffy, smelly compartment where he, I, and the rest of the Brigade staff had our sleeping quarters.

On Sunday morning, we listened in vain for news of the second raid on the Cuban airfields. There was nothing coming across Cuban radio but Castro ranting and raving, and chants of *"Paredón, paredón"*—"To the wall, to the wall," Castro's version of the firing squad.

Later that morning, I received the first of a long list of puzzling messages from Washington. I was informed that the second attack of the brigade air force had been canceled because of "political considerations." The memory of reading this message is still vivid, as is the sudden sinking sensation that came to the pit of my stomach.

I was no novice in the field of warfare. I had landed on Omaha Beach in Normandy, fought in Korea, and only recently returned from Laos. Until now, I'd had only one small worry about this invasion. It was the huge JS-3 and JS-4 Stalin tanks that Fidel had received from the Soviets. I had studied these tanks for years, and I knew that the best weapon to stop these monsters was the aircraft rockets of the brigade's B-26s. The 76mm high-velocity cannon of the brigade tanks could take them out only if they could strike them in the flanks. I also knew that if the Soviet tanks broke through the "shooting gallery" exits, they would allow Castro's forces to pour onto the beachhead.

Whoever controlled the air over Cochinos Bay controlled Cuba.

I was puzzled by this cancellation, and concerned, but, like the men of the Brigade, I had faith in the U.S. government's determination not to let this endeavor fail. I felt certain that the United States would not enter into an operation of this magnitude, where the consequences of defeat were so great, without having some alternative plan to knock out Castro's aircraft on the ground, though I had no knowledge of such a plan.

If I had been aware at the time of President Kennedy's statement, which he'd made at a press conference, that no U.S. forces would be engaged in the action under any circumstance, I would have known that there could be no alternative plan.

This was true in spite of the fact that Colonel Hawkins had written a cover letter to accompany the Cochinos plan pointing out that "this is a marginal plan. It will succeed only if all elements of the plan are left intact. Also all of Castro's fighters must be destroyed on the ground prior to the landings. If only one of his fighters is left intact, the invasion forces must withdraw at once, otherwise, this operation will result in a complete disaster."

Since my greatest concern was the Soviet tanks, I put the worry of canceled air strikes aside and spent time with Pepe discussing what I thought would be the best method of dealing with them. I explained to him that no other tank in the world could stand up to a Stalin tank in a head-to-head slugging match. The M-41s could get a few, but in the end, the Stalins would push them aside and smash their way onto the beachhead. It was my opinion that he could best employ the M-41s by covering the roads from the flank, never positioning one where a Stalin could get a direct shot at it, and striking them on their weaker-armored side. I also cautioned him never to allow his tanks to get in a slugging match. The best way to defeat these tanks was to use the ambush method, to fire and move, fire and move, and never get bottled up.

In addition, I suggested he use bazookas and land mines. The bazookas might not stop them, but I knew that most tankers, especially green ones, like Castro's, were scared to death of rocket launchers and would usually pull back when faced with them.

I tried to conduct this general discussion of military matters in a manner that would not alarm Pepe. He was extremely interested, and wanted to know if I would be available after the landing in case he needed advice. I told him I would be available for a few days, but if things went well, I would have to fade out of the picture, before the news reporters descended on the beachhead.

Pepe was not a field marshall, and he knew it. He never claimed to be, never claimed to be anything more than he was, but he was a damn fine officer and the best man for the job in the 2506 Brigade. He impressed me very much. I only regretted that I did not have time, on that short voyage, to get to know him better. After two days on the ship, I liked him. After three days and nights of the Cochinos battle, I also respected him.

Manuel Artime, the Revolutionary Council's representative to the brigade, was also on the *Blagar*. His was a famous name, not only within the brigade but throughout Cuba. Artime had been Castro's deputy chief of the Recovery Program for Oriente Province. He had broken with Fidel and escaped to the United States in the summer of 1960. I also regretted not getting to know him better.

The distance to Cochinos was getting short, and a lot of preparations were yet to be made. On the afternoon of April 16, the new camouflage uniforms of the brigade were proudly donned. Weapons and boat motors were checked, and many other last-minute preparations necessary for an operation of this magnitude were made.

At six o'clock, the invasion convoy rendezvoused near Cayo Guano. One ship, the *Houston,* was ten minutes late. She came in from due west, far too close to the Cayo Largo lighthouse, but our luck held. The radio on this outpost reported only sighting a submarine twelve miles south of the island.

The convoy formed into a column behind the *Blagar* and, just before sunset, started its run into Cochinos Bay. As darkness fell, the ships were blacked out, except for a masked stern light used to guide the ships behind.

As the last rays of the sunset bathed the ships in a golden glow, the brigade commander was presented with a Cuban flag, to run up on the stern of the *Blagar.* Everyone was assembled, the brigade staff, the UDT men, and the *Blagar's* crew. They stood at rigid attention and saluted.

Pepe and Artime conducted a moving ceremony, Artime giving an emotional speech. He spoke about how Cuban history would be made this night, how the hopes of all freedom-loving Cubans were riding with this small band of brave men. It was a short, simple ceremony, ending with a prayer for our success and safety. No man there that evening would ever forget it.

As the ceremony ended, we had our first glimpse of the two shadows that, up until now, had been seen only on the *Blagar*'s radar. Hull down, on the far horizon to the south and east of us, were the outlines of two U.S. destroyers, their bow numbers painted out. They were code-named *Santiago* and *Tampico.* Uncle Sam was watching over his chickens.

As we approached the coast, I was in the wheelhouse of the *Blagar,* glued to its radar screen, watching for the blip of the LSD. This five-hundred-foot craft had brought out our landing craft group from Vieques and was due to rendezvous with us twelve miles off the Cuban coast. Exactly on schedule, it came quickly up the column, to a position off our starboard side.

The convoy had been moving at eight knots, so as not to leave the damaged *Río Escondido* too far behind. As the LSD came abreast of the *Blagar,* the column slowed to a halt. The LSD took on a ballast of water, its stern doors opened, and the launching of the landing craft began.

The landing craft were manned by the CIA instructor group from Vieques. One LCVP moved out from the LSD to the cargo ship, to pick up the brigade landing-craft crews, the truck drivers for the vehicles on the LCUs, and the M-41 tank crews. These were distributed to their proper craft. Then the LCVPs returned to the LSD, carrying their American instructors. The stern doors of the LSD were closed, and it moved swiftly away.

We were all alone now. The lights beckoned from the horizon. We were dead on course for the mouth of Cochinos Bay.

8

Decision for Disaster

SUNDAY, APRIL 16, FOUND PRESIDENT KENNEDY AT HIS Glen Ora, Virginia, retreat. His remaining in Washington might have signaled the press that some unusual event was at hand. The press was still buzzing over the Saturday raids on the Cuban airfields and was questioning both the State Department and the White House about the "defector pilots."

The New Frontier was beginning to feel the heat of the Cuban affair, and was not happy about it. On Saturday, Raúl Roa, the Cuban foreign minister, succeeded in having a United Nations discussion on Cuba, which had been on the agenda for Monday, moved up to an emergency session that afternoon. At this session, he gave Adlai Stevenson, the U.S. ambassador to the UN, a very hard time. He charged that the United States was responsible for the air attacks and that the "mercenaries," supported by the United States, were planning further attacks.

Roa presented the committee with blown-up photographs of a defecting B-26 that had landed at Miami International Airport. He pointed out that this could not possibly have been a Cuban aircraft, as claimed, because of obvious differences in the configuration—a difference that the CIA had pointed out to the State Department when, at its insistence, the defecting-pilots scheme had been inserted in the plan. The CIA was right, for the scheme's weaknesses were so obvious that it fooled no one, not even the reporters who were allowed to examine the plane. Our planes had an all-metal nose mounting eight .50-caliber machine guns, while Castro's planes had a clear Plexiglas nose and six .50-caliber machine guns in the wings. Roa was clearly the winner in this debate.

Stevenson was also beginning to feel the heat. There has been much speculation about whether or not he fully realized, at the time of this debate, that this was only a cover story for the brigade air strikes. Many writers have said that Stevenson was unaware of the raids or the planned invasion. This seems to be true. On April 8, the CIA sent one of its top officials, Tracy Barnes, to accompany presidential adviser Arthur Schlesinger, Jr., to New York, where Schlesinger was to brief Stevenson on the Cuban situation.

Stevenson stated, on several occasions after the invasion, that the briefing given him by Schlesinger was vague and ambiguous; he was left with the impression that something would take place in Cuba, but at what date and in what manner he was unable to determine. He also said that when news of the morning raid on April 15 reached him, he had one of his aides call CIA headquarters to inquire about the CIA's knowledge of the event. The CIA, of course, was not authorized to give him anything other than the cover story, which was that this was an internal affair carried out by defecting Cuban pilots.

Stevenson's aide then contacted the State Department, which said it was still checking it out and would get back to him. The State Department informed Attorney General Robert Kennedy of Stevenson's inquiry and asked for guidance on what he should be told. The attorney general told them to stick to the cover story. So again, Stevenson was told that it was a raid carried out by Castro's own pilots. This was Robert Kennedy's sole action in regards to the Bay of Pigs Invasion.

Later that evening, Stevenson found out the truth. He had been lied to by his own government.

Stevenson said that his telephone call to Rusk on April 16 was not meant in any way as an ultimatum, as was implied by the Kennedy administration later. Rather, it was meant to let Rusk know that he now realized that he had been lied to and that he resented it.

Stevenson also expressed his displeasure at having had to debate Roa in the United Nations and forcefully defend the administration's position (that this was an internal matter, since it had been carried out by Castro's planes), only to find out later, to his embarrassment, that the planes had been flown by exile pilots under U.S. control. Stevenson added that he could not properly represent the administration's position if he was not told the facts of the matter—in other words, "no more lies!"

The most important item in his recounting of this phone call is his denial that he threatened to resign if any more air attacks were carried out, as the administration later leaked to the press. He pointed out that he could not have made this threat, since he was unaware that other air attacks were scheduled.

This is borne out by top CIA officials, who have informed me that to their knowledge, Stevenson was never informed that additional air raids were to occur, or, in fact, that there was to be an invasion. The general consensus of these men is that after the invasion failed, the administration tried to shift the blame for the cancellation of the air attacks to Stevenson.

Since the Kennedy administration supposedly canceled the air strikes based on Stevenson's threat of resignation, it is unclear whether Rusk correctly informed Kennedy as to the contents of his and Stevenson's conversation—especially since, over a period of time, Stevenson's version of their conversation had been leaked to a variety of sources by the White House staff.

The fact that bad feelings existed between John Kennedy and Stevenson was well known. In the book *Robert Kennedy: In His Own Words*, Robert Kennedy is quoted as saying, "He [Stevenson] was so unpleasant at the time we offered him Ambassador to the United Nations. The conversation with Stevenson at President Kennedy's home was very unpleasant. The President really disliked him. The President was so pleased he hadn't taken him as Secretary of State. It confirmed all he thought about Stevenson. He was really disgusted with him."

Kennedy had deliberately left Stevenson out of any discussions during the planning of the invasion. He was briefed on the subject only once, on April 8.

Late in the afternoon of April 16, the emasculation of the Cochinos plan was completed. In other written accounts of this phase of the event, it is reported that Stevenson threatened to quit if any additional air strikes were attempted. Rusk is said to have consulted with McGeorge Bundy on the advisability of canceling any further air strikes because of this supposed threat. Bundy, unaware that Stevenson had not threatened to resign, agreed that the cancellations were advisable.

Rusk phoned the president at Glen Ora and informed him of Stevenson's protest. When Kennedy asked for his opinion on the matter, Rusk recommended that the Monday-morning strikes be canceled. He also advised that no more strikes by the brigade air force be permitted until they could originate from the beachhead airfield at Playa Girón. The president agreed, and told Rusk to inform the CIA to cancel the strikes and to send Bundy to New York to pacify Stevenson.

Late that evening, Bundy informed Charles Cabell, the acting director of the CIA, and Bissell of the president's order. Both men protested the decision and asked to speak to Rusk in his office at the State Department. At this meeting, they explained their views on the serious consequences that would result from the cancellation order.

Later, in an interview I had with Bissell, I learned that Rusk would not be swayed. Rusk suggested that "the ships could unload and retire to the open sea before daylight," and "as for the troops ashore being unduly inconvenienced by Castro's air," it had been his experience as a colonel in the Burma theater *that air attacks could be more of a nuisance than a danger.*

Bissell also told me that one fact Rusk made absolutely clear was that "military considerations had overruled the political when the D-2 [Saturday-morning] air strike had been laid on. Now political considerations were taking over."

Rusk disagreed with Cabell and Bissell's protests, but agreed to call the president and inform him of their views on the matter. He made this call in their presence. Bissell told me that when Rusk was asked by Kennedy if, in view of these protests, he had changed his mind on his original recommendation, that the raid be canceled, Rusk replied that his views and recommendations remained unchanged. The president then instructed Rusk to inform the two CIA officials that the brigade air force would be restricted to missions of "tactical necessity" over the beachhead proper.

Rusk relayed the president's instructions to Cabell, but left out the part about the "tactical necessity," and asked if he wished to speak to President

Kennedy personally. Cabell declined his offer. After the invasion failed, his only explanation for this action was that he thought the effort would be useless. The two CIA officials dejectedly returned to the CIA war room to dispatch the message to Puerto Cabezas, canceling the air strike and sealing the doom of the 2506 Brigade.

Many writers have since charged that Cabell's declining to speak directly to the president was a serious mistake, referring to this as a "lost opportunity." But it seems unlikely that Cabell could have caused the president to change his mind. The record of the Cuban affair shows that from the first meeting on the subject, the president had consistently supported Rusk and the State Department in every single instance as they changed and watered down the plan. He also approved State's two previous requests to reduce the Saturday raid and cancel the Sunday raid entirely. He had done this in spite of protests from CIA planners. There is nothing in the record to indicate that this latest "decision for disaster" would have been any different.

The only difference with this latest decision was that instead of being made to satisfy "world opinion," as had the previous revisions, it was made, supposedly, to satisfy one man, Stevenson. It was a political decision, made to avoid the embarrassment that Stevenson's resignation would have caused the Kennedy administration.

The Kennedy administration had been inaugurated with the promise that it would "pay any price, bear any burden, meet any hardship, support any friend, oppose any foe, to ensure the survival and success of liberty." On this "Black Sunday" in April 1961, it failed to keep a single one of its noble promises. It did not "support a friend," the 2506 Brigade. Instead, it considered the brigade a burden too heavy to bear. When it discovered the high cost of political embarrassment, it also found it could not pay any price. Nor did it face the foe represented by Castro, and it certainly did nothing to assure the survival and success of liberty in Cuba.

When Cabell informed the paramilitary staff at the CIA of the order to cancel the air strike, there was a virtual explosion. These were veteran military men with distinguished combat records. They knew all too well what the order meant to the 2506 Brigade. Some called it an act of criminal negligence. They urged Cabell to try once again to get the president to rescind the order, or if this was not possible, to at least attempt to persuade the president to scrap the entire operation. It was the only possible way to save the brigade, which was now clearly heading into disaster.

Cabell would not make this request. His answer to this protest was "We have our marching orders."

The cancellation order was sent. It arrived in Puerto Cabezas only thirty minutes prior to the scheduled takeoff time of the strike. Rusk did authorize the paramilitary staff to allow the brigade air force to send four of its B-26s to the beachhead on Monday morning to "protect" it from Castro's jets. They were to be restricted to the beachhead proper and were not to strike his airfields. In other words, it was considered political bad form for the Brigade's B-26s to strike these jets on the ground, but it was perfectly all right for the B-26s to fly around over Cochinos Bay and wait for Castro's T-33s to shoot them down.

On Monday, that is exactly what happened. Five of the "protecting" B-26s were shot down. Eight good Cuban pilots died. This may have been the politically proper way to fight a war, according to the rules laid down by the "armchair generals" of Camelot, but in Cochinos Bay we called it murder.

At four in the morning on April 17, after receiving intense pressure from the case officer of the Cuban Project, Cabell called Rusk to request that, since the ships of the invasion fleet would have to leave Cochinos Bay at first light to avoid Castro's planes, Rusk authorize the Navy to furnish them air cover once they'd reached international waters, Rusk refused this request on the grounds that the president had pledged no American forces would become involved.

His pledge to whom? World opinion? Why should the president worry about breaking a pledge to some nebulous opinion? It had not bothered him when he broke his pledge to the 2506 Brigade in denying it the use of its own air force. For once, Cabell decided to go over Rusk's head and phone Kennedy directly. He received the exact same answer from Kennedy—no air cover, not even outside Cuban territorial waters.

At this point, I think it would be most interesting to examine the New Frontier's own written accounts of how these top officials really felt about this invasion, and their reasons for approving it.

To begin with, the president had publicly committed himself to make at least some type of effort to support the Cuban exiles in their struggle against Castro. For, in his campaign against Nixon, he had scored heavily in their famous television debates with his firm promises of support to the exiles. In his campaign speeches he had belittled the Eisenhower administration's program in regard to Cuba as being "too little and too late." His own program, he claimed, would be to "attempt to strengthen the non-Batista, democratic anti-Castro forces in exile, and in Cuba itself, who offer eventual hope of overthrowing Castro. Thus far, these fighters for freedom have had virtually no support from our government."

In a TV debate, Theodore Sorensen, Kennedy's speechwriter, explained this statement as one that "was in all candor, a vague generalization, thrown in to pad out an anti-Castro program." In other words, Kennedy did not have an anti-Castro program. It was simply campaign rhetoric, an empty promise that he should not be held to once it had served its purpose of helping elect him president of the United States.

When Kennedy took office, he quickly discovered that the Eisenhower program that he had belittled was not "too little." It called for a full brigade of these "fighters for freedom" that he had pledged to support. It was also not "too late," for they were set to invade Cuba on March 10, less than two months after Kennedy's inauguration.

When briefed on this effort by Dulles in Palm Beach, Kennedy had been, according to reports, "astonished at its [the plan's] magnitude and daring." In the many meetings on the planning and approval stages of the invasion, there was much discussion by the president and his top officials whether or not to scrap this plan and disband the brigade.

Kennedy was told by Dulles, among others, that any decision to disband the brigade would create additional problems. These men had believed his campaign promises. If they were disbanded, they would naturally feel that they had been let down by the new administration. The word would soon be spread among the exiles that they could expect no help from Washington, that the president had reneged on his campaign promises to them.

The president was faced with a dilemma. If he disapproved the plan, he felt, as Sorensen states, "it would be a sign of weakness inconsistent with his general stance."

Faced with all these problems, the president took the easy way out. As Schlesinger wrote, "Kennedy tentatively agreed that the simplest thing, after all, might be to let the Cubans go where they yearned to go—to Cuba. Then he tried to turn the meeting towards a consideration of how this could be done."

Kennedy gave the final approval for the Cochinos invasion on April 5 after rejecting the Trinidad plan as "too spectacular." Why the president approved this plan and what he really thought of it became crystal clear on April 8. In *A Thousand Days: John F. Kennedy in the White House*, Schlesinger wrote, "[Kennedy] felt, as he told me that afternoon, that he had successfully pared it down from a grandiose amphibious assault to a mass infiltration. Accepting the CIA assurances about the escape hatch, he supposed that the cost, both military and political, of failure was now reduced to a tolerable level. He added, 'If we have to get rid of these 800 [sic] men, it is much better to dump them in Cuba than in the United States, especially if that is where they want to go.' "

It seems that even at this late date, the president was still so unfamiliar with the invasion plans that he was not even aware the brigade numbered 1,447 men. Kennedy, it would seem by his statements, did not send the brigade to Cuba to get rid of Castro. He sent it to Cochinos Bay to get rid of those men!

So, as darkness descended on Washington on that Black Sunday, the final and irrevocable decision was made. Castro's airfields were to be left untouched. The 2506 Brigade was not to be recalled. It was not to be warned that on Monday morning it would have to face the full force of Castro's aircraft, all alone. Its air force, forbidden to help, would remain sitting on its runways by order of the president of the United States.

The stage for disaster was set. All that remained was for the pitiful drama at Cochinos Bay to be acted out by the doomed men of the 2506 Assault Brigade, who, at that very moment, were beginning to make out the dim outline of the coast of Cuba as they silently entered the Bahía de Cochinos.

9

H-Hour, Blue Beach

As the ships entered the mouth of Cochinos Bay, the first elements, the *Blagar, Caribe,* and *Atlantico* and the landing craft, turned to the east and headed for the lights of Playa Girón. The *Barbara J,* followed by the *Houston,* continued straight ahead for Playa Larga, at the far end of the bay. The *Río Escondido* was five miles behind, but this was of no great significance, since this ship was to be one of the last to land its troops.

The town of Playa Girón was lit up like Coney Island. High-intensity vapor lights had recently been installed at this Castro showplace. He intended it to be one of the playgrounds of the new Cuba, a resort for the masses. Many multicolored motel-type buildings were under construction. He was planning a gala opening for late May.

The landing beach was some eight hundred yards east of the town. It contained only one small building, which was situated at its center—a bodega, or grocery store.

Three miles out from the beach, the ships slowed and the convoy came to a halt. The *Blagar* lowered one of its eighteen-foot launches and a rubber UDT raft. The five Cuban frogmen destined for Blue Beach climbed down the landing nets into the launch. I went with them, along with my radio operator, Eduardo Zayas-Bazan, for it was from this launch, a hundred yards or more off the beach, that I was to make the determination of whether or not the brigade would land. If the beaches were clear, it would be signaled in; if they were heavily defended and I felt we were walking into a trap, the ships would reverse course and move quickly out of Cochinos Bay.

The launch moved slowly toward the beach, the UDT raft strapped alongside. When it was some distance away from her, the *Blagar* slowly got underway, to move to a position at the one-mile point from the beach.

The UDT men carried with them lights that could be seen only from the sea, by which they would mark the boundaries of the beach. The lights would be activated when the landing craft reached a point about half a mile off.

I had elected to go along with the launch, because I did not feel I could determine the strength of any beach defense force from the *Blagar*, which was now a mile away. I knew that when I made my decision to land, I must make it with what I saw with my own eyes. I was also prepared to go ashore with the UDT men, so as to be absolutely sure when I gave the word for the brigade to land that it would not be walking into a trap.

Those at the top might have felt plenty of concern with my decision to go ashore had they been aware of it, but I had no way of knowing that. Apparently, there was no such concern in WH-4, the CIA command from which I got my orders.

The planned landing point for the UDT men was on the seaward tip of a fifty-yard-long point that jutted out on the east end of the beach. This point contained the half-finished shell of a building, which the team could use as a covered observation point. From it they could scan the entire beach and the immediate area behind it. It was from this point that the men would move to place the beach marker lights and to scout the areas behind the beaches.

At eleven forty-five, we reached the launch position for the team. It was anticipated that the bodega, located fifty yards from that point, would be occupied, but we had come to the conclusion that at this late hour, the occupants would all be asleep. No such luck. It looked like they were having a party. There were several people wandering around. Floodlights on the corners of the little store were lighting up our landing point like daylight. We drifted a few minutes, observing them. Since they showed no signs of ending their gabfest, we turned back toward the town, moving to a point two hundred yards from the building, where the beach was in darkness, and started in.

At the release point for the UDT men, I searched

the beach with my binoculars. It was pitch black. A mass of heavy vegetation obscured the area behind the beach. There was no way to tell if one man or a thousand were waiting in the dark cover. I had to know, not guess. Therefore, I made the decision to go with the team. There was no other choice. I grabbed my radio, my Browning Automatic Rifle, and an ammo belt from the launch and slid over the side into the rubber raft with the frogmen.

We had lost precious time because of the lights and activity at the first landing point. The brigade was entering its landing craft and soon would be starting for the beach. We started in, and immediately hit hard, jagged coral outcroppings. The motor on the raft was shut off and lifted up. We began to paddle quietly toward the beach.

There were six of us in the raft. The bottom of it was filled with radios, ammunition, and beach marking lights. Somehow, in the movement of paddling, one of the marking lights switched on, illuminating the inside of the raft. It was quickly smothered and the switch checked. The switch was off—there was a short in it somewhere. Seconds later it came on again. This time when we got it switched off, I had one of the men sit on the damn thing.

It was too late. On the edge of Playa Girón, a militia outpost had seen the light. Two militia, in a jeep, started down the beach road, from our left. At this point we were forty yards from shore, and everyone but me was out of the raft in knee-deep water, preparing to go ashore.

When we spotted the jeep coming toward us, I told everyone to get down low in the water behind the raft, while I stretched flat on the raft with the BAR pointing at the beach. The jeep came on, then braked to a halt directly in front of us. It backed up and turned. Its headlights were shining straight into our faces. There was no doubt the militiamen had seen us. Before the jeep had finished its turn, I poured half a magazine into it, but the damn jeep's lights were still on.

As I was finishing off my first magazine, the frogmen had moved out from behind the raft, and they also were pouring fire into the jeep. Two BARs and four Thompson submachine guns were plowing a solid sheet of tracer bullets into the vehicle. I was on my third magazine before the jeep's lights finally went out. We learned later that the militia post had thought we were a fishing boat and were trying to guide us in.

In the sudden darkness, we moved swiftly up to the beach. One militiaman lay dead, sprawled beside the jeep. I made a quick check of the woods across the road. Empty. The brigade would land.

I called this information in by radio to the *Blagar*. Then I instructed the *Blagar* to move in to just off the beach and give us fire support. Finally, I ordered the frogmen to begin placing the beach marking lights and to tow the UDT raft along the shore toward the point of land that had been our initial objective.

The bodega now was quiet and dark, the party ended. At that moment, all of Playa Girón was plunged into darkness. Someone at the power plant had pulled the master switch. The blackout worked to our advantage, for it exposed trucks, loaded with militia, their lights on, heading for the beach. It was some time before those in the trucks realized that they were illuminated targets and cut off their headlights.

By then the *Blagar* had seen them and opened fire. The dozen .50-caliber machine guns and the two 75mm recoilless rifles twice raked the beach, from end to end. They stopped. Suddenly it was very quiet. The militiamen had disappeared.

By this time, the frogmen and I were set up in a building under construction on the point. We had placed a bright marker light on its highest point, to mark our location. From this position we could cover the entire landing area with fire.

I knew now that our greatest danger was that the militia might slip in and occupy positions in the black, wooded area behind the beach. To prevent this, I had the *Blagar* twice more sweep this area with fire. We had been taking some fire from the direction of the town, but most of it was high, over our heads. The militia was not using tracers, and without them was firing wild.

We blasted around the bodega a few times to discourage anyone from using it as cover to fire on our group. The *Blagar* was taking fire from one machine gun on the far end of the beach. It would fire only when the *Blagar* did. I notified the ship of this, but could not spot the machine gun's position. One member of the *Blagar*'s crew was hit by fire from this gun. He became the first man to be wounded at the Bay of Pigs.

After what seemed like ages, the *Blagar* called to report that the landing craft were on the way in. We had scouted out the area and found a break in the coral reef next to our point. The LCVPs were directed to guide on our light, and to use their .30-caliber machine guns as they came. This would help to discourage anyone from attempting to occupy the area.

It was a welcome sight, the streams of tracers raking the beach as the 4th Battalion came roaring in. When the landing craft grounded and the ramps dropped, the men of the brigade stormed ashore with blood-curdling yells and cheers. The pent-up emotions and tensions of the years of frustration and waiting were released. They had arrived at last, at the end of the road that led to Cochinos Bay.

Each man came ashore carrying some type of ammunition, such as a mortar shell, a recoilless rifle round, or a box of machine gun ammunition, in one hand and his weapon in the other. The ammo was dropped into piles on the beach, and the men moved on to capture Playa Girón.

Following close behind the first wave were Pepe and some of the brigade staff in a boat operated by one of my frogmen, Amado Cantillo. It was an emotional moment for the leaders. They were on Cuban soil.

I briefed Pepe on what I'd seen as we walked

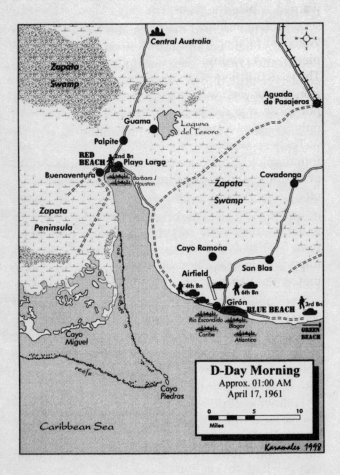

Central Australia

Zapata Swamp

Aguada de Pasajeros

Guama
Laguna del Tesoro

Palpite

RED BEACH
2nd Bn
Playa Larga

Buenaventura
Barbara J Houston

Zapata Swamp

Covadonga

Zapata Peninsula

Cayo Ramona

Airfield
San Blas

4th Bn
6th Bn

Girón
BLUE BEACH
3rd Bn

Río Escondido
Blagar
Caribe
Atlántico
GREEN BEACH

Cayo Miguel

reefs

Cayo Piedras

Caribbean Sea

D-Day Morning
Approx. 01:00 AM
April 17, 1961

0   5   10
Miles

Karamales 1998

down the beach to inspect the militia jeep that the frogmen and I had blasted as we came ashore. He wanted to use the jeep, if it was still operable, to send a team around the town to check the airfield. Well, not in that jeep he wouldn't. It was shot to pieces—everything, that is, except the headlights. Those two little jewels were still intact. The entire front of this jeep was covered with bullet holes, but not those two damned lights. They had gone out only because we had shot the battery to bits.

The jeep was useless, but behind the bodega we found an old Chevrolet that would run. One squad of the 4th Battalion piled into the old car and roared off on a side road that led around Playa Girón to the airfield.

My radio operator informed me that I had a call from the *Blagar*, requesting that I return at once. An important message had been received from Washington. As I shoved off in the UDT raft, I had that now familiar sinking sensation, because this message, I felt, could only mean trouble.

My instincts were correct. The message read: "Castro still has operational aircraft. Expect you will be under air attack at first light. Unload all men and supplies and take the ships to sea."

That elevator in my stomach was headed at full speed for the basement. Well, we were in for it. How bad it would be and what had gone wrong were things that we now had no time to speculate on. We had to get moving. For the ships to be caught off this beach in daylight by Castro's planes would be bad. Worse still would be for the brigade not to get the ammunition and supplies on these ships, for without them it didn't stand a chance. The brigade was what this mission was all about, not a few rusty old cargo ships.

The captain had already passed this information on to Pepe. He was just as shocked and puzzled as I was. I called him on the radio. He asked me not to leave. The brigade must have the supplies. I agreed with him, and promised him that we would stay as long as possible.

The Green Beach landing, by the 3rd Battalion, was scheduled for seven in the morning. I asked Pepe if he would concur in calling it off. I told him that I could put the battalion ashore immediately at Blue Beach, and he could start a shuttle service, using what trucks he had, to get them to Green Beach. That way we would have the unit ashore, intact, where it would not be as vulnerable to the air attacks. If we moved the *Blagar* and the 3rd Battalion down by sea after daylight, we would be sitting ducks for Castro's planes.

I pointed out that the *Blagar*, with her many .50-caliber machine guns, was the only real antiaircraft protection we had. If she left or was sunk, the other ships, and Blue Beach, would be unprotected. Pepe readily agreed to this, and we ordered the 3rd Battalion ashore.

Thirty minutes later, a radio message from Pepe informed me that Playa Girón and the airfield had been captured, and that the airfield was operational.

So far at least, we were on schedule in the unloading. That wasn't going to be good enough—not if we intended to get all the men and equipment ashore before the planes hit us. The unloading schedule was precise. Each ship had her own copy of it. If we followed it, we would not finish until long after daylight. The word was passed to each ship: all troops ashore as fast as possible, ammunition next.

Now trouble came from two directions. The LCVPs had been told to ease in on the beach and to watch their bottom, but they were eager to get in fast. In doing so, they had rammed the sawtooth coral at full throttle. Two of them looked like sieves, but were still going.

The other problem was the cargo ships. They didn't want to get in next to the shore, even though the water there was several hundred feet deep. In addition, they kept drifting too far out. The LCVPs had a hell of a time finding them. They were supposed to stay in one position, so that the landing craft knew from where they lay which ship to head for. When they drifted out, they changed position with one another.

I had them brought in, and marker lights rigged so the boats could tell which ship was which. The problem persisted, for no sooner did we get them in close and sort them out than out they'd drift, and we'd have to go through the same shuffle again. One of the Cuban frogmen, Blas Casares, handled this task by radio, and did an outstanding job in a very exasperating situation.

Slowly but surely, we got the flow of men moving on schedule over the beach. The two LCVPs that had struck the coral finally gave up the ghost. One beached in a sinking condition but got all its troops ashore. The other sank alongside the *Atlantico*. Luckily it was empty.

The ship's small boats were put to use along with the *Blagar*'s two launches. Pepe asked if I could get the three LCUs in with his tanks. They were originally scheduled in after daylight. The frogmen had been searching for a break in the coral large enough to get them through, but at that point had not found one suitable.

These are very large craft. When they are grounded, they require a stern anchor and winch system to pull them back off a beach. This is a tricky, extremely difficult maneuver to perform in darkness. I told Pepe this, and suggested we wait until it was light enough to see what we were doing. If a tank threw a track getting off, we'd have big problems. Pepe reluctantly agreed. I promised him that I would get things in as soon as possible.

I also informed him that there was fighting reported at Red Beach, and that there were problems with the landing boats. Rip was asking for any landing craft and tanks that we could send them. I recommended sending one of the LCUs that had two M-41 tanks aboard. He agreed, and one of the LCUs got underway.

On Red Beach, Rip was having problems of his own.

A U-2 spy plane photo of the airfield at Playa Girón, the site of the Bay of Pigs invasion. *(CIA)*

Twenty miles south of the Bay of Pigs, the commander of the 2506 Assault Brigade, Pepé San Román, raises the Cuban flag in anticipation of freeing his homeland. *(Amado Cantillo)*

Members of the invasion force test-fire weapons aboard the *Blagar.* In the foreground, frogman Amado Cantillo holds a Browning Automatic Rifle (BAR), the type of gun the author used to fire the first shots of the battle.
(Amado Cantillo)

A B-26's flight crew makes ready for departure to the invasion site. The plane's eight nose-mounted .50-caliber machine guns can be seen.
(Eduardo Ferrer)

The brigade's sixteen B-26 bombers stand at the ready in Puerto Cabezas. They bear the markings of Castro's air force so that the Cubans would think the planes were flown by defectors. *(Eduardo Ferrer)*

The railroad-equipped dock at Puerto Cabezas, Nicaragua, was the embarkation point for the brigade's fleet of six ships. *(Eduardo Ferrer)*

At the battle's end, a brigade landing craft lies dead in the water. *(Juan E. Pérez-Franco)*

One of Castro's T-33 jet fighters (originally the American F-80), which wreaked havoc on the brigade. *(Eduardo Ferrer)*

Members of Castro's air force gather in front of a British-built Sea Fury, rockets hanging from its wings. It also had wing-mounted 20mm cannons. *(Eduardo Ferrer)*

The troop ship *Río Escondido* was the first vessel sunk by Castro's air force. *(Francisco Montiel)*

The command ship *Blagar,* from which the author fought off attacking Cuban planes and where he maintained radio contact between Washington and the beachhead during the invasion. *(Juan E. Pérez-Franco)*

Robertson's assigned post, the *Barbara J,* the control ship for the invasion of Red Beach. *(Francisco Montiel)*

A view looking forward from the coning tower of the *Barbara J* of two twenty-foot landing craft used by the author and the frogmen to make the invasion's initial landing. *(Francisco Montiel)*

A World War II–era LCU (Landing Craft, Utility), one of those used to land the brigade's tanks and trucks, which were loaded with ammunition and supplies. *(Juan E. Pérez-Franco)*

Author Grayston L. Lynch as an Army Airborne captain in 1960. *(U.S. Army)*

Lynch's fellow CIA operative, William "Rip" Robertson, the only other American to accompany the Bay of Pigs invasion force.

10

The Battle of Red Beach

THE LANDING SITE DESIGNATED RED BEACH WAS LO-
cated at the far north end of the bay, directly in front
of the small village of Playa Larga. Its landing beach
was the best of all the beaches. It was sand, with a
gentle slope out to deep water. It was the perfect
model of an amphibious landing site.

The fact that the beach was directly in front of the
village was not, under the circumstances, considered a problem. Recent U-2 photos of the area had
shown that it was not prepared for defense. There
were no entrenchments or telltale signs of gun emplacements or fortifications. There were less than
sixty men in the home guard militia, and they were
equipped only with small arms and a few light machine guns.

One and a half miles to the west of Playa Larga,
around the corner of the bay, was a large construction project at Buenaventura. Castro was erecting

another of his vacation resorts similar to the one at Playa Girón. The 150 workers on this project were unarmed civilians and were not considered to be a threat to the landing force. The first structures on the beach were located seventy-five yards from the water's edge. They were crude thatch-roofed, open-sided beach shelters. Fifty yards behind them was the main village, which was a block wide and maybe several hundred yards long. It was made up of simple shacks, occupied by the fishermen and their families.

The main road from Playa Girón ran directly behind them and made a sharp turn to the north at the traffic circle called the Rotunda. This road to the north ran straight as an arrow through the small village of Palpite and the Zapata Swamp to the town of Jagüey Grande and the huge sugar mill complex called Central Australia.

The only organized military unit in the zone was based at this sugar mill, where the military headquarters of the Zapata Zone was located. It was eighteen miles north of Playa Larga and was composed of a thousand-man battalion commanded by Comandante Osmani Cienfuegos, the brother of the famous hero of the revolution, Comandante Camilo Cienfuegos, who had been killed in a mysterious plane crash in 1960.

The plan for the Red Beach landing called for the LCI *Barbara J*, which carried three UDT men, led by Rip, to lead the *Houston* up the bay to within one mile of the beach. Aboard the *Houston* was the deputy commander of the brigade, Erneido Oliva, and his small staff, and the 2nd and 5th Infantry Battalions, which would constitute the main landing force. To support them there were three platoons from the heavy weapons battalion, a 4.2-inch mortar platoon, one 75mm recoilless rifle platoon, and a 57mm recoilless rifle and a 3.5-inch bazooka platoon.

Oliva was a well-built, handsome man and a former officer in the Cuban army. His no-nonsense approach, impressive military bearing, experience, and leadership qualities made him immensely popular with the entire brigade. They had so much confidence in his ability to command that they felt sure they could handle anything Castro could throw at them. The fact that Oliva was black meant nothing to them, for the 2506 Brigade was not race-conscious or prejudiced. There were many blacks in the brigade, some in key leadership positions.

The 2nd Battalion, which was to make the initial assault landing at three in the morning, was the most experienced and best-trained unit in the brigade. It was led by a man considered the best battalion commander, a tough little fighter, Hugo Sueiro. Like Oliva, he was a graduate of the Cuban Military Academy and a former Cuban army officer.

The 5th Battalion was led by Montero Duque, also a former Cuban army officer. He had fought against Castro in the Sierra Maestra. Although well trained and experienced, Duque unfortunately was, as his later actions were to reveal, not of the same high caliber as Oliva and Sueiro.

The task of the 5th Battalion was to have been to follow the 2nd battalion ashore and mop up Playa Larga, while Sueiro and the 2nd Battalion moved to block the road to Central Australia where it entered the Zapata Swamp. After mopping up the Red Beach area, the 5th Battalion was to have left one company to occupy Playa Larga and joined the 2nd Battalion at the roadblock.

To support the Red Beach force, one company of paratroopers from the 1st Airborne Battalion was to be dropped the next morning at first light. This company was under Reuben Vera, the second in command of the 1st Battalion. The troops were to be dropped in two groups. One platoon, led by Vera, would be dropped at the north exit of the road through the Zapata Swamp to act as a delaying force. The remainder of the company was set to land north of Palpite to block the southern end of the swamp road, where the 2nd and the 5th Battalions were to join up with them to create the main battle position.

The idea was that Vera's platoon would first engage any Castro forces headed for Red Beach, and by leapfrogging his forces, bring them slowly through the swamp until they encountered the main battle line. This would have given the Brigade's B-26s more time to work them over before the forces of Oliva stopped them completely.

The plan also directed that the *Houston* and the *Barbara J* return to Blue Beach at Playa Girón as soon as the last of Oliva's forces was ashore. The

Houston would have landed a supply of ammunition at Red Beach, enough to carry the Oliva forces through the second day of action. The main routing of supplies was to be by truck convoys from the supply base at Playa Girón. The major cargo of the *Houston* contained general supplies, trucks, jeeps, and the medical staff and medical supplies to set up the brigade hospital at Playa Girón.

This was the plan when the *Barbara J* and the *Houston* arrived in position off Red Beach at 0200, on time and undetected.

At 0215, the *Barbara J* launched an eighteen-foot catamaran with Rip and the frogmen. As they eased the cat into shore, they could see a group of people in the village center, engaged in what appeared to be a loud, wild, and well-oiled party. We later discovered that this was a group of thirty of Castro's militia from Havana, who had been given a weekend pass to enjoy this vacation resort. They had been scheduled to depart for their home posts at midnight, but their group leader was drunk and could not find anyone else sober enough to drive. He had decided they would stay until the next day.

After watching the party for a few minutes, the frogmen swam in and scouted the beach area from end to end. It was empty. There were no gun emplacements and no trenches. They placed the beach marker lights and radioed the *Houston*, giving the all clear for the 2nd Battalion to come in.

On the *Houston*, the 2nd Battalion had launched the eight landing boats and the men were starting to go over the side. They sent a radio message to the frogmen saying they were on their way. Upon receipt of this message, the frogmen turned on the beach marker lights. This brought a scattering of small-arms fire from the village. It was badly aimed and came nowhere near the frogmen. They answered this fire with the .50-caliber and .30-caliber machine guns mounted on the cat, plus the fire of their own four BARs. The partying militia pulled a hasty retreat and the village was blacked out and quiet.

After waiting another ten minutes, the frogmen called the *Houston* to find out what was holding up the 2nd Battalion. They were told that there was trouble with the outboard engines on the landing boats. They could not start them, and when they did, they smoked and sputtered, and would not stay running. This in retrospect is understandable. It was exactly what we warned the JCS "logistics expert" back at Puerto Cabezas would happen if we followed his orders.

Shortly after this call to the *Houston*, the frogmen spotted several trucks coming from the construction site at Buenaventura toward Playa Larga with headlights ablaze. The *Barbara J* had spotted them as well, and had moved to a point off the west edge of the village. As the first truck entered Playa Larga, the frogmen blasted it with machine gun fire, while the *Barbara J* turned ten .50-caliber guns on the remaining trucks. This action lasted only a few minutes, and again this area was quiet and dark except for a line of burning trucks scattered along the beach road to the west.

At this time the first of the landing boats of the 2nd Battalion started arriving and unloading on the beach. Sueiro led this first group into and through Playa Larga against only a few wild shots coming from out of the darkness.

As other boats arrived, the frogmen saw that only a few of the outboard engines were operating. Those that were operational were towing two or three of the inoperative boats. To expedite this movement, the *Barbara J* launched its second UDT boat, and Rip sent his own cat boat to the *Houston* to pick up troops. Using this system, all of the 2nd Battalion and Oliva's staff group were brought ashore.

Batteries from the *Barbara J* were sent to the *Houston*, and, by using the electric starters on the seventy-five-horsepower outboards, most of them were put in running order.

Rip and his frogmen on the beach were now waiting for the 5th Battalion, as were Oliva and Sueiro, who were anxious to get started out of Playa Larga up the road to their battle positions. A call to the *Houston* by Rip, inquiring what was holding them up, brought only a cryptic reply that "we have problems."

To find out what these problems were, Rip and his frogmen took their cat boat out to the *Houston*, where they found all of the landing boats clustered along its side, but no unloading appeared to be going on.

Rip called up to the men lining the railing of the ship to start down the landing net to the boat. They replied, "We can't. We have orders to stay aboard."

When Rip asked who had given this order, he was informed that it came from Duque. Rip and the frogmen climbed aboard the *Houston,* found Duque, and asked him why he had ordered a halt to the landing.

Duque was highly excited, and in a hostile tirade he screamed out his reasons.

First, he said, he did not have enough ammunition (actually he had the same basic load as the 2nd Battalion). Second, he would not land until he was sure the area was secure and that the Castro troops did not have artillery. Third, the most transparent of his excuses, the landing boats were no good. These were the same boats that had just landed the entire 2nd Battalion with only a few engines operating. Now he had the two boats from the *Barbara J,* and most of the landing boats had their engines running.

Rip blew up. He told him, "Look, mister, it's your war and your country, not mine. If you're too scared to land and fight, then stay here and rot!"

Turning away, he told the frogmen to get back in the cat boat, saying that this group could go to hell.

As they were leaving, the frogmen were approached by a soldier, who identified himself as the squad leader of the last 2nd Battalion squad on the *Houston.* He asked if they would take him and his squad back to the beach with them. They were told to load aboard the cat boat.

As this squad started over the side, Duque ran to the rail and ordered them back aboard. He shouted that no man could leave the ship without his permission. When the frogmen pointed out to him that these were not his troops but belonged to Sueiro's battalion, Duque replied that this made no difference to him. No one was to leave the ship, and they didn't.

Rip and the frogmen returned to the beach and informed Oliva of the situation aboard the *Houston*. Oliva told him he would handle it. He called Duque and ordered him ashore. Duque refused and switched off his radio.

As daylight was now fast approaching, the problem with the *Houston* was becoming critical. It should have been unloaded and on its way to Blue Beach long before this time.

Rip called me on the *Blagar* and reported the situation. I got Pepe on the radio and explained the problem with Duque and the *Houston*. I suggested to him that we bring the *Houston* and the *Barbara J* down to Blue Beach. There we could unload them and put them under our antiaircraft protection, since we were expecting to be hit by Castro's planes early in the morning. He agreed, and the *Barbara J* and the *Houston* were told to get underway at once, and at their best speed.

Rip and the frogmen had gone back to the beach in the cat boat to inform Oliva of their planned departure and the reasons for it. They were on their way back to the *Barbara J* when the first Castro

D-Day Morning
Approx. 10:00 AM
April 17, 1961

0   5   10
Miles

Karamales 1998

plane appeared. It was a B-26. After circling the two larger ships, it came diving in in a strafing attack on the small cat boat.

Rip and his frogmen turned their .50-calibers and BARs on the plane. Although the plane's long bursts of six .50-calibers failed to touch the small cat boat, the cat boat did not miss the plane, and it banked off to the northwest with smoke pouring from it. A short time later, it disappeared into the swamp in a bright ball of fire, followed by billows of black smoke. Scratch one Castro B-26!

The *Barbara J* and the *Houston* began their dash down the bay. They had reached a point roughly six miles south of Red Beach when the second Castro air attack came in. The *Barbara J* took the two planes under fire with her .50-calibers, which now numbered fourteen. This caused the planes to break away from the *Barbara J* and instead hit the *Houston*, which had only four .50-calibers.

The planes raked the *Houston* from end to end, then fired their rockets. Most of the rockets missed, but one from the Sea Fury passed through the rear deck and exploded in the bottom hold of the ship. This blew a ten-foot hole in the stern and jammed the rudder so that it could not be moved. Water began pouring into the *Houston* from the huge hole in her bottom, and it became apparent to Captain Luis Morse that the ship was starting to sink by the stern.

Morse turned the *Houston*, by using his engines, to a heading for the sloping sandy shore of the west side of the bay. At full speed he ran her up on the sand bottom and beached her, four hundred yards from the shore. The ship was firmly aground. She would not sink, but neither could she be moved.

The *Barbara J* had stood off as the *Houston* slammed ashore. Because of her position in the shallow water, the *Barbara J* could not approach close enough to assist the *Houston*. The situation was critical, but in the next few minutes, it became even worse. Another pair of Castro's planes, a B-26 and a Sea Fury fighter, came in low from over the mangroves on the beach.

They first hit the troops of the 5th Battalion that were landing on the beach in the four surviving landing boats of the *Houston*. The boats were shot to pieces. The planes then strafed the *Houston*, and the troops in the water, who were struggling to reach the safety of the beach, and the mangrove forest behind it.

They saved their bombs and rockets for last, and used them in a one-time pass at the *Barbara J*. They made no direct hits, but from the several near misses they succeeded in springing the hull plates. She began to take on water. Her captain soon realized that the bilge pumps of the *Barbara J*, even with the addition of a portable Handy Billy (a gasoline-powered pump), could not handle the flow of incoming seawater. He radioed the *Blagar* and reported his situation.

Ryberg ordered him to proceed to Blue Beach at his best speed, where we would supply him with enough extra pumps to control the flow, and repair the sprung plates with new bolts.

The *Houston*'s radios had been shot out in the air attacks, so the *Barbara J* could not contact the *Houston* to report its own damage and the reason it must leave or sink alongside the *Houston*. This lack of communication caused the *Houston* and the 5th Battalion to believe the *Barbara J* was deserting them. It was not until much later that the men on the *Houston* learned the reason for the *Barbara J*'s forced departure.

The *Barbara J* came into Blue Beach and was pumped out. Her plates were repaired, and she was able to add her firepower to the *Blagar*'s in beating off the continuing attacks by Castro's planes.

The *Houston* was finally able to rig long lines from the ship to the beach, and landed the crew and the 5th Battalion. The ship was on fire and was abandoned.

Meanwhile at Red Beach, Oliva had finally made radio contact with Pepe. He requested permission to relieve Duque from command of the 5th Battalion and to try and get the battalion to Red Beach. This request was granted, and Oliva, after several attempts, finally gained radio contact with Duque. He ordered him to bring his troops up the beach to Playa Larga and report to his headquarters.

This would have required a march of six miles. Duque assured Oliva that he would move out as soon as he could get his unit reorganized. An hour later, Oliva called him again to ask about his progress. He was told that the 5th Battalion was starting out for Playa Larga at that very moment.

The 5th Battalion did start its march, but when it reached a point three miles from Playa Larga, it came under fire from an emplaced unit of Castro troops supported by a .50-caliber machine gun. After a short exchange of fire, Duque turned the battalion around and marched it back to the mangroves at the *Houston.*

This infantry battalion had been stopped by and had retreated from a force of exactly six men. They were the crew of the Castro patrol boat SV-3. They had removed the .50-caliber from the boat and had forted up around the small house that served as their base. Had he really been determined to reach Playa Larga, Duque could have simply moved into the mangroves and marched around this force of six men.

When Oliva called Duque again and discovered he had returned to the *Hosuton,* he informed Duque that he was relieving him of his command and told him to turn his radio over to Felix Tamayo, his second in command. Duque solved this embarrassing problem by simply switching off his radio. He gave no details to the men around him of his conversation with Oliva, and he retained command of the 5th Battalion.

At Red Beach, Oliva had placed the 2nd Battalion in dug-in positions on the road north of Playa Larga. He reported his situation to Pepe and requested additional forces to replace the 5th Battalion. Pepe told him that he was sending him a platoon from the 4th Battalion and two of the M-41 tanks.

When this force arrived, Oliva moved his troops to a better position farther up the road and dug in deep. He had been unable to contact the paratroopers of the 1st Battalion, who had been dropped north of Palpite, and was puzzled by this situation. He was unaware of what had befallen Vera's men on their early-morning jump.

There had been two planes making this drop: a C-46, which was to drop the Palpite group and continue up the road to the north exit of the Zapata Swamp to drop Vera's platoon, and a C-54, which was to drop the heavy weapons and ammunition resupply at each drop site.

The two planes came in over the west side of the bay and were passing west of Playa Larga when the first Castro B-26 that was to hit Rip's frogmen was spotted crossing their front. Both planes took evasive action and turned to the northeast, a different direction from that called for in the plan.

It seems likely that although the Castro B-26 was very close to them, it did not see them, probably because the pilot and copilot had their eyes glued on their targets, the *Houston* and the *Barbara J.* But the damage had been done; the transports had seen the B-26. Expecting other Castro planes to appear at any moment, they felt that they must get the troopers out and on the ground as soon as possible. They tuned back toward the drop zones, but now they were approaching them from the west, not by the south-to-north route they had so carefully rehearsed. All the checkpoints were gone, because they were over the Zapata Swamp.

They came in until they spotted the Playa Larga–Central Australia road and made their drops. They were off target, and the paratroopers were landed far from their planned drop sites. The C-54 with the supplies and weapons was also off target. The paratroopers were on the ground, in some cases in the edge of the Zapata Swamp, but widely scattered, and without their heavy weapons and ammunition resupply.

For Vera's men, it was a disaster from which they were never able to recover. Only a few small groups of the paratroopers were able to join up with Oliva's forces. Most of them fought in small groups or, in some cases, alone against the Castro forces advancing along the road. Vera himself landed in the swamp. He made his way to the road and fought a one-man battle against the militia until he ran out of ammunition. He was forced into hiding and eventually was able to reach Havana, where he took refuge in a foreign embassy. In 1962 he made it back to Miami with the help of the foreign embassy's personnel.

(A tremendous fighter, Vera returned to Cuba to fight again. In October 1962, Vera was on a sabotage mission in Pinar del Río. The timing of this operation was unfortunate, for the missile crisis occurred while he was still inside. The place was crawling with troops, and he was captured by Castro's G-2. He escaped from a Cuban prison farm in 1965, but was recaptured three days later. He was badly beaten by the G-2 and returned to prison. He now resides in Miami, where he is very active in the 2506 Assault Brigade Association.)

At Playa Larga, Oliva had discovered a microwave station and destroyed it. The transmitter was still warm when he found it, so he was sure it had been sending an alert to Havana from the onset of the battle. This station had not been included in the intelligence briefing he had received about the area, and he wondered how the CIA planners had missed it.

All the books written by the Kennedy apologists have exaggerated the importance of this microwave station, pointing to it as a major intelligence blunder by the CIA planners. They also report that there were several of these stations in Playa Girón. The truth is there were none in Playa Girón. Nor were there any telephones in either Playa Girón or Playa Larga.

To have believed that we could bring the entire fifteen-hundred-man brigade ashore undetected, and without Havana's knowledge, would have been naive and wishful thinking. This possibility was never mentioned or discussed in any planning session I attended. The only effect the microwave station could conceivably have had upon the invasion was that it probably allowed Castro's planes to arrive a little earlier. If the raids on Castro's airfields at first light had been conducted as planned, then the existence of the microwave station would have been irrelevant.

The first contact, with Castro's forces coming from Central Australia to Red Beach, came shortly after noon. The forward positions of the 2nd Battalion had spotted a large group of militia coming down the road in a truck, and through the trees alongside it.

The men of the 2nd Battalion were dug in on both sides of the road and well camouflaged. They had emplaced in concealed positions their heavy weapons, a 75mm and a 57mm recoilless rifle, a .50-caliber machine gun, two .30-caliber machine guns, and two 3.5-inch antitank rocket launchers. They waited patiently until the Castro militiamen were within seventy-five yards of their position. At Maximo Cruz's command, the troops opened up with all weapons.

The lead truck of the militia took a direct hit from a 75mm high-explosive round and blew up in flames. The 75mm recoilless rifle then fired a white phosphorus round, which landed in the center of the column of men. The fight was over in less than two minutes. The few survivors fled into the bushes.

The 2nd Battalion had hit the advance column of Osmani Cienfuegos's battalion and had won a decisive victory. It was two and a half hours later before the next Castro unit dared to try its luck with Sueiro's tough little group.

In Playa Larga, Oliva had been busy treating the many wounded militiamen from the night landing and collecting fifty prisoners. He employed some of the Cuban civilian workers from the Buenaventura project to salvage and repair as many of the Castro trucks at the project as had survived the blasting of the *Barbara J*, and Rip's frogmen, during the night landing action.

At 1430, Cruz's scouts reported a large column of Castro's troops advancing down the road, followed by many trucks containing troops. This was the 339th Matanzas Battalion, which was soon to become the infamous for almost being wiped out. Since Oliva had received two M-41 tanks and some of the 4th Battalion troops sent by Pepe, he felt he was in a much better and stronger defensive position than at the first encounter.

At 1445, the advancing Castro column halted a few hundred yards in front of the 2nd Battalion's position. It began setting up mortars in preparation for a further advance. It seemed obvious that the Castro troops had no idea how close they were to Sueiro's men, or that they were literally standing in the center of the bull's-eye of all the weapons of a reinforced infantry battalion.

Their situation was revealed to them as soon as they again started their advance. They were hit by every weapon of the 2nd Battalion. The machine guns and infantry weapons mowed them down in droves. The M-41 tanks and the recoilless rifles blasted the truck column into a long line of flaming rubble. Within Cuba, this event has been written about many times. It has emerged as "the Slaughter of the Lost Battalion."

It was indeed a slaughter, and was to become an even greater one, for at this moment two of the brigade's B-26s came over Red Beach and joined in the action. Firing their eight nose-mounted .50-caliber machine guns, they flew back and forth over the doomed 339th, cutting down even those who tried to flee their fire by dashing into the Zapata Swamp. After the two planes had expended their machine gun ammunition, they turned their bombs and rockets on the surviving trucks, which had been masked by the smoke of the burning column from Sueiro's men. When it was over, only a handful of the 968 men of the 339th were left to creep away and bury themselves under the mud and water of the mangrove swamps.

Oliva called the two B-26s and thanked them for their help. They told him that they must now depart the area as their ammunition was expended. As he bid them goodbye, he was startled to see the silver flash of a Castro T-33 jet as it roared over Red Beach, on the tails of the two brigade planes. The men at Red Beach stared in shocked and unbelieving silence as the silver jet quickly blasted one B-26 out of the sky and sent the other one fleeing south with smoke pouring from it.

This pair of B-26s had been code-named Puma I and II. The first plane that was hit and crashed in front of their eyes was Puma II, flown by Osvaldo

Piedra and copiloted by Joe Fernandez. They were both killed in the crash.

The other plane, Puma I, was piloted by José Alberto Crespo, with Lorenzo Perez as copilot. It had been badly damaged by the T-33, flown by the Castro pilot Alvaro Prendes. Puma I made its way out of the bay and attempted to head home to its field at Puerto Cabezas, a three-and-a-half-hour flight. Crespo and Perez almost made it. Their last radio contact with base came as they flew in darkness low over the rough waters of the Caribbean. They had reported that they had been steadily losing altitude and were now only two hundred feet above the water. Their last call was "We cannot hold it up. We are going in." Although four transport planes from Puerto Cabezas started an immediate search that lasted all night and through the next day, no wreckage or survivors were ever found.

At Red Beach, after the slaughter of the "Lost Battalion," all was quiet for some time. Then Sueiro's scouts reported that two ambulances, followed by a Red Cross truck, were coming down the road. Oliva gave the order to hold fire if they were there only to pick up their wounded. The scouts watched as the ambulances and the truck stopped at the far end of the "slaughter sector."

Their next report was that the ambulances and the truck were unloading troops and mortars, and that a column of trucks loaded with troops was pulling up behind them. Oliva ordered Sueiro's men to open fire on the group. This battle proved to be a rerun of the "Lost Battalion" action, simply adding to the by now long mound of bodies and burning vehicles, stretching for over half a mile.

A radio message from Pepe informed Oliva that he was to receive the remainder of the 4th Battalion, one company of the 6th Battalion, a platoon of mortars, and another M-41 tank. This sizable reinforcement, and the extra ammunition they were bringing with them, was welcome news. Sueiro's 2nd Battalion had fought like tigers, but now they were tired and low on ammunition.

Oliva had learned from his prisoners that there was a large force of troops and tanks gathering at Central Australia. They were planning to attack down the road to Playa Larga that night. He selected as his main battle line the Rotunda. From this position he could cover all the approaches to Red Beach. His weapons and tanks would have a wide, excellent field of fire.

When the reinforcements and ammunition arrived shortly after 1800 hours, he deployed them at the Rotunda and told them to dig in deep. All was quiet until shortly after 1930 hours, when Castro's forces opened up with a battalion of Soviet-supplied 122mm howitzers. The first rounds landed several hundred yards in front of Oliva's forces. Slowly the militia advanced them in the direction of the Rotunda.

It was fairly obvious that the militiamen had no clear idea of the exact location of Oliva's battle lines and were searching for them. The advance of the artillery shelling was at such a creeping pace that it was after 2130 hours before the first rounds fell among the defenders.

Oliva had issued orders to his company commanders to have their men stay in the trenches and foxholes and not fire until the enemy forces were clearly in sight. So they crouched and took the pounding of the 122mm howitzers for two hours. Over twelve hundred rounds landed among them, but they were so well dug in that, considering the mind-numbing, sustained artillery fire they took, their losses were light: eight or nine dead and thirty wounded.

At 2330, the barrage moved past them and continued moving south, until the rounds were landing in the waters of Cochinos Bay. At midnight the artillery stopped completely, and Oliva alerted his forces for the expected ground attack.

It was 0030 when Cruz, commander of the most forward company, spotted the first of Castro's ground forces approaching. At a distance of one hundred yards he could make out the outline of a tank coming down the road, followed by a group of infantry.

Cruz watched the force approach. He could make out the shapes of two more tanks and two more groups of soldiers. When the first tank entered the Rotunda, fifty yards away, the entire 2nd Battalion opened fire.

The first two Castro tanks (a Soviet-supplied

T-34 and a Stalin III) were quickly knocked out by the fire of Oliva's M-41 tanks and his bazookas. The third tank was hit several times and limped away in the darkness. The few survivors of the infantry that had been advancing with the tanks also faded away in the darkness.

Ten minutes later, another tank-infantry force hit, but since the wreckage of the T-34 and Stalin III tanks blocked the road, these tanks had to maneuver off the road and were hit by fire from all directions.

These tank-infantry assaults came on Oliva's forces one after another for more than an hour. Each attack was thrown back, and now there were six knocked-out Castro tanks in front of them.

At 0300 hours, the tank attacks ceased and the Castro forces launched a strong infantry attack. Oliva's entire line opened fire, and for the first time he unleashed his mortars on the screaming waves of charging militia. The line held. Castro's troops were taking heavy casualties. The infantry attacks continued for two hours. At 0530 they tapered off, and it appeared that Castro's men were pulling back.

This lull in the fighting allowed Oliva time to reposition some of his forces and evacuate his wounded. To everyone's regret, one of the seriously wounded was the gallant little company commander Cruz, who had been hit by fragments of an artillery shell that exploded only yards away from him.

The troops were exhausted after twenty-four hours of nearly continuous heavy fighting, and their ammunition was almost gone. They knew that they could not keep up this unyielding stand for much longer.

At 0545, they again heard the familiar sound of many tanks approaching and got themselves set for what they felt might be their last stand. Then for some reason the tanks stopped. Slowly the sound of their engines began to fade as Castro's forces withdrew and headed north.

That is, all but one tank, which suddenly appeared in the Rotunda and drew to within yards of Oliva's men. The hatch of the tank opened, and the tank commander dismounted and ran toward them. Suddenly he halted, then turned and ran back to his tank screaming, "It's the enemy!"

Indeed it was, and an M-41 tank blasted the Soviet T-34 tank until it exploded.

At 0550 hours, the last of the Castro tanks rumbled into the Rotunda and was hit by Oliva with a 57mm recoilless rifle firing a high-explosive round. Although the round did not penetrate the hull of the tank, the concussion was so great that the tank crew bailed out and surrendered.

As it turned out, the commander of the tank had served with Oliva in the Cuban army and knew him well. He told Oliva, "You have put up one hell of a battle, Erneido. You have whipped a very large force and have hurt them badly. I salute you. But I must warn you, there is an even larger force coming, and they are going to power their way through you."

He went on to explain that Oliva had faced a force of more than two thousand Castro troops and twenty-two tanks. He estimated that the force had suffered 70 percent casualties and lost half its tanks. Oliva's little band had numbered fewer than four hundred men and had three tanks.

Oliva now lacked one thing, ammunition. He was down to his last few tank rounds, the mortars were out of ammo, and his infantrymen had only fifty rounds per man. He contacted Pepe and informed him of the critical ammunition shortage and the size of the enemy forces that would soon be moving toward him. Pepe told him to bring his troops down to a position three miles north of Playa Girón as soon as possible to avoid being caught in daylight by Castro's planes.

Oliva knew he must move immediately. As soon as a truck was loaded, it was sent down the road toward Blue Beach. He also knew that he must disperse his vehicles, so as not to present a concentrated target for the planes that would arrive with the rising sun.

The first truck of Oliva's force that was sent to Playa Girón was shocked to discover one of the brigade trucks overturned in a ditch halfway from Playa Girón to Playa Larga. This truck contained a thirty-man, 81mm mortar platoon of the heavy weapons battalion, under the command of Enrique Ruiz-Williams. The platoon had been sent by Pepe to reinforce Oliva and had left Playa Girón at 2300 hours the night before. In their haste to get to the battle, they had been running at full speed, with their lights out to avoid detection. In the darkness they had hit a crater in the road and overturned into the ditch.

The truck was righted by Oliva's and Ruiz-William's men, and the precious mortars and ammo were returned to Playa Girón.

At Playa Larga, Oliva had finally loaded the remainder of his troops in seven trucks, on the three tanks, and in the few jeeps he had. He took his wounded and dead with him, but left two hundred prisoners he had collected. There was no room for them.

Oliva and his troops made it all the way to their newly assigned position at Playa Girón without being spotted by Castro's planes. The battle of Red Beach was over, but the battle of Playa Girón was just beginning.

11

D-Day: Action at Blue Beach

THE SUN WAS RISING OVER BLUE BEACH WHEN THE FIRST of Castro's planes appeared. The LCUs were still busily discharging their cargo of tanks and trucks loaded with ammunition across the rough coral beaches, while the LCVPs unloaded the heavy weapons battalion's 4.2-mortar crews.

As at Red Beach, the plane was a B-26. It came from the east, low over the land, and banked out over the bay, toward the ships. Its arrival was met with a solid hail of .50-caliber tracers. It broke off, wheeling back to run straight down the beach, choosing as its target one of the LCVPs that was in the process of landing the 4.2-mortar crews. The six .50-caliber machine guns of the B-26 chewed up the landing craft. The men were already out in the water and by some miracle were untouched.

One pass was all this pilot wished to chance. He

pulled out and turned up the bay toward Red Beach.

I alerted the *Barbara J* to his coming. The *Barbara J* replied that it also had been attacked by a B-26, which had departed in our direction. Reflecting on this later, I concluded we were both referring to the same aircraft, but men in battle do not have time for reflection. This is the reason battles have always been confusing affairs.

The ships at Blue Beach were now alerted for an attack from a B-26, from the direction of Red Beach. Shortly thereafter, the lookouts reported two planes coming at us from that direction. The lead aircraft we could identify as a B-26. It was headed straight at us. All guns opened up on this plane, but it neither returned the fire nor took evasive action. I took a quick, hard look at the second aircraft and now made out the familiar shape of a C-46 transport.

I yelled, "Cease fire! We're shooting at our own planes!"

This went out over the radio net, and one by one the guns fell silent, and so did we. We stood in shocked, remorseful silence as the two planes wheeled over at eight hundred feet and turned inland. We could see the open door of the C-46, a paratrooper in the jump position. It was one of the troop carriers of the 1st Battalion, heading for the drop zone beyond San Blas. The B-26 was flying escort for the unarmed transport, because it had been alerted that Castro's planes were on the loose.

We learned later, much to our relief, that only

two paratroopers were slightly wounded. One was creased on the side of the head, and the other in the posterior. Getting creased with a .50-caliber is about like being brushed by a freight train. Both men jumped.

It was difficult for the men on the ships, and on the ground, to distinguish between Castro's B-26s and our own. It was a brigade requirement that they have identical markings. In an attempt to reduce the confusion, Puerto Cabezas had painted blue bands around the wings and fuselage of our planes. Unfortunately, this was of little help, because the B-26s that we saw usually were headed straight in toward us. From this position all you see is silhouette. The blue rings were not discernible until too late.

After this mistaken attack, I sent a message to Puerto Cabezas. I asked that the pilots be told not to come within range of the ships unless radio contact was made beforehand. I said we were still having trouble identifying the aircraft. It seemed to be the only solution to the problem.

It became the practice that all B-26s would be engaged if they were coming at us in an attack attitude. This procedure obviously worked, as we shot down several of Castro's B-26s that day and none of our own.

The C-46, having dropped its paratroopers inland, came back low over Playa Girón and out over the ships of Blue Beach. The pilot obviously wanted a good look at the action. He picked a very bad time for this little sightseeing tour. At that moment, circling high above us, was one of Castro's Sea Furies. We had been watching it, waiting for it to peel off into one of its dives. Since all eyes were focused on the Sea Fury, few, if any, saw the C-46. Suddenly the Sea Fury rolled and dove straight down at the ships. Over thirty of the .50-calibers on the ships opened fire. A cone of tracers followed him down.

I was manning one of the .50-calibers on the bridge of the *Blagar*. When the pilot opened up with his four 20mm cannons, I saw that he was aiming at a target off to our left. A quick glance in that direction showed the C-46 transport heading toward us from the beach, at an altitude of three hundred feet. I also saw that the water beneath the C-46 was being churned into foam from the impact of the Sea Fury's cannons.

The cone of tracers from the ships followed the Sea Fury through its dive until we were forced to hold our fire for fear of hitting the Brigade C-46. The fighter pilot continued firing until he was forced to pull up to avoid a collision. He rolled over to make another pass at the unarmed transport. In doing so, as he reached the top of his climb, he became an almost stationary target. All the tracers from the .50-calibers converged on him. The Sea Fury seemed to hand in the air for a few seconds. This was all the ship's gunners needed. The .50-calibers tore into the plane, and it dived straight into the sea.

By another of the many miracles that seemed to

be the normal course of events at Cochinos that day, the brigade plane was untouched. It flew happily back to Puerto Cabezas, where its crew laid claim to having, through evasive action, caused the Sea Fury to crash into the sea.

The ships' crews were jubilant. They had drawn first blood, and Castro's pilots were lousy shots. This at the moment appeared to be true, but later in the day their marksmanship was to improve.

The unloading of troops and supplies at Blue Beach continued. So did the attacks by Castro's planes. All troops and vehicles were now ashore, with the exception of the 6th Battalion, on the *Río Escondido*, which had been scheduled to be the last to land.

I sent the first LCU, which had completed discharging its cargo, to bring the 6th Battalion ashore, instructing it do so in one trip. A call from Pepe, at brigade headquarters on shore, informed me that Playa Girón and its airfield were in the hands of the Brigade, and that he had taken 130 prisoners.

The LCUs had finished unloading their cargo. The vehicles, the tanks, the fuel tanker truck, and the armaments for the B-26s were in position at the airfield. Everything was set to rearm and refuel the brigade planes, but with Castro's jets in the air, none of our planes dared to land.

The 4th Battalion and the 4.2 mortars of the heavy weapons battalion had moved inland and now were linked with the paratroopers beyond San Blas. One M-41 tank and a squad of the 4th Battalion, together with a two-and-a-half-ton truck loaded with ammunition, had been sent up the coast road to reinforce Oliva at Red Beach. The 3rd Battalion had been moved down the coast road, to the east, for several miles and was dug in, with one tank to protect its flank.

Pepe had informed me that most of the civilian workers in Playa Girón had welcomed them and that some had joined the brigade as soldiers or as volunteer workers to help unload supplies.

All the troops were now ashore, and things were starting to brighten up. If we could only unload enough ammunition to see the brigade through the next day, we might be able to pull the ships out to sea, as Washington had been ordering us to do. But serious trouble was on the way.

Another Sea Fury appeared, circling high above us as the previous one had, selecting a victim. I was again manning a .50-caliber machine gun, on the wing of the *Blager*'s bridge. As the plane was circling, I noticed that one of the radio operators was standing in the doorway to the bridge with a message in his hand. I had no time now to read messages, because the Sea Fury rolled over and came down in the now familiar dive.

The gun I'd been manning had been badly overheated during the previous attack. When the Sea Fury appeared, we were in the midst of replacing it with another gun. The process was stopped when the Sea Fury rolled over, and I opened fire with the still-hot gun. The jet pulled out of his dive after striking nothing more than the fish in the bay.

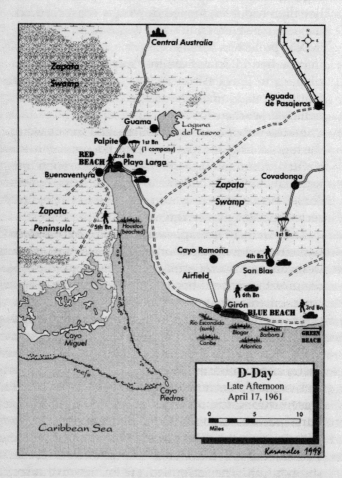

D-Day
Late Afternoon
April 17, 1961

0   5   10
Miles

Karanales 1998

The radio operator finally handed me the message. It read: "Castro's air force 100% destroyed. Do not fire on our planes. Remember they have blue bands on the wings and fuselage."

Now where in the hell had this joker gotten his information? I composed an answer: "If Castro's planes are 100% destroyed, then suggest you check Haiti, because somebody's air force is shooting the hell out of us."

I thought better of it, and threw the message, and the reply, into the sea.

Other messages were now pouring into the communications center on the *Blagar*, faster than we could decode them. Never before have so many directed so few, with so many different directives.

They were all sent in good faith, for Washington was sincerely worried. Those in charge there were desperately trying to offer any help they could. Unfortunately, their aid was restricted to advice, and at this moment advice was something we really didn't need. What we could have used was a jet fighter or two to clear the skies of Castro's aircraft.

Two B-26s were sighted heading from the southeast, parallel with the ships. As they came near, it was obvious that one of them was ours and one was Castro's, for the trailing B-26 was pouring burst after burst of fire into the plane in front. Without binoculars and with the hazy visibility that morning, the ship's gunners were in a dilemma. Which was which? They solved this by firing at both aircraft. The question of identification was quickly solved. From out of the sun came one of Castro's silver streaks, a T-33. It flashed across the rear B-26 and nailed it with a long burst. The arrogant bastard piloting it gave a victory roll and soared back up into his sun position.

The Castro B-26 disappeared into the northwest, trailing black smoke, and the brigade plane was also obviously badly hit. Feathering one engine, the pilot let down his landing gear and headed toward the Playa Girón airstrip. As he neared the runway, we were surprised to see him suddenly retract his gear and turn away from the strip. He'd seen something we had not. The T-33 pilot was coming in for the kill. Once again, he poured a long burst into the struggling B-26. The brigade plane rolled over and plowed in alongside the Girón field. A long streak of billowing red dust boiled up as it skidded the full length of the strip. An oily column of black smoke marked the end of its slide. The T-33 circled out of range, watching until the brigade plane had come to rest. Then it performed a series of victory rolls before disappearing toward Havana.

Now war is at best a brutal business, but the men at Cochinos Bay witnessed in this unequal fight actions clearly against all accepted principles of warfare. The brigade plane had been put out of action on the first pass and was desperately trying to land. We had only one word for it—murder. To us it was cold-blooded, premeditated murder. A "wounded" plane attempting to land is considered out of combat by the rules of the Geneva Convention. This was only the first of many instances to occur that caused the brigade to realize that Castro did not intend to abide by the Geneva Convention.

I should add that if the combatants wear a distinctive uniform and insignias and are formed into military units and observe military discipline, then they are recognized as an armed force and qualify for the rights and protection guaranteed by the Geneva Convention. A declaration of war is not necessary for this to be true. The brigade fit these criteria.

Miraculously, the pilot of the brigade plane survived the crash. He had been thrown clear when the plane struck the ground. For about an hour, he lay unconscious in the heavy brush alongside the runway. The men of the brigade were shocked to see the slightly burned survivor stagger onto the runway, for they were sure no one could have survived the crash.

Word began coming in on the 1st Brigade's parachute jumps. It wasn't good. North of Playa Larga, where the drops were to seal off the critical approach road through the swamp, the jumps had gone badly. Castro's planes had attacked the transports. The brigade's B-26s, flying escort, had driven them off, but the damage was done.

The troop transports, in taking evasive action, had missed the primary drop zone. The C-54s that followed had dropped the heavy weapons and follow-up supplies to the proper zone, but the troops were too scattered. In some cases, the men were dropped several miles from their intended landing zones. Many of them were never able to recover their weapon containers and extra ammunition.

Vera and his small group of paratroopers, who were to seal the road at the north end of the Playa Larga exit, were dropped directly into the swamp. After reassembling and painfully cutting their way out of the swamp to the road, they discovered that they were too late. Castro's troops were already in the exits and moving south. The paratroopers set up roadblocks and shot up and captured several of Castro's vehicles, but without their heavy weapons and extra ammunition, they could not last for long. When their ammunition was gone, they were forced to retreat back into the swamp, and the road was open again.

North of San Blas, the paratroopers of the 1st Battalion fared much better. Castro's aircraft were in the area, but the transport had dropped them in the proper zones. They were able to reassemble and recover most of their equipment and ammunition. They quickly captured San Blas and moved to seal off the two exit roads to Yaguaramas and Covadonga.

On Blue Beach, the LCUs had landed the 6th Battalion from the *Río Escondido*. They were returning to the ship to remove its deck cargo of drums of aviation fuel when a Sea Fury came screaming down from five thousand feet. Although the concentrated fire from the *Río Escondido*'s .50-calibers followed it down, it was able to fire its four rockets and escape.

Three of the rockets overshot the ship and exploded harmlessly in the water. The fourth struck the forward deck just in front of the bridge structure, only six feet short of the railing. It was a critical spot, the exact center of the fifty-five-gallon gasoline drums, which had been prepared for unloading.

The hit was doubly disastrous. Looped on brackets only a few feet from the rocket's point of impact were the ship's forward deck fire hoses. Fragments from the rocket sliced the hoses into ribbons. The gasoline drums flared. Fuel from the ruptured drums flowed down the side of the ship and into its forward hold. The hold contained over twenty tons of explosives.

Aboard the *Blagar,* I could see the thirty-foot-high flames from a very odd position—I was flat on my back, pinned under my .50-caliber machine gun, whose red-hot barrel was inches from my face.

This dangerous development was due to the changing of the overheated .50-caliber during the previous attack by a Sea Fury. My assistant had forgotten to fasten the pintle latch that holds the gun to its cradle. I had been firing this gun almost straight up at the jet when it had bucked off its cradle and crashed down on me. As the crewmen helped me from underneath it, scorched but otherwise unhurt, the first muffled explosion shook the *Río Escondido.*

The small boats of the other ships were converging on her from all directions. The courage of these brigade small boatmen, rushing to a burning, explosive-laden ship to save its crew, was amazing. They knew the ship was a veritable bomb, but they never hesitated.

They raced in, plucked the crew out of the water, and were halfway back to the *Blagar* when the *Río Escondido* exploded in a huge, mushroom-shaped fireball. The mushroom spread until it was over a mile in diameter and several thousand feet high. As it slowly lifted from the water, the stem was exposed, giving it the appearance of a nuclear explosion. The cloud continued to rise. As the mushroom stem lifted off the water, a portion of the ship's capsized stern was briefly visible. Slowly it slid out of sight, one twisted propeller still turning.

At this moment, I received an urgent call from Rip up at Red Beach. Even though he and his men were sixteen miles away, they had heard the blast from the ship exploding. They had also seen the mushroom cloud rising.

"Gray!" Rip said. "What the hell was that?"

I told him that the *Río Escondido* had been hit and had exploded.

"My God, Gray! For a moment, I thought Fidel had the A-bomb!"

Still the miracles held—not one man was lost, or even injured. But it had been a sobering experience. We were now faced with an agonizing decision. Should we follow Washington's orders to take the ships out to sea, in an attempt to save the two remaining cargo ships, or stay and try to unload the supplies that the brigade needed so desperately?

Washington had been sending messages all morning for us to leave. Up until this point, I had resisted the suggestion. Now that all the troops were ashore, there remained only the supplies and ammunition. We had lost 50 percent of them already. This made the cargo of the *Caribe* and *Atlantico* of critical importance. If they were lost, the brigade was lost. I considered ramming the ships ashore and unloading them directly on the beach. This was the only way we could be sure they would not be sunk.

After seeing what happened to the *Río Escondido,* I realized the other two ships could very well be lost in the same manner. All we would have left would be two big holes in the beach.

Another message arrived, ordering us out. This was nothing new, but the last line of the message was. It was this portion that made up my mind for me. It read: "Take all ships to sea. Navy will provide cover at 12-mile limit. Unload *Caribe* and *Atlantico* into LCUs. *Blagar* and LCUs return Blue Beach after dark and unload."

This seemed the only logical thing to do. To remain off the beach would risk everything. Unloading the ships under the now constant air attacks was a slow process. If all we had to do was go twelve miles out and unload into the LCUs, we could be back soon after dark. In fact, we could probably gain time, since unloading at that point would not be constantly interrupted. The decision was made. We would go.

I called Pepe and informed him of the plan. He didn't like the idea, but I promised we would be back after dark with the supplies. This helped to soften the blow.

As we were about to get underway, the five frogmen who had landed with me on Blue Beach called asking for instructions. I told them to stay where they were, because we would need them to mark the beach when we returned that night. We would also need their radio to contact the beach.

This decision, which seemed so logical at the time, I afterward regretted. Because of it, these five men were to spend two years in Castro's prison. When Blue Beach eventually fell, they could have escaped, for they still had their UDT raft and motor. But by that time two of them had been wounded. A sea voyage would have been too hard on them, and the other three would not leave without them.

The UDT raft was later used by five brigade members to escape from the beach. After five days at sea, they were rescued by an American freighter and taken to New Orleans.

We left the two remaining LCVPs on the beach, but took the three LCUs and the two freighters. As our convoy got underway, heading out of Cochinos Bay toward international waters, we were accompanied by the ever-present Castro air force. Attack after attack came in on the ships, but the miracles of Cochinos still held, and there was no serious damage.

At the twelve-mile limit, we were still under at-

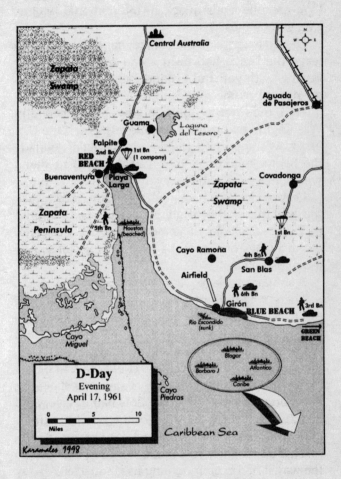

D-Day
Evening
April 17, 1961

0   5   10
Miles

Karamales 1998

tack. I called the *Santiago,* the flagship of the U.S. destroyers we'd picked up on our radar. I told her, "We are under air attack in international waters. Can you help us?"

Her answer made me realize that the decision to leave the beach had been a bad one. It was "My heart is with you, but I cannot help you. My orders are not to become engaged in any way."

Well, ours not to question why, but someone in Washington had made a terrible mistake. If the U.S. Navy was supposed to give us protection outside the twelve-mile limit, then Washington had damn well better inform the Navy of it.

I called *Santiago* back with a bitter request: "Ask the bastards if they'll allow you to stand by and pick up survivors. If someone doesn't get these damn planes off us, that's exactly what all that is left of us will be."

A similar message went to Washington.

There was nothing else to do but keep heading out to sea and wait for the Navy to get the word to give us cover, or if this was not to be, to try and shake off Castro's planes and stay afloat until dark. We didn't get Navy cover, nor could we shake Castro's planes. The only thing that saved us that long afternoon was that Castro's pilots had developed a healthy respect for the guns of the two little LCUs and would not press their attack too closely.

Castro's air force had made some big mistakes in the way it had been mounting its air attacks. All day these planes had come in by ones, on rare occasions by twos, but never in a coordinated attack. This allowed us to concentrate all our fire on one or two planes. I believe that if we had been hit by all his planes at one time, they would have sunk us all.

Another mistake was the way the planes approached the ships. The B-26s and the Sea Furies always came in on a straight northwest course, from the direction of Havana. This allowed us to spot them at long range and gave us time to get prepared. We were forced to rely on lookouts for this task, since none of the ships had aircraft search radar. Spotting the T-33 jets was something else. The jet pilots were a different breed of cat. They came only from high, out of the sun, and were so fast that usually the first warning we had was when the whoosh of their rockets told us we were under attack. By then it was already too late.

These jets never made more than one pass at a time. They would attack, then disappear, only to come back in another attack a few minutes later, always from out of the sun.

As the afternoon wore on, we were joined by one of the brigade's B-26s. The pilot radioed us, saying that although he was out of ammunition, he would stay with us as long as his fuel held out. This brave gesture saved us from at least one attack.

From far off to the west came the sound of explosions, followed by four columns of water shot high into the air. We checked our radar to see if there was a battleship firing at us. The radar was clear. Finally, one of the lookouts spotted the source of the bombardment. High above, almost a speck in the sky, was a Castro B-26 heading home. I suppose our brigade B-26 escort had backed the pilot off. His attempt to bomb us from his present altitude had created an error of something like a mile and a half.

There was one very disturbing thing about our friendly B-26. Hanging from its right wing was one of its fuel drop tanks, which had failed to release properly. The tank, attached only by its rear shackle, swung to and fro as the plane circled over us. We kept watching it, praying it wouldn't fall on us. That was all we needed now, to be clobbered by an empty fuel tank from one of our own damn planes.

Had we known what was in that fuel tank, the simple prayers would have turned into a novena. As the plane touched down on its return to Puerto Cabezas that night, the tank jarred loose and skidded almost the full length of the runway. A brigade airman who went to remove it found an unexploded warhead of one of the rockets embedded in the tank. The pilot had dropped his tanks as he came in for a strafing attack, north of Playa Larga, but the tank had not released properly. It had swung in front of one of his rocket pods, striking the rocket and snapping off its head.

In addition to this little dilemma, we then noticed that the two cargo ships, the *Atlantico* and *Cariobe*, had begun to pull away from the rest of the convoy. We had been forced to reduce our speed to allow the slower LCUs to stay up with us. I called the cargo ships, ordering them to reduce speed and stay with us. They acknowledged the order but did not reduce their speed.

The *Barbara J* was told to catch them and slow them down. She was in the process of moving up when the lookouts reported two planes coming in fast and low from the northwest. One was a Sea Fury, the other a B-26. The alert was sounded and the guns manned. When the planes had closed within three miles of the convoy, they separated. The Sea Fury climbed, and the B-26 dropped to an altitude of fifty feet above the sea. It bore in straight for the *Blagar*.

Four rockets were visible under its wings, and just above them the six deadly .50-caliber machine guns. There was a sudden epidemic of express elevators on board the *Blagar*. This guy meant business. No preliminaries for him. He was coming flat out and straight in.

No one's elevator was sinking faster than mine. His nose was lined up with the *Blagar*'s midship section, which just happened to be where my favorite .50-caliber was mounted.

The bugger was giving us no choice. Stop him or be blown out of the water. I knew we had to open fire first, and at extreme range. If we didn't get him, maybe we could at least discourage him to the point of breaking off his attack.

I started pumping short bursts at him and watching the burnout of the tracers. These, I knew, burned out after two thousand yards. When the B-26 hit this two-thousand-yard mark, I yelled, *"Fuego"*—Fire!

Sixteen .50-calibers opened up on him. These guns use a belt of one hundred rounds. When firing at Castro's planes, we always fired the entire belt without stopping. So sixteen steady streams of tracers converged on the plane.

The B-26 pilot, on the other hand, held his fire. He had us, and he knew it. He was going to wait until he was looking right down our throats and couldn't possibly miss before he blew us apart with those rockets. His patience might have served him well another time, but off Cochinos Bay, it earned him a fiery death.

The stream of tracers was boring steadily into him. His plane began to porpoise, the nose rising and falling with a slow, steady up-and-down movement. What appeared to be white smoke began streaming rearward. At five hundred yards, his patience gave out. He opened with short bursts from his .50-calibers, but his roller-coaster movement sent these bursts high over our heads or else directly into the water in front of him. He never touched the ship.

If he had held those triggers down and let his fire swing up through the ship, he would have swept our decks clean of gunners. He didn't, and now he played his trump card. At one hundred yards, he fired his four rockets. Several things took place at almost the same instant. The plane exploded in a huge fireball and smacked into the water, and the four rockets struck the water only yards short of the *Blagar*. The explosions lifted the ship's stern high out of the water.

The plane, ablaze, bounced off the water's surface and came cartwheeling over the *Blagar*'s bow section. One wing passed through the cutaway boat well section, six feet lower than the bridge. It crashed, engulfed in flames, a hundred feet from the ship. The burning elevators of the tail section crashed onto the deck, where they were quickly extinguished by the crew.

The air above the ship was filled with debris. The gunners dashed into the doorway of the bridge, seeking shelter from the deadly metal.

A long burst of 20mm fire told us that the forgotten Sea Fury was diving over our heads. We hit the deck in time to see him coming almost straight down at the *Barbara J*. The ship was fighting back, and the *Blagar* joined her. We knew she was being hit. We could see the explosions of the 20mm shells as the Sea Fury raked her from stem to stern.

The plane was dead on target. All that was left was to execute the *coup de grâce* with his rockets. Instead, the pilot pulled out of his dive and banked away hard. He knew these little ships could sting. He obviously had no desire to end up as his wingmate had—a fiery spectacle.

He circled the ships, staying well out of range, then turned to head home. It must have dawned on him that he still had his rockets. He wheeled back and fired at the three LCUs that were following the *Blagar*. It was, at best, a snap shot, from extreme range. The rockets exploded harmlessly in the sea, hundreds of yards away.

Upon his return to base, the pilot was thrown into one of Castro's prisons for his lack of effort. When he was released in 1964, he escaped to Miami and joined the anti-Castro movement. It seems he didn't lack courage, just a real belief in Castro's Cuba.

Despite all that had taken place, not a man on either the *Blagar* or the *Barbara J* was touched. Nor did either ship suffer any serious damage. One of the 20mm shells fired into the *Barbara J* had penetrated the cargo hatch. It was found embedded in a case of C-4, plastic high explosive. Luckily it was an armor-piercing round. If it had been an explosive round, the ship would have gone up in a second, for the hold was loaded with tons of ammunition.

There was one serious side effect of the attack. The two cargo ships were now leaving us at top speed. They had seen enough. Their crews were merchant seamen, not soldiers. They were concerned only with their ships' safety and their own. They ignored my radio calls to rejoin us, answering that they would wait for us at point Zulu (a reference point in the ocean, fifty miles south of Cochinos Bay). The *Barbara J* was sent in pursuit of the ships, but they were far ahead, and much faster than the LCI.

We were attacked off and on the remainder of the day. None of the attacks was pressed, and none of the ships suffered any lasting damage. One LCU was struck by a rocket, which was found in the steel deck. It had failed to explode. The crew carefully removed it and dropped it gently over the side.

One reason these attacks were not too serious a threat was they were made by B-26s. I imagine they had learned the fate of the last B-26. Reluctant to share that fate by making a close-in attack, they fired at long range, circled, and went home.

The last two circled the LCUs, then headed south, looking for the cargo ships. They found them, still fleeing south, near point Zulu, and strafed them thoroughly. Although neither ship was badly damaged and no rockets had been fired at them, this was enough to send them on to the south, without even slowing for point Zulu.

The *Atlantico* went almost a hundred miles south before it answered our calls for it to return. The *Caribe* was stopped almost two hundred miles south by a U.S. Destroyer sent in pursuit of her. She refused to heave to until the destroyer fired a shot across her bow, which meant she should heave to and prepare to be boarded. She heaved to and radioed for instructions as to where to head. She was told to return to the beach at all possible speed, which she did.

The LCIs and the landing craft arrived at point Zulu just as darkness brought an end to the air attacks. But Zulu was empty. There were no cargo ships, and repeated calls by radio brought only silence. We were now in a quandary. The brigade desperately needed ammunition. The LCIs had some, but our cargo was 90 percent weapons. What we had was a drop in the bucket—it would not begin to fulfill the brigade's needs. What it needed was the tons that were on the cargo ships.

A message concerning this latest problem was sent to Washington. Then we headed south in search of cargo ships, along with the *Santiago* and the *Tampico*, whose assistance we'd enlisted.

This might, at first glance, appear an easy task. It was not. The area south of Cuba is a well-traveled shipping lane. There were dozens of ships on the ocean that night. Since we did not know in which direction the two ships were headed, all ships had to be checked. Radar blips only tell you a ship is there. It does not tell you what ship it is. Many startled merchant ships found themselves in the glare of searchlights from the speeding destroyers. The cargo ships were found the next day by search aircraft from the *Essex*, and headed back for Cochinos Bay.

As the LCIs continued south in search of the cargo ships, we received a message from Washington. It directed the *Barbara J* to return to the beach and unload her cargo of ammunition for the brigade. Since the *Blagar* carried twice the load of ammo that the *Barbara J* did, I asked if we should go in her place.

Anticipating approval, the *Blagar* turned back toward Cochinos Bay. No sooner had we made the turn than the engines stopped. The officers raced to the engine room to discover the cause of the stoppage. They were met by armed merchant crewmen from the *Río Escondido*, who had been rescued earlier. They announced that this was a mutiny. They indicated that they did not intend to take over the ship, but were in control of the engine room and had no intentions of returning to Cochinos Bay, to be sunk a second time. They had enlisted the support of two of the *Blagar*'s crew and were armed with .45-caliber automatic pistols.

This mutiny lasted five minutes at the most. The *Blagar*'s Cuban frogmen ended it in a swift rush of Thompson submachine guns and pistols. Some heads were bloodied, and soon we had a brig full of mutineers.

This didn't end the problem. Though only a portion of the *Río Escondido* crew had taken part in the mutiny, the remainder plainly were in sympathy with them. These Cuban exiles, as I pointed out previously, were merchant seamen, not soldiers. They were terrified of Castro's planes. Many were still in a state of shock from the sinking. They had come aboard the *Blagar* wearing their life jackets, and though the jackets were now water-soaked, they refused to remove them. The *Blagar*'s crew, in a show of defiance to the planes, had made a point of having their jackets near but not putting them on. They looked on this as a symbol of their determination not to allow the planes to sink them.

The crew of the *Río Escondido* had remained huddled in the passageways and wardrooms during the day. With only a few exceptions, they took no part in the fighting. The captain of the *Río Escondido* was aboard. He had been willing to help, and he took a position on the *Blagar*'s bridge. His crew paid no attention to him. He had just recently assumed command of the *Río Escondido*. The crew figured that since there was no longer a ship, he was no longer their captain. It didn't help that he was a Spaniard, not a Cuban. That was ironic, since he was fighting and they weren't. They weren't thinking of Cuba, only of their own skins.

The *Río Escondido*'s crew were holding a meeting, trying to get the *Blagar*'s crew to side with them. They were not succeeding, but the *Blagar*'s crew were upset over it. I knew we had to remove this growing cancer before we went back and faced Castro's planes again. You don't last long in this kind of action with a halfhearted crew.

I notified Washington of the situation and turned back to transfer these "heroes" to the *Barbara J.*

Washington also was notified that because of this problem and because we had traveled so far south in search of the cargo ships, we could not arrive at the beach, discharge our cargo, and be back at Zulu before daylight. We requested some kind of air cover at daylight, for we would be alone at the bay. Our request was denied. We were told air cover was unavailable, that we should remain where we were.

Our orders were to assemble the two LCIs and the landing craft at Zulu and await the arrival of the cargo ships (if and when they were located), unload their ammunition into the LCUs at sea, and prepare for a run-in with all ships after dark, on Tuesday. So we sat and waited. The *Barbara J* and the LCUs found us, but there was no sign of the cargo ships.

Another result of the search was that it had carried us out of range of the brigade's radio, and we had lost contact with Pepe. Contact was regained at point Zulu. I was notified by the *Blagar*'s captain that contact with the brigade had been reestablished. Pepe was roaring mad, and had cursed the captain for running out on him. This was understandable. The brigade was fighting for its life. Its men knew nothing of our problems and had assumed we had abandoned them.

I talked with Pepe, explained the situation, and told him that as soon as the cargo ships returned, we would load up and come in.

All day, the ships waited for the precious ammunition to arrive. It was near dark when the *Atlantico* finally showed up—alone. The LCUs came alongside and began transferring the ammunition. The *Blagar* and the *Barbara J* launched their small boats and began transferring our ammo to the LCUs.

Rip came over in one of the small boats and joined me aboard the *Blagar*. We set up shop in the communications center in an effort to answer the flood of directives and requests for information pouring in from Washington. We were two Indians with an entire tribe of chiefs on our backs. Two very tired Indians—we'd slept only a couple of hours in the last forty-eight, and it would be forty-eight more before we would be able to get more than a few uninterrupted minutes at a time.

This may seem unimportant, and much too personal a problem to bring up in the middle of so important an event. However, no matter how important the happening, it is pretty distressing to find your forehead kissing the desktop in the middle of an important cable from Washington. One would have preferred to be alert and well turned out, but we were not. We were tired, dirty, and unshaven and still had traces of black greasepaint on our hands and faces from our night landing.

Although we were dog-tired, others were as well. I don't think Pepe ever slept. At any time of the day or night, when I called the brigade radio his voice would come back as if he had been sitting there waiting for the call. I knew he was tired—it showed later in his voice—but for the most part he was always very calm, very understanding, and very friendly. He was quite a man.

Late Tuesday morning, a message came from the Washington command group that looked like the answer to our prayers. It read: "Four unmarked jets will arrive over beachhead at 10 o'clock. Have brigade mark front lines with panels. Caution troops not to fire on these planes."

Overjoyed, I immediately notified Pepe of the message. He was jubilant. I asked him to call me the minute the planes arrived. After some delay, and more calls asking where the planes were, he called to say that they had just flown over his head. Four unmarked Navy jets had come sweeping in from the sea, all silver, shining in the sunlight. They had rocked their wings in salute as they flew over, then disappeared, heading straight in over Cuba.

None of Castro's planes were over the beachhead at that moment, but now that the brigade troops saw what they thought was jet support, they could at least breathe easier. With these jets overhead, Castro's planes would not attack them again.

Wrong!

For after a short period of calm, and salvation, the four U.S. jets appeared again, heading back out to sea. A moment later Castro's planes came in behind them, bombing and strafing the brigade positions as though nothing had changed.

Nothing had changed, at least not to save the brigade. What Washington had failed to include in the message, but I learned by contacting the aircraft carrier *Essex*, which had escorted us and was now sitting outside the fifty-mile limit (point Zulu), was that these planes had been authorized to fly one mission only, and that that mission was to *photograph* the beachhead area and not to engage in combat operations. The photo mission had been flown, and the planes were now back aboard the *Essex*. No other missions had been authorized.

This was a cruel deception to employ on the hopeful and still trusting brigade. Pepe called me. He was shocked that the planes had departed. At that moment, two of Castro's jets were attacking his area. He asked if I could contact the jets and get them to come back, this time flying lower—down where Castro's jets were, not high in the clouds as before.

I sent a report to Washington, telling of the critical need for support and asking for clarification of the planes' missions. Then I called the *Essex*. I was told that the jets would return to the beachhead. The *Essex* asked me to obtain target information from the brigade. The *Essex* wanted to know what enemy targets the brigade wanted hit and the map coordinates of these targets.

I called Pepe, notified him of this further jet support, and asked for a list of targets. These were quickly given, and I sent them to the *Essex*. This time there was no jubilation from the brigade over this message, only guarded optimism. The men had believed in the jet saviors once before, and had been cruelly disappointed. Now they were cautious. They would wait and see. The first faint cracks in their absolute belief and trust in the United States were beginning to open.

After some time had passed without word from the brigade on the arrival of more jets, I called the *Essex* to ask what was causing the delay. I was informed the jets were on their way. Later, Pepe called. I asked if the jets had arrived. He said he couldn't be sure. Some jets had been seen, but up high—nothing in the area where they were needed.

He'd wanted jet strikes on Castro's now massed columns that were closing in for the kill, not high-flying specks in the sky. Whether a second flight of jets took place over the beachhead, I do not know. Only the U.S. Navy knows for sure. Many men in the brigade saw what they described as several

Navy jets over the beachhead. Some, including Castro, reported a strike by U.S. jets on a column of Castro's troops near Covadonga that resulted in heavy losses. The brigade reported large columns of black smoke rising from this devastated area.

I believe an attack did take place, but I cannot confirm whether it was done by brigade aircraft or U.S. Navy planes, because the Navy will not discuss the matter. It is my understanding that the Navy pilots could only sit in their ready rooms and listen to the reports of the brigade and the brigade air force as they fought the air and ground battles against Castro's jets.

The pilots of the *Essex* and the *Boxer*, the other carrier in the area, were aching to get at Castro's planes. They knew that if they could catch his jets over the beachhead they could end this fight in seconds. They were frustrated, and angry, at what they knew was a disaster in the making, one their nation was creating, and could easily prevent by turning them loose for just a short while. But they were disciplined, dedicated officers, and although they disagreed with their restrictive orders, they nevertheless obeyed them to the letter. The U.S. Navy planes, one of which was hit by Castro's ground fire, did not fire a single unauthorized shot at Cochinos Bay. The pilots' record of discipline remained unblemished, but not their pride in their country.

To men in combat, a jet is a jet. Men reported Castro's jets as ours and ours as Castro's. Some even reported flights of MiGs over their beachhead, on more than one occasion. There were many MiGs in Cuba at the time. More than twenty of them were at Castro's airfields. Some were still in crates, others in various stages of assembly. But it is highly unlikely that there were any over the beachhead, because the pilots for these MiGs were still in Prague, and not due in for another ten days, as I mentioned earlier.

I called the *Essex* and asked if the jets being sent to the beach would attack in support of the Brigade. I was told, "We are launching now. This launch is armed for air-to-air combat. The next launch is for the beach. It is armed for strike support."

This information I passed on to the brigade, and we sat back to wait. I was now beginning to have my own doubts about Washington.

The Navy did not inform me that a strike had occurred, and my calls to the *Essex* brought no clarification of the matter, but since the brigade and Castro both claim to have witnessed a Navy strike, the possibility remains that Navy planes did attack.

From Washington came a cable that said, "Four F-51 fighters and a C-46 cargo plane would arrive at Playa Girón airfield at two o'clock on Wednesday morning. The C-46 would unload ammo for the Brigade and armaments and rockets for the F-51s, pick up brigade wounded, and return to Puerta Cabezas. The F-51s would fly support for the brigade from Playa Girón."

I was to notify the brigade and have the men at Playa Girón prepared to light up the runway with gasoline flares. They were to have their wounded ready to be picked up. C-46s were to drop supplies and ammunition to the brigade by parachute, at the field, starting at midnight.

Late Tuesday, Puerto Cabezas received permission to employ the American B-26 pilot instructors on combat operations. Those who remained of the brigade pilots had reached the point of exhaustion. They had been flying, or standing by to fly, since Saturday. Since Monday morning, they had been making continuous round-trip flights into the danger-packed skies over Cochinos Bay. They had lost half of their planes.

The round-trip flights required seven hours of fatiguing flying. Other long hours had been required in preparation for the flights, for briefing and debriefing. The brigade pilots had flown long, and hard, against terrific odds. They had hit Castro's forces on the ground, leaving entire columns of tanks and trucks burning in the "shooting galleries" leading to the beachhead, where they killed a thousand of Castro's Rebel Army.

On Monday night, they had been "allowed" by Washington to hit Castro's airfields, to try to knock out his few remaining jets. But it was too little, and far, far too late. The brigade air force could muster only six planes for the raid. They took off Monday, at ten at night, to hit the Cuban airfields in a desperate night-bombing raid. They knew Castro's planes would be expecting a dawn attack, and would be up and waiting for them.

At two in the morning, the planes were over the area of San Antonio de los Baños, where the jet field was located. The field and the surrounding towns were blacked out, and a heavy ground haze covered all of central Cuba. It was impossible to see the field. The planes circled and searched, but to no avail.

One of the bravest of the brigade pilots was Gonzalo Herrera. He had been in every action since Saturday morning, when he had hit Castro's planes at Santiago. He knew the field was heavily ringed by antiaircraft emplacements. If he could draw their fire, then maybe he could locate the field. So, in a desperate effort, he turned on his running lights, then his landing lights, lowered his landing gear, and circled slowly over the area where, by his calculations lay San Antonio de los Baños. He drew no fire. He discovered the reason for that in the radio conversations he was monitoring: the Cuban ground controllers were warning the antiaircraft units to hold their fire. Soon his fuel indicators warned him that it was time to head home. He rejoined his flight and the six planes returned to Puerto Cabezas without dropping a bomb.

Late that same day, brigade pilots caught Castro's forces north of Red Beach preparing for an assault on Oliva's men. They left the dead and wounded lying in long rows. Another brigade B-26 caught a PC (a 179-foot-long patrol craft) leaving its base, on the north coast of the Isle of Pines, and put four rockets into her. The PC limped back to its berth at Nueva Gerona but sank at the dock.

A Cuban navy frigate was docked east of Cochinos Bay, at Cienfuegos. She was watched, but never left port. Her 3-inch guns could have played havoc with the brigade ships. Our information assuring us she would play no part in this action proved correct.

By late on Tuesday, the brigade pilots were in bad shape, their limit of endurance having long since been exceeded. Six B-26s, three flown by American instructors, former pilots of the Alabama Air National Guard, flew to Cochinos Bay. They caught Castro's forces moving south from Playa Larga to Blue Beach and had a "turkey shoot."

A long column of tanks, trucks, and troops stretched almost the entire length of the sixteen-mile-long coast road on the east shore of Cochinos Bay. In places the columns were bunched up, two and three vehicles abreast. It was an attack pilot's dream, and these were experienced attack pilots.

They came in on the column just at sunset, picked out a seven-mile stretch packed with troops, and raked it repeatedly from end to end. They worked as a team, and methodically turned the section into flaming rubble and fleeing troops. Their ammunition exhausted, they flew back in darkness to Puerto Cabezas to prepare for another raid at dawn on Wednesday. It would be the last dawn these Americans, who had found a cause worth dying for, would see. They died that morning, caught in the sights of a T-33.

It was afternoon, on Tuesday. The *Blagar* and the

convoy still were waiting for the second cargo ship, the *Caribe,* to arrive at point Zulu for the run-in to Blue Beach. The LCUs were still unloading the *Atlantico.* It was eleven at night before they finished. Since the *Caribe* had not returned, it was decided that the *Blagar* and the LCUs would go on to Blue Beach. The *Barbara J* would remain at point Zulu to await her arrival.

It was slow going. LCUs are not very fast craft empty; heavily loaded, they could reach only six knots. We calculated our arrival at four-thirty in the morning. This would allow only one hour for unloading and our return to Point Zulu. We knew there would be enough light for Castro's jets to hit us at five-thirty.

I notified Washington of our situation, again requesting that some kind of air cover be provided for us while we were in the beachhead area. A few hours later, not having received an answer to my request, I sent a second message: "If jet cover is not furnished beginning at first light, expect to lose all ships."

Some may think this message was too alarming. I did not then, and I do not now. The brigade needed ammunition to survive. No one knew when, or if, the *Caribe* would show up with the rest of the supplies. If it didn't, what we had with us was all that was left. It was imperative it be delivered, or the brigade could hang it up.

Once again, all our eggs were in one basket. Washington must have seen this as another disaster in the making, for at two-thirty in the morning we were told to hold and return to Point Zulu.

En route to the beach, I'd received a message to pass on to the brigade. It postponed the landing of the C-46 at Playa Girón from two in the morning to four. Nothing more was said about the four F-51s that were supposed to come with it. I discovered that these four F-51s were the ones at Puerto Cabezas that had given us our early-morning reveille service. The Nicaraguan air force had turned them over to the brigade, but the long-range tanks needed to reach Cochinos Bay were unavailable. The tanks were being flown in from Florida, but did not arrive in time. This caused the two postponements of the C-46.

Pepe informed me that the lights for the strip were ready and in place, and that the wounded had been moved to the airstrip. When at first light the plane still had not arrived, the brigade surgeon ordered the wounded brought back to Playa Girón. To leave them lying there in the open during daylight was too much of a risk.

The C-46 finally arrived, but it was long after daylight. It had a Cuban pilot and an American copilot. They hurriedly unloaded their cargo of ammunition, picked up the brigade B-26 pilot who had crashed on the strip Monday, and took off for Puerto Cabezas.

Many have stated that the plane should have waited longer, that the wounded could have been brought back out. I do not agree. Any delay might have allowed Castro's planes to catch it on the field, or worse yet, the unarmed, slow plane, loaded with brigade wounded, might have been shot out of the sky. It would have been another disaster, and disasters were one thing we already had had plenty of. The fact the plane had slipped in and unloaded was a miracle in itself.

The two C-54s had dropped supplies over the airfield during the night, but some of the parachutes had been lost in the heavy woods around the field. A later drop sent some of them into the water. Most were recovered by the UDT men, but this delivery was not enough to build up the dwindling ammunition supplies.

Tuesday night I received another message from Washington, informing us that a maximum effort by brigade planes would be flown in support of the beachhead at dawn on Wednesday. Once again Pepe was requested to mark the brigade's frontline positions with panels. I radioed these instructions to Pepe.

What we were not told was that the White House had given permission for unmarked jets, from the carrier *Essex*, to fly escort to keep the sky clear of Castro's planes for exactly one hour. No explanation was given.

I later learned from Bissell that Admiral Arleigh Burke, chief of the Navy, had called the president out of a black-tie affair he was attending to request U.S. Navy air support for the supply ships so that they could make a run into the beachhead with the brigade's much-needed ammunition and supplies. At first the president refused the Admiral's request, citing his promise that no U.S. forces would be used in Cuba. He said, "We just can't become involved."

Bissell said Admiral Burke's response was "Goddammit, Mr. President, we are involved. We put those people in there and promised to aid them. We can't just wash our hands of them and walk away."

The president relented and gave approval for the use of the *Essex*'s planes for one hour beginning at first light, 0530 to 0630.

The brigade force was made up of three B-26s, two flown by Americans—one by Riley Shamburger and Wade Gray, the other by Leo F. Baker and Thomas W. Ray, CIA instructor pilots on loan from the Alabama National Guard. The third plane was flown by the indestructible Gonzalo Herrera. It was all they could muster. A fourth plane was forced back by a bad engine.

The brigade planes arrived at the rendezvous point at 0530 and headed for the beach. No Navy planes were spotted. They could not wait for the jets, as their fuel supply was limited to just enough to allow them to strike and return. Someone somewhere had made a miscalculation. The jets sat on the deck of the *Essex*, the pilots in her briefing room. The message sent to the *Essex* read not 0530 to 0630 but 0630 to 0730. Our B-26s had come over the carriers an hour too early.

The mistake, made in Washington, is not the kind men readily admit to, since it cost the lives of the four Americans. My personal investigation of this matter indicated that the man responsible for writing and sending this message was Jake Esterline, the CIA's chief of the Cuban Task Force (WH-4). It appears that he became confused with the difference in time at Puerto Cabezas and the beachhead, since they were in different time zones. This should not have been a problem, since messages of this type are always sent in Zulu time, which is the same throughout the world.

Castro's jets jumped the B-26s over the beachhead. The last calls heard from the American pilots were to their jet cover to come to their aid, each having a T-33 on his tail. One of the B-26s crash-landed on the little dirt strip at the Central Australia sugar mill, north of Playa Larga. Uninjured, one of the Americans came out of the plane with his .45 blazing, as Castro's militia, firing on the plane, closed in. He died under fire, but as Castro's men later described it, "He died like a man."

The other American B-26 went down at sea, in flames. The two pilots parachuted into the water. They were picked up by Castro's men and executed. Proof of this appeared in a photo sent to several Latin American newspapers by Prensa Latina, Fidel's propaganda arm of the media, along with an explanation saying that the pilots had been killed when their plane crashed into the sea. The picture showed the two Americans lying side by side on canvas, their clothing wet, their Mae West life jackets inflated, and they were missing their boots. Each had a small-caliber bullet hole in his forehead that was very evident in the picture. Dead men do not inflate life jackets, nor can they remove their boots. Had they died in the crash, as Castro wanted everyone to believe they had, their life jackets would not have been inflated and their boots would still have been on.

The Cubans saw the mistake in the first photo and took a second one with the life jackets deflated. The CIA obtained a copy of both pictures and sent copies of both to those Latin American newspapers friendly to the United States and thus discredited Castro's claim that the pilots had died in the crash.

Gonzalo Herrera made his strike beyond San Blas. He flew back to Puerto Cabezas at a hundred feet above the water, his plane riddled with thirty-eight bullet holes and one engine out. This was the last brigade plane to fly over Cochinos Bay.

It was at this hour that the *Blagar* and the LCUs rejoined the *Barbara J* at point Zulu. The long-lost *Caribe* was back in the fold. We began unloading the *Caribe*'s ammunition into the LCUs, filling them to capacity.

About noon, I received a message from Washington. The Navy had been authorized to move in on Wednesday night, using the landing craft of the U.S. Marine Amphibious Force, afloat just to the south of us, to remove the brigade from the beachhead. The destroyers were to support this evacuation with fire, if necessary. Two of them, the *Santiago* and the *Tampico,* were on their way into Blue Beach to reconnoiter the area. I was told to pass this on to Pepe.

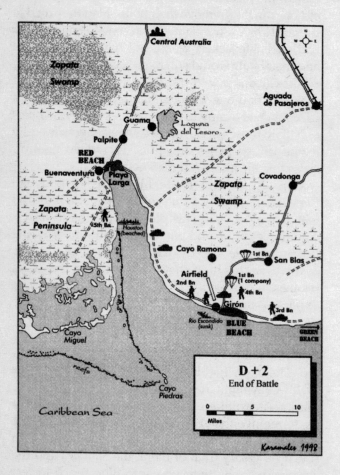

Central Australia

Zapata
Swamp

Aguada
de Pasajeros

Guama

Laguna
del Tesoro

Palpite

RED
BEACH

Buenaventura

Playa
Larga

Covadonga

Zapata

Zapata

Swamp

Peninsula

5th Bn

Houston
(beached)

Cayo Ramona

1st Bn

San Blas

Airfield

2nd Bn

1st Bn
(1 company)

4th Bn

Girón

3rd Bn

Río Escondido
(sunk)

BLUE
BEACH

GREEN
BEACH

Cayo
Miguel

reefs

Cayo
Piedras

Caribbean Sea

D + 2
End of Battle

0   5   10
Miles

Karamales 1998

Now, how do you tell a man that you cannot support him, without risking involvement, in his fight to free Cuba, but that you will, at all costs, come in and get him out?

I told him in the best way I could: "Remember, Pepe, that if things get too bad we will come in and bring you out."

Pepe's reply was: "No, Gray, we will not leave this island. We will fight to the end here, if we have to. Thank you, but we will not evacuate."

He gave me his last situation—it was bad. Castro's troops were closing in on him from all sides, and his ammunition was almost gone.

This was more than we could take. Without asking permission, we fired up the *Blagar*, the *Barbara J*, and the LCUs and headed for Blue Beach. We notified Washington of our move, but no one stopped us. At our speed, we figured we could arrive at five Wednesday evening. We might be sunk, but it didn't matter. It was clear that the brigade had only hours to live if we didn't move in.

After two in the afternoon on Wednesday, the last hours of the brigade can best be described in the message I received from Pepe and sent on to Washington. It read: "Tanks closing on Blue Beach from north and east. They are firing directly at our headquarters." Then: "Fighting on beach. Send all available aircraft now!" And: "In water, out of ammunition. Enemy closing in. Help must arrive in next hour."

I told Pepe we were on the way and would arrive

at five. I asked him if he could hold on till that hour. He said he would try, but at two he radioed that Castro's tanks had broken through, and that he was destroying his maps and equipment and taking to the woods.

His last words were: "I can't wait any longer. I am destroying my radio now."

The radio went silent. It was over.

I sent this information to Washington, then tried calling the beach on all channels, but all contact with Cochinos was lost. The brigade's fight was ended. Its men were not defeated in battle, nor did they surrender. They simply ran out of ammunition, and the fighting slowly died away.

As the firing died, they slipped away in small groups, into the woods and swamps around Cochinos Bay. They were sure that when Castro's forces saw they were no longer firing, they would end it in one fast rush, but they did not. In fact, Castro's troops did not move forward at all. They were too fearful of being sucked into a trap. I later learned that they had figured the brigade's strength to be ten thousand men. From the handful of prisoners they had been able to capture, they knew the brigade was certainly still intact. Therefore, at Playa Girón, there must be ten thousand men waiting for them to charge into a trap.

At that very moment they saw a sight that convinced them they were facing an even larger force. Two U.S. destroyers came racing into Cochinos Bay. They were the *Santiago* and the *Tampico* on their reconnaissance mission for the evacuation of the brigade—an evacuation that had been refused, and that was now impossible without radio contact.

Not only did Castro's forces not advance, but the commander of the column on the coast road from Playa Larga ordered a full retreat.

The destroyers entered Cochinos Bay with crews at General Quarters and guns pointed shoreward. They turned and passed in front of Playa Girón heading east. Castro's forces on this flank of Playa Girón under the command of Comandante José Ramón Fernández did not fall back. They opened fire on the destroyers with the Stalin tanks and heavy artillery.

The destroyers were untouched, and ignoring the fire, they continued the reconnaisance of the beach. Satisfied, they wheeled out and moved off-shore, just as the heavy artillery was finding the range.

The last shots fired at Cochinos Bay were a concentration from Soviet-made artillery guns at U.S. Navy destroyers. The Soviet presence in the Caribbean was no longer just a threat, it was a reality!

As the destroyers left Cochinos Bay, they saw brigade troops trying to escape the beach in a sail-boat. They could not stop to pick them up, for not only were they under heavy artillery fire, but Castro's planes were circling the dying beachhead, strafing the troops trying to escape in anything that would float.

The planes did not choose to attack the two destroyers. They could shoot back. The struggling troops in the water, without ammunition, were a more suitable target for these brave pilots.

Just before sunset, the *Blagar* and the brigade ships saw a lone plane approaching them from the direction of Cochinos Bay. The guns were manned, but it was identified as the brigade air force's lone air rescue plane, an old World War II—era PBY, flying a search pattern, looking for survivors.

There were survivors, as we found out later, but for now, the brigade ships, with the two destroyers as escort, sadly turned away from Cochinos Bay.

Many have called the Bay of Pigs Invasion a fiasco. It was not a fiasco—it was a tragedy. For the first time in my thirty-seven years, I was ashamed of my country.

12

Rescue

ALL DAY THURSDAY AND FRIDAY, MY SHIP, THE *BLAGAR*, with me and my remaining frogmen, Cantillo, Soto, and Casares, and her sister ship, the *Barbara J*, with Rip and his surviving frogmen, Pruna, Bentancourt, and Font, had cruised the waters south of Cuba. Standing on her deck, which gently rolled with each swell, I lit a Lucky Strike and gazed aimlessly out over the horizon.

How typical the last two days had been. We had received orders to almost every port in the Caribbean. No sooner were they received than they were countermanded. No one seemed to know what to do with us.

Earlier that day, the Navy had taken the LCUs on to Key West. The *Caribe* and *Atlantico* had taken aboard the LCUs' Cuban crews and the survivors from the *Río Escondido*. We were glad to see these malcontents go.

We had just finished transferring our wounded to a destroyer, along with a Castro pilot who had been aboard the *Tampico*. He'd been picked up when he'd parachuted out of his crippled B-26 over the ship. His story was that he'd been shot up by one of the T-33s when he'd strafed Castro's troops on his way out.

No one had any reason to doubt him. He stuck to his story even after arriving in Guantánamo, where his name had been checked by the CIA. Not until he was flown to the United States and was faced by a CIA man he knew from Puerto Cabezas would he finally admit his true identity. He was a brigade pilot. He had been told to use a cover story if he was forced to ditch and was picked up by other than a brigade ship. He followed that cover story to the bitter end—long past what common sense called for.

"Excuse me, sir." One of the communications crew interrupted my thoughts. "We have a report from the *Santiago* indicating a skunk headed in our direction."

A "skunk" is Navy lingo for a surface craft of unknown nationality. We'd seen a lot of skunks in the last few days, none of them oceangoing.

"The destroyer reported that she'd chased them away. It was manned by troops in green uniforms and was flying a Costa Rican flag."

"So now the Costa Ricans are after our hide as well," I joked. "What's the status?"

"Apparently they're still trying to get through."

We joined the men in the radio room. A communiqué from the *Santiago* indicated that she and another destroyer had charged the invader repeatedly. They'd headed it off, only to find it making another attempt.

The invader had run down the Costa Rican flag and proceeded to run up every flag in the Western Hemisphere, finally displaying a white flag.

The *Santiago* radioed us that it was placing itself between us and the skunk in an attempt to stop it. If this failed, the *Santiago* would fire a shot across its bow. If it continued after this warning, the *Santiago* would sink it. To reinforce this implied threat, carrier jets came streaking in at the little ship a hundred feet above the water.

By now we could see the ship and make out its blinker signal. It read, "Call off the damn Navy. We're friendly." It turned out to be Nino Diaz's group. So much for an escalation in the war. We were only too happy to welcome them back to the fold.

A few hours later, we received orders to proceed to Vieques Island, Puerto Rico. I retired for the night, only to be awakened at four in the morning by another of the crew.

"Sir, we have a message for you from Washington."

The message directed Rip, the frogmen, and me to transfer to the *Santiago*. Our planes had spotted survivors of the *Houston* and the 5th Battalion in the swamps on the west side of Cochinos Bay. We were to mount a rescue mission and bring them out.

"Get Rip on the radio for me," I said. Running my hands through my hair in lieu of a comb and tucking my shirttails into my pants, I followed the crewman to the communications room.

The radio cracked and Rip's voice boomed over the speaker. "You got any idea what time it is? Having trouble sleeping?"

"Orders from headquarters," I replied. "Looks like they found a few strays for us to round up."

It was a good mission. We decided we would go, but only if we were given assurances that the information was correct and current. Too many people had been let down in the last few days by false promises.

We cabled this request to Washington. We received a return cable from the director of central intelligence, Allen Dulles, himself, indicating all information correct and current.

"You can't get much higher than this unless it's from God," I said, and we went off to gather our gear.

Just after dawn, we loaded up our UDT rafts, equipped with eighteen-horsepower silent motors. Weapons, radios, and everything else we could pack were loaded onto the rafts. We were lowered over the side of the LCU into a very rough sea, where we waited for the *Santiago* to come to us.

She came, all right, with her bow aimed straight at us, or so it seemed. We paddled like mad to get out of the way of the knife-edge bow, but the more we paddled the more she turned. The *Santiago* finally slid to a stop. We paddled over and climbed the cargo nets the crew had dropped over her side. Once everyone was safely aboard and the gear stored, we joined the captain on the bridge.

"What the hell kind of maneuvering do you call that?" I inquired.

"Sea's pretty rough," the captain said. "I thought I'd bring my bow past you and let you slide down the side of the ship to the net. You boys sure know how to make things difficult for yourself."

I thanked him for his concern, but pointed out that we preferred the more conventional means of coming aboard, especially since our nerves were a little tight from the strain of the past five days.

The *Santiago* took us to the *Essex*, where we were transferred for a planning conference. The Navy was now authorized to conduct this "humanitarian effort" with all available ships and aircraft. The only restriction placed on the operation was that the frogmen, Rip, and I be the only ones to actually land on Cuban soil.

Now that the battle was over, we had more ships and planes in Cochinos Bay than we could use. If only we had been given just one of these jets a few days earlier, there would have been no need for a rescue mission.

We were bitter, bitter and saddened by what we had seen. If we could contribute some act of decency to an otherwise shameful episode in our history by this rescue mission, then by all means we wanted to do it.

We were briefed on the *Essex*. Aerial photos indicated the area to be mainly swamp, stretching south twelve miles from the sunken *Houston* to small brush-covered keys that curved west for another twenty miles. It was an awfully big area for only two Americans and six Cuban frogmen. Navy planes, flying as scouts, were to locate the survivors for us.

My three frogmen and I transferred back to the *Santiago* and headed for Cochinos Bay. Rip and his men went aboard the *Tampico*.

All night we searched up and down the island chain. The mosquitoes fed ravenously on us, and the air hung with the smell of death, but in the darkness we were unable to detect any activity on shore.

Just before dawn, we moved into Cochinos Bay, and at first light we lay off the sunken *Houston*. Rip and his crew closed to within a thousand yards of the island chain and started their search. Off the *Houston* it was quiet, the shore deserted. Nothing moved, nothing but the *Santiago* and flight after flight of Navy fighters orbiting over Cochinos Bay, a signal to Castro that this was one show to which he was not invited. It would be best if he and his jets stayed home and celebrated their great victory over what they now claimed to the world's media was the combined fleets of the United States and all its armed forces.

We launched our rubber raft and moved into shore. Nothing moved. We eased slowly along the beach flying a U.S. flag, hoping the survivors would respond by approaching us and not shooting at us, although at this point I really wouldn't have blamed them if they chose the latter course of action. The *Santiago*, in a similar attempt, ran up her holiday flag, the largest she had.

Damn, where were they? I strained my sight for a sign of somebody, anybody. We learned later that many of the survivors along that seemingly deserted shore saw the flags, but thought it was a Castro trick to lure them out. When we landed and moved to the edge of the swamp, they moved deeper into it. These were frightened men. In this swamp for over a week, with little food or water, hunted and strafed by Castro's planes, they were wary and tired of running. Only one man was spotted. He was seen from the *Santiago*, which reported to us that he had walked to the beach, taken one look at the destroyer, and run back into the brush. Was he a friend or a foe? We didn't know and couldn't turn back and look for one running man. There were two hundred others from the brigade and the *Houston* somewhere in there. We would have to find the main concentration of them if we were to get all, or even a sizable number of them, out.

Over our radios, we could hear the conversations of Castro's troops as more and more units were ordered into action. They were moving into the north end of the swamp and starting to sweep south toward us.

It was not until the *Santiago* left us and moved out of Cochinos Bay, to come in close to shore off the chain of islands, that the first survivors were spotted. There were five of them, waving frantically from the beach. The *Tampico* sent Rip and his frog-men in to get them. The tattered men swam and waded out to meet them, overjoyed and crying with relief, saved from what they thought was certain capture and, in all probability, death at the hands of Castro's militia.

We were now alone in Cochinos Bay, for the reefs along this section would not allow the *Santiago* to follow us. All morning we searched without finding a man. At last we came out to the island chain and the two destroyers.

That afternoon, after a quick sandwich and some cold drinks aboard the *Santiago*, we moved back to shore and started walking the beaches looking for footprints or any other trace of the elusive survivors. The day was scorching hot, and the burning white sand of the keys soon forced us to work in shifts. Two men searched the shore while the other two rested in the raft that was eased along, just off the beach, behind them.

It was a damn long day, and all we had at the end of it was a dozen or so survivors between the two rescue teams.

Before dawn of the next day, we were at it again. We were now assisted by two more destroyers and additional planes. The propeller-driven Navy ADs were being flown almost on top of the water. Their pilots flew along the shore looking under the overhanging mangroves for any signs of life. And they found them. In pairs and groups of three, and sometimes one man, all alone. When the ADs spot-

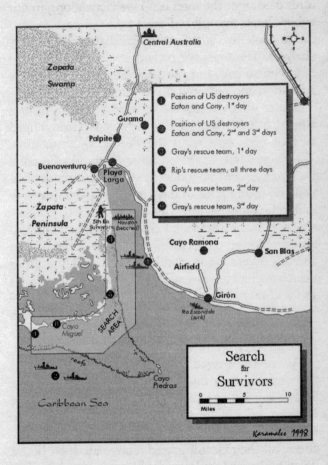

Central Australia

Zapata
Swamp

Guama

Palpite

Buenaventura

Playa
Larga

Zapata
Peninsula

5th Bat
Survivors

Houston
(beached)

Cayo Ramona

Airfield

San Blas

Girón

Río Escondido
(sunk)

SEARCH
AREA

Cayo
Miguel

Cayo
Piedras

Caribbean Sea

1. Position of US destroyers
   Eaton and *Cony*, 1st day

2. Position of US destroyers
   Eaton and *Cony*, 2nd and 3rd days

3. Gray's rescue team, 1st day

4. Rip's rescue team, all three days

5. Gray's rescue team, 2nd day

6. Gray's rescue team, 3rd day

Search
for
Survivors

0   5   10
Miles

Karamales 1998

ted a survivor, they would notify us by radio, through the *Santiago*. Then they would make pass after pass over the men until we came along in our rubber boats and picked them up.

We took the survivors immediately to the destroyers. The ones we picked up the first day had not been so bad, but the later ones were in terrible condition and required prompt medical attention.

Most were completely naked, their clothes ripped from their bodies, which were covered head to foot with cuts from the needlelike vegetation. Their feet were lacerated so severely by the coral that many could no longer walk. They'd had practically no food for eight days and had been forced to drink the brackish salt water.

As a former Special Forces officer, schooled in survival techniques, I knew that a person could live in these swamps for months if need be. During our searches I had discovered fresh water in many holes in the coral rock formations and tops of tree stumps. The sand bottoms off the beaches were littered with edible shellfish that needed little more than cracking open on a rock.

All of the brigade's men had been given this training, but only one five-man group put it to use. They were found in very good condition. Even after having covered thirty miles from the *Houston* in four days, they still had their weapons, their canteens, all their clothing, and, above all, their boots. They had spent the daylight hours lying in shallow holes scooped in the sand under the overhanging mangrove trees. They had traveled only at night on the hard sand, by the water's edge. They had to cross the many channels and cuts that divide the keys. Some of these channels were two hundred yards across, with tides that surged through them in swift rushes. They gathered the dry brush and bound it together with rope made of strips of cloth torn from their underwear. Holding on to the sides of these makeshift rafts and kicking their feet, they propelled themselves to the other side. The rafts were necessary because none of the men could swim. They were able to accomplish this journey primarily because they had a strong and determined leader, a fifty-year-old crewman off the *Houston*.

Castro did not care for this humanitarian effort of the New Frontier. His ships now lay off the coast behind ours. They formed a semicircle on the far horizon, like a group of hungry vultures waiting for scraps. The vultures were mostly small craft such as PT boats. Since our destroyer fleet now numbered six, they could only sit waiting patiently in the burning sun.

Ashore, Castro's Soviet-built helicopters, armed with machine guns mounted in the doorways, circled over the swamps, slaughtering the frightened and desperate survivors. We would catch glimpses of this murder as long bursts from the machine guns echoed through the swamps throughout the day.

For some ungodly reason, no action was taken by our guardian aircraft against them. In an attempt to see how far he could push these unwelcome Americans who now controlled a section of his coast almost as long as the Cochinos Bay beachhead, Castro sent two of his Sea Furies down from Havana.

I was in the radio room of the *Santiago*, having just delivered aboard a group of survivors. "Listen to this," the radioman said, putting the ensuing action on the loudspeaker for all to hear.

Castro immediately discovered that his little foray with the Sea Furies was a mistake. A considerable force of Navy jet fighters moved in on the two planes, escorting them the full length of Cochinos Bay. There were Navy jets above, below, and on both sides of them. In every direction the Sea Fury pilots looked, there were Skyhawks riding along like an honor guard. Still the Sea Furies came on.

The destroyers went to general quarters, racing out to deeper water to get maneuvering room. We could hear the Navy Skyhawk leader radio for instructions from the *Essex* as to when and under what conditions he was allowed to "dump" these two invaders. He was told to take action only if they continued their forward progress, dropped below five thousand feet, and entered an area of five miles from the destroyers.

"Seven thousand and closing," the flight leader began, calling off the altitude, as the Sea Furies continued dropping toward the ships. "Six thousand. Five thousand and seven miles."

The next transmission was a disgusted "The bastards are turning off."

As the Sea Furies turned back, the Skyhawks saw them safely on their way.

We heard a final communication between the *Essex* and the Skyhawks, asking if they thought the Sea Furies had seen them.

"Affirmative," came the reply. "We gave them a close flyby to bid them adieu. I guarantee you those two jokers will have gas on their stomachs tonight!"

Castro now knew that he could not push the U.S. Navy, no matter how many fleets he claimed he'd defeated.

While Castro screamed loud and long over the Cochinos invasion, he never said a word about this American force that literally took over the west coast of Cochinos Bay and held it for three days. This was obviously not out of sympathy for the humanitarian effort of the operation. His lack of protest in this matter stemmed from the same reasoning the Soviets used in not mentioning the U-2 flights until they shot down Gary Powers. To do so would be an admission to the world that Cuba was powerless to prevent these intrusions. Communists are not prone to admit to any weakness.

The rescue effort lasted for three days. It seemed like three weeks to me, and I'm sure to the rest of the men. I cannot give a chronological account of this effort. To me, it all blended into an unending series of trips to the beach in the rubber rafts; long, hot hours in the brush of the swamp and islands; seeing too many scarecrow survivors.

We took sleep in short snatches. A sailor would

come in to wake us, only to return minutes later to find us still fast asleep. The Navy treated us royally, but we were only six men. We'd been going hard for a week before this effort started. Now after three days and nights, we were fast approaching exhaustion. In fact, we were beginning to approach the state of the men we were rescuing.

Some of the events stand out clearly. These I will relate as I remember them. As to which day they occurred and in what order, I cannot say.

I remember one man. We picked him up on the beach. He was so thin, skin and bones. My heart went out to this scarecrow. Two years later, I saw him in Miami. To my amazement, he still looked like the skin-and-bones derelict we'd picked up off Cochinos Bay. He laughed at my surprise, and told me this was his normal weight. He was six feet tall and had never weighed more than 125 pounds in his life.

Another one was delirious when we found him. He tried to throw a grenade at us, thinking my Cuban frogmen were Castro's *barbudos* and I was their Russian adviser. We finally got him aboard the *Santiago*. He thought she was a Soviet ship and openly cursed every "Russian" who came near him. Later that day he became rational and thanked everyone for his rescue. That night, I dropped in to see him. He was huddled in his blanket in one corner of the wardroom. When I spoke to him, he called me a damn Russian and withdrew deeper into his blanket. He was out in left field again. But he fully recovered before the operation was over.

I was aboard several different destroyers during this period. As a rule I was treated well on all of them. On one in particular, I was greeted like a VIP. It seems there had been mention of a "Gray" in a lot of their radio traffic. The sailors asked me if I was that same Gray.

I said, as far as I knew, I was the only Gray in the area.

Unfortunately, they had mistaken me for a General Gray, who was somewhere around this fleet of Navy ships. I learned this by accident, and wondered if I should set them straight on the matter. I decided against it. First off, they might be so angry at this "impostor" that they would throw me overboard. Secondly, I kind of liked the idea of being a general. After all, how many times in a lifetime does a mere Indian get this kind of opportunity? Not many. So, I was a general for a day in Cochinos Bay and thoroughly enjoyed every minute of it. I was sorry to have to leave.

"General, come back and see us anytime," they said in farewell. I thanked them, but avoided this destroyer afterward. It is not wise to push your luck. A day of being a general would have to suffice for this lifetime.

One of my frogmen, Amado Cantillo, and I had a close call. We were searching one of the islands when we got a call from the destroyer informing us that a Castro helicopter was headed our way. We sprinted into a large clump of bushes that overlooked a three-hundred-yard-long clearing. Positioning our Thompson submachine guns, we waited.

The whump-whump of the rotor blades increased in volume as the helicopter approached our position. Moments later, a Soviet-built chopper came into view above the clearing, heading straight for us.

"Come on, baby, just a little closer," I prayed, under my breath.

Thompsons are short-range weapons, and I wanted a sure shot at him. I didn't get it. When he was two hundred yards away, he suddenly turned, dropping out of sight over the trees to our left. Back in the swamp, we could hear the sound of his machine gun, as he continued his "rabbit hunt."

The most heart-wrenching incident of the entire mission occurred on the last day. The search planes reported a lone survivor, sitting under a mangrove tree, slowly waving a white cloth on the end of a stick. We moved cautiously in on this survivor. Castro's forces were very near on their sweep to the south of this swamp. The fact that the man did not move from his sitting position under the tree when he saw us approach made us feel it might be a trap. We called for Rip and his crew to join us, since they were nearby. As we moved in, we could see another man lying on the ground near the seated man, who still continued to wave the small white flag.

Rip's group landed off to one side, to provide cover. My men and I moved in to the survivor. The man lying on the ground was dead. The other one was close to joining him. He'd been drinking salt water and could neither stand nor talk.

Rip and his men dug a grave and buried the dead man. Cantillo carried the survivor, like a baby, to the boat. Fresh water was trickled down his parched throat. He was unable to swallow. Slowly, drop by drop, we were able to get a pint of water into him. By gently massaging his throat, we got him to swallow another pint.

He couldn't taste the water and kept trying to talk. Finally he was able to form a few words that were almost a whisper. Cantillo bent over him, then straightened up and was silent.

I asked him what the man had said.

Turning to me with tears in his eyes, Cantillo said, "He wants to know if we won."

I felt tears come to my eyes as well. After regaining some semblance of composure, I said, "Tell him we lost the battle, but not the war."

We took good care of the man until we could get him back to the ship, where he received proper medical treatment, which allowed him to survive his ordeal.

Soon we were to lose the battle of the rescue mission too.

During and after this event, it was evident that the brigade members were never confused as to who had let them down, but they never blamed Americans in general. Especially not Rip and me, who had fought alongside them and had clearly adopted their cause as ours. In fact, they treated us as heroes and looked to us for advice and guidance for years afterward.

The next morning, as we were preparing to make another dawn landing, we were told to stand down. The effort was over. During the night, Castro's men had landed on the islands. Planes reported the islands alive with troops. His vulture ships had moved in to the beaches. They were now lying offshore all along the island chain leading out of Cochinos Bay.

The U.S. Navy does not give up without making a maximum effort. The Navy had permission to use all available ships and craft. The submarine was called in and plans were made for another effort. It was to be made the following night, deep into Cochinos Bay near the *Houston*. It was there, it had been reported, that the main body of the 5th Battalion was concentrated.

Cochinos Bay is thousands of feet deep. A submarine could run submerged up its full length. I was told to take my frogmen and go aboard this sub for a conference on the coming mission. We launched in our rubber boat and waited for the sub to surface. Up it came, long, black, ugly, and very deadly looking.

After a long bout with our outboard, which seemed, like us, to be on its last legs, we made it to the black hull and climbed aboard. Rip and his crew were already aboard and below. As we entered the conning tower, we heard the sound of escaping air from our rubber boat.

"What the hell are you doing with that, sailor?" I shouted.

"It's to go below, sir," he replied.

The captain, who'd heard the ruckus, announced that his orders were for us to stay aboard, and that he was ready to submerge.

"Captain," I said, "no offense, mind you, I have nothing against conferences on surfaced submarines."

I have always suffered from claustrophobia, as did one of my frogmen. Some kind of defect in the number of our marbles, or whatever it's caused by. Anyway, somehow I didn't think a trip in a diving sub would do either of us much good.

"But," I continued, "if this conference is to be held in the briny deep, well, I'll just pass on this little excursion. Unless, of course," I warned him, "you don't mind a few more hatches in your vessel."

We retrieved our raft and returned to our destroyer, where we promptly fell into the first good night's sleep we'd had in a long, long time. Sometime later we were awakened by clanging bells and slamming hatches as the destroyer went to General Quarters. When we sleepily asked the cause of all this racket, we were told that the fleet had been alerted and was moving out to sea. The sonar had just picked up a Soviet submarine entering Cochinos Bay.

The shooting of helpless survivors in the swamps was not the only atrocity perpetrated on the 2506 Brigade at the conclusion of the battle. One of the more cruel and despicable acts of the conquering Cuban Rebel Army, as ordered by Comandante Osmani Cienfuegos, occurred at Playa Girón after the survivors had been flushed out of the woods and were being shipped to Havana.

The prisoners were to be taken to Havana in a forty-foot semitrailer. Cienfuegos ordered one hundred men put in the trailer. When his men complained and even pleaded with him that there wasn't room for that many, Cienfuegos ordered them to jam fifty more men into this metal oven.

The prisoners were so tightly packed in the trailer that it required all the strength their captors could muster to shove and push them back into it and seal its door shut. With the sun beating down on this unventilated, overcrowded rolling prison, Cienfuegos ordered the trucks on to Havana.

The truck took its good old time, eight hours, to cover the distance to Havana. Lack of air and the unbearable heat caused many of the men to pass out. By the time the truck reached its destination and its doors were opened, ten men were dead, and the rest were nearly so.

13

The Road Back from Cochinos

THE FOLLOWING DAY, THE NAVY INFORMED RIP AND ME, now berthed on the *Santiago*, that it had orders to send us back to Washington as soon as possible. A helicopter from the *Essex* plucked us off the stern of the destroyer with its winch, in a little maneuver that I did not wish to become accustomed to, and set us down on the flight deck of the *Essex*.

We flew to Guantánamo, and later that same night reached Jacksonville Naval Air Station. Here we were sidetracked. There was no plane waiting to continue us on our journey, as we had been told to expect. A few hours later, the reason was found. The message regarding our arrival had been so highly classified that only the base commander could read it, and he was off somewhere on an inspection trip.

Our escort called Washington. He asked if he could send us on by commercial air and was told no. Under no circumstances were we to go by that route.

Rip and I had a little conference. We were officers in the CIA, but nowhere near the super grade to have aircraft stand by just to fly us to Washington. We decided that somebody somewhere didn't want the two "Indians" wandering off the reservation.

Finally, a plane was found, a big Convair transport with only three seats. We were the only passengers. We piled newspapers on the floor and went to sleep on top of them. When we awoke, cold and stiff, we were coming into Anacostia Naval Air Station, across the river from Washington.

Rip and I were not quite prepared for official Washington. We had lost our utility combat clothing to the brush of the Cochinos swamps and were dressed in lightweight short-sleeved khaki clothing given to us by the officers of the *Essex*. Our paratrooper boots were cracked, and cut from the coral, and were almost white from the salt water of Cochinos Bay.

My personal possessions, a toothbrush, some cigarettes, and underwear, were in a cardboard box tied with string. Rip's were in a once-white Navy seabag that he had dug up somewhere on the *Essex*. It looked as though it had been used in cleaning her bilges. We were certainly not dressed for Washington. The color of our skin was a good indication that we had not been there for some time. It was burned a deep brown by the weeks of blazing tropical sun.

It was late April. Washington, as we were to discover when the door of the plane was opened at two in the morning, was not a land of sunshine. In fact, it was freezing cold, as was apparent from the long topcoats worn by the three CIA men who met the plane.

We "Indians" were home safe, if not sound, and were driven to our wigwam. What a wigwam—a suite at the Shoreham Hotel. The "chiefs" were being awfully nice to us braves, and we wondered why. We had been at the center of an important event, but a losing one. Chiefs don't go out of their way to be so kind to losing warriors. We had done the best we knew how, but in no way considered ourselves heroes.

As Rip said, "Hell, they know we didn't do anything that a good Marine fire team leader couldn't have done, and they'll feel he wouldn't have lost either."

We entered the elevator at the Shoreham from the basement entrance, off the rear parking lot. When the elevator stopped at the first floor and picked up a group of late-partying dignitaries, our odd attire and luggage drew some pointed stares from the tuxedoed gentlemen and their mink-clad wives. In fact, their noses shot straight up in the air.

To keep them from suffering a bad case of whiplash, I thought I would relieve their obvious suffering in the company of such ragged peons. I turned to our escorts and asked in a rather loud voice, "What floor did you fellows say that plumbing was out on?"

The dignitaries relaxed, and the danger of whiplash was prevented. We were simple maintenance men, there to see to their comforts and to keep their johns unplugged. Not some upstarts who meant to mingle with their betters.

After reaching our suite, we broke out a fifth of Jack Daniel's, supplied by our escorts, and proceeded to refight the battle of Cochinos Bay. This time it was amazingly easy. It required less than half the fifth to wipe out every last one of Castro's jets. By the time the last of the bourbon was downed, we had given the Rebel Army such a beating that it was in full retreat. This little task out of the way, we went happily to bed, delaying our triumphant march into Havana till the morrow.

The following morning, we were told that we were to be outfitted by Uncle Sam, at no cost, since we had been plucked away from our clothing without notice. Beautiful—bring on the tailors. Soon our measurements were recorded and the suits were ordered.

Rip indicated to me that he wanted to slip out for a while. So while I engaged our escorts in the other room, he eased out, and was gone before they knew it. When his absence was discovered, there was deep concern. Where had he gone? I didn't know, and that was the truth.

I must explain, before someone gets the wrong idea, that we were not prisoners, and never considered ourselves as such. We knew Agency procedures, and realized that it was more for our own protection than anything else that we were not to be out on the street without an escort. People dressed as we were stood out like sore thumbs in Washington, and especially around the Shoreham Hotel. We knew this, but we had been out in the boondocks for a long time and, just for fun, made a little game out of bewildering our patient and friendly escorts, who in a few days were very happy to see us go. The problem was that they just never seemed to appreciate our humor.

Rip had "escaped" so that he could go into Washington and purchase his own suit of clothes. He said, "I'm old enough to dress myself."

We each had several hundred dollars, but Rip's weather-beaten appearance caught the eye of a man near Raleighs, in downtown Washington's main business section. The man came up to him and said, "Is that you, Rip?" It was an American businessman whom Rip had known several years before, while living in Managua, Nicaragua.

Rip allowed as how it was indeed he, and considered saying something to explain away his strange attire, but couldn't think of anything appropriate or believable, so he said nothing.

The man, noting his embarrassment said, "Rip, I don't know what the problem is, but it seems you have fallen on some hard times. Here is my card and my hotel number. Call me and I'll see if I can't get something going for you."

After he left, Rip looked at the card and saw a twenty-dollar bill had been attached to it. Well, so much for a good cover story.

When he returned to the Shoreham, a new escort was with us who had never seen Rip. He was in the bathroom when Rip came back dressed in his new suit. The new escort came out and discovered the two of us in a deep, guarded conversation in the next room. He coughed, and cleared his throat to get my attention, signaling me into the other room. He was upset, and wanted to know who this guy was that I was talking to.

Being one who never could resist the temptation to add a little spice to a rather dull forced confinement, I answered with my best straight face, "Hell, I don't know. I thought he came with you."

That did it. He punched panic buttons one through five and approached Rip with all the official airs he could muster, demanding to know who he was and what he was doing there.

Rip took one look at my straight face and began to explain the rights of a free press, and its privileges of not revealing its sources of information. This sent our escort into a higher orbit—he had allowed not only a complete stranger into the suite but a news reporter at that.

We might have carried this into a series with reruns, but these were our own people, and so we explained the situation and brought him back down to earth. For some strange reason, he never really seemed to trust us after that.

Now our fun was at an end, for our serious debriefing began. For the next two days, we told the CIA officials of the Cuban Task Force what had happened in Cochinos Bay, and they, in turn, told us what had happened in Washington. Both sides appeared to be amazed when the full story of the causes and effects of the cancellations of the air raids became clear.

Up to this point, we still had no idea who had canceled the raids, or why. We sat in absolute shock when we were told that it had been the president himself who had called them off.

The Washington men were equally shocked when they heard of the full effects of Castro's planes. Tears came into their eyes when we told them of the last hours of the brigade, and of the suffering of the pitiful group of survivors that we had brought out of the Zapata Swamp. The only heartening observation we were able to share with them was that the brigade had fought magnificently. Outnumbered in every battle by at least twenty to one, it had inflicted heavy casualties on Castro's forces, at a rate of more than fifty to one.

We all wondered what would have happened had the air strikes not been canceled, and if the brigade planes had ruled the air over Cuba. In a three-day battle, the brigade had hurt Castro badly, and with ammunition meant for only one day of fighting. What the men could have accomplished if they had had all their ammunition supplies and all their aircraft we could only speculate. Speculation or not, in our hearts we were sure they would have won the battle of the Bay of Pigs. But they did not have the ammo and the planes, and they had lost.

Now we were called upon to tell the New Frontier how they lost, not why they lost. This the administration could decide for itself later. We were summoned to appear before an investigating committee set up by the president to determine all the facts about this disaster and report its findings to him.

For this committee, he had selected as chairman General Maxwell Taylor, former chief of staff of the U.S. Army and now retried. With him were Admiral Raleigh Burke, chief of naval operations, and Allen Dulles, director of central intelligence. The fourth member selected by the president was his younger brother Robert F. Kennedy, the attorney general.

This selection disturbed me. I could understand the first three members, but the selection of his brother, who was in charge of the Justice Department and had no mandated role in such affairs, was, I felt, an indication that the groundwork for a cover-up had been laid.

I knew that if the full and true story of the Cochinos affair was made public, it would be a heavy blow for the New Frontier. I did not expect them to make this story known—I expected them to cover it up. But I did not expect them not just to dodge the blame but to place it on the shoulders of the very persons who had warned them against canceling the air strikes.

I was soon to see this committee in action, for I was set to appear before it the following Monday morning at nine o'clock.

I arrived at the Pentagon, where the committee

was conducting the hearing, shortly before nine. After a short wait, I was ushered into the hearing room. I recognized General Taylor, Admiral Burke, and Dulles from many years of seeing their pictures in the press. At first, I did not recognize the young man slouched in a chair at the hearing table, in a white shirt, with his tie pulled down and his sleeves rolled up.

I was introduced to Bobby Kennedy.

I had read of his casual manner of dress, but was not prepared for this. This Indian always visualized his chiefs as dressed for the part, with full war bonnets and eagle feathers.

It surprised me that there was no microphone or recording equipment to record the testimonies, or a stenographer in the room to type a transcript of the day's proceedings. I later learned from Admiral Burke that the official transcript of these proceedings was constructed by General Taylor and Bobby Kennedy after each day's proceedings, supposedly from memory. This leaves a very wide window for omissions and misinterpretations of testimonies.

The day I testified, I thought General Taylor conducted the hearing in a very fair and efficient way. As I told of what had happened at Cochinos Bay, he would time and again comment that "it all goes back to the planes. Everything that went wrong started at that point, and was caused by them."

This was good enough for me. If he knew this important fact, the report would have to reflect the truth.

But Robert Kennedy's questions started out to be meant to support the idea that the invasion would have failed even without Castro's air strikes. This was something that was impossible to prove. At this point, I made a statement that I felt ended this line of questioning. As far as Mr. Kennedy was concerned, it clearly ended any idea that I might be of assistance to his cause.

I told them that I wanted to make it clear that I was before the committee not just as a government employee but as an American citizen, and a very angry American citizen. I felt very strongly that the Cochinos plan had been sound and had been successful up to the time of the first Castro air attack. From that point onward, many things went wrong, none of which would have happened had the Castro planes been destroyed on the ground, as planned. Therefore, any explanation for the failure other than that we were almost destroyed by Castro's planes was wrong. So was any suggestion that it would have failed anyway.

As one might expect, this ended my role as a witness, and I was quickly excused. I now know from others who testified before the committee that this same line of questioning was pursued by Kennedy with them.

It would be very interesting to see the original transcript of the Taylor Commission Report, which is still highly classified. A sanitized, chopped-up version was released a few years ago, and a declassified section of the report was published in Luis

Aguilar's book *Operation Zapata*. I checked what was supposed to be my testimony in the book and found that it had been altered and chopped to pieces so badly that I could hardly recognize it. Three and a half hours of testimony had been reduced to just over two paragraphs.

I left the hearing still angry. I was sure that the statement I had made there had ended my employment with the U.S. government. But I was wrong. Mr. Dulles saw me and told me that he thought I had done a good job, and that I had a job with him as long as I wanted it.

I did want the job. I had no grudge against the Agency. It had, in my opinion, done as good a job as it could in an intolerable situation. I stayed on in the CIA for ten years, and I was happy that Rip also chose to stay. He was a good man. I could, and did, learn a lot from him.

But while we stayed, our superiors in the Agency and others in the Department of Defense did not.

To support their "myth" of how this disaster was created and by whom, Bissell, the brilliant chief of operations of the CIA, the man who had created and directed the U-2 program and who had warned of the disaster to come at Cochinos, was fired.

Dulles was given a decent interval before being eased out. General Lyman Lemnitzer, chairman of the JCS, was reassigned to NATO, and Admiral Burke was given early retirement.

But the men who had written both the Trinidad plan and the Cochinos plan, and whose chief had written the prophetic warning that a disaster would result if the air raids were canceled, suffered the most. These were career military men. Most were graduates of West Point or Annapolis. They were the best the Defense Department had to offer. But they were returned to their services with their careers in ruins. Many were full colonels and were already on the selected list for promotion to brigadier general. These promotions had to be approved at the White House before they were sent to Congress for confirmation. They were never made.

To give credence to the myth that the New Frontier was creating, these "advisers" had to be made to appear to have been wrong. They were the ones who had led the New Frontier and its young president down the garden path, and who had supposedly assured him that the invasion would succeed without any American air support.

To support the myth, heads had to roll, and roll they did, but not one of these heads belonged to a New Frontiersman.

On the first of May, I watched on television the big Mayday victory parade Castro was putting on in Havana. There were troops, tanks, and artillery guns by the thousands passing in front of Castro and his viewing party. But at the end, all eyes were turned skyward, for out of the east came streaking a large flight of fast swept-wing jets.

The MiGs had reached Havana. They would be followed by ballistic missiles.

14

Rewriting History

To sustain the myth of how, and why, the Cochinos invasion was lost, the New Frontiersmen began grinding out book after book on the Kennedy years. All contained at least one chapter on the invasion.

Arthur Schlesinger wrote *A Thousand Days: John F. Kennedy in the White House.* Theodore Sorensen wrote *Kennedy.* The supposed "bible" on the subject, Haynes Johnson's *The Bay of Pigs: The Leaders' Story of Brigade 2506,* was the worst of the lot. Johnson, a well-known journalist and columnist, was most known for his support of liberals and Democrats. His version was so loaded with errors and untruths that it should have been labeled fiction.

These "military experts" discovered some bizarre reasons for the failure of the invasion, and other, even more outlandish reasons why it could never have succeeded in the first place. Since the true key to the failure was the watering down of the plan and the cancellations of the proposed, and approved, air strikes prior to the landing, their analysis of this will be examined first.

Not one of the three provides even one word about how many air strikes were proposed and canceled by the New Frontier because of State Department objections. Nor do they mention that five strikes of sixteen planes each—strikes at first light on Saturday, Sunday, and Monday and last-light strikes on Saturday and Sunday—were approved by President Kennedy at the final full-scale meeting on April 4. Two of these, the last-light strikes on Saturday and Sunday, were later canceled by the CIA because the State Department objected to them on the basis that it would make things too hot to handle.

They also omit the fact that the State Department, on April 13, persuaded the president, after this final approval, to reduce the first strike of sixteen planes to six. This emasculation of the plan was done without a full-scale meeting on the matter and over the objections of the chief CIA planners.

Bissell informed me later that the president had informed him that Rusk had objected to the number of planes in the raids. The president asked Bissell if he could perform the task with six planes. Bissell replied that he could not. After numbers had been tossed around, Bissell had to accept an offer of eight planes. Bissell remarked to me that it was more an order than an offer.

The State Department allowed the CIA to add

two more B-26s to the strike when it was pointed out that this reduced plan had completely omitted the strike at Santiago Airport in Oriente, where there were three Castro planes based, a Sea Fury, a B-26, and a T-33 jet fighter.

The State Department, of course, is famed for its expertise and knowledge of military strategy, tactics, and weaponry.

Since the Nino Diaz diversionary force was to land on Saturday night, fifty miles from this base, to expose them to the untouched planes was to risk losing the entire Diaz force.

It was later learned that the State Department had arrived at the limit of six B-26s simply because this was the number of B-26s in Castro's air force. The outlandish restriction to six planes was motivated by the New Frontier's fear that the United States would be exposed as having had a role in the invasion. This fear of exposure so dominated their thinking that it became an obsession. It became their primary concern in any discussion of changes to the plan. They were far more concerned about exposure than about any military requirements, regardless of their importance, and whether or not they were so critical to the success of the invasion that without them it could very easily fail. In short, they feared exposure more than they feared defeat.

In the records of these meetings and proposals for reductions and cancellations that so emasculated the original plan and eventually led to its disastrous failure there cannot be found a single indication that the objectors and emasculators gave the slightest thought to a fact that was so obvious that it should have been immediately detected by even the most amateur of these armchair generals: that if the plan did not succeed, the exposure they so feared would most assuredly occur, and that a successful invasion was the one and only means of preventing this most horrible of nightmares. For if the invasion had been carried out as originally planned and fully supported, it had a good chance to succeed in overthrowing Castro.

A successful invasion could have won the approval and acclaim of the entire free world. The fact that it had been backed and directed by the United States government could have won the New Frontier praise and respect. They could have won that praise and respect if they had acted boldly, without fear and with the national interest of the United States uppermost in their mind.

Instead they were timid and fearful, and they heaped shame and ridicule not just on themselves, who justly deserved it, but on the entire nation.

The apologists conveniently omitted the fact that the State Department also pushed through, at the same time, a requirement that a "cover story" be concocted to explain, for "world opinion," that these air strikes were carried out by defecting Castro pilots. The cover story that was approved by the Kennedy administration, and inserted, despite the strenuous objections of the CIA air staff, was the pseudo Castro B-26 plan. When the cover story fell apart, as predicted, it was the CIA air staff that got the blame.

Another important point, conveniently overlooked by Schlesinger, Sorensen, and Johnson, was that the two planned and approved air strikes, before the landings, had been necessitated by State Department meddling with the plan. The CIA and JCS had proposed, in both the Trinidad and Cochinos plans, one mass air strike. Twenty-two B-26s, using rockets, bombs, and napalm, would destroy Castro's planes on the ground, at first light, on the morning of the invasion.

These three apologists refer to the Saturday-morning raid, which had been cut from sixteen planes to six at the last minute, as having been conducted as planned. Then they proceed to belittle it for destroying only half of Castro's planes.

When it came to the "decision for disaster," the cancellation of the Monday-morning strike, the Kennedy apologists waffled, sideslipped, and performed miracles of acrobatic sophistry in a futile attempt to downplay and explain away the president's decision to sign the death warrant of the 2506 Brigade.

Brigade Commander José "Pepe" San Román said that President Kennedy told the brigade leaders, when he met with them in West Palm Beach, Florida, after the invasion, that he had made this decision because "Russia and China were threatening action, if not in Cuba, then perhaps in Berlin, Laos, or Vietnam."

Had the president really believed that the Soviets would give up their foothold in the Western Hemisphere without one word of protest? They had threatened action in these places many times before, so what was so special about this latest saber-rattling?

Sorensen insists, though, that this decision was "consistent" with the president's policy that the Cuban affair not be allowed to jeopardize larger United States interests.

What larger United States interest? Did Kennedy actually believe that a threat by the Soviets that they might take action in Berlin, Laos, or Vietnam was of larger interest to the United States than the reality of a Soviet satellite state only ninety miles from the United States? One year later, when the Soviets placed intercontinental ballistic missiles in Cuba and aimed them directly at the United States, he suddenly realized that the largest and most important interest jeopardized was the United States of America itself.

Sorensen says that this was "consistent with the president's policies, stated unequivocally, both publicly and privately." Maybe it was consistent with his policy, but it was in direct contradiction to his publicly written ideals.

In his book *Why England Slept*, Kennedy said: "We cannot tell anyone to keep out of our hemisphere unless our armaments, and the people behind these armaments, are prepared to back up the command, even to the ultimate point of going to war. . . . There must be no doubt in anyone's mind, the decision must be automatic. If we debate, if we question, if we hesitate, it will be too late."

In April 1961, the president and his New Frontiersmen were "the people behind these armaments." They were not prepared to back up the command to the Soviets to keep out of our hemisphere. They debated, they questioned, they hesitated, and it was indeed too late. Far too late. Too late for the "dumped" 2506 Brigade, too late for the people of Cuba, and too late for the United States. The Soviets had won their foothold in our hemisphere. Castro remains in power today.

This was the same president who had taunted Richard Nixon in their TV debates, during the election campaign, with "If you can't stand up to Castro, how can you ever be expected to stand up to Khrushchev?"

When the chips were down at Cochinos Bay, Kennedy not only failed to stand up to Castro, or to Khrushchev, but he would not stand up to his own State Department, and pliantly approved request after request from State to water down the invasion plan. The cancellation of the only remaining air strike against Castro's jets, a cancellation that doomed the 2506 Brigade, cost the lives of many good men, and one year later was to bring the world to the brink of nuclear war.

But the New Frontier apologists shrugged off Kennedy's momentous decision as being of little importance, and of lesser consequence.

Sorensen wrote in *Kennedy* that "the President's postponement of the Monday morning air strike thus played only a minor role in the venture."

The air strike was not postponed. It was canceled. The cancellation was not minor, it was catastrophic. This postponement myth was used by many of the administration apologists, including Robert Kennedy, who stated in a *U.S. News and World Report* interview published on January 28, 1963: "There was supposed to be another strike on the airports on Monday morning. The President was called about whether it should take place, as there was a stir about the matter [in the UN]. He gave instructions that it should not take place at that time . . . and in fact the attack on the airports took place late that day."

This is untrue, and Robert Kennedy, at the time he made this statement, knew it was untrue.

The Monday-morning raid was canceled thirty minutes prior to the planes' scheduled departure from Puerto Cabezas. Late Monday afternoon, after Castro's jets had sunk the *Houston* and the *Río Escondido,* and had shot down three of the Brigade's B-26s over the beachhead, to which they had been restricted by presidential order, and after repeated requests from the CIA that they be allowed to strike the airfields, the president finally authorized a strike of four B-26s against the airfield at San Antonio de los Baños, to take place at two o'clock Tuesday morning. The four planes arrived over the target area. They could not attack, for the area was completely blacked out, and a smoke haze and low clouds covered all of central Cuba. The airfield could not be seen.

Since their instructions were that they could bomb only the airfield and must, at all costs, avoid hitting any civilian areas, they returned to Nicaragua without dropping a single bomb or firing a shot.

Although these pilots searched for the field to the full limit of their fuel supply, and one even turned his lights on in an attempt to draw fire from the antiaircraft batteries encircling the airfield, Haynes Johnson casts a slur on his bravery by referring to this mission as being "aborted," in the same manner as the Nino Diaz operation, in the Oriente deception landings, which he says were aborted primarily "because of bad leadership." The Oriente landing "feint" may well have suffered from bad leadership, but it was not alone. The government of the United States also was lacking in good leadership, and in honesty.

If Sorensen truly believes that the president's cancellation of the Monday-morning strike had only minor effects, then he should certainly have no objections to sitting down with the sons and daughters of the ten Cuban pilots and four American pilots who died under the guns of those untouched Castro jets, and explaining to them that the deaths of these brave men were due to a "minor" decision made by President John F. Kennedy.

Schlesinger, to bolster his version of the minor

role of this cancellation, writes in *A Thousand Days*: "Kennedy came later to feel that the cancellation of the second strike was an error. But, he did not regard it as a decisive error, for even on the most unlikely assumption that the second strike achieved total success, and wiped out Castro's air force, it would still have left 1,200 men against 200,000!"

Schlesinger could also explain to these families that the brigade's sixteen B-26s, each armed with eight .50-caliber machine guns, eight 5-inch rockets, and ten bombs, could not have destroyed the Castro air force of two T-33 jets, three Sea Furies, and two B-26 bombers on the ground. In fact, if the sixteen brigade planes had destroyed only the two T-33 jets, the battle could have been won, for without the jets the others would not have lasted very long. No brigade planes would have been shot down by Castro's planes. All the brigade planes were shot down by the two Castro T-33 jets.

As for the 1,200 men facing 200,000, Schlesinger implies that Castro was prepared to strip all of Cuba of every last soldier and send them against the brigade. He said that he sent twenty thousand men against the brigade. But if the brigade air force had been able to eliminate Castro's fighters and could have operated its own aircraft off the Playa Girón airfield, it really might not have mattered if Castro had sent all two hundred thousand men at once. Their only possible entry to the beachhead was down the three narrow exit "shooting galleries." With napalm and bombs, the B-26s would have packed these eight-mile-long death traps with burning tanks, trucks, and men.

In just three days these twelve hundred men, and the few B-26s that were allowed into action, had killed five times the number of troops that Castro had lost in the entire two-year fight against Batista. They wounded fifteen times the number wounded in that two-year war, and they did it with only one day's supply of ammunition.

To the New Frontier, the 2506 Brigade represented a "disposal problem," to be dumped in Cuba. But to the Rebel Army of Fidel Castro, it represented a highly dangerous military organization.

To show that the invasion would have failed even if the air strikes had not been canceled, the military experts dug up long lists of "mistakes, blunders, and inadequacies." Haynes Johnson writes that the ships provided for the invasion were "inadequate." These ships were there only to transport the brigade to Cochinos Bay and put them ashore. This they did, so what else could he expect of them? They were inadequate in one respect, though. They did not float very well, and sometimes exploded, when hit by Soviet-made air-to-surface missiles.

He complains also that the number of planes was inadequate. The size of the brigade air force was limited by restrictions placed on the CIA by the State Department. This same State Department, by its objections, reduced, then canceled forty of the forty-eight planned and approved sorties of this "inadequate" air force. Size is of little importance when this air force was left sitting on its runways by presidential order, at a time when it was most desperately needed by the brigade, the very unit it had been formed to support.

Johnson, like Sorensen and Schlesinger, complains that the Cochinos Bay areas was also inadequate. If the New Frontier wanted a better invasion area, then why didn't they accept it when it was offered to them in the Trinidad plan?

Another of Johnson's "serious handicaps" was that messages from the fighting zone at the Bay of Pigs took too long to reach the top level at Washington. He gives them the name "military chain of command," and says the messages went "from Girón to *Blagar,* from *Blagar* to the American destroyer, operating under the code name *Santiago,* from *Santiago* to Washington Command Group, and then to their final destination, the White House."

Now, I hate to take issue with such a self-made military expert as Mr. Johnson, but since I wrote and sent every message from this fighting zone, I am forced to disagree. I was in constant voice contact with brigade headquarters at Girón. And from the *Blagar* I was in instant radio contact with Washington. All messages from the beach were in Washington in a matter of minutes. There was no chain of command through *Santiago,* and there was no filtering back of messages as he says. There was never a time gap from Cochinos to Washington to our many requests for aid.

There was, however, a "minor" communications problem: all we received from Washington in answer to our requests was broken promises and empty words. It was not the lack of communications from Cochinos that contributed to the disaster. It was a lack of courage and of decisive leadership in the Kennedy administration.

In retrospect, I now realize that I should have sent only one message from Cochinos Bay, early on Monday morning when the last man of the brigade stepped ashore. The message should have read: "Mission accomplished. Your disposal problem has been solved. The 2506 Brigade has been successfully dumped into Cuba."

Schlesinger lists several reasons for the disaster. First, he says, Castro's men "spotted the invasion at almost the first possible moment." Big deal! The first of Castro's men spotted the invasion force when it was less than forty yards away, and they died ten seconds later. It took three and a half hours to notify Castro. Schlesinger fails to point out that exactly seven hours after these patrols spotted the invasion force, the brigade had seized a beachhead forty-two miles long and twenty miles deep, at the cost of less than a dozen men killed or wounded. It had killed fifty of Castro's troops and captured two hundred more.

Then, Schlesinger says, Castro's "planes reacted with speed and vigor." They certainly should have—they were left untouched by order of the president of the United States. If this "Do not disturb" order had not been given, they would have been turned into a pile of smoking rubble at first light on Monday morning, Yes, this "reason" did indeed cause the disaster. But to say that Castro's planes "reacted with speed and vigor" is to give them undue credit.

Castro first learned of the landings at 0315 on Monday morning, three hours and thirty minutes after his patrols had spotted the invasion. Yet the first Castro aircraft did not arrive over the beachhead until 0625, a full three hours later. This is speed?

This first aircraft, a B-26, had so much "vigor" that it avoided the large armed ships and attacked instead an eighteen-foot craft of the UDT men, who shot it down with their lone .50-caliber machine gun. Castro's planes were certainly decisive, but speed and vigor they lacked.

Another reason Schlesinger gives is that Castro's "police eliminated any chance of sabotage or rebellion behind the lines." Since the 2506 Brigade had never expected or depended on any type of uprising or rebellion for at least two weeks, this had nothing whatsoever to do with their defeat. And Schlesinger says that Castro himself "never panicked. . . . His performance was impressive." Schlesinger seems to be very easily impressed, so letting the last part of that sentence go for now, let's examine the first part.

After Castro was informed of the landing at three-fifteen in the morning, he gave a multitude of orders and directions, then raced off for the military headquarters at the sugar mill at Central Australia, north of Playa Larga. When he arrived, he determined that the attack at Playa Larga was only a diversion. He was then informed that there was another landing occurring in Pinar del Río Province, three hundred miles from Playa Larga. This he declared the main invasion.

What does the unflappable Castro do? Why, he dashes off madly to Pinar del Río, of course, and he dispatches Ché Guevara and a large force of his men to that invasion site. What he found on his arrival was that he had been drawn away from the main invasion by a "sound and flash" deception staged by the CIA.

This deception Castro himself spoke of as "a large fleet of ships and landing craft, with an aircraft carrier." He identified the aircraft carrier as the *Essex*. It was all an illusion. The *Essex*, at the time, was five hundred miles from Pinar del Río. There were no ships, there were no landing craft, and there was no invasion force. Castro puzzled for years over just how this illusion was created. If he hasn't already found out, I will be happy to tell him:

With mirrors, Fidel!

Castro may have seemed "impressive" to Schlesinger, but to Guevara's men he looked like a damn fool who was taken in by a deception, and who had sent them charging two hundred miles to search for an invasion that never was.

Schlesinger says that Washington miscalculated

Castro partly because of "a series of failures in our own intelligence." These failures in our intelligence were that "we dismissed his air force and forgot his T-33s."

What he fails to make clear is just whom he is referring to when he says "we." I suppose one must discover this on his own by a process of elimination. The CIA and the JCS had never forgotten Castro's air force, for they had been requesting strike after strike to destroy it, almost as fast as the president had been canceling them. And the CIA and JCS didn't forget the T-33s. This leaves only the New Frontier to fill the "we" role.

If Schlesinger and the other "Knights of Camelot" had been at Cochinos Bay, I could have refreshed their memory about these forgotten T-33s. They were, Mr. Schlesinger, those bright shiny planes that made that funny noise when they flashed by you as they fired those weird-sounding rockets that blew large holes in our "inadequate" ships and "inadequate" planes. I guarantee you, Mr. Schlesinger, that you would never make the mistake of forgetting them again.

Yes, there were failures in intelligence. I agree with this statement wholeheartedly. But my idea of whose intelligence failed is different from Schlesinger's.

Schlesinger finds much to criticize in the brigade's tactical planning, too. For example, "We put too much precious ammunition and communications equipment in a single ship." This overworked, lame, and completely untrue charge has been kicked around by the New Frontier apologists for so long that it has been accepted as gospel. Schlesinger is referring, although he avoids saying so, to the sinking of the *Rio Escondido* on the morning of the 17th by Castro's planes. This ship contained a ten-day supply of ammunition for the brigade, as did the *Atlantico* and the *Caribe*, which were not sunk. There were two other cargo ships due to arrive within a matter of days, each containing a fifteen-day supply of ammunition and arms for fifteen thousand men.

The communications equipment he speaks of was an elaborately equipped trailer that was to serve as the brigade's communication center. It also contained a powerful commercial radio station that could broadcast to all of Cuba. This trailer was indeed lost when the *Rio Escondido* blew up. But what Schlesinger does not tell his readers is that a duplicate of this communications trailer had been constructed by the CIA and was aboard the *Atlantico*.

The Kennedy administration carried this myth to the extreme when it sent two White House aides to Gettysburg, Pennsylvania, to brief former President Dwight D. Eisenhower on why the invasion failed. They blamed the CIA for "putting all the brigade's ammunition and communications on one ship." Eisenhower, in a 1962 *New York Times* interview, later remarked that "even a new 2nd Lieutenant would know better than that." He was later enlightened by a friend, Bill Pawley, who told him the true story of what happened at the Bay of Pigs. Eisenhower was furious that he had been lied to and stated that the real cause was that Kennedy had lost his nerve.

To substantiate his claim that the president's cancellation of the Monday-morning air strike was not "a decisive error," Schlesinger writes that "the Brigade's air power was already in decline because of the scarcity of pilots."

This claim is false. The Monday strike had been limited to eight planes because of the State Department's request. The brigade air force had sixteen fully manned B-26s ready for takeoff at Puerto Cabezas when the president's order to halt the raid was received. It had on hand another three B-26s with pilots, which could have been sent on this mission if it had been allowed.

It was not the brigade air power that was in decline. It was the will and determination of the New Frontier.

On the same page, Schlesinger makes some speculation as to what might have occurred if this second strike had not been canceled. He says it "might have protracted the stand on the beachhead from three days to ten; it might have permitted the establishment of the provisional government; it might have made possible the eventual evacuation of the invading force." But, he says, "There is certainly nothing to suggest that it could possibly have led to the overthrow of the regime on the terms which Kennedy laid down from the start—that is without United States armed intervention."

This line of reasoning of why the invasion was futile to begin with might have had some validity except that Schlesinger forgets the brigade air force just as he forgot Castro's T-33s. If the second strike had been made, Castro would no longer have possessed an air force and the brigade would have.

With the Brigade B-26s operating from the beachhead airfield, Castro's Rebel Army could not have broken through the three shooting gallery exits in ten days, or even in a hundred days. With the provisional government in the beachhead, recognized by the United States, the regime of Fidel Castro could have been doomed instead of the 2506 Brigade.

As for Schlesinger's suggestion that this might have allowed the "invading force" to be evacuated, let me remind him that I passed Washington's offer of evacuation along to the brigade commander on the third day of the Cochinos battle. His answer was that he would never evacuate. What Schlesinger does not seem to understand is that the men of the 2506 Brigade were fighters, and that they were Cubans, and that they had come to Cuba to fight, not run.

Schlesinger also states that the plan was not prepared politically to succeed. He claims that its eventual success, even if its military problems had been solved, would have depended on an internal uprising against Castro. Schlesinger and the others charged that the CIA through "intelligence failures" miscalculated the popular support for Castro's army within Cuba—that it grossly overestimated the number of dissidents and their willingness to rise against Castro at the onset of the invasion.

There never was an uprising contingency included within the early stages of either plan. This is something Schlesinger and the others seem to be unwilling or unable to understand. Most of them seem to forget that even before the invasion and subsequent mass arrests began, Cuban prisons were bulging to the seams with over fifty thousand "enemies of the state." When mass arrests began, Castro filled the prisons to capacity. Lacking prison facilities for his many detractors, he filled movie theaters, sports arenas, open ball parks, and unused hospitals, and finally ended up with several thousand of them in open fenced fields, with no water or sanitary facilities.

It was of interest to the CIA staff that six thousand prisoners were placed in the old tuberculosis sanitarium at Topes de Collientes on the peak of the Escambray mountains above Trinidad, our first choice for a landing site. If we had gone in at Trinidad, these six thousand men would have been of great value to the brigade.

From April 15 until April 18, Castro's security forces arrested and imprisoned 250,000 Cubans. This made a total of 300,000 "enemies of the state" in a country with a population of just over six million, or one out of every twenty Cubans. These numbers are well documented by both U.S. sources and the admission of the Castro government. Some of the critics include these figures in their writings, but fail to draw any significance from them.

To put this in greater perspective, we can compare it to the population of the United States, which was around two hundred million at that time. If this had occurred in the United States, it would mean that our president would have arrested and imprisoned ten million people. How popular would that have made him?

I might add that this mass roundup of dissidents did not, by any means, bring in all those opposed to Castro. A great part of the underground was never touched, and almost none of the CIA infiltration teams were caught. Most Cubans familiar with conditions inside Cuba at the time feel that for every one arrested there were at least two more who opposed the regime that were missed.

Schlesinger also said it could not succeed politically because the CIA, "had developed its operation in a different political atmosphere and on different political presuppositions" from those which "Kennedy had well defined . . . in the Alliance for Progress and the White Paper."

He also charges that the CIA had put together a "nonpolitical military expedition . . . excluding the radical exiles and neglecting the internal resistance." In other words, the 2506 Brigade was too conservative and nonpolitical to have won!

It seems strange that such a learned military expert and historian as Schlesinger would overlook the fact that the 2506 Brigade was a military organization. Once in a battle, politics and military matters do not mix well. Any cursory examination of history will substantiate that fact. The goals of the battle need to be defined and clearly understood.

The leadership of the brigade was conservative, he says. If by this he means that they were all anti-Castro and anti-Communist and had also been anti-Batista, then that statement is correct. The brigade was not where the leadership problem was.

He complains that the brigade excluded the radical exiles. The radical exiles he is referring to were men like Manuel Ray and others of the "Fidelismo without Fidel" brand of political philosophy. The only thing this group wanted changed in Cuba was its leadership. They did not object to the policies of Castro, but to the fact that he and not they was running the country.

The Kennedy administration had ordered the CIA to include Ray, and his MRP radicals, in the provisional government over the heated objections of the CIA and the entire Cuban exile movement. Some of these radicals had been sent to the brigade in Guatemala, and had promptly fomented and led a mini-mutiny against the brigade leaders.

This attempted coup was squelched and the twelve ringleaders were imprisoned on an island in the center of the Petén Swamp in Guatemala. The brigade had planned to have these men sent to the beachhead after the provisional government had been established for legal trial for mutiny. When the invasion failed, they were flown to Miami, where they were acclaimed heroes by the radical left movement, and released.

According to Schlesinger's theory, the CIA was badly prepared to win the battle of the hearts and minds of the Cuban supporters of Castro. He fails to point out that first and foremost was the task of applying sufficient military pressure on Castro's regime to enable this hearts-and-minds battle to have any hope of success.

Besides being "misconceived politically," Schlesinger charges that the invasion was also "misconceived technically," in that it was "clearly beyond the limits of disownability." He continues, "Unless we were prepared to back it to the hilt, it should have been abandoned. When the president made it clear time after time that for the most cogent reasons we would not back it to the hilt, the planners should not have deluded themselves into thinking that events would reverse this decision or that the adventure would succeed on its own."

The only *backing* "to the hilt" that the 2506 Brigade expected or requested was that it be allowed to fight with its full force, which included the brigade air force, which Kennedy denied it in order to prevent political embarrassment to his administration.

The only *request* the brigade made was included in the message the special emissary of the president, Colonel Jack Hawkins, sent from Guatemala as the brigade was debarking for Cuba. It read, "The brigade officers ask only for continued delivery of supplies."

Both Schlesinger and Johnson include Hawkins's

report in their books. That is, all but this vital sentence. Why didn't they include this portion of the message? Because doing so would have undermined their claim that the brigade was promised support "to the hilt" and that it expected U.S. armed intervention. Before the invasion there was never a request made by the brigade or the CIA planners for U.S. armed intervention, and none was expected. Neither the brigade nor the CIA planners asked for "backing to the hilt." The backing the brigade got was not "to the hilt"; on the contrary, what it got was the shaft.

In addition to being the president's emissary, Hawkins was a veteran of the U.S. Marine Corps and chief of the paramilitary branch of the CIA Cuban Task Force for the invasion. He was the man who developed the Trinidad plan, which required four months to complete. When this plan was rejected, he developed the Cochinos plan in the four days allowed him by Kennedy. He had objected strongly to the rejection of the Trinidad plan, but had, like the good Marine officer he was, obeyed orders and come up with as good an alternate plan as was possible under the restrictions placed on him by the White House.

When Hawkins submitted this plan, which I read later, he sent it with a covering memorandum, which stated that the Cochinos plan and the invasion area had less chance of success than had the Trinidad plan; that it was a militarily marginal plan that could succeed only if all of its elements were left intact; and that the air strikes to destroy Castro's planes on the ground were of such vital importance that if they were canceled, or if they failed to destroy all of Castro's fighters, the invasion would result in disaster.

Nowhere in any of the New Frontier's publications was there any mention of this warning.

The invasion failed because of the very acts that Hawkins had warned against. Though he did not make the decision for the changes that caused the failure, this fine officer, with a brilliant combat record, was given the major share of the blame by the Kennedy administration.

Before his assignment by the JCS to aid the CIA in planning the invasion, Hawkins had been on the selected lists for promotion to brigadier general. These promotions must first have White House approval before being sent to Congress for confirmation. Hawkins was never promoted, and he retired in 1964 still a colonel. He was made a scapegoat for the mistakes of others.

Schlesinger's complaint that the invasion could not be "disowned" brings up several questions. First, if it had succeeded there would have been no need or desire to disown it. After the defeat, Kennedy stated that "there is an old saying that victory has a hundred fathers and defeat is an orphan."

Had the Cochinos invasion been successful and Cuba liberated, this victory would have had a thousand fathers, including the entire Camelot Round Table. No one in the New Frontier would have disowned it. As soon as the smoke cleared they would have rushed to Havana to congratulate the new government, reminding it that this was all brought about by the "to the hilt" support of President Kennedy and the New Frontier. They would also, I am sure, have offered some sound political advice to these new rulers of Cuba, including a reminder to put more radicals in their administration.

Schlesinger had been opposed to the invasion plan from the start. He had written two memorandums to the president, one on April 5 and the other on April 10, outlining the reasons for his opposition. His principal objection was that since, in his opinion, the brigade could not overthrow Castro on its own in one swift blow, the struggle could only develop into a protracted civil conflict. This, he felt, would lead to the danger of U.S. involvement. The Brigade, unable to do its task alone, would be forced to call for U.S. armed intervention, and certain members of Congress would support the request, which would "make it politically hard to resist the demand to send in the Marines." But, according to Schlesinger, the Marines would be unable to do the job, since "the *Fidelistas* could be counted on to fight to the end."

My only advice to Schlesinger on this matter would be: "Tell that to the Marines."

Any encounter between Castro's *fidelistas* and the U.S. Marines would have been short and very swift. The end of the *fidelistas* would have fought to would have come quickly.

I would also like to remind Schlesinger that on the last day of the Cochinos battle, seven thousand of these *fidelistas* were sent into headlong retreat when they saw one lone U.S. destroyer rushing toward the coast to Playa Girón, and they did not stop until they had fallen back sixteen miles.

Schlesinger saw the fidelistas not only fighting to the end, but retreating into the Sierra Maestra mountains for a prolonged stand. Then the Russians would come to their aid by enlisting "volunteers in José Martí and probably even Abraham Lincoln Brigades" and would "seek to convert the conflict into another Spanish Civil War."

This "war" that Schlesinger envisioned would have other, even more serious consequences. It would, because of our "bullying intervention," turn the greatest of all forces, world opinion, against us and "might recklessly expend one of our greatest national assets—John F. Kennedy himself."

Not only is this brilliant military theory pure hogwash, but Schlesinger's insinuation that the United States armed forces could not defeat Castro's ragtag Rebel Army in one quick decisive blow is an insult to America's fighting men. One year later, these same armed forces were poised for an invasion of Cuba during the missile crisis. Schlesinger wrote no such memorandum to the president in protest of this planned invasion.

Some readers may suggest that I am being rude to Schlesinger, and that some of my questioning of his theories is impolite. This is absolutely true. I have a license to be rude and to make impolite inquiries. In Schlesinger's own words, "The Bay of Pigs gave us a license for the impolite inquiry and the rude comment."

Schlesinger closes his chapter with an observation that must win for him the grand prize in logic. He states, "But no one can doubt that failure in Cuba in 1961 contributed to the success in Cuba in 1962." He was referring, of course, to the victory of the New Frontier in the Cuban Missile Crisis.

This simply overlooks the fact that had there been no failure in Cuba in 1961, there would have been no missile crisis in 1962. There would have been no Soviet satellite in the Western Hemisphere in which the Soviets could have installed their missiles. If this is the way victories are assured, then perhaps we could have carried his logic a bit further and engineered a defeat in the Cuban Missile Crisis in 1962, which would have assured us total victory in the nuclear holocaust it would have brought on in 1963.

The failure in 1961 was just that, a failure. But not a total failure, for it did accomplish for the New Frontier a solution to one of its problems. It got rid of the 2506 Brigade.

Their "dumping" into Cuba was flawless!

One problem the Kennedy administration had thought they'd solved was that of what they contended was an uncontrolled, irresponsible, free-wheeling CIA. This myth was as great as the administration's other myth about Cochinos, but it was necessary for one myth to support another. Because of this, the Agency was under such tight control, that any function larger than a fast trip to the john had to be presented in multiple copies to committee after committee until it was given final approval by the Committee to Control Committees. The committees came and went, changing names and members so fast that I am sure some of them missed approving a plan for the simple reason that no one knew of their existence. There was the 40 Committee, the 303 Committee, the Foreign Intelligence Operations Board, the 707 Committee. They were now the advisers and we were the doers.

Over and above the seeming necessity to tighten control over the CIA came another priority—getting rid of Castro and his Communists had become an "obsession" of the New Frontier and Kennedy.

To accomplish this task, the CIA, on Kennedy's orders, began a massive buildup of its Miami station. Dubbed JM WAVE, the station, at its peak, was the largest CIA station in the world. On its payroll were 450 staff agents and support elements, and two thousand Cuban nationals. In comparison, a normal overseas CIA station's staff consisted of no more than five to thirty people.

JM WAVE was so large that it was organized on

the style of the CIA's headquarters in Langley, Virginia, with divisions of all Agency branches represented. It was housed in seven buildings, three large warehouses, and three ammo bunkers at Richmond Field, once a World War II Navy blimp base, located ten miles south of Miami. At that time, Richmond Field was under the control of the University of Miami, which leased the entire reservation to the CIA. This area is now the Miami Zoo. Our main headquarters, housed in the largest of the complex's seven buildings, oversaw, among other things, a radio station that was so large it could cover all of the Caribbean and most of Latin America, a land link to Langley and Washington, and a huge maritime branch, which supported our seaborne operations.

Rip's and my home, the Special Operations Division, was the largest branch. SOD's mission was to conduct all the penetration operations into Cuba. This covered everything from commando operations to the insertion of agents and the running of supplies to resistance units in the Cuban mountains.

Although Castro had made sweeping arrests of three hundred thousand Cubans during the Bay of Pigs Invasion, the resistance movement remained very much alive, and there was no shortage of willing new recruits. In fact, we found that after the invasion the resistance to Castro was more widespread than ever. However, recruitment into these resistance groups was handled differently now, for their leaders had learned a bitter lesson about unwarranted trust and betrayal from within, and were more cautious about whom they recruited and, more important, whom they trusted.

Rip and I were ordered to form a commando group from those men left over from the U.S.-based infiltration groups and the members of the 2506 Assault Brigade who had been rescued or had otherwise made their way out of Cuba after the invasion. (The remainder of the 1,250 members of the brigade languished away in Cuban prisons until they were ransomed by the Kennedy administration.)

We later divided this group into two groups. One of the groups, with Miguel Orozco as its chief, was under Rip's command, and a second, led by Roberto San Román, brother of the 2506 Assault Brigade's commander, Pepe San Román, was under my command.

Roberto and sixteen other men had escaped from Cuba in a sailboat in the last hour before Castro's forces overran the beachhead. They sailed for two weeks before they were rescued south of New Orleans. Seven of the seventeen died at sea for lack of water, and another died on the rescue ship. I had four of the men who'd survived this ordeal in my group. They harbored a great deal of hatred for the Castro regime and a burning desire to liberate their country.

All of my men were highly motivated and thirsting for action. Unfortunately, at first all we could offer them was a lot of intensive training and a few missions to Cuba to deliver arms and supplies to the internal resistance groups. Finally, word came down from the White House to begin offensive operations against Castro. The orders even contained the words "set Cuba aflame."

This was the beginning of a secret war waged against Cuba, which, until it ended with the closing of the Miami station in 1967, saw over 2,126 operations run by JM WAVE against Castro and his regime. A total of 113 of those operations was conducted by my commando groups. These operations, and my part in the Cuban Missile Crisis, require a book in themselves, which I am currently writing.

Chapter Notes

CHAPTER 1
Into the Bay of Death

The description of the arrival of the 2506 Assault Brigade is from the author's own experiences and recollections. The information on Castro's forces landing in Cuba and his first months in the Sierra Maestro mountains was obtained by personal interviews with Julian Jose Marti Perez, son of Crecensio Perez, the guide who was waiting for Castro on the beach in Cuba. Perez lighted several bonfires to attract the *Granma's* attention but to no avail. It was Perez who rounded up Castro's men after they were scattered by Batista's soldiers, who had attacked them and chased them into the mountains. For three months, he provided them with food and other materials. For his service to Castro, Perez was made a commandante in the Rebel army. His son,

Julian, was made a captain and served under Raúl Castro until 1963, when he defected to the United States. There, he joined an anti-Castro commando group called the Commando Mambises, which was headed by the author, who was the group's CIA Special Operation's case officer. The events surrounding Castro's march into Havana after the fall of Batista were told to the author in interviews with Francisco Montiel and several of his men, who served in the Rebel army at that time, and in interviews with Capt. Manuel VillaFaña, who was the first chief of the Rebel air force. Montiel and VillaFaña later served with the 2506 Assault Brigade, Montiel as the commander of the 6th Battalion and VillaFaña as the chief of the brigade's Liberation air force. Accounts of the State Department's actions are mostly from former Ambassador Earl B. Smith's book *The Fourth Floor*. Information was also found in *New York Times* articles written by Herbert Mathews, which ran in 1960, news reports out of Havana, John F. Kennedy's *The Strategy of Peace*, and Arthur M. Schlesinger's *A Thousand Days: John F. Kennedy in the White House*.

CHAPTER 2
The Charade

Information for this chapter was gathered from the many news reports of the time; from Bill Moyer interviews used in the making of CBS Reports' documentary "The CIA's Secret Army"; from a Dwight

D. Eisenhower speech given in Groton, Conn.; from Ambassador Earl B. Smith's book *The Fourth Floor*, from interviews with CIA case officers stationed in Havana at the time; and later, from interviews with Richard M. Bissell, Jr., deputy director for operations, and other personnel involved with the Bay of Pigs Invasion at CIA headquarters, where the author was employed.

CHAPTER 3
The Light Brigade

This chapter's information came from the first TV debate between John F. Kennedy and Vice President Richard M. Nixon; from interviews with officers of the 2506 Assault Brigade both before and after the invasion; from interviews with Richard M. Bissell, Jr., CIA deputy director for operations; CIA instructors to the brigade; Capt. Eduardo Ferrer, a member of the brigade's Liberation air force; and from CIA files of the brigade's and the brigade's Liberation air forces' formation, which the author had to familiarize himself with before carrying out his duties as case officer to the command ship *Blagar*.

CHAPTER 4
The Trinidad Plan

Data for this chapter were gathered by studying the Trinidad Plan and from interviews with Richard M. Bissell, Jr., the CIA's deputy director for operations.

Bissell was in charge of this operation; he knew the details of the Trinidad Plan and the actions that were taken by the parties involved with it intimately.

CHAPTER 5
Change of Plans

Information for this chapter came from interviews with Richard M. Bissell, Jr., CIA deputy director for operations; and with Admiral Arleigh Burke, chief of Naval Operations and a member of the Joint Chiefs of Staff; from Arthur M. Schlesinger's book *A Thousand Days: John F. Kennedy in the White House*, and from Haynes Johnson's book *The Bay of Pigs: The Leader's Story of the Brigade 2506*.

CHAPTER 6
Trampoline

This chapter's information developed from the author's personal experience; conversations with William "Rip" Robertson, the author's CIA counterpart; and interviews with CIA operation's people at CIA headquarters.

CHAPTER 7
En Route to Cochinos

Material in this chapter came from the author's personal experiences; interviews with Richard M. Bissell, Jr., CIA deputy director for operations; conversations with Col. Jack Hawkins, USMC; and the commanders and men of the 2506 Assault Brigade.

CHAPTER 8
Decision for Disaster

Information for this chapter was drawn from personal interviews with Richard M. Bissell, Jr., CIA deputy director for operations; Edwin O. Guthman and Jeffrey Shulman's *Robert Kennedy: In His Own Words*, Arthur M. Schlesinger's *A Thousand Days: John F. Kennedy in the White House*; the John F. Kennedy–Richard Nixon television debates; and from a television debate in which Theodore Sorensen was a participant.

CHAPTER 9
H-Hour, Blue Beach

Material for this chapter came from the author's personal experiences.

CHAPTER 10
The Battle of Red Beach

This chapter's information was drawn from the author's personal experience; personal interviews with William "Rip" Robertson, CIA case officer to the *Barbara J*; and with José "Pepe" San Román, 2506 Assault Brigade commander; and Erneido Oliva, deputy commander of the brigade.

CHAPTER 11
D-Day: Action at Blue Beach

Information for this chapter was compiled from the author's personal experiences; conversations with William "Rip" Robertson, CIA case officer to the *Barbara J*; interviews with Richard M. Bissell, Jr., CIA deputy director for operations; Admiral Arleigh Burke, chief of naval operations; and the commanders and many of the men of the 2506 Assault Brigade.

CHAPTER 12
Rescue

This chapter's details came from personal experience of the author; personal interviews with William "Rip" Robertson, CIA case officer to the *Barbara J*; Amado Cantillo, 2506 Assault Brigade frogman; and members of the crews of the destroyers *Eaton, Murray,* and *Cony,* who were involved in the rescue mission. The episode involving the inhumane trucking of the brigade prisoners to Havana was told to the author by Col. (Ret.) Juan Lopez, USA, one of the brigade officers who was a prisoner in the truck. He later served in the U.S. Army.

CHAPTER 14
Rewriting History

The information for this chapter was drawn from personal experiences of the author; personal interviews with CIA personnel involved in the Bay of Pigs invasion; 2506 Assault Brigade members involved in the invasion; excerpts from John F. Kennedy's *Why England Slept*; Theodore Sorensen's *Kennedy*; Arthur M. Schlesinger's *A Thousand Days: John F. Kennedy in the White House*, and from articles in the *New York Times*, 1962, on Dwight D. Eisenhower and *U.S. News and World Report*, Jan. 28, 1963, on Robert Kennedy.

CHAPTER 15
Epilogue

The information for this chapter came from the author's personal experience.

Bibliography

Books

Aguilar, Luis. *Operation Zapata*. Frederick, Md.: University Publications of America, 1981.

Andrew, Christopher. *For the President's Eyes Only*. New York: Harper-Collins, 1995.

Catledge, Turner. *My Life and The Times*. New York: Harper & Row, 1971.

Dulles, Allen. *The Craft of Intelligence*. Westport, Conn: Greenwood Press, 1977.

Ferrer, Eduardo. *Operación Puma*. Miami: International Aviation Consultants, 1975.

Gross, Peter. *The Life of Allen Dulles*. New York: Houghton Mifflin, 1994.

Guthman, Edwin O., and Jeffrey Shulman, eds. *Robert Kennedy: In His Own Words*. Toronto and New York: Bantam, 1988.

Hunt, Howard. *Give Us This Day*. New Rochelle, N.Y.: Arlington House, 1973.

Johnson, Haynes. *The Bay of Pigs: The Leader's Story of Brigade 2506*. New York: Norton, 1974.

Lasky, Victor. *J.F.K.: The Man and the Myth*. New York: Macmillan, 1963.

McCullough, David. *Truman*. New York: Simon & Schuster, 1992.

Meyer, Karl, and Tad Szulc. *The Cuban Invasion*. New York: Praeger, 1962.

Nixon, Richard M. *Six Crises*. Garden City, N. Y.: Doubleday, 1962.

Phillips, David A. *Night Watch*. New York: Atheneum, 1977.

Rusk, Dean. *As I Saw It*. New York: Penguin, 1991.

Schlesinger, Arthur M., Jr. *A Thousand Days: John F. Kennedy in the White House*. Boston: Houghton Mifflin, 1965.

———. *Robert Kennedy and His Times*. Boston: Houghton Mifflin, 1978.

Shoenbaum, Thomas J. *Waging Peace and War*. New York: Simon & Schuster, 1988.

Taylor, Maxwell Davenport. *Swords and Plowshares*. New York: Norton, 1972.

White, Theodore. *The Making of the President 1964*. New York: Atheneum, 1965.

Wise, David. *The Politics of Lying*. New York: Random House, 1973.

Wyden, Peter. *Bay of Pigs: The Untold Story*. New York: Simon & Schuster, 1980.

BIBLIOGRAPHY

Interviews

Carlos Betancourt, Underwater Demolition Team (UDT), 2506 Assault Brigade

Richard Bissell, CIA deputy director of operations

Admiral Arleigh Burke, chief of naval operations, Joint Chief of Staff (JCS) representative

Amado Cantillo, Underwater Demolition Team (UDT), 2506 Assault Brigade

Captain Robert R. Crutchfield, U.S. Navy, commander destroyer squadron

Eduardo Ferrer, squadron commander, 2506 Assault Brigade air force

Carlos Font, Underwater Demolition Team (UDT), 2506 Assault Brigade

Colonel Jack Hawkins, paramilitary chief, Cuban Task Force

Gonzalo Herrera, B-26 pilot, 2506 Assault Brigade air force

Enrique Lamar, chief of Underwater Demolition Team (UDT), 2506 Assault Brigade

Armando Lopez-Estrada, company commander, 1st Battalion, 2506 Assault Brigade

Francisco Montiel, commander, 6th Battalion, 2506 Assault Brigade

William "Rip" Robertson, CIA case officer

José "Pepe" San Román, commander, 2506 Assault Brigade

Roberto San Román, commander, heavy weapons battalion, 2506 Assault Brigade

BIBLIOGRAPHY

Hugh Sueiro, commander, 2nd Battalion, 2506 Assault Brigade

Reuben Vera, company commander, 1st Battalion, 2506 Assault Brigade

Manuel VillaFaña, commanding officer, 2506 Assault Brigade air force

Eduardo Zayas-Bazan, Underwater Demolition Team (UDT), 2506 Assault Brigade.

Index

INDEX

SONG OF JOY

Elaine L. Schulte

Serenade/Serenata
BOOKS
of the Zondervan Publishing House
Grand Rapids, Michigan

A Note from the Author:
I love to hear from my readers! You may correspond with me by writing:

       Elaine L. Schulte,
       Author Relations
       1415 Lake Drive, S.E.,
       Grand Rapids, MI 49506

Earth's crammed with Heaven
And every common bush afire with God;
But only he who sees takes off his shoes—
The rest sit round it and pluck blackberries.

Elizabeth Barrett Browning
Aurora Leigh

CHAPTER 1

AMY CURTIS FELT A shiver of excitement as a sudden flash of light swept the walls of the already sunlit living room. It was only the reflection from a car pulling into the driveway, she told herself as she finished vacuuming the carpet, yet her sense of anticipation lingered.

She turned off the vacuum cleaner and quickly wound up its cord, grateful that the empty house gleamed, that the new owners would find everything spotless. It seemed strange to be leaving this house in which she had spent most of her twenty-two years. She had always imagined herself, like her older sister Valerie, leaving home to walk into the arms of love, to marry someone special; instead, she would be venturing into the unknown—alone.

Outside, a car door slammed. That would be Valerie now, coming to collect her with this last load of moving cartons. Gramp's old two-bedroom stucco house had sold at last, and the weeks of packing and moving were drawing to an end.

A knock at the front door startled her. Who would be knocking? Surely not Val . . .

Amy hurried to the screen door, flipping her long dark hair over her shoulders. Recognizing the man standing there, she felt her mouth fall open slightly as if she were—as her grandfather would have teased—catching flies.

"My, my, you look surprised," Mark Marston said with a hint of amusement playing around his narrow lips. He slid his sunglasses up into slightly wavy dark brown hair that gleamed with reddish highlights in the California sunshine.

It was a moment before she thought to open the screen door. "I–I was expecting Valerie."

"I've come instead," he responded in his confident, rich baritone. "I hope you don't mind."

"No—of course not—" She was all too aware of her grubby cleaning clothes: old cut-off jeans and a faded turquoise shirt that had once matched her eyes. At least she was slim now, she thought gratefully. With the weight loss she had even acquired rather elegant cheekbones, accentuated by fashionable hollows. Despite her own impressive height, she noted again how Mark towered over her. He looked striking as usual, wearing a blue polo shirt that enhanced the startling sapphire hue of his eyes and displayed the breadth of his shoulders. "It's been months since I've seen you," she finally said into the lengthening silence.

He raised a brow in reflection. "Must have been Christmas."

"Yes . . . when the wedding was announced at your parents' house." She recalled that their uneasy conversation had centered upon their future roles as maid-of-honor and best man in Valerie's wedding to his younger brother Thom—and not much else.

"We thought the bride-to-be needed a rest, so Mom talked her into going to bed," Mark said, explaining his presence at her doorstep. "We don't want Val backing out at the last minute from sheer exhaustion."

Amy laughed. "Little chance of that, but she *has* been overdoing it." She moved aside a bit too quickly to let him into the house, embarrassed to have kept him standing outside and wishing that she didn't always react so awkwardly around Mark. He was terribly attractive

8

and eight years older—thirty to her twenty-two. But then, she had never known quite how to act around men. They had always gravitated toward her svelte sister. Now, since the tragedy Mark had experienced and the ensuing changes in him, she felt especially gauche. "I thought you were still in Los Angeles."

He smiled, his even teeth white against his tan. "Oh, American Holidays, Inc. won't fold up just because the president decides to take an occasional long weekend. And it isn't every day that the Marstons welcome two such lovely ladies as houseguests. The family is gathering just for that purpose."

"How nice . . ." Amy was uncertain as to whether Mark was pleased or not; he had probably come home—and here—at his mother's request. Despite some semblance of the old charm in his initial greeting, he had changed so much since the tragedy five years ago that it was difficult to read the real meaning behind his words.

For example, she wondered what he was thinking now. He continued to gaze at her with perplexity before a flicker of realization lit his face. "I hadn't decided until now what was so different about you. You've lost a lot of weight, haven't you?"

She shrugged. "I couldn't eat when Gramp was sick."

"That explains it. . . . I'm sorry to have missed the funeral."

"Your parents helped enormously, and I know you were in New York—"

"Yes . . . well—" His tone changed. "Let me give you a hand with packing what's left."

"It's just these cartons, the vacuum cleaner, the mop, and a broom in the kitchen. Not very thrilling, is it?" Heat crept up to her cheeks. Since when did boxes of household articles have to be thrilling? Since Mark had come to pick her up and had noticed that she was no longer *chubby* Amy Curtis?

Effortlessly shouldering one of the boxes, he appraised her again, a vaguely sensuous light passing from his eyes to hers as if considering whether or not she might be fair game, or if there were another man in the picture. What a ridiculous notion!

9

She rushed on distractedly. "Moving in with your family for a few weeks seemed our only option. The new owners of this house have to be in tomorrow, and my apartment by the university isn't quite finished." It struck her that he might think she was imposing, taking advantage of his parents' generous hospitality.

He paused only an instant. "It does seem to be the most sensible thing to do. After all, in a little over two weeks, you'll be part of the family." Turning, he headed for the front door with the carton perched on a broad shoulder.

But I won't actually be part of the Marston family, she fretted as she hurried to the kitchen. Valerie was the one who would become Mark's sister-in-law and the daughter-in-law of his parents. If it weren't for her love for Val, she might resent the rapidly approaching wedding, maybe even feel hurt that Valerie would be leaving Southern California to move to Virginia—in a sense, abandoning her. She knew well that feeling of loss. Twenty years ago their parents had been killed in an accident, and Gram and Gramp had taken in the two little girls, then five and two, and reared them as their own. Gram had died a few years later. Now Gramp had, as he called it, "gone on to Glory" too.

Shaking off her unhappiness, Amy focused on her immediate duties but found her thoughts drifting again to the touch of Mark's gaze upon her only moments ago. In all the years she had known him, he had never looked at her like that. . . .

"Everything all right?" he inquired as he returned for the other carton and the vacuum cleaner.

Startled, she realized that she had been staring at a kitchen cabinet. "Oh! Yes, of course. I–I'm afraid I've been daydreaming." She set off determinedly for the back door. "I'll just lock the doors and windows and be right with you."

Minutes later, when everything was locked up and she had gathered the last of the cleaning supplies, Amy cast a lingering look at the familiar rooms of the only house she remembered. Her throat tightened. Through Gramp's illness, his funeral, and the selling of the house, she had refused to cry. Keeping a stiff upper lip had seemed imperative. *Don't break down now!* she warned herself— *especially not in front of Mark!* But she could no longer restrain the hot tears that sprang to her eyes.

"Here, use this." Mark offered his neatly folded handkerchief, but his voice sounded stiff and stern. "Crying doesn't solve anything, you know. It might be an old cliché, but it's true."

She swallowed with difficulty, blotting away the tears. "It's just—the memories. Even after Gramp died, it seemed he was still in the next room, but now it's so final. It's so terribly clear he's no longer here." Glancing at Mark to see if he understood, she found him frowning, his eyes glacial.

"If the house is all locked up, let's go."

"But—"

"A fast getaway doesn't hurt nearly so much."

It does hurt! It hurts dreadfully! Amy objected silently, but she knew from his tone of voice that there was no point in arguing with him, no point at all.

Once outside, Amy was suddenly aware of the spectacle she must be making for passers-by as she rushed out the door, mop and broom in hand. What an inglorious exit, after all of Valerie's attempts to mold her into a lady!

From next door, Mrs. Brockaw waved. "See you at the wedding!"

"Yes! Good-by, Mrs. Brockaw!" They had spoken at length this morning, and there was nothing to do now but to return the older woman's wave. The Brockaws would be driving across the country in their camper to attend the wedding, accompanied by their son Rob, whom Amy had begun to date in the past month. In fact, Rob would be here now, helping her with the move, if he hadn't been called out of town on business.

"What do we do with the house keys?" Mark asked.

"We have to drop them off at Santa Rosita Realty, then take the boxes and cleaning supplies to the mini-warehouse. I hope you don't mind."

"No problem," he replied. He strode across the small crabgrass lawn toward the driveway, as if to quickly deliver her from the source of her grief, but Amy was unable to resist turning back for one last look.

The house was just a small California stucco on a narrow city lot, but they had been happy here—she and Valerie and Gramp. She noted that the hibiscus bushes near the front steps were covered with red blossoms, and bursts of purple bougainvillaea bloomed against the white chimney wall.

"No backward glances," Mark warned as he helped her into the familiar red van advertising "C's Catering"—his mother's business. "They don't do any good."

He probably was unable to cope with weepy females after the torment he'd been through. He was no doubt castigating himself even now for allowing himself to be drawn into Amy's situation. But that was *his* problem, she thought resolutely. She hadn't asked for his help!

While Mark made his way around to the driver's seat, Amy darted one final look through the van's open window. The afternoon ocean breeze was rising, rustling fronds on the palm trees that lined the streets and towered over the old houses. She knew that she would always remember this scene and this moment when her future was so uncertain. As the breeze gathered strength, the palms she had always envisioned as sentinels seemed to be waving farewell.

She dug in her handbag for a tissue to dab away the dampness clinging to her lashes.

"I warned you about backward glances." Mark's tone brooked no argument as he started the van. Worse, his dark glasses masked not only his blue eyes, but the expression in them, making him appear callous, uncaring.

She donned her own sunglasses. "Don't you ever look back?" Amy kept her voice even as they drove away.

"No," he said bluntly. "I don't."

She almost blurted, *Then why have you changed so?* but held her tongue. His entire life seemed colored by what had happened to that girl. She decided not to pursue the thought.

He looked directly ahead, preoccupied with his task of maneuvering the van through the late afternoon traffic, and she took the opportunity to study his profile, noticing how his fashionably cut hair angled slightly onto his high forehead. His nose was straight, patrician. Her eyes wandered to his high cheekbones, to his angular chin, then to his narrow sensuous lips. There was a confidence about him that appealed to Amy as he wheeled the van through the maze of cars and trucks around them.

Apparently unaware of her scrutiny, he said, "The owners of the condo I've been leasing are returning from Europe early, so I'm moving back home until after the wedding."

"I didn't know you'd be there," she said almost too quickly, as if to clarify the fact that she was not moving in because of him. In fact, if she had known, she might have had second thoughts about accepting his parents' invitation—not that the house wasn't large enough to accommodate all of them quite easily.

"I just found out this week."

What was *that* supposed to mean? That he hadn't had time to make other arrangements? That he hadn't moved home so she could pursue her childhood infatuation? Was he careful now to keep women at a distance, or was she reading too much into the situation?

She realized she was sitting bolt upright and forced herself to relax against the van's warm black vinyl seat. After a while she cast about for a safe topic of conversation. "Will you commute to L.A. every day?" His national travel agency, which specialized in tours for foreigners visiting the United States, was headquartered in West Los Angeles.

"No, I'll be out of town a lot. As a matter of fact, I'm flying up to San Francisco next Monday."

She felt strangely relieved. "Sounds like fun!"

He chuckled. "You don't have to look quite so pleased that I'm leaving."

"Pleased?" she hedged. "Why should I be pleased?"

"Somehow I've gotten the impression you don't like me very much."

"Don't like you? Of all the peculiar ideas!" It was true that she didn't quite know how she felt about him now, but most of her life she had idolized him. "Why should I dislike you?"

"I'm sure there must be a dozen good reasons."

"You've been—almost an older brother." Well, until five years ago, he had been. After that, the camaraderie had ceased; he had grown silent during their visits to the Marston home on those rare occasions when he was around, although she felt certain that his aloofness was not caused by anything she or Valerie had done.

Braking for a traffic light, Mark studied her thoughtfully, and she had to look away at the restaurants and shops along the Coast Highway before she could continue. "Your entire family has been wonderful to Valerie and me all of these years since my parents died. And they helped so much with Gramp. I don't know how we could have managed without . . . all of you."

The light changed to green, and nothing more was said about her feelings. Instead, an air of tenuousness hung between them as they drove through Santa Rosita's downtown traffic. After knowing each other for so many years, they were acting like strangers.

Finally Mark broke the silence. "I'm glad the wedding's been moved to Virginia."

"I am too. After Gramp died, it seemed senseless to have it in Santa Rosita, especially since our only relatives live on the East Coast. Most of yours too. And with Thom receiving his doctorate from Princeton just days before the wedding, then going to work in Washington almost immediately, it was the logical thing to do."

To make the new plan even more practical, Thom's aunt—and, of course, Mark's too—had graciously offered to hold the wedding in her historic home in Alexandria, Virginia, a suburb of Washington, D.C., the same house in which their parents had been married. If Aunt Alicia had the same flair for creating occasions as their mother, Catherine, the festivities would be not only

14

memorable but marvelous. The drawback to the new plan was that the expense of the trip would cut severely into Amy's small savings account. And, of course, the cross-country flight would make the distance between her and her sister seem even more pronounced. Soon she would be alone—truly alone. . . .

The smell of salt air wafted in on the warm afternoon breeze, and the surging Pacific Ocean shimmered a silvery blue, reflecting scattered clouds that momentarily veiled the sun. It would be a beautiful sunset, Amy thought as she reclined on a chaise lounge on the patio of the Marstons' two-story white Spanish ocean-front home.

Beyond the low stucco wall with its old brass lanterns was a sandy beach, then the vastness of ocean. Great waves gathered in the distance and crashed to shore. If she could only listen to the music of the sea long enough, its rhythms might soothe the growing emptiness within her.

Valerie, ever the serene one in the family, was sleeping in their room upstairs. Not wanting to awaken her by opening the closet and drawers to which they had transferred their clothing in the past two days, Amy still wore her old clothes. And Mark, after depositing her at his home, had departed for the airport to pick up a friend . . . evidently a female friend since his mother had called after him, "Be sure to invite her for dinner, though it's just going to be spaghetti out on the patio!"

Who *she* might be was a matter of speculation. Amy hoped it wasn't Glynia, the exotic model who sometimes visited her mother and stepfather next door. Long before Glynia had become a model, she and Mark had been childhood friends, though she'd been known then to their fellow classmates as that "kooky Gloria Anne Bennington."

Mark's mother, Catherine Marston, tiptoed across the Mexican tile patio, carrying a vase full of yellow roses to the round redwood table. She cast a concerned glance at Amy, then sighed. "Oh, I had hoped to find you sleeping. You've looked so tired lately."

Amy sat up with a twinge of guilt. "I'm fine . . . truly. Please let me help with dinner."

With a firm shake of her head, the older woman placed the roses on the dinner table. "Thanks, but everything's under control." The liveliness in her brown eyes and her slim figure in the moss green shift belied her age; only streaks of gray in her auburn hair and smile lines curving around her mouth hinted that she was past fifty. She crossed the patio and lifted Amy's feet back onto the chaise lounge. "At least put your feet up."

Amy lay back, reluctantly enjoying the rare experience of being pampered. "Thank you. I think I've forgotten how to relax."

"Then I'm going to see to it that you remember!" Catherine warned with a laugh.

Amy felt a familiar rush of love for the woman. She recalled a long-ago picture of her mother and Catherine going off to grade school with their arms around each other; they had been best friends all of their lives—until her mother's death. Afterward, Catherine had tried to fill that tragic gap in the two young lives, indulging what she called her need of feminine support. "I'd never survive without you girls," she had often insisted. "I'm the only woman in this houseful of men!" It was indeed a male household—her husband, Mark, and Thom.

Now Catherine said, "The ocean will do wonders for you, Amy, dear. Blows the cobwebs away. It always has for me."

"I've wondered what your secret is. How you could run your catering business, this enormous house, community activities . . . and a thousand and one other things!"

"The ocean helps, but I pray a lot too!" Catherine responded with a wry expression.

Amy forced a smile, uncomfortable as usual at the mention of Catherine's faith. Amy knew her comment was meant to be taken literally. Catherine Marston did pray a lot and aloud, especially when they were catering a big job; it appeared as if she expected God to be interested in even the minutest details. Still, it was amazing to see how well the woman managed everything and still had time for others. She and Valerie had been working for C's Catering since high school, earning generous wages during the frantic hours of putting together everything from wedding receptions and elegant dinner parties to political barbecues for thousands of guests. Slowly, very slowly, they had earned enough money to pay their way through college, though due to her work and Gramp's illness, Amy had been unable to study full-time and still had another year to go for her bachelor's degree.

"You've really turned down all catering jobs this month?" Amy asked.

"Absolutely. I've referred every one of them. We've even declared a moratorium on gourmet cooking to save time and energy for wedding preparations. We'll survive on family fare this next week. Now, try to nap before dinner."

"I'll try." Amy closed her eyes obediently. It was the rare individual who objected to Catherine's loving suggestions. *If ever I have a family of my own,* Amy thought, *I hope I can be just like Catherine Marston.*

In the past few years, however, her energies had been directed toward getting through Santa Rosita State College and embarking on a banking career. Unexciting as banking might be, it was a field in which women seemed likely to climb the career ladder more readily than in many others. If only she could follow her real interests—but there was no great demand for poets nor short story writers nowadays, not that there ever had been. She wished she felt more direction in her life.

As she listened to the ocean's roar, it reminded her of the fascinating conch shells she held to her ear, and then of her father. A literature professor, Dr. Curtis had underlined Dante Rossetti's "The Sea-Limits" in one of the books she often read to bring him closer to her.

Familiar lines returned to her: *Consider the sea's listless chime . . . the murmur of the earth's own shell . . .* Between dozing and waking, other lines swirled through the mist of her memory: *Gather a shell from the*

17

*strewn beach and listen at its lips: they sigh the same
desire and mystery, the echo of the whole sea's speech.*
As the afternoon sun slanted onto the patio, she rolled
over sleepily. There was another line in the poem. . . .
What was it? *No quiet, which is death's* . . . The light
filtering through her eyelids dimmed.

The familiar scene reappeared. She was two years old,
still in her stroller that silken summer evening. Her
family crossed the street, eating their after-dinner ice
cream cones. Valerie skipped along just ahead, singing
lustily, "The farmer in the dell, the farmer in the dell—"
Quite suddenly brakes screeched and a car careened
toward them.

"Run!" her father shouted.

She felt the stroller propelled in the direction of the
curb, heard her mother's labored breathing just before
the shocking sound of metal on flesh. Then the sound of
gears meshing in reverse, and a car raced away from the
scene.

"Call an ambulance!" a man yelled.

Amy looked down at her parents from the stroller, not
comprehending why they lay on the street nor why a
crowd had gathered. Her father was smiling, seemingly
in sleep. An expression of wonder filled her mother's
face.

Moments later, someone murmured, "They're gone."

"What do you suppose they saw?" a woman asked
into the hush.

Then someone was lifting her from her stroller and
Valerie was crying. "These poor children. To lose
both—"

"No!" Amy cried as darkness drifted over her parents'
motionless bodies. "No!"

Horrified, she sat up before realizing she had been
dreaming—the terrible, haunting dream that had lodged
itself in the depths of her mind, to be played out again
and again when she was most exhausted.

Mark's voice came from the side of the patio. "You
have them too, don't you?"

Brushing away perspiration from her forehead, she

glimpsed him on the patio swing. In his tan swim trunks, a white terry beach jacket, and scuffed brown leather sandals, he seemed relaxed, as if he had been swinging and observing her for some time.

"Have what?" she inquired groggily.

"Nightmares. Bad dreams."

She sat up straighter, slowly coming fully awake. "You have bad dreams?"

"Occasionally." His eyes were hidden by the dark glasses again. He rose from the swing and headed for the oak table where a tray of tumblers and a pitcher had been placed near the yellow roses. He poured two glasses of lemonade. "I thought it might be of some small comfort to know you're not the only one who suffers from them."

"I–I suppose it does."

He handed her the cool drink. "I thought you might be thirsty."

"Thank you. I am." She dropped her eyes to avoid seeing her own reflection in his sunglasses.

Why had Mark told her about his nightmares? She sensed that it was a rare occurrence for him to make himself so vulnerable, and she felt strangely close to him. She sipped the icy, tart drink, and recalled the old Mark as he returned to the patio swing. Five years ago he had brimmed with fun and laughter; there had been a light behind his eyes. She could easily imagine how an unstable eighteen-year-old clerk in his office might fall in love with him. Erika had—

"Apparently Valerie and Thom haven't changed their minds about getting married," Mark said, adroitly changing the subject that occupied both their minds.

"No-no, certainly not Valerie! She walks at least six inches above the ground." Amy smiled, setting her gloomy thoughts aside.

Mark added with a chuckle, "And Thom sounds just as bad when he so much as mentions her name over the phone."

"It must be wonderful to be in love," Amy ventured in an effort to keep the conversation light, then wished she had kept that particular comment to herself. He must truly think her naïve and unsophisticated!

Mark sipped from his glass of lemonade. "I wouldn't know."

Mark Marston had never been in love! She found that very difficult to believe. Yet everyone knew he had certainly not loved Erika. Poor Erika . . .

"I *do* know," he injected with rare enthusiasm, "that the best thing after a nightmare is a good swim. How about it? There's plenty of time before dinner."

"That *would* be an eye-opener." She rose and started across the patio. "I'll be back in five minutes."

He glanced at his watch and looked up with a skeptical grin. "I'm going to hold you to that."

"Five minutes!" she responded with a laugh and hurried into the house.

Upstairs in the beam-ceilinged guest room, Valerie was still asleep in her twin bed. Amy quietly stripped off her blouse and jeans and pulled on a yellow maillot, then took a few swipes at her hair with the brush.

When she returned to the patio, Mark rose from the swing, pulling off his beach jacket. "Four minutes! I can't believe it!" His mocking tone changed as he took a second look at her. "What? No bikini?"

"Not for real ocean swimming!" She turned and ran across the warm sand. If he was disappointed in her modest one-piece suit, that was his problem; she did not intend to provide entertainment for him or for any other man. As it was, she received more than her share of stares. Having been slightly overweight most of her life, she was unaccustomed to such scrutiny; it seemed an invasion of privacy. Still, she was sorely tempted to gape at Mark's magnificent physique, displayed to advantage in his brief trunks!

Resisting the impulse, Amy splashed into the cold shallow water for some distance, then dove into a wave and swam out strongly through the incoming breakers. Beyond the surf, she turned onto her back for a rest. She lay there for a long time, watching the gulls that soared overhead, their mewling cries in counterpoint with the pulsing sounds of the sea.

"I forgot you were on a swimming team!" Mark called

out some distance away. "I gave you too much of a head start."

Brushing her hair from her face, Amy joined him, lazily treading water and no longer self-conscious with only their shoulders bared above the rolling swells. It seemed as if they had stepped back in time to the days when, as the oldest child, Mark had been placed in charge of the younger ones—herself, Valerie, and Thom.

"Unfortunately, I don't swim every day anymore," she confessed.

"A pity. But it's not obvious. You have a good stroke."

"Thanks." She turned her attention to a sailboat gliding by in the distance. "I love it here," she said, half to herself. "The ocean . . . the sand . . . the sun . . ."

"Gets in your blood, doesn't it? When I'm home, I swim every day, even in the winter."

She remembered him, slicing through the wild waves of a winter storm years ago, but now he appeared at peace as the swells lapped at his broad shoulders. The undulating water lifted them as if they were in a watery cradle, and she noticed that his eyes seemed even bluer today. His gaze caught hers, and she quickly averted her own eyes toward the horizon.

Overhead, a vast expanse of sky stretched out to embrace the earth, the sun, the entire galaxy and whatever galaxies lay beyond. Time itself seemed suspended. For a moment, a transcendent moment, Amy felt aglow with joy, It seemed almost as if she had touched the heart of the universe, and even when the wonder passed, she sensed a peace she had never known.

"Your poetic streak is showing." Mark observed.

He must have noticed a glow about me, she thought.

She licked salt from her lips and smiled. He had always teased her about her serious side. Well, she didn't care. Nothing could disturb the perfection of this day. She swam away, exulting in her own strength as she carved a path through the pulsing waves. There was an underlying confidence, too, an almost mystical certainty that the water would not betray her. Odd as it seemed, in some ways she felt safer in the ocean than she often did among people on land.

A memory drifted back to her . . . moments from long ago. Mark must have been a teenager, because she had been about eight at the time. They had been swimming out through the breakers when a huge wave caught her, tossing her wildly while she thrashed about in helplessness and terror. Suddenly strong arms plucked her from the wave, holding her so that her head was above water while she coughed and sputtered. Mark . . . it was Mark, his face contorted with concern.

"Are you all right, Amy?" he had asked. "Are you all right?"

Gulping deep draughts of air, she could only nod in reply. It was more than simply choking on water; it was the sensation of being in his arms. She adored Mark, had even confided to Gramp that she would marry him someday, but now—now he had even saved her life!

"You're going to have to practice, if you insist on trying for long-distance swimming," he had scolded gently.

"I will, Mark . . . I promise!" The sun shimmering on the surface of the water cast him in bronze. A golden Apollo. In that wonderstruck moment she might have promised him anything. "I'm going to take more swimming lessons, maybe even diving lessons. I'll be the best swimmer you've ever seen!"

"Good girl. Let's see you give it another try right now."

Despite her fear, she had plunged in again to please him. From that day forward she had been intent upon becoming an expert swimmer. Year after year she had worked toward that goal, always with the thought of pleasing Mark in the back of her mind until, one brutal day, she realized she was much too young for him. There were other girls, older and wiser than she—girls his own age. Then the girls were becoming women—beautiful, sleek, worldly women—who knew just how to please Mark. And she was still Amy—chubby little Amy

22

Curtis—who could merely outswim anybody in her junior high class.

When she circled back to the place where Mark was treading water, he eyed her quizzically. But if he had been about to ask a question, he had apparently changed his mind. "We'd better start back."

"Race you to the beach?"

His boyish expression might have belonged to that sixteen-year-old so long ago. "You're on!"

She turned and stroked hard through the water, positioning herself to catch a great wave, then body-surfed to the shore. Regrettably, Mark was a good three lengths ahead of her. Splashing toward the beach just behind him, she noticed him waving to someone on the beach in front of the house.

Following his gaze, her spirits sank. Glynia! Even from this distance there was no mistaking the well-known model who wore outlandishly chic clothing and the vulnerable face of a child. She was dressed in a red and black Indian-print sundress, its handkerchief hemline dipping below one knee and rising to the middle of a lovely thigh. Her incredible mane of black hair curled wildly about her head, and her widespread eyes imparted the incongruous appearance of innocence.

"Are you joining us for dinner after all?" Mark asked her.

Glynia's voice was low and sultry. "I thought I might, since you invited me so sweetly on the way from the airport."

So he *had* picked her up at the airport, Amy thought as she approached them. "Hello, Glynia," she said, mustering a smile.

Glynia nodded slightly, but her jade green eyes registered no recognition. It was possible that the lovely model didn't remember her from their few brief encounters at the Marston home. Like Mark, Glynia was eight years older, and had undoubtedly regarded her only as one of the Curtis sisters—the plump one—who often visited the Marstons after the death of their parents.

"Where was your last fashion shoot, Glyn?" Mark asked.

"New York. Why?" She looked puzzled.

"I thought maybe you'd been shopping in the wilds of Africa." He eyed her jewelry with a grin.

Amy surveyed the outrageous pieces as they walked across the sandy beach to the Marstons' patio. One pale green icicle of an earring dangled to Glynia's collarbone; her necklace was fashioned of primitive beads in the color tones of her dress, and another necklace, a cord with a clawlike pendant, hung over the angular ruff of the strapless bodice.

Glynia smiled indulgently at Mark and caught his arm lightly in hers. For a long moment their eyes held, hers dancing with secrets.

So that's what's going on in Mark's personal life, Amy thought as she hurried toward the patio. It was becoming abundantly clear that the sooner she forgot her childhood crush, the better.

Mark called out something behind her, but it was impossible to hear above the ocean's roar.

"I have to wash my hair!" she shouted in reply and ran on, her feet sinking into the dry sand on the incline to the house. No doubt he was making some excuse for joining Glynia. Well, Amy fumed, *she* certainly had no intention of coming unhinged over him, of doing something rash like that other girl—like Erika.

CHAPTER 2

HURRYING ACROSS THE PATIO, Amy decided that she especially wanted to avoid Catherine Marston. The woman knew her too well not to notice that something was amiss. She detoured past the kitchen and family room, taking a roundabout way through a wrought-iron gate to the courtyard and then up the inner courtyard stairs.

As she dashed into the bedroom, Valerie turned, her hazel eyes wide with surprise. "Oh, Amy, I wish you didn't burst around so."

"Sorry. It's just that I'm pressed for time."

Valerie, lovely in her white eyelet sundress, shook her head hopelessly, her sleek honey-blond curls not quite brushing tanned shoulders. "You're still in your swimsuit, and it's almost time for dinner!"

"Well, there's nothing I can do about it now. I have to shower and wash my hair." She should have turned down the swim with Mark . . . but his offer had been irresistible.

"You'll never get your hair dry."

"I hoped you might braid it for me—"

"But I was just going down to help." Valerie cut her protest short, and let out a soft breath, smiling indulgently. "Well, all right, although I don't know how you're going to take care of all that hair when I'm gone."

"Thanks, Val." Amy didn't know how she would take care of a great number of things alone, but she didn't want to consider that now. As for her sister's less-than-subtle campaign to persuade Amy to have her hair cut to a more manageable length, she was determined not to give in. It seemed that she had always capitulated in everything else. Besides, during her years on the high school swimming team, she'd had to keep her hair shorter than most boys', and she was enjoying the feeling of femininity her luxuriant long hair gave her.

"I laid out your turquoise sundress," Valerie was saying.

"Thanks." Amy hurried to the adjoining bathroom before she said something she'd regret. The dress was exactly right for dinner on the patio, of course, but she would have preferred to have chosen it herself. There would be a thousand reasons to miss Valerie soon, yet one blessing too: in her role as older sister, Valerie was always ever-so-sweetly dictating Amy's life.

When Amy hurried downstairs later, wearing the turquoise sundress, her hair was still damp despite blow-drying. She brushed back the tendrils that had curled about her face and headed for the patio, finding Valerie and Catherine Marston conversing in low tones.

Catherine's face turned a bit pink. "There you are, Amy." Her slightly guilty tone of voice suggested that Amy had been the topic of their conversation. No doubt they were discussing her future.

Well, she would survive on her own, Amy told herself, raising her chin with determination. In any event, there was no choice in the matter. She attempted an independent air as she said, "I decided I didn't want my hair braided after all, Val," then quickly added, "What can I do to help with dinner?" The patio table was already set with the salmon-colored place mats and napkins Valerie had sewn for the Marstons to match the rim of their stoneware dishes.

"You could spread the herb butter on the bread slices—," Catherine began, but was interrupted by the ringing of the front doorbell. "Now who could that be?"

"Uh, I think I'll call Thom," Val said as she glanced at her watch. "It's after nine in Princeton."

For a split second, from the way Catherine and Valerie were acting, Amy suspected a conspiracy of some sort. *Oh, Amy!* she moaned inwardly. *Won't you ever stop writing scripts for daydreams?* Her active imagination was working overtime again.

She followed them into the spacious beam-ceilinged kitchen with its island work center, over which hung a vast array of gleaming copper pots and pans and other utensils. The mingled aromas of garlic, onions, herbs, and tomatoes wafted from a huge copper pot in which the spaghetti sauce simmered.

While Catherine went to the door and Valerie to the den to call Thom, Amy settled at one of the tall barstools at the workcenter and began to spread herb butter on the French bread slices.

She could hear Catherine chatting with the unexpected guest as they came down the hallway. "Look who's here to see you, Amy."

"Rob." Amy hardly knew what to say. Rob Brockaw had been in meetings in the Midwest all week, representing the research company for which he worked.

"Hi." He appeared ill at ease but thrust a green foil-wrapped pot of white and yellow daisies in her hands. "These are for you. I tried to fly back early from the conference to help you with your move, but I couldn't get away."

"Thanks, Rob. How thoughtful of you." She accepted the pot of daisies, burying her face in their wild fragrance.

Odd that he would visit her here when he scarcely knew the Marstons. In the many years Rob and his family had lived next door to Gramp's house, he had all but ignored her. Like so many of their friends, he was Valerie's age and had fancied himself in love with her sister until she announced her engagement to Thom. Yet

27

recently he had begun asking Amy out—first to a community concert, then for a day at the zoo in San Diego, and last week to attend a dinner party at his boss's home. But he had never so much as tried to hold her hand. He was merely an old friend—the boy next door. He even looked the part, with his light brown hair and brown spaniel eyes.

Now those eyes glowed from beneath nice bushy brows. "I remembered that you like daisies."

"Yes—thank you." It occurred to her that Valerie might have suggested Rob show up, but she quickly dismissed the notion. Surely Val wouldn't go *that* far.

"Daisies seem just right for you," Rob was saying.

Amy smiled ruefully. "I suppose they do. If women could be characterized by flowers, Valerie would be a white gardenia, Catherine a . . . yellow rose . . . and I'd be a daisy."

His color deepened. "But that's not what I meant!"

"Oh, I love daisies!" she insisted hastily. Why, oh, why didn't she ever think before she spoke!

Across the work counter Catherine stirred the bubbling spaghetti sauce. "You two go out on the patio, and I'll finish the herb bread."

Amy protested, "But I haven't helped at all with dinner—"

"Nonsense, you always do more than your share. Besides, dear, you're supposed to be relaxing." She turned to Rob. "We'd be pleased if you'd join us for dinner. It's only spaghetti, but enough for an army. I scarcely know how to cook for a small group anymore."

He looked delighted. "Thanks, I'd like to—if you're sure it's no bother."

"It's no bother at all," Catherine insisted. "Now, outside with you two!"

As Amy and Rob stepped out onto the patio through the French doors, she shook her head, "They're going to spoil me."

"Good. You could use a little spoiling. You've had a pretty hard time—with your grandfather and all."

When Amy glanced at Rob, she found his expression

quite serious. Flustered, she blurted, "Since when have *you* cared?"

"Since I took a good look at you, I suppose. You're really a very pretty girl, Amy, and pretty girls shouldn't have worry lines on their foreheads."

A very pretty girl? She wondered if he found her as attractive as Valerie. But Amy was distracted from her thoughts by the stunning realization that Mark and Glynia were seated on the patio swing and had obviously overhead Rob's last comment. Although she was certain that her face was bright red, Amy pressed on. "I think you both know Rob Brockaw."

Mark had changed into tan slacks and a royal-blue knit shirt, open at the neck. He rose to shake the younger man's hand, the creases near his lips deepening as he smiled. "Haven't seen you in years, Rob," he said, his eyes shifting to regard Amy curiously.

"Well—" Glynia stretched, her green eyes gleaming, catlike. "I didn't know you two were an item."

"Yes—," Rob began.

"We're just old friends." Amy objected.

Mark interrupted them with a sweep of his hand. "Sit down and make yourselves comfortable."

Rob ignored the invitation. "I thought you were living in L.A.," he said with a slight edge to his voice.

Mark quirked an eyebrow. "Not at the moment. My plans have changed."

Amy settled uneasily on a nearby rattan couch, perching on the salmon terrycloth cushions, and was grateful to find Rob following her lead.

After a moment Rob remarked, "Nice view."

"Lovely," Amy agreed. Discomfited by the interchange between the men, she tried to focus on the sea gulls wheeling against the blue sky. The ocean breeze rustled palm fronds above their heads, and beyond them, the white-crested waves rushed onto the beach.

Glynia continued her hushed conversation with Mark as if no one else were present. Amy recalled having heard that if one spoke very softly, the audience would draw nearer. She herself had never tested the theory, but

29

then she had never been very clever about playing games with men; in any event Glynia's seductive murmur had completely captured Mark's attention.

Rob turned to Amy. As if taking his cue from Glynia, he lowered his voice. "I mentioned to Mom that you might like to stay with us until your apartment is available."

"With you? But I'm fine here—"

"Unfortunately we have just the two bedrooms at home," he continued, "but we can work it out."

"But, Rob, we're fine. Really!"

"I hope so." He glanced at Mark and Glynia before he continued, "If things don't work out here, you can use my room. I'll sleep on the living room couch."

She caught herself blinking hard, then trying to hide her astonishment. "I appreciate your concern, but there's no need—" What on earth was going on in Rob's head? And why did he think things wouldn't work out with the Marstons?

Valerie stepped out onto the patio, carrying a glass container of grated cheese and the small wooden salad bowls. "How nice to see you, Rob." She smiled at him, then at Mark and Glynia with whom she had apparently spoken earlier. After placing the cheese and the salad bowls on the table, Valerie chose a rattan chair between the swing and the couch, her golden presence melding the two couples into a companionable group. Amy felt a rush of love for her sister. How serene she had become lately.

Mark looked at her appreciatively. "And how is Thom? I take it you've had your evening chat."

Valerie beamed. "Happy. Almost as happy as I am. Just sixteen more days until the wedding!"

"My little brother is a fortunate fellow," Mark said with a smile.

Glynia turned a petulant look on Mark. "I never expected to hear those words coming from you! I thought you didn't believe in marriage."

With a smooth push of his tan loafers, Mark set the swing in motion, his color deepening faintly. "Only in special cases, like this one." He smiled at a thought and turned to Valerie. "I can already imagine the two of you taking Washington by storm—Thom, with his brilliance; and you, with your beauty and sweetness."

"Now, Mark—," Valerie objected, obviously pleased, while Amy reflected upon Glynia's comment. Evidently Mark didn't believe in marriage, or so he had told Glynia. If she had designs on him, nothing had come of it—at least not yet. There was something about Glynia—her glamour perhaps—that made her seem an unlikely partner for a lifelong commitment.

Later, Dr. Marston stepped out on the patio with his arm around Catherine's trim waist. "I see we have the four most beautiful girls in the world assembled here."

Catherine smiled wryly and shook her head at her husband. "Why do I always invite the beautiful ones?"

"Because you adore me?" he inquired with a grin.

She nudged him gently with her elbow. "Because I trust you," she returned, and he laughingly kissed the top of her head.

It was always a pleasure to see the two of them together, Amy thought. They radiated love. But there was something more. It was as though they had embarked together upon an adventure through life, no matter where it took them. Certainly Mark must agree that his parents modeled the best that marriage could be.

Dr. Marston turned to kiss Valerie's cheek, then stepped over to Amy. "What a pleasure to have you here." The glow of welcome in his blue eyes was confirmed by a fatherly hug.

Amy's vision blurred and for an instant she wished he were really her father and that this house was more than a temporary stopping place in her life. "Thank you for— for inviting me too." Soon this day would be over, she reminded herself, firmly gaining control of her frayed emotions. Years from now she would recall it as the day she took her first step into the future, and that the Marstons had eased the transition for her.

"'Our tent is your tent,' or whatever the old adage is," he replied lightly.

"Tent—?" She smiled at his understated description of the magnificent ocean-front house full of family heirlooms. "It's scarcely a tent, Dr. Marston." For some reason, while Amy had always felt comfortable calling his wife by her first name, she had never been able to call him "James." It was always "Dr. Marston," the eminent surgeon.

As Mark shook hands with his father, Amy noted again the strong resemblance between the two men—the same sapphire blue eyes, straight patrician noses, high cheekbones and angular chins. Even the same narrow sensuous lips and the deep creases beside them when they smiled. Dr. Marston's hair, however, was predominantly gray, and he was not quite as tall as Mark. It occurred to her that Mark would look like his father when he neared sixty, and that he would still be a very handsome man.

Catherine announced, "And now if I can coax all of you to the table—"

Later, seated between Mark and Rob, Amy was disconcerted when everyone joined hands to pray. At home, grace was never said at meals, and despite her Sunday school experience as a child, she was not sure she believed in God. Those long-ago lessons of a loving Father seemed irrelevant for these harsh times. Moreover, it was peculiar to be holding Mark's and Rob's hands in this fashion. She listened, uncertain of the words.

For all the glory of Thy way . . .

To her right, Rob was silent; nor did she hear Mark or Glynia praying.

For Thy protection night and day . . .

Dr. Marston's voice rang clear and strong, as did Catherine's and Valerie's. Since her sister had begun attending church again this year, Amy had noticed an unusual change in her. Or perhaps it was just because Thom was a believer. He was, after all, the son of Catherine and James Marston—former medical missionaries—and the grandson of the late Dr. James Marston, Sr.—once pastor of the largest congregation in Santa Rosita.

32

For roof, tree, fire, and bread and board,
For friends and home, we thank Thee, Lord. Amen.

As they dropped their hands, Amy glanced at Mark. He looked embarrassed, uncomfortable. She supposed he was no longer a believer, or maybe he was just outright angry with God. She couldn't really blame him; she was angry herself. If God existed, why had Erika thoughtlessly done something that would affect Mark for the rest of his life? And why had Amy's own parents been killed by that drunken driver? And why had Gramp suffered so before he died of cancer? It all seemed grossly unfair.

"Your salad," Rob said, passing it to her.

Jarred from her thoughts, she thanked him and noticed that Val was serving salad while Catherine filled plates with spaghetti. Reaching for the basket of herb bread, Amy started it around the table, then the bowl of grated cheese. She forced the anger from her mind and tried to focus on the lovely setting and the pleasant ocean breeze. There probably wasn't a lovelier place to be dining in all of Southern California—or anywhere else, for that matter.

During dinner, the conversation turned to Mark's trip to San Francisco on Monday and the news that his secretary's husband was being transferred and she had given notice that she would be leaving her position at American Holidays, Inc. "I'd counted on her to do some research for me in San Francisco next week," he said with disappointment.

"Perhaps you can hire someone after you get there, dear," Catherine soothed.

"I'd prefer using someone from out of town—someone who could see the city through the eyes of a first-time tourist."

"How about taking Amy?" Dr. Marston suggested. "She enjoys writing. She might be just the person who could see San Francisco from a foreign tourist's point of view."

Mark turned to her. "Actually, I considered asking you at the beach this afternoon. Would you be interested?"

33

Amy felt her eyes widen in surprise. "I–I don't know. I've never been to San Francisco."

"All the better," he replied. "I need a research assistant who can view the city from a fresh perspective."

Everyone at the table shifted their attention to her. She noted Glynia's disapproval, Valerie's silence, Rob's frown.

Turning to Mark, she asked, "What would I be expected to do?"

"Scout out locations with special appeal for foreign clients of American Holidays. Find problems that might confront them—and suggest solutions. Then prepare a written report so we can compile an itinerary of the most important tourist attractions. My secretary has already finished reports on L.A. and San Diego. You could use them as guides, although they could stand some improvement. She's a good secretary, but not the world's best writer."

The trip sounded intriguing, and writing, of course, had always been a passion with her, though she supposed she would have to bone up on the art of writing reports on travel. Certainly Mark intended this trip as nothing more than a business proposition, or he wouldn't have mentioned it in front of his family and Glynia. Besides, it had been his father's idea. But for some reason, she had a reservation.

"Thank you, Mark, for your confidence in me, but I'd like some time to think about it."

"Fine, but I'll have to know soon. You'd be paid a research fee and expenses, of course. We can discuss that later, if you're interested."

She nodded, relieved when the conversation drifted to other topics. The offer sounded almost too good to be true—being paid to see San Francisco, considered by many to be the most beautiful city in the United States. And with Mark! Years ago she would have leaped at the chance, but so much had happened since those carefree days. They had both changed. In just this one day, Amy had witnessed so many different facets of his personality.

Carefully winding spaghetti on her fork, she realized that Rob was watching her. She turned to smile at him, but his expression remained somber as he leaned toward her.

"I want to talk to you before you decide."

She was so amazed at his presumption that she could think of no reply.

"I'm serious, Amy."

She nodded, more to silence him than anything else.

To her left, Mark and Glynia were engaged in rapt conversation about Glynia's latest modeling job, though Glynia's attention strayed for an instant, her jade eyes narrowing in Amy's direction.

As if aware that he had spoken out of turn, Rob said, "It's going to be strange not to have you living next door."

"I know. I'm still wondering if I'll ever adjust to an apartment after living in Gramp's house most of my life," she said casually, more and more bewildered by Rob's attitude. She bit into her herb bread, turning to listen to the others as they spoke of more familiar things—the weather, the upcoming county elections, the national news. To her relief, nothing more was said about moving, nor about Mark's invitation for her to accompany him to San Francisco.

After dinner, Amy insisted on clearing the table, partly to give herself time alone to consider Mark's offer. Yet, as she placed the dirty dishes and silverware in the dishwasher, her mind played tricks on her. How could she make a decision if she couldn't even sort out the pros and cons of the matter? Gradually she calmed herself enough to think clearly.

Rob's disapproval had been evident and, undoubtedly, others would consider it improper for her to travel with a man. Valerie, for one. Yet the trip sounded so perfect for her—just what she needed after the long months of caring for Gramp, and it would challenge her writing skills. Both the negative and positive aspects of the decision whirled through her head. If it were any other man but Mark. . . . At last the kitchen was spotless, with

35

only the copper pot full of spaghetti cooling on the stove, and there were no more excuses to remain inside.

At that moment Catherine stepped in through the French doors. "I thought we'd have lemon sherbet and chocolate chip cookies for dessert," she said, starting for the enormous stainless steel refrigerator-freezer that was often used for her catering jobs. "Didn't I promise family fare?"

"There's something very comforting about spaghetti and chocolate chip cookies," Amy agreed. "Let me help." Good. A little more time would be gained to delay the decision about San Francisco, which was still circling elusively in her mind—and to avoid the confrontation with Rob.

Carrying out the dessert, Amy felt a pang of dismay to see that Mark and Glynia had changed into swimsuits and were dragging her parents' small sailboat across the beach. While the rest of them devoured sherbet and cookies, Mark and Glynia sailed away, the bright red and white sail billowing.

After dessert Valerie excused herself, and Rob asked the Marstons, "Would you mind if Amy and I took a walk along the beach?"

"Certainly not. Go right ahead," Dr. Marston replied with a curious look at them. "Catherine and I usually stroll after dinner ourselves."

"Thanks. Excuse us then," Rob said, rising from his chair.

Amy saw no other course than to accompany him. In any event, it was a beautiful evening, and cerise-stained clouds near the horizon promised a magnificent sunset.

She and Rob walked over the sandy hillside and down toward the ocean. Trying to forget the unsettling issues before her, she gazed out at the bright blue Pacific. Great waves gathered in the distance and roared in upon the beach, crashing and rushing toward them, only to foam into pearly patterns in the sand at their feet. Catherine had said the ocean always had a calming effect on her. Now, however, it seemed to reflect the turbulence of Amy's thoughts.

They wandered along the beach in silence for a time before Rob ventured, "I hope you don't mind my not asking you first about a walk . . . but I was afraid you'd refuse."

"Why would I?"

"I don't know. Maybe it's because everything seems so different now that you're staying here. I'm not always the most tactful person either. I suffer from what your grandfather called 'foot in the mouth disease'."

She smiled wryly. "I suppose you're going to issue a warning about my going to San Francisco."

"Not very subtle, am I?"

"It's just that I'm not sure I understand your concern."

"No, I suppose you don't." They strolled quietly on past the other beach houses, then beside the rugged cliffs, listening to the ocean. After a while he began nervously, "I don't know quite how to tell you that— that I've grown to like you very much, Amy—"

She had not expected any kind of a declaration, nor had she ever seen such a vulnerable look on Rob's face. "I like you, too, Rob. But—"

"I know we've always been more like brother and sister, living next door to each other, but lately I've come to feel differently about you."

No! I don't want to hear this now! she wanted to say, but then it was too late and his arm was around her, turning her to him in the warm evening breeze.

"Oh, Amy!" he whispered hoarsely against the ocean's persistent roar.

She was aware only of spreading streaks of pink and orange as the sun began its descent into the sea, then she closed her eyes, and his lips met hers. She knew she should pull away, but something in her yearned so desperately to be held, to be kissed, that she found herself yielding.

His mouth was soft at first, hesitant, then sweetly demanding, and she found herself slipping her arms around his neck and her lips responding with such an amazing surge of passion that the brilliant colors of the sunstruck clouds seemed to blaze through her.

Rob pulled away, catching his breath. "I had no idea you'd feel this way too."

I didn't either! she thought. All through her teen years she had only imagined what it might be like to be kissed by a real man. There had been only a few sloppy kisses at parties, delivered inexpertly from boys rejected by the slender, pretty girls. It was different with Rob, whose hands still gripped her shoulders, whose brown eyes revealed that he meant to kiss her again.

Once more, his familiar face tilted down toward hers, his eyes closing, his lips poised above hers. Over his shoulder, a bright object bobbing in the swelling ocean caught Amy's attention. It was Mark and Glynia in the sailboat!

Amy pressed both hands firmly against Rob's chest. The sailboat was precisely where she and Mark had treaded water this afternoon, a good distance away. Nevertheless, she felt certain they were watching.

"What is it? What's wrong?" Rob asked.

She shook her head helplessly.

"Amy—?" His voice was full of confusion, compounding her own.

"Oh, Rob, I don't know—"

"But, I thought . . . you seemed to . . ." Sensing her dilemma, Rob drew a deep breath. "Surely this wasn't your first kiss, Amy."

"Not exactly . . ." How embarrassing that he should think so. Couldn't she do anything right where men were concerned?

He looked momentarily relieved. "I don't want to rush you," he said, apparently still unaware of the sailboat on the horizon. "Maybe we should start back."

"Yes, we'd better."

She wanted to extract her hand from his as they strolled back along the beach, but it would seem odd after having returned his kiss with such wild abandon. Looking out at the ocean, she realized that Mark and Glynia were sailing in to shore, and that the sunset was a disappointment. A typical May cloudbank had rolled in, shrouding the promise of a wondrously hued sky. Without fanfare, the sun slid out of sight.

They walked along silently, absorbed in their own thoughts. As they approached the Marston house in the last lingering rays of light, Rob said, "I care about you very much, Amy, and I'm awfully concerned about your being with Mark. Just the thought of you two going to San Francisco alone worries me sick. You know his reputation."

She eased her hand from Rob's, but he continued undaunted. "Women throw themselves at him. Everyone talks about it. You know about that girl, Erika—"

"But that wasn't his fault," Amy responded, dismissing doubts that flickered in the deepest recesses of her mind.

"How do you know?"

She shrugged. He would probably have a difficult time believing her if she told him that Catherine—Mark's mother!—had explained what had happened. Nor would Rob understand her belief that Mark was a fine man, despite the anger that often ignited him now. Besides, it had all happened when Mark was working in New York. How could people here pretend to know?

"Mark Marston's type takes advantage of women— especially innocent ones," Rob persevered. "I suppose someone like Glynia could handle it, but I don't think you should go with him."

"I appreciate your concern, Rob," she said more stiffly than she had intended, "but I'm going to have to make my own decision." She only hoped that her decision would be the right one. There had been too many disappointments in her life already, too many cloudbanks obscuring the sunsets.

When they returned to the patio, Catherine and James Marston were sitting on the swing, enjoying the evening. In the descending darkness, the old brass lanterns on the low wall glimmered softly, imparting such a nautical air to the patio that it seemed they had stepped onto the deck of a ship at the edge of the sea.

"Did you have a nice walk?" Dr. Marston asked.

"Yes, thank you," Rob replied, sending a bright flush to Amy's cheeks.

"Very nice," Amy added nervously, although it wasn't quite true. The walk—and Rob's declaration and kiss—had only added to her confusion.

Catherine glanced out toward the ocean. "Here come Mark and Glynia."

Amy watched the two of them drag the small sailboat along the sand to the edge of her parents' patio. Minutes later, an outdoor floodlight illuminated the impressive Bennington house of wood and glass. Glynia's mother and stepfather were visiting in the south of France for the month and would stop on their return in Virginia to attend Valerie's and Thom's wedding. What had brought Glynia from New York to an empty house? Amy wondered. Mark's presence in Santa Rosita? And if so, why was it any concern of hers?

As Amy and Rob settled on the couch, the French doors opened and Valerie carried out a guitar. "I was feeling so lonely that I hoped you'd sing for us," she said to Catherine. "It would remind me of the nights Thom and I have spent here with you."

"We haven't sung together in a long time," her husband added. "It's just the night for it."

Catherine patted his arm and took the guitar to the chaise lounge. Sitting down, she ran her fingers lightly over the strings, then twiddled one of the tuning pegs. "There. That's a little better. Any requests?"

Valerie suggested, "How about *Greensleeves*? That seems to suit the evening."

Catherine sat back thoughtfully, then began strumming, her melodious contralto voice blending with the chords of the guitar and the deep symphonic chorus of the sea. " 'Alas, my love, you do me wrong, to cast me off . . .' "

As they all joined in the refrain, Rob caught Amy's hand in his. Again, she felt reluctant to pull it away. The next moment Mark and Glynia stepped onto the patio, Mark's eyes taking in the cozy twosome. He quickly turned away, seating Glynia and taking the chair opposite her. Amy took the opportunity to withdraw her hand from Rob's, hoping no one would conclude that there was any kind of commitment between them.

The voices blended harmoniously to the rousing strains of "Michael Rowed the Boat Ashore" and "I'd Like to Teach the World to Sing." Then Catherine chose "Evergreen," dedicating it to Valerie and Thom, humming the haunting melody until she had quieted the singers and there was not another sound except the mellow strings and her voice. When the poignant words of love filled the night air, Amy felt such an aching in her heart that her eyes stung with tears. Feeling Mark's gaze upon her, she quickly looked out at the approaching fog that crept over the ocean, blotting out the stars overhead. It was as if they alone had floated away to sea, as if all of them had embarked on an ethereal dream.

" 'Now the day is over,' " Catherine sang into the stillness, " 'night is drawing nigh, shadows of the evening steal across the sky.' " A brass lantern glimmered just behind her, softly silhouetting her lovely profile. " 'Jesus, give the weary calm and sweet repose, with Thy tenderest blessing, may mine eyelids close.' " It was obvious that she was no longer singing for them, but singing to God like a loving child, her voice full of trust and joy. " 'Through the long night watches, may Thine angels spread their white wings above me, watching round my bed . . . When the morning wakens, then may I arise, pure and fresh and sinless in Thy holy eyes.' "

Her soft and lingering "Amen" hung in the air, and Amy knew that it was not just to hear Catherine's voice that the others begged her to sing, but to glimpse her wondrous faith. It occurred to her that if she had such faith herself, she wouldn't be wallowing about in indecision; she would be asking God for answers. And perhaps she would have Catherine's inner joy. She recalled that the older woman had once said, "Joy is the song of love that God plants in one's heart."

After a while Catherine sighed. "Bedtime for us."

Rob rose with them. "Thank you for a delicious dinner and a beautiful evening." His words were heartfelt. "I don't know when I've enjoyed myself more."

Dr. Marston shook his hand. "Our pleasure."

Joining her husband, Catherine added, "Yes, Rob, we

41

hope you'll come again," before they bade everyone a good-night and made their way inside.

"Guess I'd better head home too," Rob decided. "I'm tired after that trip."

As Amy walked with him out to his car, he asked, "Are they always like that . . . so loving?"

"Dr. and Mrs. Marston, always," she replied, but her thoughts ran on, *Mark is another matter.* "They're a very special family."

He gave an odd chuckle. "I think I'm jealous."

"Why should you be?" She hoped he understood what she was implying: *that she was not committed to him or to anyone else, nor did she want to be!*

Despite the impression she had tried to convey, when they arrived at his car he attempted to draw her into his arms.

"No, Rob, please—"

He backed away reluctantly, brows furrowed with confusion in the dim driveway lighting, then climbed into his brown Mustang. "See you tomorrow?" he asked hopefully.

"I don't know what the Marstons have planned yet."

"I'll phone." He turned the key in the ignition, still searching her face.

"Fine."

She watched Rob back his car out of the driveway, suddenly realizing that she should have mentioned his daisies again, but he was already edging into the street, the car's headlights piercing the grayness of the night. In its beam, she noted that Val had parked Gramp's old blue Chevy to the side of the Marstons' garage.

On the patio she found Mark waiting to lock the gate, apparently having seen Glynia home along the beach. It seemed a long moment while they gazed at each other through the billowing fog. "I hope you'll go with me to San Francisco," he urged in his rich baritone.

"I don't know—" She wanted to go! Oh, how she wanted to! Yet perhaps it was better to play it safe.

"We haven't discussed your pay," Mark continued. When he named the amount, she was astounded. The sum was as unreal as the fog swirling around them. That much for exploring a city and writing a report on it? She could certainly use the financial help. The probate attorney said it would be a long time before Gramp's estate was settled, and that there would not be much left after taxes, fees, and medical bills. There was little to occupy her time in Santa Rosita now since her part in the wedding plans was completed. Moreover, she truly wanted to see San Francisco.

"Thank you, Mark," she found herself saying, "I think I'll take you up on your offer." She wasn't sure whether her reply was prompted by the money . . . by the spell of the evening . . . or by her endless attraction to him.

"Fine. Good-night then . . . Amy." His voice caressed her name. It was as if he had called her *dear* or *darling* for the first time.

"Yes . . . good-night." She turned away abruptly and hurried into the house, scarcely seeing Rob's daisies as she fled through the kitchen, then upstairs to the sanctuary of her room.

CHAPTER 3

ON SUNDAY MORNING the whole Marston clan, including Valerie, gathered to see Amy and Mark off to San Francisco. There was a last-minute flurry of hugs and kisses and promises to keep each other posted.

"Whew!" Mark sighed, nosing the blue BMW northward. "You'd think we were leaving forever."

"In a sense, we are, I suppose," Amy mused as she gave a final wave. "Maybe that's why the rite of waving good-by has lasted through the years. We never know if we'll see the others again or, if we do, how all of us might have changed in the meantime."

He turned a wry grin on her. "The poet speaketh."

"Guess I've done it again," she laughed.

More important at the moment, she thought, "the poet" was grateful to be getting away. Yesterday hadn't been easy. The pressure had mounted with Valerie's warnings about Mark's sophistication, his reputation with women. Rob, who had taken her out last night for a hamburger and a movie, had echoed Valerie's concern. And Glynia, who had spent most of yesterday with Mark, had glared at her furiously.

Mark asked, "Mind if I turn on the radio?"

"No—not at all," she murmured, feeling suddenly

aware of Mark's masculinity, so close now within the compact car.

Moments later, soft music swirling from the radio heightened the aura of intimate proximity. Directing a hasty glance at him, she decided that it must be her imagination, that he had no special motive for choosing romantic music. Indeed, Mark's attention seemed riveted on the road ahead.

They ventured a few tentative remarks about the possibility of rain, then shifted to a discussion of the scenery and occasional bits of news from the radio. As they passed the university district, Amy pointed out the new apartment building in which she would live after the wedding, and Mark mentioned that it was very near the church his grandfather had pastored.

Halfway to Los Angeles he said, "I have to stop at the condo to pick up my secretary's reports and gather some other things together. You can freshen up there if you'd like."

Amy nodded. She *was* curious to see how he lived, though she knew Rob would be appalled if he knew she was contemplating a visit to Mark's apartment. A phrase from an old nursery rhyme hovered disconcertingly: *"Step into my parlor, said the spider to the fly."*

Last night during her date with Rob, she hadn't been able to summon the courage to tell him she was going to San Francisco until they pulled into the Marstons' driveway.

"You mean you're really going with that guy?" Rob had asked incredulously.

A bubble of laughter escaped her. "Yes, of course. I'm not going alone."

It was obvious that he didn't find her amusing as he turned off the motor and frowned into the darkness. "I suppose there's nothing I can say to make you change your mind?"

"No, Rob—I've already given my word."

He opened his car door angrily, but at the Marstons' front door his mood softened. "Amy—," he whispered pulling her into his arms, "—please don't go. Please take my word for it—Mark Marston is a—"

45

"But I've promised," she interrupted. "I've known Mark practically all my life. Besides, this is strictly business."

"I hope so," he yielded with a note of helplessness. As his head inclined toward hers, she ducked, causing his kiss to land awkwardly somewhere in the vicinity of her left ear. But he held her an instant longer before moving away. "I hope so."

Amy's thoughts returned to the present, and she glanced uneasily at Mark, then out the car window.

Sunday morning traffic was light on the San Diego Freeway, even in the outskirts of Los Angeles. Mark took the Santa Monica Boulevard off-ramp and drove beyond Century City before pulling up beside a tall tan stucco building, a "skyscraper" by West Los Angeles standards.

"I'm impressed," she said as he helped her out of the car. "I didn't expect anything quite so elegant."

"Oh, I'm only leasing, piling up a lot of useless rent receipts."

Exactly what she'd soon be doing, Amy thought with a pang of regret.

Inside, only a few people wandered through the small marble lobby. Mark and Amy took the elevator to the top floor. Stepping out into the posh corridor, she noted a swimming pool, artfully landscaped with potted trees, shrubs, and flowers.

"You didn't tell me you had the penthouse!"

"Albeit leased," he reminded her. "The owners should be back from Europe midweek. Fortunately they're letting me store most of my things here until I can find somewhere else to live."

As he unlocked the condo's shimmering stainless steel double doors, Amy couldn't help imagining that they were entering an expensive vault. Something within her recoiled at the cold austerity of the ultra-modern entry. The living room was a vast expanse of brown carpeting, white leather couches and chairs, dangling silver mobiles, and outrageously modern paintings, heavily daubed with yellow and orange oil paints.

46

"What do you think?" Mark inquired.

"The plants are lovely—"

He chuckled. "I take it you're not wild about the decor."

"It's just that it's such a contrast to the antiques in your parents' house—"

"The furniture belongs to the owners," he explained, "but the place has been ideal for me. And within walking distance of my office." He eyed the furnishings critically. "The space-age decor has been an interesting change, but in the words of the old cliché, 'It's a nice place to visit, but I wouldn't want to live here.'"

She felt strangely relieved. She too preferred rooms that looked warm and inviting—more hospitable.

He opened the draperies, and she was stunned by the view of the city and distant foothills through the sparkling floor-to-ceiling windows. "What a magnificent view of Los Angeles!"

He smiled. "That's what I enjoy most too. Now, if you'll excuse me—" He headed for the adjoining den to use the telephone. "The bath is down the hallway," he said, "and there's instant coffee in the kitchen cabinet over the microwave."

"May I make some for you?" Amy asked, but he had already disappeared into the next room.

"No, thanks," he called out. She could hear the staccato sound of digits being dialed on the touchtone phone.

She found her way to the bathroom. Now was a good time to use the facilities; the drive to San Francisco would take most of the day.

The bathroom was no less modernistic, with its enormous white marble tub and Jacuzzi. A wall-to-wall mirror reflected the browns and white of the room, the monotony relieved only by a dish of lemon yellow soaps. How utterly unhappy she would be to live in such a stark place, she thought. As she brushed her hair, she noted another color: green. A filmy nightgown of jade green was hanging on a hook behind the bathroom door.

Appalled, yet fascinated, she felt herself drawn to

examine the gown. Embroidered in exquisite letters on one side of the deeply plunging bodice it said: Glynia.

Oh, Mark! Amy's heart cried out. *So it is true! I didn't believe . . . I thought you were different. Why couldn't you be—special?*

As they drove away from the condo, Mark donned his sunglasses. Behind them, he could assume any guise he chose. There was no way to read his true emotions. Suddenly Amy felt completely out of his league. It was obvious that he traveled the fast lane, where the so-called sophisticates sped through life. She felt unexpectedly angry.

After a long silence he asked, "Anything wrong?"

How transparent she must be, she thought, and carefully ignored his question. "Did you pick up your secretary's reports on Los Angeles and San Diego? I thought I might read them on the way."

"They're on top of my briefcase in the back seat," Mark replied, watching the light traffic as they headed back for the freeway. "In the manila envelope. There's a folder full of tourist information on San Francisco too."

Amy unfastened her seat belt and leaned over the headrest. The manila envelope was just beyond her grasp. Well, there seemed to be no other way to retrieve it but to turn around in her seat, kneeling as best she could. Not a very ladylike position, especially in her tan dress with its straight skirt, she thought. The car swerved and she found herself thrown against Mark's shoulder, his touch jolting her like an electric shock.

"Sorry," he apologized abruptly.

She caught her breath and moved away. "It's . . . all right." Envelope in hand, she settled back into her seat. Hopefully he was unaware of his galvanizing effect on her.

Surveying the nearby traffic, she wondered why Mark had swerved. There were no cars particularly close to them, nor had he changed lanes. Had he been that intrigued with her indecorous position? Maybe she really didn't know Mark anymore. Unnerved, she refastened her seat belt.

As they merged back onto the freeway, she was grateful to have the material to occupy her mind. The reports were not terribly well written, as Mark had clearly warned. But Amy was confident of her own writing ability, so she felt no real qualms about the work ahead. Instead, the pressure she was feeling came from Mark's nearness.

After Los Angeles and its sprawl of endless suburbs disappeared behind them, they curved for miles through green and tan foothills, seemingly entering another country.

Mark turned and smiled at her. "When I'm out here," he said, "I always feel as if my responsibilities are over and I can look forward to adventure ahead."

"What sort of adventure?" she inquired a trifle warily.

He darted an odd glance at her. "Travel is an adventure. Don't you agree?"

"I'm afraid I haven't traveled enough to know," she retorted and turned to the reports again. Why on earth was she letting him get under her skin? Why couldn't she forget things that were none of her business—things like Glynia's nightgown hanging on his bathroom door?

Before long, they were descending into the San Joaquin Valley, a flat land filled with rectangular green fields of irrigated alfalfa, tomatoes, cotton, and crops neither of them could identify. Occasional palo verde trees and tamarisks grew at the roadsides, and, here and there, windbreaks of eucalyptus trees swayed over distant farmhouses.

Amy decided to interrupt the uncomfortable silence. "Gramp, Valerie, and I drove through here once on the way to Yosemite," she said. "He used to take us camping. Have you ever done any camping?"

"With the Boy Scouts."

"Of course! I forgot you were in scouting."

He added thoughtfully, "It seems a long time ago."

"Looking at you now, it's hard to believe that you were once a—boy, let alone a Boy Scout."

He gave her an amused glance. "I'm not *that* old."

She laughed. "Actually, I didn't mean it entirely as a

joke." She tried to explain. "It's just that time seems to have no meaning. What I'm trying to say is . . . recent events sometimes seem to have taken place eons ago. Yet, on the other hand, I remember moments from my childhood as if they happened yesterday." For example, she thought, the frequent dream in which she vividly relived the death of her parents. But she didn't want to dwell on the past. "Tell me about your scouting days."

Their conversation moved between childhood recollections and the scenery of the valley. Slowly Amy's distrust diminished as she pondered the stories Mark was sharing. How unlikely it seemed now that he had ever been shy among other children, or apprehensive about swimming in a river or about learning to ski. Whenever silence fell, she returned to her reading matter. It seemed a pleasant enough way to spend the morning.

It was well after lunchtime before Mark pulled off the freeway for gas at what appeared to be the world's largest rest stop. They climbed out of the car to stretch, and he slid his dark glasses up into his hair. "Hungry?" he asked, studying the fast food restaurants nearby.

"A little."

"I'm afraid none of these places looks very enticing."

"But your mother packed a lunch for us."

He grinned. "She didn't tell me."

"Apples and crackers and cheese. She said you were especially fond of apples." For some reason Amy was reminded of the biblical account of the temptation of Adam and Eve and their infamous apple, and she almost laughed aloud. Shrugging off the notion, she continued, "The bag is in the trunk."

"Would you mind eating in the car?" he asked as they went around to the back of the car. "We could save time if we drove straight through. We can eat on the way—if you'd help me."

She suspected this was not the first time Mark had traveled alone with a woman. A mental picture of the glamorous Glynia, feeding Mark a cluster of ripe grapes rose, unbidden, and Amy felt a twinge of resentment.

"It's an old family custom," he explained, unlocking

50

the trunk, "especially when driving through the San Joaquin Valley. The valley may be an agricultural marvel, but it's not one of the garden spots of the world. If you recall, the faster the ride's over, the better."

She nodded in remembrance, her resentment fading. It would be a dreary drive if one traveled with less . . . intriguing company than Mark. "Far be it for me to interfere with a . . . *family* . . . custom," she replied with an attempt at levity.

"We'll make up for it tonight at dinner." He peered into the brown sack among their luggage. "Here it is. There's even the little cutting board and an old knife. Let's buy something to drink in the station."

As they resumed the drive, Amy served lunch from the brown bag spread across her lap. There was a special warmth to the ritual of spreading cheese on wheat crackers for him, their fingers touching as she handed them to him—and later the slices of apple.

"My fingers are getting cheesy," he said, wiping his hands on a tissue. "Would you mind putting the food into my mouth?"

"Another old custom?" she inquired wryly.

"Yes, come to think of it."

"Well, here goes," Amy laughed as she fed Mark a cracker with cheese.

At first he was restrained as she placed the bits of food in his mouth, but then a sense of mischief overcame him and he pretended to nip at her fingers. She laughed at first, but his expression changed as his eyes met hers with sudden passion.

"Mark, please—"

"This is much nicer than eating in a rest stop," he said, casting an appreciative glance at her and ignoring the huge trucks roaring by.

"Eyes on the road," she said with uncertainty.

"And if I'd rather look at you?"

"Better watch the road—"

He smiled, the creases around his lips deepening far too engagingly.

He'd merely been teasing her, she decided, and it

51

wouldn't do to take him seriously. Not now. Not with the evidence of a romantic relationship with Glynia hanging in his bathroom. This was not the Mark she had adored. Suddenly she wondered what their room arrangements might be when they arrived in San Francisco. Why hadn't she asked about them at yesterday's breakfast when he'd explained the details of her job? She cast an apprehensive look at him as he finished his lunch, realizing how quickly the old attraction had reasserted itself—even though she should be outraged by his behavior.

As if reading her mind, his mood turned somber, his angular chin slowly taking on a stubborn expression as he concentrated on his driving. Apparently the pleasant interlude was at an end. He had been friendly, had even seemed interested in her. But something had changed and he had withdrawn once again.

Amy's mind darted to her conversation with Dr. Marston yesterday.

She'd been strolling along the beach with him, and he'd said, "Val has strongly hinted that she disapproves of your going to San Francisco with Mark, but I think she has the wrong impression of him. A lot of people do."

Amy gazed out at the ocean. In their bedroom Valerie had made her feelings quite clear. "Mark is different from the rest of the family, Amy—different and dangerous. He's chosen to follow another path for his life, and if you're not careful, you could get hurt."

Over the sounds of the surf, Dr. Marston continued. "Mark's a lot like I used to be."

"Like you used to be?"

He laughed at her amazement. "Believe me, there are no rebels like preacher's kids!"

"But you were a medical missionary—"

"That was after my rebellious stage, and after I married Catherine."

Amy shook her head. "It's hard to believe you were ever a rebel."

Dr. Marston smiled. "Faith can make a lot of surprising changes in a person."

"I suppose so," she replied politely, unconvinced.

Mark blasted his horn at a passing truck as it cut too closely in front of them, jarring Amy from her memories.

"Idiot!" he growled, his brow furrowing in disapproval.

His mood did not seem to be improving, she thought, returning to the brochures and articles in the manila envelope. The envelope included paperwork for the Travel Agents' Convention and Conference that Mark would be attending, and there was even a page entitled, "Spouses' Activities." Perhaps these tours would be a good way to see the city for the first time, if she was allowed to participate. The Spouses' Schedule of Events included a welcoming coffee, followed by tours of the city, Victorian homes, Filoli Gardens, Alcatraz, wine country, Chinatown, and special activities like a Chinese cooking class and a shopping excursion.

After another glimpse of Mark's obdurate expression, she decided not to inquire about the tours now; she could check on them with the Spouses' Activity Chairperson in the morning. Or perhaps she could arrange for tours on her own through the hotel. He had been so quiet since lunch that she was beginning to wonder if he was already regretting having brought her along. If she only knew more about men!

Hours later, as they approached San Francisco, Amy pulled out the area map and her notebook. Better to make too many notes than not enough, she thought, and began to record her impressions as they drove through Livermore, then the suburbs of Oakland. Traffic grew steadily heavier until they were hurtling through four lanes of cars and trucks in downtown Oakland. In the distance she spotted the twin towers of a high-arching bridge spanning an expanse of brilliant blue water.

"The Bay Bridge?"

"Yes."

"Then, according to the map, that's San Francisco Bay! It's all going too fast—"

Amy struggled to capture visual images on paper—"driving through the sky on the long Bay Bridge," "the perfect marriage of God's creativity and man's ingenuity," "sailboats skimming the surface of the sea; freighters plowing a watery furrow," "Gates of splendor—the Golden Gate Bridge," "sunstruck city." At last, she put down her pen, forgetting her notes.

"It's magnificent—"

She was only vaguely aware of Mark's reflective smile as he said, "Yes, that it is. One of the most beautiful cities on earth."

"Now I see why everyone raves about it—"

Suddenly they were driving down into the breathtaking city, merging with the five o'clock bustle of homebound shoppers and workers who spilled out of shops and towering office buildings, surging impatiently around traffic lights at each block. People streamed into noisy buses and subway stations, many of the men wearing suits, the women in dark business attire; these urbanites exuded energy even at the end of the workday, filling their city with a shimmering excitement.

"We're staying just off Union Square," Mark offered, calm despite the impossible traffic.

Amy located the hotel on her city map. "Thank goodness you know the way!"

"I've been here a few times," he commented in that understated way of his.

"So I assumed." She suspected that he was amused with her naïveté. Well, she would most certainly manage. He had revealed so little about his plans, with the exception of attending the travel agents' convention, that she would simply have to find her own way around to do the research.

Minutes later they drove through scenic Union Square, surrounded by some of the world's most elegant shops, then pulled into the hotel's carriage entrance.

Uniformed attendants took charge of the car and luggage, then led them to the hotel's spacious lobby, a bastion of old-world luxury with its ivory marble floors, Oriental carpets, dark wooden columns, and potted palms.

"Tired?" Mark asked her.

54

"A little. But you must be exhausted after all that driving."

"Not bad. Excuse me. I'll see about our registration."

"I'd prefer to register for my own room—"

"I'll take care of it," he said firmly and started for the registration counter.

Feeling a flutter of panic, Amy sat uneasily on an antique couch next to a potted palm. If Mark's plans were unsuitable, she would simply demand a change.

She gazed about the lobby. At the far end a string quartet was playing semi-classical music in the lounge. Behind her a hallway led to the elevators, sedate shops and a dining room. It was without a doubt the most exquisite hotel she had ever seen. It would be sure to impress foreign visitors, too, affording them a glimpse of old San Francisco. She pulled out her notebook to jot down ideas for her report.

When she looked up, Mark was approaching with a bellman in tow. There was a curious intimacy suggested by their luggage, placed side by side on the portable rack. "All set."

In the elevator Amy noticed the stares of the other occupants. Did they think that she and Mark were newlyweds? Or that they—? She wondered what his grandfather, the minister, would say about the impression they might be giving. Oh, why had she agreed to come?

As the bellman let them into a seventh-floor suite, Amy felt as if she had walked into the pages of an exclusive house and garden magazine. The small living room, furnished with antiques, commanded a lovely view of the city and the bay. Doors on either side led to small but elegant bedrooms, each with its own bath. But she would never need all this space! Mark was being more than generous.

She opened her mouth to tell him so, when the bellman interrupted. "I hope this will be satisfactory, sir."

Mark turned to her, his blue eyes holding a question. "All right with you, Amy?"

Her mouth remained open! Mark expected to share this suite with her!

"Sorry about the mix-up sir," the bellman was saying.

Amy found her voice. "Mix-up?" she echoed stupidly.

"Through some error, they had booked us in one room." Mark looked uncomfortable.

"Happens in the best of hotels," the bellman injected hastily. "I'm surprised this suite was available, with the hotel so full."

"Yes," Mark agreed. "I made sure of that. What about it, Amy? It appears we have no choice."

She exhaled slowly. Was this a ruse? After the disturbing discovery of Glynia's nightgown earlier in the day, she hardly knew what to believe. But she supposed this arrangement was not much different from staying in the Marston home, with Mark's bedroom just down the hall from the guest room.

"I—I suppose it's all right."

The bellman showed them the television set, concealed behind the doors of a lovely walnut armoire, then placed the luggage in their rooms. Mark quickly handed the man folded bills.

"Thank you, sir," the bellman said, backing out with curious looks at both of them.

What must he really be thinking? Amy wondered again. Nowadays everyone seemed to assume the worst.

"I guess we ought to unpack," Mark suggested, still looking chagrined. "I've made reservations for dinner at eight in one of the dining rooms. I hope that's not too late for you."

"No, eight is fine." She didn't recall ever having seen Mark embarrassed, and it made her feel awkward too. "Besides, there's food right here in the room. Your favorite—apples," she added, handing him the bowl of fruit that had been placed on the coffee table.

As he reached for a red apple, she could not resist saying, "Just like Adam and Eve—" She caught the incredulous look on Mark's face. "Oh, dear! Now I've done it!"

He burst into laughter, and she couldn't help smiling, though she knew her face was crimson.

"Now *that* I didn't expect from you," he said, still chuckling.

56

At least her blunder had relieved the tension between them. Selecting some grapes, she headed for her room. "See you later," she tossed back, though not as blithely as she had intended. Of all things to have said to Mark— and under these circumstances! Adam and Eve, indeed! She was instantly sobered by another thought from her Sunday school days. After the temptation in the Garden of Eden had come the fall.

Closing the bedroom door behind her, Amy noticed the lock. She turned it as slowly and quietly as possible, but the bolt slid into place with a loud snap, the sound no doubt carrying into the living room. Now Mark knew she didn't quite trust him, she thought ruefully. And maybe it was just as well! She had no intention of allowing him another easy conquest. *Her* nightgown would never hang on his bathroom door!

CHAPTER 4

POISED TO LEAVE HER bedroom for dinner later in the evening, Amy glanced in the full-length mirror and was again pleasantly surprised to find the reflection of a slender young woman. She paused an instant longer to coax wisps of dark brown hair into curls to frame her face. Her hair, caught back in a soft coil at the nape of her neck, helped to achieve a semblance of sophistication as did the touches of turquoise eye shadow that heightened the color of her eyes. The white silky dress she had chosen, with its modest V-neck, long sleeves and slightly flared skirt, made her feel deliciously feminine.

She knew very well that her "look," as the fashion magazines termed it, was likely that of an ingénue dressed for cosmopolitan San Francisco. Unfortunately, she did not have the high-fashion flare of a Glynia, nor did she really want to resemble the models in the more outrageous fashion magazines. Despite her best efforts to effect an appearance somewhere between Glynia's glamorous one and her own, she hadn't quite brought it off; she still looked everlastingly and hopelessly unsophisticated . . . and young.

A tremor of anticipation stirred through her, and she took a deep breath to steady herself. She must not seem too eager. She allowed her eyes to sweep the bedroom, decorated in ivory, pale sea-green, and shades of peach. The room was neat, her belongings put away; there had been time to unpack, shower, and dress at leisure, but now it was seven-thirty. Mark had turned on the television set in the living room some time ago and was obviously waiting. Moreover, she was starved.

Catching up her white clutch bag from the bed, she hurried to the door. When she attempted to unlock it, the bolt snapped back into place loudly. She stepped out into the living room, expecting a wry comment from Mark.

But he quickly rose from the pale green couch, his eyes filling with undisguised admiration. "Don't you look lovely!"

"Thank you, Mark," she smiled, pleased by his sincere compliment. "You look nice yourself." To her own ears, her reply sounded abysmally trite. What would Glynia have said? And how did a woman tell a man that he was strikingly handsome, and that it didn't make a particle of difference if he were wearing jeans or a three-piece navy blue suit as Mark was tonight? His dark hair was neatly brushed, his face freshly shaven, and she had to quash an overwhelming urge to touch one of the creases by his lips with her fingertips.

"Thanks. Ready to go? It's a little early, but we could peruse the hotel shops before dinner."

"Fine. I'm eager to learn my way around."

He switched off the travel documentary on the television set. "Since we'll be so busy the rest of our time here, I haven't planned a big evening out tonight."

"Isn't it strange? I don't feel at all tired. Too excited, I suppose."

He leveled an ironic look at her, but said nothing, and she reminded herself that she must be more careful in her choice of words.

In the hallway he said almost too casually, "Oh, by the way, Rob phoned."

"Rob phoned? Here?"

"Yes, apparently he wanted to make sure we'd arrived safely."

"But you didn't call me—"

"I knocked on your door, but you didn't answer. It sounded as if your shower was running."

"Oh, you didn't tell him that I was in the—shower?"

He smiled broadly. "No. Only that you didn't answer when I knocked on your door." As if reading her thoughts, Mark added, "That seemed unsettling enough for him." He couldn't quite maintain a straight face.

She glared at him. "Thanks so much."

"Not at all," he responded with amusement.

"Any other calls?" It would not be surprising to hear that Valerie had phoned too, since everyone apparently assumed little Amy was unable to handle her life without help.

"No, just Rob. Don't tell me there's a whole string of boyfriends!"

"No . . . and Rob's not a boy. He *is* twenty-five years old!"

"I beg your pardon," Mark returned, not looking terribly apologetic.

Since he seemed so entertained by Rob's call, she was tempted to ask if he had talked to Glynia, but held her tongue. Besides, she was unsure whether she really wanted to know what transpired between the two of them.

Fortunately the elevator was empty so there was no one to scrutinize them on their descent.

Stepping out into the elegant lobby, Mark checked his watch. "We have twenty minutes for window-shopping along the way."

"Wonderful!"

Minutes later, they passed impressive hallway windows displaying the latest designer clothing, luxury toys, expensive candies, and perfumes. "'Window-shopping' is the most accurate term for it!" Amy laughingly exclaimed. "Marvelous purchases for your foreign tourists to take home, if they happen to be very wealthy! I suppose this hotel is top dollar or franc or yen?"

He nodded. "It's one of the most expensive, but we try to arrange tours to meet all budgets. . . ." He paused.

"Travel agents, of course, receive lower rates for convention visits such as this."

"The Marston streak for honesty coming out in you?" she teased, thinking that another man might have exploited a stay in such an elegant hotel just to impress her.

"Honesty?" He chuckled. "There's only been one minister in the family as far back as we know. Who knows what renegades lurk in my family tree?"

Mark has chosen a different path, Valerie had warned.

As they passed the hotel's sundries shop, Mark said, "I forgot to pack toothpaste." He eyed her small white clutch purse. "Do you suppose there'd be room for a small tube in your purse?"

She thought about offering to share her own toothpaste, but that would surely be inviting disaster, since he would have to wear a path to her door. "If it's very small."

"Maybe we'd better take care of that now," he said. "The shop might be closed by the time we've finished dinner."

She followed him into the brightly lit area and, as Mark made his purchase, Amy investigated the rack of paperback novels; several looked interesting, but there would be little time for casual reading on this trip. When she looked up, Mark was at the cash register, paying the bill, and two attractive women shoppers were eying him with great interest.

Mark must have noticed their attention, for he flushed under his tan as he strode over to Amy and handed her the toothpaste. "I hope you don't mind."

"Not at all." She tucked the small carton in her purse, thinking that at least he had the good grace to be embarrassed when women ogled him so brazenly while he was in the presence of a date . . . or, for all they knew, his wife.

Outside the shop, Amy suggested, "Tell me about the tours. I think I ought to know more about what American Holidays has to offer." She knew very little about the business—only that Mark had used money inherited from Catherine's mother to buy the agency when it was

61

foundering, and that he wanted to put his education in finance and international relations to use.

While they made their way toward the dining room, Mark expounded upon the business and the countries from which most of his clients came—England, Germany, France, Japan, and Australia. The interests of the foreign tourists varied as widely as their nationalities. There were art and theater buffs, tennis and golf enthusiasts, bicyclists and hikers, culinary devotees—

"There are the tourists who want to ride through the country and see everything through bus windows, and the real travelers who want to experience places on their own," Mark explained. "It's a juggling act, trying to please everyone."

"Like everything else, I suppose, there's far more to it than meets the eye," Amy commented. "I'll do my best, though, Mark. I promise you that."

"I wouldn't have asked you if I hadn't thought so." He turned a dazzling smile on her. "Even when you were a little thing, you always aimed to please."

"I'm surprised that you remember."

"I remember a great deal about you."

"You do?"

He grinned. "I do."

She might have asked precisely what it was that prompted such amusement, but they had arrived at the entry of the hotel dining room.

The maître d', resplendent in a black tuxedo, greeted them. "Good evening, sir, madame."

Their reservation was obviously in order, and he promptly led the way through damask-covered tables with crystal goblets and gleaming silver. Amy, with Mark behind her, was acutely aware that admiring eyes followed their passage through the sumptuous room.

After she was seated, Mark sat down across the table from her. The intensity of his gaze was disquieting, and she quickly looked away, pretending an inordinate interest in the antique wall tapestries and murals painted on the coved ceilings.

"I've never seen anything so exquisite. It's like a palace!"

"I've always thought so, except tonight it seems unusually palatial . . . perhaps because I'm escorting a princess."

"Now, Mark—" Attempting to make light of his comment, Amy hurried on. "I do feel a little like Cinderella, though. It was Friday, just two days ago, that I was scrubbing Gramp's kitchen floor when you came for me . . . and here I am now. It seems unreal, as if I might blink and this magnificent room, this enchanted city, you—everything will disappear."

He smiled, the creases around his lips deepening. "You're beautiful enough to be Cinderella."

Now thoroughly unnerved, Amy was grateful for the interruption of the waiter who had arrived with their oversized menus.

Mark's compliments were exhilarating, and she was enjoying them all too much. It behooved her to keep in mind that she was here to work, and that life would be returning to normal soon enough after the wedding . . . and that she would be returning to a new and empty apartment—alone. Still, such a magical evening deserved at least one wish and, before she knew it, that wish had slipped into her consciousness. Perhaps something wonderful would happen. Perhaps Mark would come to love her as she had loved him for so many years. If only he hadn't changed—

Over his menu Mark remarked, "I'd give quite a lot to know what you're thinking."

Ignoring the blush rising to her cheeks, she asked boldly, "How much?"

"A quarter?" he teased.

She laughed. "Very tempting."

"I recall when it worked."

"I do too!" She was relieved that the conversation seemed to be taking a healthier turn. Years ago Mark had bribed her with a quarter to paint the patio swing so he could play baseball with his friends. "It was a neat trick. I'll bet you learned how to avoid responsibility by reading *Tom Sawyer*."

"No doubt," he said with a chuckle. "Except I'd prefer to think that I was learning the art of delegation."

"I'm not sure you could have talked me into painting an entire fence."

"I might have tried if I'd had a fence to paint. As a matter of fact, I've been remembering more and more about us, some of it entirely reprehensible on my part. I don't know how you put up with me."

Put up with you?! Amy couldn't believe he hadn't suspected her true feelings. *I thought you were the most wonderful being on earth!* Outwardly, she kept a firm grip on her emotions and answered with cool detachment. "Oh, it was difficult, but I managed. You weren't so bad—for an adolescent." Even Glynia couldn't have topped that bit of repartee.

Studying her menu again, Mark was hidden from view. What an idol she had made of him . . . and he had probably considered her a chubby little nuisance. Well, she still had to watch her weight, which was most unfortunate as the hotel dining room specialized in continental cuisine. When the waiter returned for their order, she ordered the medallions of veal with shallots and mushrooms instead of the calorie-laden lobster thermidor Mark had recommended.

Dinner began with dispatch, a busboy pouring tinkling ice water in their crystal goblets, their waiter presenting thick warm slices of French bread and the delicious house paté. Over crisp tossed salads their conversation turned to company business. Mark would soon be requiring additional reports on Eastern cities to add depth to some of the more extensive tours.

"Maybe you could write the reports for those too," he suggested. "I'll be stopping in Philadelphia and Washington, D.C. between Thom's graduation and the wedding, then going to Boston and New York right after. At least, consider it."

"But you haven't even seen my first report," Amy protested, though she felt a surge of excitement at the prospect. "In all fairness, I think you ought to see my work first . . . and I'll need time to think about it too." She stalled, reluctant to commit herself to spending more time alone with Mark until she knew the outcome of this trip. "But I appreciate your confidence."

"There's no need for a decision yet." A glint of concern in his eyes gave the impression that he might already be having second thoughts about the offer. "You've never been back East, have you?"

She shook her head. "Would you believe that I've never been out of the state of California?"

"All the better. The last thing I need is a jaded traveler. This business takes someone with enthusiasm, energy, and a healthy dose of curiosity about people and places." He studied her thoughtfully, then was diverted as the waiter arrived with their main courses.

Perhaps Amy knew little about travel, but working for Catherine's Catering had piqued her interest in gourmet cooking, and she did know that the veal in its delectable French sauce was marvelous. She laughed ruefully. "I've heard about jaded travelers, but I doubt that I'll ever be bored with food!"

He smiled at her over his lobster thermidor. "You don't strike me as the type who is easily bored."

"Thank you . . . I guess." She felt a flutter of nervousness under his scrutiny, and quickly changed the subject. "Tell me what I should see, do, and know about San Francisco."

"Now that's a tall order. It's quite a place."

As he launched into a discussion of the city and its environs, Amy made mental notes of the places to investigate: Union Square, Ghirardelli Square, Fisherman's Wharf, The Cannery, Golden Gate Park, Chinatown, Muir Woods, Sausalito—the list seemed endless and exotic.

Over coffee and their shared dessert—a generous slice of chocolate-topped cheesecake—Mark continued to wax eloquent about the touristic possibilities. He concluded, "I want you to take a fresh look at the city, to see it not only from a woman's viewpoint, but from that of a first-time tourist. Most of our foreign tourists will see it only once."

"I'll try," she promised, hoping that she would do the work justice.

After calling for the check, Mark added, "I'll have some time off to show you around."

"Oh—?"

"Do you mind?"

"Of course not," she replied. "It's just that I was assuming you'd be too busy with the convention . . . that I'd be on my own." It struck her as strange that he had not told her sooner.

As he ushered her out of the dining room, his fingers lightly touched her elbow, sending a small tremor through her arm. Her eyes darted to his face and found him looking as startled as she felt. "Thank you for the— the marvelous dinner."

"My pleasure," he responded, his blue eyes glowing with warmth.

For an instant she thought he was going to reach for her hand, and she quickly transferred her white clutch bag to render her hand unavailable. Apparently he was unaware of her deliberate maneuver; instead, he cast a skeptical glance at her white high-heeled sandals. "Are you up to a stroll around Union Square?"

"Of course. It sounds like a good way to walk off dinner and to start my report," she replied in a light-hearted yet businesslike tone. She would have to keep her mind on the job at hand, she reminded herself as they crossed the hotel lobby, and now was as good a time as any to begin.

Outside, the air was surprisingly still and warm, and the sidewalks no longer crowded with homebound pedestrians. Lights softly illuminated the park in the middle of Union Square, highlighting the lawns, trees, and flowers, and imparting an atmosphere of serenity in the midst of the city.

As they strolled along together, a comfortable camaraderie settled between them, and Amy found herself conversing easily about the shops and their wares with Mark. He seemed knowledgeable about everything from the precious gems to the fine crystal and china and even the housewares displayed in store windows.

"I thought men didn't especially care about such things."

"Must be a family trait . . . knowing a little about everything, but never quite enough about anything."

"A Renaissance man?"

"Hardly. You ought to know better than that."

"But I don't really know you well," she objected, "and it seems so strange not to—after all these years." For an instant she wished she had held her tongue, then to her relief she found Mark smiling at her.

"It does seem odd," he agreed. "I suppose it's because there were so many years between us."

"But I'm not a little girl anymore, Mark."

His face took on a wry expression. "So I've been noticing."

"Well, it's about time!"

Probably he interpreted her protest as a bid to be considered an equal, nothing more. Yet, their exchange seemed to have cleared away the last vestiges of tension between them.

As her high-heeled sandals tapped on the sidewalk, Amy realized that this was the first time all day—possibly the first time in years—that she had felt entirely at ease with Mark. The constant strain she had experienced in his presence had vanished in the evening air. It was as if their relationship of years ago had been changing subtly, shifting to a new plateau . . . as if they were no longer strangers.

After their stroll around Union Square, they walked down to California and Market Streets, then back again, enjoying the sights and the sounds of the city.

"Guess we'd better turn in," he sighed at last.

At his words she felt a small stirring of alarm. "Yes. It's going to be a busy week."

Upon reaching the hotel, her uneasiness grew. Alone in the elevator with him, she couldn't think of a thing to say. Mark, too, was silent. When the doors opened, she exited in the wrong direction.

"This way," Mark said, waiting patiently.

Once again, she felt the heat stealing into her cheeks. His gaze rested on her an instant too long, and she glanced away. The air around them seemed charged with a peculiar electricity.

As they stepped to their door, he quickly unlocked it

and stood aside to let her into the dimly lit room. She moved past him, her shoulder brushing against his suit jacket, imparting such a physical jolt that she caught her breath. She hurried into the living room and heard Mark close the door behind them.

"Thank you for a wonderful evening," she managed to say evenly before starting for her room.

"Amy—" His low voice caressed her name as it had that foggy night on the patio, and she turned to him like a leaf bending to the wind.

"Yes?"

His eyes darkened with passion, and, as if in a dream, they moved toward each other. His arms opened and her shoulders stiffened only a trifle as his hands gripped them, drawing her to him. He was so close that she could feel his warm breath waft through her hair.

"Mark—" But her protest was only half-hearted. Her pulse pounded wildly in her ears and, instead of resisting, she found herself tilting her head up to his. As their lips met, his hands splayed across her back, lifting her to him, and she felt such a rush of happiness that all resistance vanished.

Mark! her heart cried out, *Oh, Mark!* She felt his chest expand. Her hands encircled the strong column of his neck, threading her fingers through his hair. It was as if theirs was the first kiss on earth and that she had waited through all eternity to receive it—like Adam and Eve—

Quite suddenly the thought of the hapless biblical pair and the afternoon's *faux pas* with the apple brought Amy to her senses. Firming her resolve, she pressed her hands against Mark's unyielding chest. "No—," she said against her own wishes.

He backed away instantly, the expression on his face revealing his remorse. "I didn't intend to—"

He didn't intend to *what?* To hold her? To kiss her? For things to get out of control? She hadn't planned for this to happen either, but it had! Turning from the consternation clouding his face, she hastened to her door.

"Good-night, Mark!" She brushed her fingers across

68

her lips as if to erase his imprint. Her mind was whirling. Opening her door she turned and found him still gazing at her.

He looked as uncertain as she felt. "Good-night, Amy."

She shut the door behind her, quickly flipping the lock, although this time she was uncertain whom she was trying to protect. All she knew was that, after she had idolized him for so many years, Mark had kissed her. It seemed far too wonderful to be true. So why should she feel so confused? And why had he said . . . *that he hadn't intended to?*

CHAPTER 5

THE NEXT DAY AS Amy stepped into the living room, Mark was watching the eight o'clock news on television.

"Good morning," she called cheerfully as though nothing momentous had happened last night, as though their breathtaking kiss had simply been an illusion. Her eyes dropped from the curiosity in his expression to his clothing, finding a casual urbanity about his navy blazer, white open-necked shirt, tan slacks, and leather loafers.

"You're looking bright-eyed," he said, rising from the couch. "Ready for breakfast?"

Nodding, she answered with a twinge of nervousness, "All set for a hard day's work." Glancing down at her own navy suit and tailored white blouse, it occurred to her that their matching ensembles might appear planned, though it apparently didn't occur to him as his approving gaze roamed over her slim figure.

He started toward the door.

"Shall I turn off the TV?" she asked, just behind him.

"Yes, thanks—I forgot."

She headed for the armoire that housed the TV set, and he added with a note of apology, "It appears that I forgot something else . . . I forgot myself last night too. I didn't intend for—that to happen."

"Well, if you think *I* intended such a thing—," she sputtered. This was really the limit. Hadn't Mark made himself abundantly clear last night? In the ensuing silence she said, "Oh, well, what's a little kiss between two old friends. The best thing to do is to forget the whole thing."

Mark echoed her private thoughts. "Is it that easy to forget?"

She had lain awake remembering every detail of the evening, particularly their kiss, but on such treacherous grounds an indifferent answer seemed her only resort. "Why not?"

From the pained reaction on his face, she knew she had erred again. If only they could somehow begin the morning all over again! This was not at all what she had hoped.

He lifted an eyebrow. "At least I know it's not the first time you've been kissed."

"And what is that supposed to mean?"

"I couldn't help seeing you and Rob on the beach Friday night."

Nonplussed, she hurried past him to the door. "That wasn't 'intended' either, as you put it." Did Mark assume that she allowed men to kiss her indiscriminately?

He closed the door behind them, his forehead furrowed. "It's not that I didn't enjoy kissing you."

She averted her eyes to the corridor's creamy wallpaper so that he wouldn't see that she had enjoyed it too, but he must have read her expression because his voice deepened and caught huskily, "Amy—?"

She swallowed hard, her instincts telling her that a single word or gesture would trigger another embrace. But then he would probably say he didn't *intend* that either! *The road to Hell is paved with good intentions*, Gramp had always warned, and she supposed it was true, particularly in the realm of love.

She started irresolutely down the corridor. Never having rehashed a romantic encounter with a man, she could already see that it was dangerous ground, fraught with ruts, and that she would likely stumble even more if they pursued the subject.

Entering the crowded elevator, Mark tried to slip a protective arm around her, but she edged away. The memory of Glynia's nightgown in his bathroom only yesterday morning returned to her now like a specter. She concentrated on the elevator's blinking floor numbers, trying to resist the inclination to luxuriate in his nearness. Perhaps it was only physical attraction she was feeling.

"I thought we'd eat in the coffee shop." The moment they stepped out into the lobby, Mark nodded toward a charming trellised doorway. Here, the interior designer had avoided the hotel's more formal decor in favor of a cheerful and inviting warmth.

Amy began to relax. Waiting at the door to be seated, she wondered what Mark might be thinking. That he had made a monumental mistake last night by kissing her? That he should never have brought her to San Francisco in the first place? She opened her shoulder bag and extracted a tour map, but it was a long time before she could focus clearly on the maze of streets, hills, and famous landmarks.

When they were settled amid ferns and antiques at a small corner table, Mark bestowed a conciliatory smile upon her. "I'm glad I don't have to eat breakfast alone this morning."

She looked at him over her menu, still feeling annoyed. Did he mean that he preferred to eat breakfast in her company—or would just any woman do?

Ignoring his remarks, she shrugged guiltily, then turned to watch the busboy pour their coffee; at least its aroma helped to dispel her irritation with Mark and with herself. What a mess she was making of things this morning.

After the busboy left, Mark continued, "I simply said that I don't like to eat breakfast alone, and you looked at me like thunder. I don't know what you're assuming, but the fact is that I've never enjoyed eating any meal by myself in a restaurant."

"I'm sorry. Since I seldom dine in restaurants, I really don't know. No doubt I'll learn all about being alone when I move into my apartment next month."

He gazed thoughtfully at the steam rising from his coffee cup. "I don't imagine you'll be alone for long."

"I'm not quite sure I know what you mean."

"As Rob mentioned Friday night, you're very beautiful. He or some other fellow will move in with you—"

She interrupted angrily. "What makes you think I'd allow a man to move in with me?"

"Isn't that what everyone is doing?"

"I don't care what everyone is doing!" she retorted.

He sat back in his seat with a slow smile. "I don't think you'll be so different . . . once you accept the fact that men find you . . . desirable."

"If you think that's a compliment, you're badly mistaken!" She couldn't believe this kind of talk coming from a minister's grandson . . . the son of missionaries. To avoid his eyes, she sipped the hot coffee, her hands trembling.

"You'll change," Mark assured her.

If he had been baiting her, he had certainly succeeded, she thought as she rose from the table in a huff. "You're wrong . . . I'm not that kind of woman!" she flung at him, hurrying to the buffet to escape this upsetting confrontation.

He was behind her in a moment, following her through the Victoriana and greenery to the next room, his low voice compelling. "Look, Amy, I'm sorry. It wasn't fair of me to goad you like that, but I didn't sleep well last night."

She glanced up at him through her lashes, not quite hiding her astonishment. Taken aback by his candor her anger began to subside, though she didn't intend to let him off too easily. "You're right, Mark, it wasn't fair, particularly since you don't seem to know me very well. . . . You were testing me, weren't you?"

"Maybe."

"Then I hope you know where I stand."

"You didn't leave much doubt." His slow grin did funny things to her heart. "Truce?"

"Truce," she agreed gratefully. They had had a lovers' quarrel—of all things.

"Perhaps you *are* different, Amy."

"I guess I am," she said, mustering a small smile before turning to the buffet.

It was a glorious display—mounds of fresh pineapple, grapes, strawberries, oranges, grapefruit, bananas, a variety of melons, and assorted juices. Great copper lids crowned pans of scrambled eggs, hash browns, corned beef hash, bacon, sausages, hot cakes, cheeses, and even small steaks. At a table nearby, trays were heaped with freshly baked breads, croissants, rolls, and muffins.

She filled her plate with a little of everything and found that Mark's plate was piled even higher. Their tentative smiles were given and received in an atmosphere of reconciliation. Today might turn out fine, after all.

The state of truce lasted through breakfast and during their invigorating walk in the early morning sunshine to the Moscone Convention Center where the travel agents' convention was being held. The air had cooled during the night, and, when they stopped for a light on a street corner, Amy had to hold down her skirt against the sudden gusts of wind.

Mark grinned as the fickle breeze whipped his hair. "Not balmy Southern California, is it?"

"Not quite!"

San Francisco by day was entirely different from the mellow mood of the evening before. The city throbbed again with energy as workers flooded into shops and offices, and tourists, bedecked with cameras, wandered out of their hotels reading street maps. Excitement, it seemed, beckoned around every corner.

At the convention center's registration counter Mark quickly checked on the day's meetings, then the available tours, booking Amy on outings for Tuesday, Wednesday, and Thursday.

"But what about today?" she inquired as they stood at the tour reservation counter.

"There's nothing of importance for me to do until

three-thirty, and the welcoming dinner isn't until tonight. I thought this would be a good time to show you around."

"Oh?" she asked, but he was preoccupied with the paperwork. She had been under the impression that she would be researching the city on her own.

"Why, Mark Marston!" exclaimed a stunning blonde with a southern accent. "Ah was hopin' you'd be heah. Ah haven't seen you in ages!"

Just behind her were several others, equally delighted to see Mark again. He quickly introduced Amy to a stately brunette from New York, a platinum beauty from Minneapolis, and the blonde from Atlanta, appropriately named Dixie. They examined Amy with interest when Mark called her "an old friend from home." She had already noticed that the composition of the crowd flooding the convention center included far more women than men—and that apparently a great many of the prettier women knew Mark.

As he signed up for the three-thirty meeting, Dixie said to Amy, "Ah do hope you aren't going to deprive us of our favorite escort. Mark is always such a deah to take us around at the conventions. You know how it is— women alone in a big city."

Amy smiled with difficulty. "I'm afraid you'll have to ask Mark. I don't know his plans."

"You don't?" Dixie replied, her blue eyes dancing. "Aren't y'all stayin' together?"

Amy blushed. "Not exactly—"

Mark interrupted, "All set. See you ladies at the meetings."

Dixie called after them, "Y'all have fun—heah? Ah know you will."

Amy caught Mark's sidelong glance and pretended not to have noticed. Unsure what to think of this most recent episode, she decided to reserve judgment.

"Let's get started—," he said hastily, "and the best place is aboard a cable car."

Not waiting for a response, he took her arm and ushered her outside. Launching into the history of San

Francisco's most famous attraction, Mark told her that someone had taken pity on the poor horses that had sometimes slipped and broken their legs on the steep hillsides—hence, the first cable cars.

When the two of them arrived at the stop, early morning commuters still crowded the red cars, and Amy and Mark had to wait their turn.

"Where are we going?" she inquired as they boarded the next available car.

"Pier 39, Ghirardelli Square, Fisherman's Wharf," Mark replied, looking relaxed, almost carefree. "We'll do some of the footwork for your report today. You'll have plenty of bus and boat riding the rest of the week."

The seats filled quickly, and they were forced to hang onto straps just as the cable car bell clanged, and the noisy, shimmying ride down the middle of the street began. Swaying on a strap beside Mark, Amy didn't object to his arm around her waist, finding protection and security in its steadying strength.

The cable car operator chatted loudly with the passengers, calling out street names and amusing items of information.

"They're usually characters," Mark commented.

"A dash of local color," Amy laughed. "I'll be sure to include him in the report. No doubt your foreign clients have 'characters' in their countries too."

She also made a mental note to mention the ever-changing views. Beyond the downtown area, houses and apartment buildings climbed the steep incline, presenting the beautiful scenes she had often seen of the city in magazines and on television.

While they clanged to a stop an engaging scene took place near the site of an excavation. A little old lady was clambering over the rubble with the help of a workman who had just crawled out of a manhole in the street. As she reached the other side, she turned and waved her thanks. The workman smiled and bowed as the woman proceeded to make her way up the precipitous sidewalk.

"That's San Francisco for you, folks," the cable man laughed. "You'll leave your hearts here."

The riders groaned at his attempted humor.

All too soon the invigorating ride was over, and the passengers were disembarking at Pier 39—an old docking area that had been transformed into a nautical tourist attraction with weathered gray buildings. At the entrance, calliope music from a colorful carousel floated through the salty air, imparting a carnival mood to the setting.

Amy pulled out her notebook and headed for a nearby bench. "Do you mind? I'd better start making notes now or I'll never be able to remember everything."

"Good idea," Mark agreed, settling down beside her. His warm hands brushed her neck as he reached beneath her long hair to turn up her suit collar. "Don't want you to get a chill."

"Thanks—," she began, but his hands were still on her shoulders, drawing her to him. A long look passed between them, and quite suddenly, for a breathless instant, his lips pressed hers before he released her.

"Oh, Mark—" She sat back to catch her breath, savoring the slightly salty taste of his lips, the clean smell of his aftershave. It was awhile before the calliope music intruded and she remembered that they were in a public place.

"Sorry," he shrugged. "You always look so tempting that I just couldn't resist."

Tempting! What had gotten into him? Perhaps it was only the carnival atmosphere. But she returned his smile before quickly opening her notebook.

"Business before pleasure?" Mark observed.

"Something like that." It escaped Amy how she could possibly concentrate on the report with Mark sitting beside her, especially when she so wanted to touch the creases of amusement playing around those sensuous lips.

Suddenly the blonde—Dixie—came to mind with her parting words: "Y'all have fun—heah? Ah know you will." Just how much *did* Dixie know about Mark? Amy steeled herself against his disconcerting presence and her own imaginings and began to write.

77

Later, as they wandered through specialty shops selling everything from coats of arms and kitchen equipment to woolens and toys, they discussed where they might have lunch. There was a plethora of restaurants, both American and international, in addition to those specializing in seafood. Pier 39, it appeared, was a must for foreign tourists to San Francisco.

At the end of the pier they sat upon a weathered wooden bench to enjoy the unfolding panorama of the bay. "The view alone is worth the trip," Amy sighed, then extracted her notebook once again, jotting down notes to orient tourists who would be seeing this scene for the first time: *To the left, beyond the bay, are the green hills of Marin County . . . to the right, Angel Island. . . .* Later, when she was alone, she would record the effect of the moment upon her senses. Or was this delicious giddiness caused by the nearness of the man beside her?

They rose and stood together at the railing. "It's all so breathtakingly beautiful, isn't it?" she asked, but as their eyes met, the deeper significance of her words flashed between them. She turned to blink away a sudden blur of tears.

"Is the lady hungry?" Mark's hearty voice belied the tender look of a moment earlier. "Methinks, if we follow our noses, we're sure to find nourishment."

Amy had to laugh in spite of herself. "How can you be hungry—after that enormous buffet this morning?"

"The fresh sea air, my dear. Does wonders for the appetite."

"And the waistline!" Amy moaned. But she followed Mark dutifully to a seafood restaurant overlooking the sparkling water.

Though Mark insisted she try at least a taste of his golden rings of deep-fried calamary with a tartar sauce, she held firm and ordered only a small tomato and anchovy salad with vinaigrette dressing. Served with the city's renowned sourdough bread, it proved to be an excellent choice.

Outside the window of the restaurant Amy could see

the Golden Gate Bridge arching through the sky, carrying cars to the green hills of Marin County. Closer at hand, hundreds of sailboats and yachts skimmed the waters of the bay, while the heavier ships of commerce plied their course through the deeper channel. So many people going about their daily affairs . . . so much happening in the world around her . . . yet she felt strangely detached from all of it.

Mark was speaking to her. "Dessert? Amy, would you care for dessert?"

A waiter hovered nearby, pen poised to take her order. "Oh, no, thank you. I couldn't eat another bite."

Shaking off the wistful mood, she gathered her belongings and left the restaurant with Mark, stepping out into the bright sunlight of reality.

They strolled along the bay to Fisherman's Wharf, where the fish market and famous seafood restaurants overlooked another sea of masts. A fisherman, wearing a parrot on one shoulder and a patch over his eye, shouted, "Seafood cocktails, mateys! Shrimp! Crab! Clam chowder!" He turned to Amy. "How about it, pretty lady?"

She gave a laugh and patted her trim tummy. "Sorry! We've just eaten—again!" It occurred to her, however, that this "fisherman-pirate" was another character to enliven the information about San Francisco for foreign visitors.

"We'll be back another time," Mark was saying. He caught Amy's hand in his as if it were the most natural thing in the world to do.

How wonderful it felt merely to have his warm hand engulfing hers, Amy marveled as they wandered along the bay. They stopped for a while at the Cannery, an old brick building that had been renovated. While retaining the charm of its past history, the structure now housed modern specialty shops and restaurants with sidewalk tables, where a juggler entertained the passing crowds. Beyond, in Golden Gate Aquatic Park, there was a wine museum and a maritime museum. Torn between tourist attractions, spectacular scenery, and Mark, it was all Amy could do to make sensible notes.

In Ghirardelli Square they saw the famous chocolate factory with its chic shops that, according to Mark, had inspired renovations of old buildings all over the country. She took detailed notes, not forgetting to describe the well-known fountain with its bronze mermaid.

"I'll be back in a minute," Mark said and departed before she could ask where he was going so abruptly.

She concentrated on her notes, then was amazed to see him return with a bouquet of pink roses which he presented to her with a courtly bow.

"Oh, Mark, you shouldn't have!"

He slipped an arm around her waist. "But the color reminded me of your cheeks when you blush."

She obliged again, dipping her head to inhale the sweet perfume of the petals. She could scarcely believe it. Never before had men given her flowers. Yet on Friday, Rob had brought her daisies. And now these.

"Time for dessert," Mark announced.

"But I told you I couldn't possibly eat dessert!"

He laughed, pulling her lightly to her feet and leading her to the Ghirardelli ice cream parlor. "You'll find room for this."

Inside, Amy was intrigued by the old-fashioned tables and chairs. In the rear of the huge room, men stirred chocolate in huge vats, turning out chocolate bars with the antique equipment just as it had been done in the early days of the factory.

Overcome by the rich aroma, Amy said, "Well, maybe I could manage a small dessert after all."

"I thought so," he said with a grin. "What will it be?"

They both chose chocolate concoctions topped with whipped cream and nuts, and carried them out to a round marble-topped table on the adjacent patio. In the shade of sprawling trees, they devoured every mouth-watering bite.

"It was far too delicious," Amy pronounced.

"So are you," he returned.

"Oh, Mark—" She simply didn't know how to handle the rash of compliments he had been bestowing on her all day.

At length he checked his watch. "Two-thirty. I'm afraid it's time to start back."

"Yes, I suppose it is." She rose reluctantly, wishing the glorious afternoon could go on forever. Still, they would be taking the cable car back downtown . . . and Mark had told the fisherman with the parrot on his shoulder that they would return someday. She could carry that thought with her . . . along with the fragrant bouquet of pink roses.

Leaving Mark at a cable car stop near the hotel, Amy continued on alone, city map in hand. It seemed a perfect time to explore the exclusive shops lining Union Square. Mark had mentioned that his foreign clients might appreciate a few comments about each of the major stores. Making her way from one elegant shop to another, she took extensive notes. Her only purchase was a lovely turquoise scarf she found on sale, persuaded only slightly by the saleslady's insistence that it matched her eyes to perfection.

She returned to the hotel by five, carrying her roses for which the housekeeper provided a crystal vase. Since tonight's welcoming dinner at the travel agents' convention would commence at seven with a social hour, there was time for a bubble bath.

At six o'clock she heard Mark enter the suite. "I'm home!" he called out, and she couldn't help thinking how much like a husband returning from the day's work he sounded to her.

"I'm dressing—," she replied spontaneously, then wondered whether announcing that fact was such a brilliant idea.

Mark hesitated only an instant. "I'll be ready in half an hour."

She entered their living room first and sat down on the elegant couch, hoping he would approve of her dress; she had made it herself for Val's wedding festivities. A lovely shade of peach, the gown was extremely flattering, with its bias layers skimming her hips to swirl just below her knees.

81

When Mark stepped into the room wearing a midnight blue suit, he smiled with pleasure. "You're even lovelier than the roses," he said, glancing at the bouquet on the coffee table. Catching her hands in his, he drew her slowly from the couch. She thought he would kiss her, but he noted her fresh lipstick and evidently changed his mind. Perhaps just as well too, she thought, hurriedly grabbing her purse and leaving the room with him.

When they arrived at the San Francisco Room of the convention hotel, the predinner social hour was well underway. Dixie and her friends spotted them first.

"We've saved y'all seats at our table. Ah do hope that's all right."

"We *all* thank you," Mark mocked. "I wanted to discuss the latest travel scene in the South with you anyhow. Which reminds me, I need to find Tony Sanca to set up a dinner. Have you seen him?"

"At the buffet, where else?" she responded with humor, then grew serious. "Just wait until y'all see what's new with him."

Mark raised a speculative eyebrow, but didn't inquire. Excusing themselves, he took Amy's hand, and they threaded their way through the crush of people.

"Tony!" Mark called, recognizing the fiftyish man holding court near the sumptuous array of canapes; he held a drink in one hand and an hors d'oeuvre in the other.

Tony waved at Mark, a diamond ring gleaming from his little finger, but continued his animated discussion with a younger man.

"I'll have to get to him later," Mark said.

At seven-thirty everyone settled at round damask-covered tables in the adjacent dining room, and an army of busboys and waiters began to serve the prime rib dinner. Amy, unsure of what to expect, found herself quickly admitted into this congenial circle of friends who met only occasionally but obviously with great enthusiasm. After their initial curiosity about her relationship with Mark was appeased, the conversation turned to business: the last convention in Dallas, new promotions by the Mexican tourist bureau, last month's tour of China, the devaluation of the *escudo* in Portugal.

"How exciting it all sounds!" Amy said as Mark caught her eye. "I'd never really considered travel from behind the scenes. It's fascinating!"

"I hoped you'd be interested," he responded with pleasure. "I believe it was Augustine who said, 'The world is a great book, of which they who never stir from home read only a page.'"

"And don't forget the old adage about the bee," Dixie put in. "'A bee, though it finds every rose has a thorn, comes back loaded with honey from his rambles . . . why shouldn't other tourists do the same?'"

"That's new to me," Mark said, chuckling with the others.

"The only reason ah happen to know it," Dixie admitted, "is because ah happened to quote it in my last client mailing."

Delightful as Dixie was, Amy couldn't help wishing the woman didn't have quite so much in common with Mark.

After dinner a rousing speech was delivered from the head table, then there was an announcement of the meetings and seminars to be held the rest of the week.

When it was all over, Dixie suggested with a facetious sparkle, "Why don't y'all come to my hotel suite to continue the—ah—discussion at hand." The invitation was accepted with alacrity.

As if in explanation, one of the other female travel agents said to Amy, "We all love Dixie."

Amy pasted on a smile. "How nice."

Yet several hours later, in Dixie's suite, Amy learned that her envy of the lovely southerner was unfounded. Dixie was happily married and spoke glowingly of her husband at home. So she *was* just a friend of Mark's, Amy thought with a great flood of relief. *Just a friend.*

It was midnight when Amy and Mark returned to their hotel suite. In the taxi on the way back, Mark had been thoughtfully distant, as though turning something over carefully in his mind. But in the suite the pink roses on the coffee table were a fragrant reminder of the afternoon they had spent together.

He drew her slowly into his arms. "I'm not so sure," he murmured, his breath warm in her hair, "that this is such a good idea."

"But it is!" she protested. "Oh, Mark, it's a wonderful idea."

His arms tightened, crushing her against him. Exhilarated by the events of the day, Amy lifted her lips to his, initiating a fervent kiss.

Almost immediately he backed away. "Good-night, Amy." And, as she stood watching in dismay, Mark strode purposefully toward his room and closed the door firmly behind him.

"Good-night, Mark," she called faintly.

Oh, what must he think of her now? She had practically forced herself on him. Would she never learn how to act, what to say, what *not* to say to a man? Perhaps her reckless declaration had already driven him away.

She glanced at the bouquet on the coffee table. Since she had placed them there that afternoon, the beautiful roses seemed to have drooped ever so slightly. And, as if in confirmation of her fears, a single petal fell, drifting slowly to the floor.

CHAPTER 6

AFTER BREAKFAST IN THE hotel coffee shop the next morning, Amy decided that her passionate faux pas had not cooled Mark's ardor after all. Perhaps he had only been concerned with protecting her from herself!

"If only we could spend the day together," he said wistfully as they exited into the hotel lobby. "You'll be all right, won't you?"

"Of course."

He dropped a warm kiss on her cheek. "See you then at six." He paused. "Amy—"

Her heart thumped erratically. "Yes?"

His gaze fastened on her for a long moment. "At six," he repeated and smiled tenderly at her before he took off.

He must realize by now how much she loved him, she reasoned; yet there was still an atmosphere of quiet constraint on his part. For one thing, he had not told her he loved her, nor so much as called her "dear" or "darling," although the endearing sound of them filled his voice when he pronounced her name.

But there would be time to ponder her situation later. Right now, she thought, glancing at her watch, there was a tour bus to catch. Just as she stepped outside, the bus was pulling up to the hotel entrance. Work would be a pleasant diversion from her thoughts, for never had she expected to find a job so enjoyable.

After picking up tourists at the major hotels, the tour began with the civic center, opera house, and Old Mission Dolores; later, there was a stop at Twin Peaks for a panoramic view. Once Amy and her fellow tourists had snapped pictures, they drove on through the lushness of Golden Gate Park and visited the Japanese Tea Garden. The drive continued along the Great Highway to the ocean, where they stopped for a seaside look at seals sunning on the rocks near Cliff House. Then it was on to the Presidio and across the Golden Gate Bridge to Vista Point for another view of the bay and Alcatraz Island. By the time they reached Fisherman's Wharf and Pier 39, Amy felt very much at home. It would be easy to capture on paper the various impressions of a place she had already come to love.

As the week progressed, the pattern of the days fell into a comfortable routine. After breakfast together, Amy and Mark parted to go their separate ways until evening, when they dined with his colleagues and business acquaintances in some of the city's fabulous restaurants. It was wonderfully romantic, although Amy was still uncertain about Mark's feelings for her—beyond the obvious physical attraction.

On Wednesday she toured Muir Woods, visited the giant redwoods, walked the picturesque streets of the artists' seaside colony of Sausalito, and was back just in time to take the narrated Bay Cruise. Returning to the suite at four o'clock, she was surprised by Mark's arrival within minutes after hers. "You're early!"

"I skipped out on a dull meeting," he replied, giving her a fast hug. As if a warning bell sounded in his head, he stepped back almost too quickly. "Are you up to climbing Nob Hill?"

"Yes, of course—it's still on my list of places to see." She tried to sound enthusiastic, but Mark's indecisive attitude toward her was puzzling. At times, he seemed passionately attracted to her, then suddenly withdrew for no apparent reason; at other times, he appeared to think long and hard before even holding her hand, then was overcome by passion. Gramp would probably have said, "He's blowing hot and cold." That's what he'd said about Thom's actions toward Valerie for a period during their courtship. If Mark's ambivalence weren't so unnerving, Amy might have smiled it off as a trait of the Marston males. Still, it was such a joy to be in his presence that there was no point in being downcast.

Outside, Mark took note of her high heels and asked the doorman to flag a cab.

It wasn't too many minutes later that they were driving up the almost perpendicular street, and she understood why Mark had decided to take the cab. "I had been warned that San Francisco was hilly, but this is ridiculous! I'm sure there must be mountains that are not this steep!"

Mark chuckled. "And that's not the only reason for the term 'steep.'"

Glancing around at the elegant hilltop hotels and apartments, Amy said, "I see what you mean. Only millionaires could afford to live here." Catching sight of a tall spire, she gestured, "That's Grace Cathedral. I've read about it. Could we stop here? I'd really like to see it."

He cocked a quizzical brow. "May I ask why?"

"It's an historic landmark," she explained a trifle defensively. "Besides, don't you think that some of your tourists would like to know a little about it? I suppose that some of them are Christians, and others might be interested in the architecture—"

"You're right," he replied with a nod. "Now you see why I need a woman's perspective."

She blinked. "What does being a woman have to do with it?"

"It seems that women are usually more intuitive . . . more open and religious than men."

"I agree with your first point . . . but more religious? How do you reconcile that theory with the fact that your father was a medical missionary—and your grandfather, a minister?"

"Ministers and missionaries are the exception," he responded easily. Obviously he had thought the matter through. "Besides, in both instances in my family, the men were married to very spiritual women."

"Really?" Mark continued to surprise her.

"Would you like to take a look at some of the hotels?" He took her hand, drawing it through his arm.

"I'd love to." But her mind was not wholly on the grand old structures sprawling atop Nob Hill.

As she walked with Mark alongside Huntington Park, she was mentally reviewing their conversation. It didn't make sense. Why should women be different from men in matters of religion? Or did she mean Christianity? Catherine had once defined religion as "man's search for God," and Christianity, as "God's reach to mankind." *Well,* Amy thought, *at any rate, if women were indeed "different," she certainly wasn't one of them.* She opened her notebook and turned her attention to Mark's comments about the hotels.

Later, when they headed for Grace Cathedral, she made notes about its north tower—the Singing Tower— named for its carillons. As they approached the cathedral's magnificent doors, she remarked knowledgeably, "The Ghiberti Doors of Paradise. They're copies of the bronze doors from the baptistry of San Giovanni in Florence, Italy. It's said that when Michelangelo saw them he told his friend Ghiberti, 'They are so beautiful they could grace the entrance to Paradise.'"

Mark darted a pleased glance at her, looking more impressed with her research than with Michelangelo's veneration. "That should be of interest to our Italian tourists. Perhaps we'll add the cathedral to some of our itineraries. The doors should at least be mentioned in the San Francisco brochures."

Together they examined the panels depicting Old Testament accounts of the creation of mankind and of early Jewish history. There were Adam and Eve—their creation, sin, and expulsion from the Garden of Eden— as well as Cain and Abel, Noah after the Flood, Moses receiving the Ten Commandments on Mount Sinai, and other biblical events that seemed familiar, even after long years away from the teachings of her church. Amy was strangely moved by the sense of reverence conveyed by the artist.

"Someone donated quite a lot of money to have those doors made," Mark commented.

She nodded uncomfortably. "I'm afraid I don't quite understand why people would bequeath their entire estates to churches . . . or become ministers . . . or missionaries, for that matter. My parents and Gram were devout Christians, and Gramp believed in the end too, though he didn't talk much about it, and now Valerie—" She confronted Mark with the issue that had been surfacing more and more often lately. "*You* must understand why people become so thoroughly convinced about Christianity."

He shook his head. "You'd think so, coming from a family like mine. But as far as I know, it boils down to one thing: they say they have accepted Christ as their Savior. They feel a call."

A call. It was a nebulous word, indistinct. What exactly did it mean? Did God actually speak to these people? And, if so, did He speak audibly? Or did He use that "still small voice" mentioned in her Sunday school lessons? She found herself saying, "There must be something to it, or there wouldn't have been so many ministers and missionaries—and other Christians through the centuries."

"Yes—let's go in." Mark evaded further discussion by moving into the cathedral.

Then Mark failed to understand too, she decided with a faint sense of disappointment as she accompanied him into the majestic sanctuary.

Just beyond the main door, her eyes fell upon the baptismal font, which was no doubt stationed there because baptism was the sign—the sacrament—that some Christians claimed to be necessary for salvation. But was baptism everything? Both she and Valerie had been baptized as infants, yet Amy always struggled with the vague notion that the ritual itself had not made her a true Christian . . . nor had those years in Sunday school when she attended the classes, but gave no thought to the meaning of the Scripture or its place in her life. A quotation came to her now: "Baptism is the outward sign of an inward work." Had there been any "inward" work—some change in her heart? Or had her baptism been merely an empty formality?

She turned to the cathedral's nave, which rose skyward like a great inverted ark. Here and there among the pews, a few people prayed. Late afternoon sunshine beamed through the stained-glass windows, the rays shimmering with opalescent tones across the wooden pews. As she and Mark started down a side aisle in the awesome silence, organ music burst forth, resounding through the cathedral like a great heavenly voice.

Amy must have given a start because Mark commented with a smile, "Someone must be practicing."

"Yes, so it seems."

"Something by Bach, I think." He added, "I used to visit Grandfather's church sometimes after school and, when the music surprised me like that, I would pretend that . . ." He hesitated, then chuckled, ". . . that God was playing the organ."

She smiled, trying to visualize Mark as a small boy, but her memories carried her back in time only to his teen years. "How little I really know you—"

"You haven't missed much," he said unhappily. His eyes darted toward her in a momentary appeal, betraying a flicker of guilt that made her reach out her hand to his. As he clasped it, his expression filled with a warmth as intimate as their touch.

"I happen to think you're very nice," she responded softly before they moved down the aisle, still holding hands.

The majestic music became less overwhelming and quite natural to the cathedral, although it prolonged her interest in that small boy who spent occasional afternoons in his grandfather's church. "You must have learned quite a lot about Christianity as a child."

Mark glanced up toward the stained-glass windows.

"Yes, I suppose I did. There was even a time—I must have been six or seven—when I decided that I would be a minister like my grandfather, a time when I thought I had a great deal of faith." His chin quivered with sudden emotion, but he quickly subdued it.

"Oh? Following in your grandfather's footsteps?" she mused, then, aware of the growing stiffness of his lips, immediately regretted her question.

His reply was abrupt. "Yes, I suppose that was it."

She suddenly perceived at least a part of what was bothering him. It was guilt. Guilt that he hadn't followed up on that childhood vow or sense of mission.

The organist repeated a series of runs, and after a moment Amy spoke softly, "I'm sorry, Mark, I shouldn't have said that. I always seem to leap mouth-first into everything."

"It's all right."

But it wasn't all right, she brooded as they continued up the aisle. It was obvious that he was guilt-ridden and that the guilt spanned a much longer period of time than the incident with Erika.

Mark interrupted her thoughts, pointing to the magnificent windows filtering a rainbow of light through the colorful glass panes. "Two styles of windows."

"Oh, do you know about them?" Amy asked brightly. "Give me the tour."

She thought Mark looked more grateful for the shift in their conversation than for the opportunity to impress her with his knowledge. As he explained the glorious windows, it appeared evident that he knew a great deal about Christianity as well. But something was missing. Catherine had once said that the average distance between the head and the heart was approximately eighteen inches—that being the difference between an intellectual Christian and a true believer.

Amy trailed behind him, admiring what he termed the clerestory windows that were devoted to human endeavor. There were windows honoring John Glenn for exploration, Henry Ford for industry, Robert Frost for letters, Albert Einstein for natural science, and numerous others.

Later, as they passed the high altar, it occurred to her that perhaps she should pray, but Mark was already moving on. Following him through the iridescent light cast by the stained-glass windows, a feeling of peace and happiness descended upon her. She sensed that Mark felt it too.

When at last they strolled out onto the grounds, however, he said nothing more about their visit to the cathedral, but surprised her with another mention of his trip to the East Coast.

"I hope you'll decide to do the research for me in Philadelphia and Washington, D.C. before the wedding. I can't imagine finding anyone else who would do it so conscientiously."

Mark wanted her with him, she thought happily, but he just wasn't quite ready to commit himself fully enough to say so.

"Will you do it?" he persisted.

What a fool she would be to pass up such an opportunity. She gazed deeply into his blue eyes. "Yes, Mark—I will."

Something leaped within her at the hope that these simple words of acceptance pledged in front of the cathedral were only the first of other vows yet to come.

The Thursday tour of the Napa and Sonoma valleys lasted nine hours, and Amy returned to the hotel exhausted and just in time for a fast shower before dinner. Somehow she had managed to visit most of San Francisco and surrounding places of interest since Sunday night. There were, of course, more tours such as the eleven-hour visit to Monterey and Carmel, but it was humanly impossible to go that far afield on this trip, nor did Mark expect it. Indeed he seemed extremely pleased with her research and organization of the report thus far. He had already called his office to set up the arrangements for her to accompany him to Philadelphia and Washington D.C.

Hurrying into the hotel lobby, Amy glanced at her watch. It was nearly six-thirty. Their dinner with Tony

92

Sanca and his wife was scheduled for seven. "Tony's a little brash," Mark had warned, "but he's a good businessman. I think you'll especially enjoy his wife. They're an older couple, but Ruby's truly a gem."

"You did it again, Mark. Bad pun. Ruby—a gem," she had chided him.

They arrived just a few minutes late at the hotel's rooftop dining room, overlooking San Francisco and the bay. Amy wore her white silk dress, the same dress she had worn on that first memorable evening with Mark. She followed the maître d' through the maze of tables, with the promise of another such evening before her. If Ruby were at all like Mark's other friends, it was sure to be delightful.

"There you are, Mark!" his friend Tony said, rising from the table, drink in hand.

And that must be Ruby . . . although something about the young brown-eyed blonde with Tony rang false, Amy thought as she was seated. Hadn't Mark mentioned that Ruby was older?

Tony's voice was thick with a New York accent, his words slurred. "I'd like you to meet my friend, Sondra."

Amy nodded toward the voluptuous blonde in her deep-cut black dress, trying not to gape. "How do you do?" Her tone was clipped and formal. *Don't jump to conclusions, Amy,* she admonished herself. *Appearances can be deceiving.*

"Pleased to meet you," Sondra replied, assessing Amy with a lift of one arched brow.

Mark appeared genuinely astonished. It seemed immediately apparent that Tony was either separated from his wife—or cheating on her. He was at least fifty years old; Sondra, no more than nineteen. They made a ludicrous picture, Amy thought, holding hands like teenagers, the diamond ring on Tony's plump finger sparkling.

Mark broke the uncomfortable silence. "And where are you from, Sondra?"

Her brown eyes danced, and she turned a provocative smile on Mark. "Oh, I live here in the city." Her voice took on a sultry note. "How about you, Mark?"

"Now—wait just one minute, Sondra," Tony warned. "I know Mark's a big handsome fella, but you're with me. Don't forget I'm the guy who's picking up your tab this week."

Sondra sent him a petulant look. "Big spender—paying for our hotel room and food."

"And that get-up you're wearing, as I recall!" Tony shot back. "Right down to those straps you call shoes!"

Amy swallowed hard and turned to Mark, who seemed to be recovering as graciously as possible under the circumstances. She was thankful when the waiter arrived with their menus, although by now she had lost her appetite. If only she and Mark could have dinner alone. . . . She forced herself to concentrate on the menu, deciding upon a crab salad.

"Is that all you're having?" Mark asked.

"I'm not very hungry." She appealed wordlessly to him, but there was nothing that could be done. Mark had mentioned Tony's importance to his New York travel operation. They would obviously continue the evening with the other couple, Amy concluded; she would simply have to make the best of it.

"Tony's taking me to Carmel this weekend," Sondra remarked to Amy. She squeezed his hand again. "Aren't we having a good time, hon?"

"That we are!" Tony agreed, then turned to Mark with a conspiratorial wink. "I'm counting on you to keep this under your hat."

Mark nodded uneasily, quickly glancing out the window again.

"You from around here too?" Sondra asked Amy, after taking a look at her ringless left hand.

"No, I'm from Santa Rosita . . . south of Los Angeles."

"Oh, you two must be together too," Sondra said with a relieved laugh. "I thought you might be married."

Amy's indignation rose. How dare the woman make such a sordid insinuation. "I'm conducting research for Mark's firm," she corrected firmly.

"Sounds like as good an excuse as any," Sondra said

with a meaningful glance at Tony, who cheerfully raised his glass and announced, "I'll drink to that!"

If only Mark would *say* something, Amy thought, her resentment mounting by the moment. Suddenly she rose, excusing herself from the table. She had to get away from the disgusting couple, if only for a few minutes.

She swept through the dining room, not stopping until she reached the hallway. To her surprise, she found that Mark had followed her.

"Listen, I don't like the situation any better than you do," he said, his eyes darkening ominously, "but you don't have to act so—superior!"

"Superior!" she flung back. "If you were any kind of a gentleman, you wouldn't have involved me in such a situation!" Turning on her heel, she ran blindly to the ladies' lounge.

Inside, Amy was too furious for tears and sat in stiff dismay on a couch. Why had Mark let this happen? It wasn't as if she didn't know that some married men picked up women when they were out of town, but why was Tony flaunting his affair so flagrantly? Amy knew she was far from perfect, but she did know the difference between right and wrong, and her standards of morality were high. Now she and Mark had been placed in a compromising position, and Sondra was trying to tar them with the same brush!

She'd simply stay in the lounge until Mark returned to the table, then take a cab alone to their hotel. But a thought occurred to her, and she opened her white evening bag. Of course—it had been too small to hold her wallet. She had no money with her for a cab!

Amy made a swift appraisal of her appearance in the mirror. Aside from her apparent chagrin, she looked the same. Yet circumstances had changed so radically. Somehow she would have to endure the remainder of the evening. Gathering up her courage, she took a moment to brush her hair back behind her ears and gloss her lips.

She started for the dining room again. As she approached the table, there was a glimmer of relief in Mark's eyes as he rose to seat her. Did he suspect that she might have fled?

95

Fortunately the two men resumed the business discussion that had prompted their dining together in the first place. After unsuccessfully attempting to divert Tony from the topic, Sondra occupied her time with picking at her food, smoking, and staring out the window.

By the time the unpleasant meal was over, Sondra and Tony had downed a bottle of wine with their dinners in addition to the cocktails, and were eager to hit the nightclubs.

"Come on along, Amy," Tony urged. "A good time won't hurt you!"

Amy suspected her idea of a good time and Tony's were vastly different. Why was it that so many people seemed so anxious to drag others down their particular alleyways of life? Well, she would not be a part of it.

"What do you think, Amy?" Mark asked, as if nothing were amiss.

"I'm a little tired," she managed to reply evenly. "I think I'd prefer to return to the hotel. I have to pack too." She supposed she must seem an awful dullard to them—Mark included. Suddenly she couldn't resist a gibe, "But please feel free to go along with your *friends*." At the furious look in Mark's eyes, she realized she had pushed him too far.

"Fine!" he replied. "We'll drop you off at the hotel, then I think I'll just do that. Sounds like great fun."

Heartsick, she turned away and followed Sondra and Tony through the dining room. What a fool she was to have made such a big thing over their relationship. On the other hand, Mark had made it obvious that he preferred their company to hers. Apparently Valerie and Rob had been right all along about Mark Marston. His family background might be impeccable—but he marched to a different beat.

The next morning, as they began the long drive home, Amy was still despairing over their clash of the evening before. How could Mark have been so insensitive? Conversely, she herself was not blameless. She had mishandled everything again.

Darting a glance at Mark in the driver's seat, she winced to see the angry thrust of his jaw. They had breakfasted separately this morning, then he had checked them out while she sat in the suite stewing over her stupidity. If anything, he had seemed even more irate than she.

Once the bustling city was behind them, the scenery passed in a blur: San Francisco Bay, Candlestick Park, the Cow Palace Convention Center, then foothills rising to meet an overcast sky. On the car radio an announcer was forecasting rain. What else? It suited their black moods perfectly.

"I guess I'll work on the report," Amy said, opening the manila envelope on her lap.

There was no answer from the driver's side.

Well, if he wasn't speaking, she would have time to write, she thought, and forced her attention to the task at hand. After struggling with the introduction, the report began to take shape, the words falling neatly into place.

Nearing Paso Robles, Amy looked up momentarily to gaze out at the live California oaks dotting the green hillsides where placid sheep grazed. In contrast to the high-voltage electricity flashing between the occupants of the car, she found the scene peaceful and serene. *If only things had worked out differently*, she said to herself . . .

Her thoughts were jolted by the sight of a huge semi-trailer truck immediately ahead. It had slowed to start a long incline, and instantly Mark hit the brakes to avoid a collision.

"No brakes!" he yelled, pumping furiously.

Terrified, Amy tensed against the seat as the huge rig loomed before them. Acting instinctively, Mark swung the car around the laboring truck. Fortunately there was no oncoming traffic, and she released her breath in a long sigh.

Mark shifted down, muttering, "I should have flown."

"Why didn't you?"

"Because I was fool enough to bring . . ." His vehement words trailed off significantly.

". . . to bring me along?"

97

"If you want to put it that way—yes," he retorted, finally maneuvering the car off the road and bringing it to a stop.

"You can put it any way you want to!" She was shaking with anger and fright. "But don't worry, I won't commit suicide over you like Erika did!" The words were no sooner uttered than she saw Mark's face pale, and the realization of her hasty comment dawned with sickening finality. "Oh, Mark . . . I'm so sorry!"

"Well, it's out now!" he flared, turning off the engine and pulling himself out of the car. "I suppose you've been thinking about that all along!"

Stung by the rage in his voice, she blanched. If she had tried for a lifetime, she could not have touched on a more sensitive subject. "I'm truly sorry."

Without a backward look, he slammed the door and stalked down the road.

"Mark!" she called after him, but now he had broken into a jog, probably heading for the nearest service station. She climbed out of the car. "Mark!" She watched him run on as if he didn't hear . . . or care. And now it was beginning to rain. *Oh, Amy,* she reproached herself, *how could you have said those things?* It was true that you always hurt the one . . . you love. A sob caught in her throat, then another and another until she gave way to a torrent of hot tears.

Five hours later, after having waited for parts to be delivered to the small service station and then for the repair work to be done, they were underway again. When Amy glanced in the mirror on the car's visor, her eyes were still red. Maybe he would listen to her now.

"It wasn't your fault about Erika . . . everyone knows that she'd been seeing a psychiatrist for years . . . and that you had never been more than a friendly boss to her. It's—it's just that she was so unstable and had a crush . . . an irrational fixation on you—"

"Drop it, Amy." Mark's voice was flat and even.

"But I *am* sorry," she persisted miserably. She would never to be able to repair the damage inflicted by her tongue this time. She closed her eyes in despair.

Shaking off her despondent mood, Amy picked up her writing tablet and, by the time they arrived in Santa Rosita, the report was completed. If nothing else, she knew she had done a good job with the assignment, though it was small consolation to her now.

Darkness had fallen, and, as they drove into the Marston driveway, she was relieved to see that the house was dark too; the family had probably gone out for dinner. At least she would not have to explain the obvious rift between herself and Mark, although *rupture* was the more appropriate word.

She would deal with explanations tomorrow. Tonight all she wanted to do was to throw herself into bed and sleep for a week, forgetting the last few hours. But would Mark ever forget—or forgive her?

CHAPTER 7

"AMY?" VALERIE WHISPERED.

Amy rolled over in bed, blinking awake. *Where am I?* she thought, struggling to orient herself. Dark wooden beams supported the ceiling of the spacious white bedroom; arches curved over oaken doors. At the open French windows, birds twittered from a California pepper tree in the courtyard, and the surf was rolling onto the beach not too far away.

Peering around, she saw her sister sitting on the other twin bed. The bed was already made, its green and white leafy spread trailing down to the moss green carpeting. Of course—they were back at the Marstons' house. She and Mark had returned last night after having quarreled over that couple. She sat up slowly.

"I thought I was still in San Francisco. What time is it?"

"Ten o'clock," Valerie replied, looking crisp in white culottes and a yellow knit top that enhanced her honey-blondness.

Amy yawned and stretched. "Guess I overslept."

"I wasn't sure whether I should wake you, but everyone else has been up for hours, though I'm not sure about Mark."

"I didn't realize I was that exhausted," Amy said, trying to ignore any thought of him. "I hope they haven't waited breakfast for me."

"No, everyone's on their own for breakfast today. Catherine and I are going shopping and thought you might like to come along. We're flying back East tomorrow—remember? There's still so much to do before the wedding and not much time left."

"Oh, Val, thanks—but I have to wash some clothes and pack for the trip." She desperately needed a quiet day, she thought as she stood and smoothed her blue cotton batiste nightgown. "I can't quite believe it—tomorrow we'll be back East."

"I can't believe it myself—tomorrow I see Thom!" Valerie was radiant at the thought, then her attention shifted again to Amy. "How did it go in San Francisco?"

"The research went very well. San Francisco is wonderfully interesting. I took tours all through—"

"That's not what I meant and you know it!" Val interrupted with a laugh.

Amy started for her closet, dodging her sister's penetrating gaze. "If you're referring to a great romance between Mark and me, your worries are over." It was pointless to mention that, for a time at least, she had been tempted. "There's nothing doing."

"Oh?" Valerie asked, not sounding entirely convinced. She hesitated, then added, "I once had a terrible crush on Mark, and I've always assumed that any female who comes within ten feet of him is instantly attracted. I was afraid you'd be one of them. And Mark is so different from the rest of his family. He's changed so dreadfully—since Erika."

"There's nothing doing," Amy insisted. After yesterday that much was certainly true, but she wished her sister had not brought up the dead girl's name again. Moreover, she didn't want to hear any more of Val's sage pronouncements.

"Well, if you say so. I just wish you didn't sound quite so vehement about it. It makes me all the more suspicious."

"It's just that I don't enjoy being grilled, Val."

Valerie allowed a soft sigh to escape her. "I'm sorry. I guess I still feel somehow responsible for my little sister."

Amy replied with a forgiving smile, "Don't I know it!"

"I suppose my sense of responsibility must strike you as overbearing at times."

"Sometimes," Amy admitted as she started for the shower, "but I love you anyhow."

"Thanks—I love you too." Valerie gave her a warm hug and hurried out of the room.

Later, under the stinging spray of the shower, Amy was determined not to dwell on the mess she had made of things with Mark. She fervently hoped to stay out of his way today, although there would be no chance of avoiding him during the wedding festivities. When an opportunity presented itself, however, she would certainly tell him she had decided not to make the trip to Philadelphia and Washington, D.C. with him. It seemed a shame, though. She had always wanted to visit Philadelphia. Well, it wouldn't be a total loss. She would see a little of Washington, since the wedding party would be staying in the nearby suburb of Alexandria, Virginia.

When she returned to the bedroom to slip into her blue sundress, she discovered that Valerie had made the bed for her. As always, it was difficult to remain annoyed with her sister for long; theirs had never really been a bumpy relationship. On the other hand, her relationship with Mark was a different matter altogether; bumpy was hardly the word for it, swinging as it did from the heights of ecstasy to the depths of anguish.

On the way downstairs the aroma of fresh-perked coffee greeted her. Hopefully Mark would not be around. She peered into the kitchen. It was empty. At the counter, breakfast was laid out: a cold tray with strawberries, sliced melons, and fresh pineapple; a basket with oversized blueberry and bran muffins; boxes of cereals. Amazing how hungry she was after yesterday's debacle, but then she had skipped dinner, too tired to fix something for herself . . . or to risk spending another moment alone with Mark.

Taking a stoneware plate, Amy helped herself to strawberries, a melon slice, and a bran muffin. She was about to settle on a barstool next to the kitchen work counter when her eyes were drawn to a picture hanging on the wall near the French doors. A beam of sunshine sparkled on the glass protecting the framed picture . . . no, it was a sampler, recently hung, for she hadn't noticed it before. The embroidered words were simple cross-stitching:

> Earth's crammed with Heaven
> And every common bush afire with God;
> But only he who sees takes off his shoes,
> The rest sit round it and pluck blackberries.
> *Elizabeth Barrett Browning*

The first two lines make sense, she thought. *Earth reflects the beauty of Heaven in nature—flowers, trees, shrubs.* She smiled, remembering the unforgettable sights she had seen in San Francisco only this week—the bay awash with the colors of the setting sun, the melding of blues as sapphire sea met azure sky—and, closer to home, the flaming bougainvillaea.

The third line, however, struck her as perplexing—unforgivable for an aspiring poet. She mulled it over: "But only he who sees takes off his shoes . . ." He who sees what? The beauty in a bush? As for "taking off his shoes," she searched her memory. . . . Wasn't there an account in the Bible of a prophet who took off his shoes during a supernatural phenomenon? A burning bush? That was it! The prophet was Moses, and it was God in the bush that burned but was not consumed. In reverence for the holy ground on which he stood, Moses had taken off his shoes!

"Lovely, isn't it?" Catherine asked as she entered the kitchen through the French doors.

"Very!" She examined the yellowing linen and embroidered green leaves and blackberries encircling the verse. "It looks old."

"I found it in the attic several months ago and had it framed. Sarah, my mother-in-law, embroidered it years ago."

103

"The minister's wife?" Amy asked.

"Yes. James remembers her working on it when he was a boy. It seems a wonderful thing to keep in the family. I'm only sorry we didn't find it sooner, but maybe . . . just maybe there's a reason for that too."

Amy turned from the sampler and pondered the meaning of the poet's words. It occurred to her that if she could "see" God as her parents had and the Marstons did, she might not feel so empty; perhaps she wouldn't have allowed herself to be taken in by Mark just because she yearned so desperately for love. Embarrassed to find Catherine watching her, Amy asked, "Aren't you going shopping with Valerie?"

"In a minute. I had some last-minute packing to do. Val rode with James on his way to the hospital. But you're right—I'd better get going. Have a good day, dear."

Amy had just settled down to breakfast when she heard footsteps coming down the hallway to the kitchen. A tremor ran through her, covering her with goose bumps. Mark? Taking a bite of the melon, she stiffened her shoulders.

When he spoke, his voice held a hard edge. "Mind if I join you?"

"Of course not," she replied, compelled to look at him. His expression was dour. She'd try once more. "Mark . . . please forgive me—"

"Let's forget it," he responded abruptly and poured himself a cup of coffee.

But would *he* be able to forget? Amy wondered. Her crack about Erika had been horrendous . . . as difficult to forget as the love that had flared with such passion between them. Well, it was over, and there would be no better time than now to tell him of her decision about the next assignment.

"Mark," she began unsteadily as he sat down on the stool at the opposite end of the counter. "I've decided that I . . . can't possibly go with you to Philadelphia and Washington D.C."

He frowned. "My office has already made all the

arrangements. You agreed to do it, and I expected you to honor your commitment.''

Cradling her cup carefully, she sipped her hot coffee. ''I'm certain you can find someone else.''

He swiveled on the barstool to face her, and his stern gaze softened. ''And if I don't care to?''

Just at that moment a knock sounded at the French doors, and Glynia strolled in. She wore a minuscule white bikini, her untamed black hair curling around her all-too-perfect face. ''Well, isn't this an intimate little scene?'' she said, then laughed lightly at Mark. ''It seems to take care of your aversion to eating breakfast alone.''

Amy almost dropped her coffee cup and the dark liquid sloshed onto the counter. Mark had made such a big thing about hating to dine alone, but apparently she was not the first woman to have heard that story. What other old lines had he fed her?

The phone rang and Amy reached across the counter for it, trying to ignore the kiss that Glynia was dropping on Mark's cheek.

''Marston residence,'' she managed.

''Amy? It's Rob. . . .'' He hesitated, then asked, ''Are you there?''

''Yes, of course I'm here.''

''Oh. You sound odd. I guess you're not alone.''

''No, I'm not.''

''I'll be brief. I was hoping to take you out for dinner and maybe to a movie tonight.''

''But we're leaving tomorrow morning for the wedding—''

''So am I,'' he put in quickly. ''We won't make it a late night. You'll have plenty of time to pack today.''

''Yes, I suppose so,'' she agreed, noticing that Glynia had perched on the barstool beside Mark and was pouring herself a cup of coffee. It would be a good idea to get out of the house tonight. ''Thank you, Rob. I'd love to go.''

After replacing the receiver, Amy excused herself. ''I've some things to do before the trip,'' she explained. ''Just leave my breakfast, please. I'll finish it later.''

"Sure," Mark replied with a speculative glance.

Glynia, on the other hand, flashed a calculating smile.

That evening, as Amy and Rob drove out of the Marston driveway, she felt a sense of relief in escaping Mark's presence. He—and Glynia—had spent most of the day on the patio just outside the laundry room window. It had been decidedly uncomfortable to be washing and ironing clothes with the two of them forever in sight—particularly Glynia in her white bikini.

"Val mentioned that you're going to do some more research for Mark in Philadelphia and Washington," said Rob, turning onto the highway.

"Oh? Well, I don't know. It's not definite. . . ." She paused, wondering how on earth her sister had heard about it.

Rob slid a curious look at her, then turned again to his driving. "How was the trip to San Francisco?"

"Fine. Just fine." She wasn't up to rehashing that episode in her life. "Could we possibly stop by my apartment? I'd like to see if they're making any progress. It's supposed to be ready in just over a week."

"Sure thing," Rob replied. "I wanted to get an early start so we wouldn't be rushed, so we could stop now if you like."

"Wonderful." Only last week the thought of moving into the empty apartment had filled her with such loneliness. Now she considered it more a haven—a retreat from Mark and the turmoil he had caused her.

As they pulled up outside the Spanish-style apartment building, a crew of landscapers were planting bougainvillaea against the white stucco. They had already put in hibiscus and bottlebrush bushes on the small incline sloping down to the sidewalk and red geraniums as a ground cover. Rob helped her out of the car, turning an annoyed look on the workers who eyed her with appreciation.

Inside, the pungent odor of fresh paint assailed them. The manager, an attractive fiftyish Mrs. Smithers, was busily moving in. "Go on upstairs, honey," she urged.

"The painters are finishing your place today. It's been a real challenge getting everything coordinated, but it's going to be worth it. Just wait till you see the nice parklike view from your living room window."

Upstairs, the painters were finishing the white walls of Amy's studio apartment, while in the bathroom, two plumbers were installing an equally pristine white bathtub. Dark wooden cabinets had already been hung in the minuscule kitchen.

"What parklike view was Mrs. Smithers referring to?" Rob inquired.

Amy looked out the sliding door and beyond the small enclosed balcony. "It appears that Mrs. Smithers means the street meridian's ivy and trees."

Rob chuckled, then looked around the apartment again. "And on the same positive note—it appears you won't have much cleaning to do."

"True." After living in the Marston home, the apartment seemed little larger than their kitchen and the adjoining family room. "But it's all right," she announced with determination. "By the time I'm through with it, it's going to be a real home.'"

"Sure it will," Rob consoled.

Later they stopped at a Mexican restaurant for a tostada dinner, then on to a movie, a spy thriller. Amy had read the book and was chagrined to see that the story had been changed to enhance the risqué element. It was embarrassing to sit with Rob through the smoldering love scenes. As far as she was concerned, the story line had been ruined.

On the way home Rob sensed her displeasure and apologized. "I guess we should have seen the science fiction movie." Adroitly changing the subject, he chatted about his work.

Amy appreciated his thoughtfulness and was content to listen, prompting him to continue with an occasional question. Gramp would have approved of Rob. She could hear him now . . . "A fine young man, Granddaughter." And indeed he was—caring, hard-working, and with more than his share of intelligence, albeit in the area of science, which unfortunately did not interest her.

As they pulled up at the Marston house, the outdoor lights were ablaze.

"They certainly lit it up tonight," Rob remarked, turning off the car's engine.

Amy shifted nervously in her seat, recalling their passionate kiss on the beach. No doubt Rob would expect another. Unconsciously she reached for the door handle. The door opened easily.

Startled, Rob climbed out and hurried around to help her out. He caught her hand in his as they strolled up the sidewalk to the front door.

Amy turned to him with a smile. "Thank you for a lovely time, Rob. I guess I'll see you in Virginia next weekend."

Under the bright light, Rob's brown eyes glowed with warmth. His hands cupped her shoulders and drew her to him.

The door cracked open loudly, and Mark stood there, towering over them. "I wondered who it was," he said, gazing at them curiously. "We have a house full of wedding presents. Can't be too careful nowadays."

Self-consciously, Rob dropped his hands. "I suppose so." The disappointment in his voice was evident.

"It's late," Mark added in a paternal tone. "We have to leave for the airport tomorrow morning by eight o'clock. It's going to be a busy week."

Amy bristled, certain that Mark had stationed himself near the door to interrupt their good-night kiss. "It's only ten o'clock, Mark," she reasoned, appalled at his nerve.

"Oh?" He glanced at his watch innocently. "It seemed much later."

Rob looked dubious. Finally he drew himself up and nodded politely. "See you next weekend in Alexandria, Amy."

"Yes. See you then." She stepped into the house, darting an indignant look at Mark. When the door was closed behind them, she turned on him, outraged. "Really, Mark! That was unforgivable. I can't believe you would—"

The blue of his eyes darkened with passion, and suddenly his arms were around her, crushing her against him, his lips putting an end to her tirade.

"Mark!" she protested at last, twisting away so violently that it took him by surprise. He backed off for an instant, and she seized the moment to sidestep his embrace. "You have no right!" she flung over her shoulder, rushing from the hallway and up the stairs.

What on earth had gotten into him? With any other man she might attribute such actions to jealousy, but certainly not with Mark who could have any woman he wanted. Whatever the case, she must make it perfectly clear that he had no claim on her. She refused to fall victim to any more agony over him! And . . . in the unlikely event that he thought meeting her at the door was some kind of joke . . . she was definitely not amused.

The next morning Amy tried valiantly to keep her distance from Mark. But as they climbed into the catering van—the one vehicle commodious enough to hold all of the luggage and the cartons of wedding gifts—she found herself sitting in the back seat between Valerie and Mark. The only diversion was Valerie's nervousness over what she might have forgotten.

"Don't tell me you're finally getting wedding jitters," Catherine commented laughingly from the front seat. "I thought for a while you might be the world's only exception to prenuptial nerves."

"I suppose that's all it is," Valerie replied uneasily, "though it's strange to be leaving Santa Rosita too. I wonder when I'll be back here again."

"In no time at all," Catherine assured her. "We're hoping the two of you will come home for Christmas."

Amy thought of Val's confession in their room this morning. "I'm suddenly terrified, Amy. What if after all this time apart Thom has changed his mind and doesn't want to marry me? Or what if our marriage turns out to be a terrible mistake?"

Amy had tried to reassure her sister, knowing how

109

many years Valerie had loved Thom. She marveled that Val would question her decision at the last moment. It seemed impossible.

Now Amy patted her sister's hand. "Valerie never gets the jitters," she said to Catherine. "She's the one who's always composed."

"I don't know about that," Val replied ruefully.

Mark turned to Amy. "You strike me as composed."

"I do?" Between Val's last-minute nerves and the episode at the door last night, she felt anything *but*.

"Yes, particularly as a researcher," Mark continued.

"Oh, that's different. That's dealing with words on paper," she began, then nearly lost all semblance of composure as Mark casually slid an arm around the back of her seat. What was he up to? Perhaps he had been jealous of Rob after all . . . but would he ever forget her terrible crack on the way home from San Francisco?

"Mark tells me you did an outstanding job on the San Francisco report," Dr. Marston injected.

Valerie spoke up proudly, "Amy has always been an excellent writer."

"Yes," Mark agreed, "excellent."

Amy turned a chilly look on him. After last night's embarrassing performance, she didn't know what to think anymore. Only one thing was certain: she would do no more research for Mark Marston. He would simply have to find someone else.

Sunday morning traffic was still light in Santa Rosita; even the freeways were surprisingly uncrowded as they approached the Los Angeles airport. Amy felt a flutter of excitement as Dr. Marston parked the van. Within minutes, they were sitting on an airport bus, then unloading beside the terminal.

When they finally boarded the plane, she found herself seated at a window, an empty seat between herself and Mark; his parents and Valerie occupied the seats just ahead of them. How had that happened?

Shrugging, she extracted a paperback novel from her carry-on bag and tried to read, but felt Mark's eyes on her. Finally he pulled the airline magazine from the seat pocket in front of him and opened it, thumbing through it distractedly.

As the plane taxied to the runway, Amy felt a great lump growing in her throat and clutched the armrests.

"Scared?" Mark asked with a twinkle in his blue eyes.

"Of course not!" she retorted, though it was only her second time to travel by plane. Years ago, Gramp had flown with her and Val to Northern California to visit old friends.

Amy turned to watch their take-off, the plane ascending rapidly as they flew well out over the ocean before banking east. Beneath them, the placid Pacific gave way to the sprawl of Los Angeles with its miles of freeways teeming with toy cars. From this vantage point even the canyons looked like small indentations in the crust of the earth, and the foothills like ripples in a tan ocean.

Shortly after the fasten-seat-belt light blinked off, the flight attendant served a midmorning snack of orange juice and nuts.

Mark sipped from his cup of coffee, lifting his gaze to study her. "I suppose I owe you an apology for last night."

"Yes, you do. And you owe Rob one too." But it was more than Mark's standing there at the door like a watchdog that bothered her. She had desperately wanted to end the entanglement between herself and Rob, and Mark's tasteless performance had only served to prolong the matter. There had been little sleep for her last night.

He hesitated, strangely uncertain. "I'm sorry."

"I'm sorry that it happened too. Just as sorry as losing my temper about Tony and his—his girlfriend in San Francisco, and my making that remark about Erika. We're both sorry. Now let's just let everything go at that."

"And if I don't particularly want to let things go at that?"

"I don't care to play games anymore!" Amy's voice rose. "I'm not Glynia or one of the other women in your life!"

From the seat in front of her, Val's head swiveled.

111

Hoping her sister hadn't overheard her heated exchange, Amy turned blindly to the window, but there was nothing to see except thick white clouds.

"Amy—," Mark whispered, taking her hand from the armrest.

She tugged herself loose. "Please leave me alone!" What a way to begin Valerie's wedding week—a quarrel between the maid of honor and the best man. Amy buried her head in her book.

Hours later, when she put down her paperback for lunch, Mark attempted to resume conversation. "About the research job in Philadelphia and—"

"I told you. I'm afraid you'll have to find someone else," she stated firmly.

"Let's try again," he began, "It will be strictly a business proposition. I'll even throw in a twenty percent raise to cover your—grievances."

"One hundred percent wouldn't be enough!" she returned, amazed that he would be willing to buy his way back into her good graces. "As for your suggestion that we have a *businesslike* relationship, I'm willing to substitute the word *pleasant,* but I'm not working for you again."

His eyes took her measure. "Then pleasant it is."

She turned to her lunch—a delectable spinach quiche, croissant, and salad—and was able to eat much of it.

Mark kept his word. He was a perfect traveling companion for the remainder of the flight to Newark, the most convenient airport to Princeton.

Deplaning behind Valerie, Amy again sensed her sister's nervousness. Fortunately Thom was not as mercurial as his older brother, nor was he as handsome, she thought with a wrench of her heart. Thank goodness Val had settled for the steadier of the two brothers! Of course, Thom had never faced the tragedy of a girl committing suicide over him. It was bound to have an effect. She wondered whether Mark often thought about it.

As they hurried through the disembarking area, Valerie clutched Amy's arm. "Do I look all right?"

"You look beautiful," Amy assured her, noting that her sister's cheeks were pinker than usual. "Just wait—everything's going to be wonderful. Thom's probably feeling a little nervous too."

On the other side Amy caught Mark's look of undisguised amusement and turned away. What did *she* know about brides and grooms and wedding jitters? She supposed he was thinking.

Approaching the lounge, Mark peered out over the waiting crowd, his height giving him great advantage. "There's the anxious groom!"

"Where?" Val asked apprehensively.

Spotting Thom's mop of auburn hair, Amy waved. "There he is, Val, at the front of the lounge." Scrutinizing the deplaning passengers, Thom did indeed look as unnerved as Valerie, Amy thought.

Val and Thom saw each other at the same instant. Dropping her carry-on case, Valerie fairly flew the last few steps, throwing herself into Thom's open arms. "Oh—Thom!" she cried happily, "I thought this day would never come!"

Amy's eyes misted over as she collected her sister's things and tried to avoid overhearing their happy reunion.

"No crying," Mark chided her as he helped gather up Val's belongings. "You're only allowed to cry at the wedding."

"I'm not crying," she insisted with a sniff.

Thom turned to Amy with his familiar lopsided grin. "Who's not crying?" he asked, dropping a brotherly kiss on her cheek. He was still holding a radiant Valerie, who looked as if she had never harbored a moment's doubt about the wedding.

Amy laughed through a new threat of tears. "Me . . . I'm not crying! Oh, Thom, you'd better be good to my sister!"

"I will, Amy. I promise." His brown eyes shone with sincerity, and he moved on to embrace his parents.

When all of the luggage and cartons were collected, Thom led them and a uniformed skycap to the parking lot. He had leased a station wagon to carry everything, and Mark had arranged for a sports car for his drive to Philadelphia and Washington.

"I'll drive Amy so you four can thrash out the last-minute arrangements," Mark offered. "That is, if the newlyweds-to-be can stop gazing at each other long enough to think."

"Wait a . . ." Amy tried to object, but it was too obvious that Mark's plan made perfect sense.

Within minutes the cars were loaded, and they drove off for Princeton, Mark's red Corvette tailing the station wagon.

At length he turned to her. "Tired?"

She nodded. Here in New Jersey evening was upon them and, despite the three-hour time difference, nightfall was welcome. "Yes. I'm exhausted, and if you don't mind, I'd like to skip dinner. I just want to go to bed."

"Didn't you sleep well last night?"

She shot him an incredulous look. "Please turn on the radio." She wasn't about to discuss her lack of sleep over him again; she'd fallen into that trap before.

Once the industrial area of Newark was behind them, the last lingering rays of sunshine disappeared too, and there was little to see as they drove through the countryside. Amy rested her head against the seat and felt herself doze off for an instant, blink awake, then slowly doze again.

It seemed only a short time before they arrived at a colonial hotel on the outskirts of Princeton. She sat up drowsily. "I thought it would take longer—"

"You were sleeping," Mark explained as he pulled into the hotel's parking lot.

She considered refuting his statement, but it wasn't worth another argument. Moreover, he was apparently right.

"By the way," he added, "you snore."

"I do not!"

He laughed as he opened his car door and climbed out. "Very softly."

By the time Amy was settled in the room she was to share with Valerie, she was ready for bed.

"Won't it look awfully strange if you don't come down to dinner, Amy?" Valerie was clearly disturbed. "Please come down with us, even if you're not hungry."

Amy inhaled deeply. "Well, if it's really that important to you, Val, I will."

"You know, I'm not sure I believe there's 'nothing doing' between you and Mark. Sparks are flying all around you two. It might not be romance, but it certainly is *something* . Please, Amy, try not to fight with him—at least until after the wedding."

"I'll try," Amy promised reluctantly, hurrying to freshen up.

Downstairs in the dining room, she found herself paired with Mark at the table. The six of them—Val and Thom, Catherine and James, and she and Mark—fell naturally into couples. She decided she might as well accept the situation gracefully; the two of them would be thrown together most of this graduation and wedding week. In any event she would only eat a salad and then excuse herself. Tomorrow they were to make the rounds of the campus and the town of Princeton, then on Tuesday Thom would receive his doctorate. She would make it clear to Mark tonight that she was traveling on to Alexandria with his family as originally planned—and most definitely not accompanying him to Philadelphia, nor to Washington D.C.

The meal was served promptly. To Amy's surprise, she heard Dr. Marston suggesting, "Shall we give silent thanks? This family has much for which to be thankful tonight." The warm glance that swept the table encompassed all of them, including Amy.

She bowed her head slightly and closed her eyes, concerned with whether other diners were watching. Lifting her eyes after a respectable interval, she marveled to find that no one seemed to have noticed. Yet why did she find the Marstons' prayers so disturbing?

As she tried a forkful of the delicious chilled crabmeat, Mark murmured, "I really need you to do those reports for me. Won't you reconsider?"

"Thanks for the compliment," she replied icily, "but I'm not going."

He looked pointedly at the others. "And what are they all going to think—especially since they know my office has already made the arrangements?"

Noting Val's happy expression as Thom whispered in her ear, Amy recalled the promise she had made to her sister. Pasting a smile on her face, she kept her voice light. "I really don't know what they'll think. I only know that I'm not going with you."

A muscle twitched near his chin. "Let's discuss it after dinner."

"Too late. I'm going to bed immediately after dinner."

He hesitated. "Then I'd like to see you to your room."

Across the table, Dr. Marston raised a quizzical eyebrow, and Amy nodded pleasantly. Still smiling, she whispered to Mark, "You most certainly will *not* see me to my room."

"At the very least, we might try to be civil this week for Valerie's and Thom's sake," he returned.

"All right," she conceded, "but *no* Philadelphia and *no* Washington D.C. either."

After finishing her crab salad, she excused herself. "I'm terribly tired," she apologized as she rose.

The men stood and Catherine Marston smiled. "Of course, dear. Run along. We won't be far behind you."

"If you'll excuse me too," Mark said, "I'll see Amy safely to her room."

Dr. Marston nodded, his blue eyes twinkling.

Did he suspect what this son of his was up to? Amy wondered hopelessly as Mark followed her out of the dining room. Mark looked so like his father, but it seemed improbable that James Marston had ever been as devious as his son.

Once they had left the dining room, Amy's temper flared. "*That* was not terribly subtle."

"Under the circumstances, I thought I handled it very well," Mark replied lightly.

"Oh, you did?"

"The proper line," he corrected with a smile, "is '*Oh, you did—did you?!*' "

"Thank you ever so much," she returned, though not

116

as icily as she had intended. "You're always so— helpful."

The elevator was crowded and people watched them curiously; it reminded her of their stay in San Francisco, which had been so blissful until that last evening and the trip home.

Stepping out onto her floor, Amy took a quick look around and turned to Mark. "Thank you for your concern, but you can see there's no one lurking in the shadows, so please feel free to go on to your own room."

"That's easy. It's next to yours," he responded, pausing at her door while she dug out the key.

She unlocked the door, intent on escaping into her room, but before the door was fully open, Mark's arms were around her, turning her to him, one hand behind her neck, his fingers in her hair.

"Let's try again, Amy," he pleaded, his voice low and compelling. She struggled for only an instant before yielding to the sweet demanding pressure of his lips on hers.

When she finally broke away, she whispered breath- lessly, "Kissing is all very lovely, but Mark, this won't work. It just won't work!" She rushed into her room and closed the door firmly against him.

Leaning against the door, her heart thundered as she heard him continue down the hallway before pausing to insert his key in the next lock. She must not get involved with Mark again. His kind did not believe in permanent commitments. And what could these passionate encoun- ters do but continue to tear her emotions to shreds?

CHAPTER 8

"GOOD MORNING, AMY."

It was Mark, holding the door of the station wagon as she hurried from the hotel entrance. His voice was friendly, his slow smile reminiscent of last night's encounter.

She avoided meeting his eyes, and addressed the entire group with a cheerful, "Good morning, all!"

Their equally cheerful greetings lifted her spirits. Having missed breakfast to evade Mark, she had been wondering uneasily what the day might bring. Apparently it would be a light-hearted outing with the Marstons, even though she would have to sit beside Mark as they toured Princeton. But only for one more day. Thom's graduation would take place tomorrow morning, then Mark would depart for Philadelphia—alone!

Thom was driving, with Val nestled happily beside him in the front seat, Dr. Marston on Val's other side.

Amy climbed into the back seat beside Catherine.

"Isn't this a gorgeous day!" Catherine exclaimed. "Thom swears that we've brought California sunshine with us. Their weather has been wretched until now—rainy all spring."

"Yes, it's beautiful," Amy agreed politely.

A sudden beam of sunlight struck a gold cross suspended from a thin chain around Catherine's neck. The older woman had purchased the necklace years ago while on a pilgrimage to the Holy Land with a group from her church. Again Amy was reminded of Catherine's faith and frequent admonition to count one's blessings . . . a timely idea since the situation with Mark was becoming increasingly uncomfortable. At the moment Amy's chief blessings appeared to be the sunshine and the simple fact that she was not alone with Mark this morning. His family served as a welcome buffer.

Mark moved in beside her, their shoulders touching lightly, his long well-muscled legs crowded against the front seat. "You're looking lovely as usual," he commented.

His masculine aftershave assailed her senses, but she managed an even, "Thank you."

Her turquoise silk blouse with tiny cape sleeves, white linen skirt, and white sandals had seemed appropriate for their leisurely day, and she had twisted her long hair loosely and anchored it to the crown of her head. But if Mark assumed that she had dressed to impress him, he was mistaken!

As they drove off for Princeton, she resolved to keep her eyes on the scenery. The countryside, green and luxuriant from the wet spring, held the fragrance of the purple and white lilacs blooming along the roadsides. Catherine, who had lived in the East as a child, enthusiastically pointed out unfamiliar flowers and trees.

After a while Amy felt Mark's gaze and turned to him with annoyance, but his conciliatory expression was disarming. She dropped her eyes in self-reproach and, when she looked up at him again, she managed a faint smile before turning away. It was unfair to fault him alone for last night's kiss. Perhaps if she had more experience with men, she would know how to deal with what was obviously a mere physical attraction for him. It appeared that his relationships with women never progressed beyond the physical, since at thirty, he had yet to make the commitment of marriage. Perhaps he never would—with women like Glynia at his beck and call.

From the front seat Thom detailed the scenic high-lights. As they passed by great dairy farms, he explained, "Some of these dairy farmers commute by helicopter to Wall Street daily—" He paused for effect. "That's where they earn their *real* cream."

"Oh, Thom!" the group groaned in unison.

He laughed. "I see I haven't lost my touch."

"Not yet," Mark added wryly. "Keep trying."

Here and there clusters of older houses lined the roadsides, then there were the ghosts of what had once been great estates with peacocks strutting the grounds. Almost all of them had been scaled down, even sub-divided in some areas into luxurious developments at prices Amy found appalling, though Thom managed to find the humor in that aspect too.

Not for the first time, she marveled that two such dissimilar people as Thom and Valerie had fallen in love. For one thing Val was not known for her sense of humor, but so enjoyed Thom's that she made a wonderful audience for him. Nor was Val as intellectual as Thom, who appreciated her artistic flair and sensitive nature. In their case it was a matter of opposites attracting and complementing each other, Amy concluded. Love was not only a many-splendored thing, she mused, but an extremely illogical one as well.

When they arrived in Princeton, its small-town simplic-ity and tiny downtown park, featuring an unpretentious bronze statue of a boy reading a book, did not quite disguise the area's underlying wealth.

"Understatement is the key here among the country gentry," Thom explained.

"You'd fit in well someday," Mark injected, "with your doctorate in economics."

Thom winked at Val. "Maybe when we're old and gray. Right now, Washington D.C. seems far more enticing."

Dr. Marston put in a jovial, "No cracks about the old or the gray," and Catherine reached forward to pat his silvery head.

How congenial they were, Amy thought, pleased that her sister would have a real family at last.

Beside her, Mark inquired conversationally, "What do you think of the East Coast so far, Amy?"

He was simply trying to be pleasant for his family's benefit, she thought, and decided to respond in kind. Gazing past him at the quaint town with its English village flavor, she remarked, "If the rest of the East Coast is like this, I'm impressed."

Thom said, "Unfortunately, Princeton will spoil you. It doesn't get any better."

The only *unfortunate* note of the trip thus far, Amy grumbled to herself, was Mark's constant presence, his nearness still unnerving her. At the moment she felt such energy flowing between them that she was tempted to lean against his strong tan arm, to touch his smoothly shaven jaw, to trace the creases around his lips with her fingertips. She closed her eyes, recalling his kiss. Feeling his gaze upon her, she blinked and found him smiling at her, as if he had read her mind.

Quickly she pretended an intense interest in the campus. Thom was pointing out Carnegie Lake, then the university's neo-Gothic Graduate College and its impressive Grover Cleveland Tower. As Thom parked the station wagon he insisted, "Everyone has to climb the tower. The view from the top puts the surroundings into perspective." Amy began to wish she had worn hiking shoes instead of the flimsy sandals.

Thom parked near the stately stone buildings housing the resident students, and he and Valerie went off in search of the tower key. In the meantime Amy wandered about, struck with the grotesque gargoyles overlooking the Graduate College's arched entrance. When Thom and Valerie returned with the key, they led the way into the stone tower, his parents trailing behind them.

"Aren't you going up, Amy?" Mark asked, waiting at the door.

"Yes—of course." She hurried to join him and entered the cool interior of the gray stone tower. Climbing the narrow spiral staircase with Mark just behind her, she could hear the others, chatting and laughing, their voices echoing in the confined space.

They had made quite a head start. Perhaps she should try to catch up with them, she thought, rushing up the worn stone steps.

"What's the great hurry?" Mark called.

He was the cause of her great hurry, Amy thought, pushing herself even harder. "I thought we might—" Suddenly her sandal slipped. "Oh . . . !" she cried out, her ankle turning and catapulting her into a fall toward the steps.

"Amy!" Mark grabbed her, staggered, then braced himself against the tower wall.

She clung to him, eyes closed in relief, pressing her face into his shoulder, into his warm masculine scent. "I'm sorry," she apologized, trembling. "I nearly took you down the steps with me."

"Amy . . ." he murmured, holding her close.

It was more than mere passion in his voice that stopped her from pulling away. "Yes . . . ?"

His voice filled with wonder. "I think I love you!"

Stunned by his words and the surrealistic setting, Amy felt herself spinning backward in time—back to her childhood, when her dearest wish had been to know Mark's love. Perhaps she was only conjuring up that childish wish again . . . simply daydreaming.

When she made no reply, he repeated huskily, "Did you hear me, Amy? I said I think I love you."

She whispered, "I heard you." Leaning away from him, she was amazed at the vulnerable expression on his face, an expression so unguarded and full of tenderness that she was weak. For a long moment they gazed into each other's eyes. "I don't know what to say," she finally responded, then, "Oh, Mark, I've waited so long to hear you say those words. I've—I've loved you all of my life."

With a shudder of joy, he gathered her closer. His admission had changed everything between them. There was hope after all . . . hope that he was open to love, that he felt far more than physical attraction and simple friendship for her.

From up above Thom called out, "Hey, you two! You're missing a great view!"

Mark said for Amy's ears only, "The view from here isn't bad either." Then, dropping a kiss on her forehead, he called up the winding staircase, "We're on our way!"

She smiled tremulously before he kissed her again, his lips warm and tender. Reluctant to leave his embrace, she finally forced herself away and continued up the winding stone stairs, scarcely believing what had happened. The phrase echoed in her mind: *I think I love you.* How strange that Mark's uncertain declaration had not been sealed with a passionate kiss, but rather with wide-eyed vulnerability.

When they joined the others atop the tower at a bright sunshiny window overlooking the campus and golf course, Amy thought she had never seen any place so beautiful in her life. With Mark beside her, tentatively holding her hand in the presence of his family and Val, Amy suspected rather strongly that the beauty of the view was enhanced by her happiness.

Mark's parents tried to act as if nothing had changed; Val leveled a warning look at Amy; and, on the way down the tower steps, Thom turned back to Mark with a wide grin and pointed out sotto voce, "You're wearing a trace of lipstick, pal."

Mark squeezed Amy's hand. "Thanks, but there's not much sense in wiping it off just now. I hope to be wearing more soon. Go on ahead. We'll be down."

"Whatever you say," Thom replied with an agreeable chuckle and continued down the tower steps. "Just don't hold us up too long."

"We don't promise to hurry!" Mark called after him with a laugh.

Amy shook her head ruefully, extracting a tissue from her handbag. "Fortunately, Thom exaggerates. It's even less than a trace of lipstick." She handed him the tissue.

"I hadn't planned to need that just yet," he whispered, taking her in his arms again. "I know a good thing when I find it."

"Me too," she whispered, "Me too."

The rest of the day passed, dreamlike, and Amy happily acquiesced to Mark's plea that she accompany him to Philadelphia and Washington D.C. "Your San Francisco report was excellent," he said. "So much travel writing is terribly reportorial and dull, but you brought an emotional touch to it . . . . a poetic touch too. You brought the city and its people alive for our readers."

How could she refuse with a compliment like that? How could she refuse when she never wanted to leave his side again? How could she refuse when she loved him with all of her heart?

The next morning dawned bright and clear. There was rejoicing when Thom graduated with honors under great sprawling trees among the ivy-covered halls of the university. Later there was a flurry of picture-taking—Thom, resplendent in his cap and gown, against a bower of purple blooming rhododendron; Thom and Valerie giving the victory sign; Thom and the rest of the family sharing the joy of his triumph.

With Mark at her side so attentive and loving, Amy thought she would burst with happiness. Val and Thom, caught up in each other and the festivities, made no comment, though Val occasionally darted concerned looks in their direction. Mark's parents wore a perpetual smile, embracing all of them.

That afternoon Amy and Mark set out for Valley Forge in his red Corvette, but the marvelous glow that had surrounded them had already begun to flicker. For one thing, Mark had never declared himself beyond that tentative *I think I love you*, and now his expression had turned contemplative as they drove down the turnpike. It struck her more and more forcefully that perhaps he was not at all sure he loved her, that he might have even changed his mind.

The smell of newly mown grass along the turnpike filled the warm air with an earthy reassurance, and she reached over to touch Mark's arm. "What are you thinking?" she ventured.

He shrugged uneasily. "Nothing much."

"Then why the thoughtful expression?"

"If you really want to know," he began, "I've been wondering if we've let things get out of control."

"Out of control? I don't quite understand." There had been nothing more than a few fervent kisses and embraces between them.

He frowned, staring straight ahead at the road. "I think we ought to simmer down."

She swallowed hard. "But I thought you were happy too. It was your idea to . . . to kiss me in the tower . . . and to tell me—"

"Yes, it was," he admitted. "And it's my fault for letting my feelings get the better of me. I apologize, though I'm not entirely sorry, either. It's just that I think we ought to back off, give ourselves time to see how we really feel."

She was so stricken that she hardly knew what to think or say. Finally the words came from beyond the lump filling her throat, "If you think so, Mark—"

He caught her hand. "I'm glad you're not furious. You have every right to be. But I just don't think we should rush into anything—"

Rush into anything! When she had spent most of her life loving him? Arguments and pleas leaped to mind, but it was useless. It would be impossible to force a commitment from him, nor would she want to.

Suddenly she knew precisely what was troubling him—the wedding! Val's and Thom's imminent wedding. Mark was frightened, whether he would admit it or not. He was surely not the first man to fear the prospect of marriage, particularly after having evaded it for so long. An old saying Gramp used to quote about bachelorhood came to mind: "A bachelor's life is a splendid breakfast, a tolerably fat lunch, and a most miserable dinner." But Mark evidently didn't see it that way.

The countryside disappeared in a blur. Trying to ignore the ache in her heart, she dug out her notebook. If she didn't occupy her mind now, she would surely give in to the tears that threatened. If only she hadn't agreed to this assignment, she would be on her way with the Marston family to Virginia. Now she would have to endure this trip stoically, for under no circumstances would she let Mark know how he had hurt her.

Later they drove into the green fields of Valley Forge National Historical Park and stopped at the Visitor's Center. The ultra-modern architecture of the underground building made a startling contrast to the Revolutionary era portrayed in its exhibits. That, she decided, was precisely how she must appear to Mark—cool and sleek and impervious to the pain hidden in her heart.

Inside, she gathered up brochures and took rapid notes from the placards describing the displays. "I suppose your foreign visitors ought to stop here first," she managed in a steady tone. "This is a good refresher course in American history."

"If they learned it at all," Mark added, his voice cool. "At the very least, they should stop here and at Washington's Headquarters."

"The Washington Memorial Chapel might be interesting too," she dared to suggest, since the Grace Cathedral in San Francisco had proved a successful addition to the itinerary.

"Possibly," he replied shortly, "although I've never been there."

Returning to the Corvette, Mark held the door for her but made no further comment. After their lovely interlude at Princeton, his cold aloofness made little sense. Possibly there was far more to his taciturn manner than his wanting to cool their relationship to a simmer.

"Don't you feel well, Mark?" she inquired, genuinely concerned.

His tone held a trace of anger. "I feel fine."

Well, I don't! she felt like flinging at him. However, if he intended to give her the silent treatment, she could play that game too. She opened her notebook.

Few tourists were about and Amy was thankful for the excuse of taking notes as they followed the park map. Special stops featured cannons and log cabins, where costumed "Revolutionary soldiers" wearing white breeches, white colonial-type shirts, and red vests explained the reconstructed settings. Between stops,

126

they drove at a leisurely pace through the battlefield. Amy had always enjoyed the study of history, and, despite her unhappiness, she experienced the illusion of riding through the 1700s.

Near George Washington's Headquarters, a friendly park ranger led them through the countryside with a small group of tourists, enthusiastically explaining everything from the history of the area to the stake-and-rider fence zigzagging around the handsome old stone house that had served as the president's quarters.

In the house, furnished much as it had been for Washington and his aides and officers, the ranger told of the Continental Army's epic struggle to survive against terrible odds—hunger, disease, and the unrelenting forces of nature. Hearing Washington's own words was especially moving: "To see men without clothes to cover their nakedness, without blankets to lie upon, without shoes . . . without a house or hut to cover them until those could be built, and submitting without a murmur, is a proof of patience and obedience which, in my opinion, can scarcely be paralleled."

"It does make history come alive, doesn't it?" Mark asked thoughtfully.

"Yes," Amy agreed with a shiver, "all too alive. I can just see those poor men in their tattered clothes, without blankets in the snow, far from home and family. . . ." Strange how insignificant one's own problems seemed when contrasted against far greater calamities, she thought.

Mark was looking at her oddly, and she wondered if he had forgotten their differences for a while too. Or was he only amazed at how quickly she had managed to rebound after the emotional battering he had given her?

Stepping outside, they wandered across the road to overlook Valley Creek and the rushing waters of the distant Schuylkill River. "Valley Forge seems a good half-day excursion for tourists visiting Philadelphia for several days," she said as they moved on.

"Remind me to check on how that's being handled with the agents I'm going to be interviewing," Mark ordered.

She nodded and jotted it down, tempted to slap him with a stinging, "Yes, *sir!*"

As they drove on, Amy pondered the beauty and living history surrounding them. Impressive as it was, how much more she would enjoy it if Mark were not retreating from her now.

Later, they parked at the stately memorial chapel and its nearby bell tower, where carillons pealed out the notes of "The Old Rugged Cross," the melody ringing across woods and fields. Letting himself out of the Corvette, Mark said rather abruptly, "I'll inspect the museum and you can take the chapel."

It seemed, more and more, that he was reverting to past behavior—shutting her out, avoiding contact with her. Or was he wrestling with a guilty conscience, sidestepping the possibility of a confrontation with God in the chapel? Mark had, after all, admitted that there was a time when he decided to be a minister like his grandfather, a time when he'd had a great deal of faith.

Amy grabbed her notebook and handbag and climbed out of the car without waiting for him, allowing the soothing music of the carillons to quiet her confusion.

She headed through the parking lot for the chapel, aware that the rift between them was widening by the minute. Why? Was Mark incapable of sharing a lasting love because of the resentment within him?

She forced her attention to the majestic gothic chapel and bell tower. Clear and pure, the final notes of the familiar hymn filled the air, and Amy recalled the words: *I will cling to the old rugged cross and exchange it someday for a crown.*

If she only had this kind of faith, perhaps the future would seem less frightening, and the present, less painful. She recalled that Catherine often played an old-time gospel record in which Robbie Hiner sang the hymn with overwhelming love and faith. How was it that some people found such peace in their relationship with God . . . and others—like herself—never quite grasped the meaning of faith?

Onward, she reminded herself, and entered the chapel,

open notebook in hand. Duty called and, since she had agreed to do the report, she would complete the research.

Inside, the chapel was startlingly beautiful. The floor, constructed of squares of black and white marble, shone with the luster of years, its checkered pattern interrupted only by bronze commemorative plaques in the three aisles. Despite the quiet intimacy of the sanctuary, there was an atmosphere of reverent grandeur that drew the worshiper's gaze toward the towering ceiling, where rich wooden panels were embossed with emblems of the states. Colorful flags hung from high above the white chancel with its carved and gilded cross; above the cross, an archway of stained-glass panels enhanced the gemlike magnificence of the place.

Amy held her breath. Though this was a sight to impress Mark's foreign visitors, there was more to the memorial chapel than its beauty. She sensed instinctively an aura of peace and joy and . . . grace . . . though the meaning of the word eluded her.

She dropped her eyes to the elegant gothic pews, carved in what was possibly walnut. A brass plaque on the side of one of the pews read: "To the glory of God," then listed a memorial name. Moving from pew to pew, Amy saw that the words were repeated, like a litany: "To the glory of God." How many loved ones had grieved over the deaths of those who had died for the sake of creating this country? How many hearts had been broken? Yet they had been able to dedicate those lives "to the glory of God."

As she recorded her impressions, Amy was vaguely aware of a woman sitting in a nearby pew. When she looked up again, she noticed that a pair of crutches was propped against the end of the pew. The woman was smiling, her eyes so full of love and light that her face seemed luminescent. There was an ethereal quality about her that reminded Amy of the great old paintings of the saints. Was it true that suffering could bring one closer to God, enabling joy to transcend pain?

Amy moved on toward a prominent wall plaque,

finding George Washington's prayer for the country. "Almighty God, we make our earnest prayer that Thou will keep the United States in Thy holy protection—" She read with a curious reverence, especially noting the ending: "Grant our supplication, we beseech Thee, through Jesus Christ our Lord. Amen."

There seemed no question that George Washington had been a Christian. She vaguely recalled having seen reproductions of a famous battlefield painting, depicting him on his knees in prayer. It occurred to her that, throughout the centuries, presidents had turned to God in times of national crisis, and she found her resistance crumbling. If presidents and statesmen felt the need for prayer and could humble themselves to place their petitions before God, shouldn't she? Not tonight or tomorrow or another day—but now.

Settling into a pew, Amy ran her hand absently over the lustrous reddish-brown wood before closing her eyes. How did one begin? *Heavenly Father,* she tried out the words she had heard others use, not quite sure she had the right to address Him as *her* Heavenly Father. *If You are really there . . . if You can hear me . . . please make Yourself known to me. I've made such a mess of things. I need the peace that . . . that others talk about . . . that Catherine Marston has. I need to know that You care what happens to us, that You forgive us. I want to believe in You. And, oh, if You would only work out things between Mark and me—*

Amy knew that she was not making such a good job of the prayer, and that she might as well end it. What had Washington said? *. . . through Jesus Christ our Lord. Amen.*

She opened her eyes slowly, hoping that something miraculous had happened. But nothing seemed to have changed except that the woman with the crutches was gone. The chapel was just as it had been before, though not as serene now that a group of school children had filed in with their teachers. Rising, Amy started for the chancel door, stopping only for a final glimpse—to capture the chapel's beauty in her memory.

Outside, Mark sat in the car, his impatient look making it plain that not only had he been waiting for some time, but that nothing had changed with him, either.

As they followed the drive that wound along beside the Schuylkill River, Amy noticed that smokestacks were interspersed with the church spires and housetops protruding above the trees. "Apparently Philadelphia's old settlements were built along the river for navigation and power in those days," Amy said into the silence between them.

"Typical of the old eastern cities," Mark returned evenly, his eyes on the expressway traffic. "It's still a major seaport today. The Schuylkill runs into the Delaware River at the edge of the city."

"So I see on the map." She felt like a schoolgirl receiving instruction from her tutor. Mark seemed determined to remain remote. She jotted down some notes.

Before long they were in downtown Philadelphia—a thoroughly modern city—and there was City Hall, topped by its famous statue of William Penn.

Caught in a traffic jam, Mark idled the motor of the Corvette. "We're staying near Independence Hall. I have a dinner appointment at seven, but you shouldn't have any trouble finding your way around after I get you oriented."

"Oh, I wouldn't think of putting you to the trouble," Amy insisted. "I'm quite capable of taking care of myself. Little Amy isn't as helpless as you may think." The moment the words were out, she wished that she could recall them.

Mark cast a skeptical look at her and turned back to the traffic, which was finally beginning to move. "I have an interview with a tour agent."

"You don't owe me any explanations. This is strictly business." But she couldn't help thinking that if he had wanted to be with her, he would have found a way.

Mark swung the car into the fast lane. "Tomorrow night I'd like you to join me. We'll be entertaining a couple."

131

"Don't feel that you have to include me."

"Amy—?" He touched her hand tentatively, and she pulled it away, turning to gaze out of her window at the City of Brotherly Love. How ironic, she thought, when she and Mark were engaged in a bitter cold war.

"Listen, Amy," Mark began, "it's my fault that our little discussion has been blown out of proportion. I wanted to back off—but not this far."

"Oh, no?" she returned heatedly. "Then why the silent treatment since Valley Forge?"

"I've been thinking—"

"Well, so have I!" she flung back. "I've been thinking that you're all for love as long as you don't get too close to a—" She almost said "lifelong commitment," but bit off the words.

"To what?" he demanded.

"Too close emotionally."

There was a thoughtful pause. "Maybe you're right, but this is not the world's best time for discussing the matter—not in the middle of this traffic."

"We had plenty of time on the way!" she fumed. What was wrong with her? Her emotions roiled on from anger and hurt to regret. "Oh, why can't we get along? What triggered the fight *this* time?"

"I believe I mentioned a dinner engagement," he replied blandly.

Feeling hopelessly childish, she peered out the window, scarcely seeing the rush-hour activity. She hadn't wanted to make this trip with him to Philadelphia in the first place, but he had coaxed and wheedled and kissed her until she had agreed. Well, she wasn't the first foolish woman who had fallen in love with her boss. Erika had been another—

Mark interrupted her thoughts. "Very honestly, after the scene you made in San Francisco over Tony and his date, I was afraid you wouldn't appreciate the man I'm interviewing tonight."

"The scene *I* made? What about *them*?"

Silence hung heavy between them during the remainder of the drive through the city. Finally Mark pulled up in the registration parking space of a red brick Georgian colonial hotel, and Amy let herself out of the car.

"I'd prefer to register myself. No more suites." She waited a moment for Mark's reaction, but when he said nothing, she hurried on, "In fact, I want to be on an entirely different floor!"

It seemed to take forever to process her registration and transfer her luggage to the room. But when she was at last alone, Amy threw herself onto the bed and cried out her anger and frustration. When the phone rang, she was sobbing too hard to answer; besides, she wasn't about to give Mark the satisfaction of knowing she had shed a single tear over him!

Finally, she wiped her eyes and blew her nose. The best thing to do at a time like this was to take a long hot shower. That therapy had been known to bring her emotions under control before.

Later, she changed into white slacks and a peach sleeveless knit shirt. Donning dark glasses, she hurried outside. It was only a few blocks to Independence Square, and, as she walked, her spirits lifted. Whether it was the brilliant sky or the soft June breeze blowing around the old red brick buildings that bestowed the calming effect, she didn't know; perhaps it was the ambience of a bygone era. Suddenly she felt a kinship with those other women from the past who might have experienced similar heartaches in this very spot, where the streets looked like illustrations in history books she had read as a child.

Finding a bench in Independence Square, she pulled out her research notes. It was from here that the Declaration of Independence had first been read publicly in July 1776. Indeed, Philadelphia had been the nation's first capital. John Adams had called the city "happy, peaceful, elegant, and hospitable." As she sat there pondering those words, she felt that they were still true at least in part, for she felt a sense of deep peace.

At length, she checked the map. Tonight she would locate the historical building recommended for tourists and wander along the Delaware River; tomorrow she would cover the tours. As she stood up to leave, Amy felt a bit of a spring in her step, a hint of renewed energy.

When darkness fell she returned to the hotel, pleased to have made so much progress with her research. Exhausted, yet feeling vestiges of her earlier tranquility, Amy decided to skip dinner and fall into bed. She opened her door and flicked on the light switch. Then she saw it on her dresser—a huge bouquet of red roses.

Her chest felt suddenly constricted and her thoughts tumbled wildly. The fragrance of the magnificent roses overwhelmed her, and her fingers trembled as she reached for the card. *Please forgive me,* it read, and was signed simply, *Mark.*

Happiness began to surge through her, but she caught herself up short. How could she possibly risk being hurt again? Whenever she was too available, he backed off. It was wiser not to rush into his arms. Besides, it was entirely possible that Mark's simple request for forgiveness did not imply love, that he was only interested in patching up their friendship. But why would he send her *red* roses—a symbol of love? She debated the possibilities endlessly until at last she changed into her nightgown and lay down exhausted in bed.

The next morning Amy carried the memory of the roses with her to breakfast, but there was no sign of Mark in the hotel coffee shop. Disappointed, she turned to mapping her course for the day: Independence Square tours including the Liberty Bell, Dolly Todd Madison's house, Betsy Ross's house, Christ Church, Elfreth's Alley, Head House Square, a fast lunch at the famous Bookbinders' Restaurant, then over to the City Hall Tower—for a unique view of the downtown area—and, last, the Council for International Visitors. How could she possibly see it all? She'd need to get started.

After the excellent introductory film at the Independence Square Visitors' Center, her timing for each tour was perfect. Everywhere she looked there was a bit of history. If only her report could convey the excitement she was feeling.

At noon, while lunching on delicious clam chowder at Bookbinders' near the wharf, Amy especially missed Mark. The popular restaurant was jammed with tourists and locals, many of them dining in pairs, and she felt saddened to be alone when it was just the sort of place one wanted to share. The restaurant's historic decor took her back to days of tall-masted ships at the river, horse-drawn wagons pulling loads of goods, horses and buggies, and children rolling hoops through colonial crowds.

After lunch she arrived at the old red brick Christ Church, from which an ornate white steeple pointed skyward. Stopping in the small gift shop to pick up a brochure and post cards, she was astonished to learn that among those who had worshiped here were George Washington, Thomas Jefferson, Benjamin Franklin and many other signers of the Declaration of Independence, seven of whom lay buried in the adjacent cemetery.

As Amy stepped into the simple white interior of the church, a hush fell within her. She walked slowly up the middle aisle toward what the brochure called the first Palladian window in the country, stopping at George Washington's pew. Alone in the church, she saw no reason why she might not sit down in it; she sank onto the red cushion. A brass plaque proclaimed:

Here worshiped George Washington,
General-in-Chief of the Continental Armies
First President of the United States
Martha Washington
from 1770–1797
The pew was voted by the vestry in 1797 to the use of
John Adams
Second President of the United States
It was occupied at a religious service by
Lafayette
on his second visit to America, 1824.

The signers of the Declaration of Independence had certainly been a godly group, she thought with some surprise. Had they, too, experienced the peace and tranquility she felt here now?

CHAPTER 9

DESPITE THE UNPLEASANT CIRCUMSTANCES of her arrival in Philadelphia, Amy regretted the time for their departure. The city had been fascinating beyond her expectations, and she had enjoyed last night's dinner as she and Mark slowly, almost wordlessly, made amends.

"I really liked the Engles," she said, gazing out at the passing scenery.

"So did I," Mark agreed. "Ed seems just right for the job."

After a morning interview with Ed Engle, Mark and Amy had taken Ed and his wife out for dinner in the evening. The topics of conversation had ranged far beyond the tourist industry. The attractive couple had even introduced the subject of religion.

Donna Engle, an amber-eyed redhead, had enthused, "Our marriage, which was fast becoming a disaster, changed when we accepted Christ as our Savior. In fact, our newfound faith has changed our entire lives!"

"It's made that much difference?" Mark asked, genuinely interested.

Ed Engle, so darkly attractive that he occasionally performed in local television commercials, fondly squeezed his wife's hand.

"I'd have never believed it myself. I was always on the fringes of the church, trying to edge in occasionally, but I had such a mistaken impression of Christianity. I suppose that's common when you're on the outside looking in." He chuckled. "If I'd known what an adventure it would be, I'd have turned my life over to the Lord years ago!"

Amy hoped to hear more, but Mark quickly maneuvered the conversation around to the tour agency business. It struck her again that he seemed determined to avoid the subject of religion. Yet at the end of the evening, he hired Ed as his new agent for Philadelphia, despite Ed's lack of expertise with foreign tourists.

Mark explained after the Engles left them in the hotel lobby, "I suppose I really hired Ed because I trust him, and trust in an employee is money in the bank." He had darted a look at her. "It seems that not everyone is trustworthy."

Now what did he mean by that? she reflected later in her room. That he had been throwing out confusing signals? That he had let her down?

Now, driving toward Delaware Bay, they discussed the upcoming wedding. "Can it only be three days away?" Amy asked with amazement. "This entire trip has flown by so quickly."

"Yes . . . far too quickly." His dark glasses disguised his intentions so effectively that she was surprised when he reached for her hand. Reason warned her to pull away, but his hopeful smile deterred her. "I'm afraid you can't really trust me," he said, "I'm as confused and torn by all of this as you must be."

"I want to trust you, Mark, but I don't understand. . . ." Her voice quavered threateningly and she forced herself to continue, "I just don't understand what's been happening with you!"

He slowed the car, pulling off onto the shoulder of the road and stopping. After shifting into neutral, he gazed at her thoughtfully. "What's been happening is that I've been falling in love with you more and more every day."

"Oh, Mark—are you sure?"

"I'm sure, very sure." Gathering her into his arms, she was only vaguely aware of the restraint of the seat belt. As their lips met, her heart overflowed with forgiveness for the anguish she had endured. The car, idling under them, intensified the fervor of their kiss, and she scarcely heard the blaring horns of cars whizzing by. This time there had been no hesitation in his voice. This time he had clearly stated, *I've been falling in love with you.*

If only this blissful moment could last forever . . . if only nothing ever came between them again. But a niggling doubt zigzagged through her mind and quite suddenly her lips trembled. As Mark pulled away in surprise, she burst into sobs.

"What is it?" he asked with concern. "What's wrong?"

"I can't imagine what got into me," she apologized, reaching for a tissue to blot her tears. What an unromantic spectacle she had made of herself.

"I must admit, crying was not quite the response I expected," he said, his eyes full of consternation. "Are my kisses so bad?"

Smiling tearfully, she shook her head. "They're wonderful! I don't know what's wrong with me. . . . I'm sorry, Mark."

He let out a deep breath. "Well, I think I know, and I must have been an idiot not to see it before. You've been under too much emotional strain since the San Francisco trip . . . for the last few months, for that matter. With your grandfather's death, selling his house, finding an apartment, getting ready for Val's wedding . . . and now me . . . well, it would be too much for anyone. I'm afraid I haven't helped at all." He turned from her and shifted the car into gear. "*I'm* the one who's sorry." Glancing behind them, he swung the car back onto the road and accelerated with a burst of speed fueled by his self-contempt.

"You are not an idiot!" she protested. "I think you're just as confused as I am by . . . by all of this."

He kept his eyes on the road. "But that doesn't make it fair for me to tear you apart too!"

She slipped her hand under his on the steering wheel.
"I'll be all right now. I promise, I'll be all right."

He drew her hand to his mouth and kissed it. "If my
family knew how I've been treating you, they'd never
forgive me."

"But it's my fault too . . . and they'll never know—
unless you tell them. Besides, there have been so many
happy moments too."

"When, for instance?"

"Just being with you," she said simply, "and sometimes when you look at me without those sunglasses on.
You must have the most beautiful blue eyes in the
world."

He grinned.

Something within her compelled her to say, "I love
you, Mark."

A kaleidoscope of emotions rushed across his face.
"Don't you know you should never admit that you love a
man?"

"I guess I don't know a great deal about men," she
confessed.

"Thank goodness for that! Though I'm not sure there's
ever been a woman alive who didn't intuitively know
more about men than they do about themselves."

She removed his right hand from the steering wheel
and kissed it. "Maybe I'm an exception."

He smiled. "After that display, I doubt it very much."

She rested her cheek against the warmth of his hand.
Loving him did seem the most natural thing in the world.
But then she'd had a great deal of experience at that—
since she was seven, at least.

As they drove over the great bridge connecting Delaware Bay with Chesapeake Bay, she set the unhappy
memories firmly behind her, basking in the warmth of the
moment—and the splendor of the scenery. There were
inlets grown thick with reed and cattails, then the Kent
Narrows Bridge, and finally the majestic silvery Bay
Bridge, thrusting itself skyward over the blue waters of
the bay. As they crossed the bridge, great sea-going
freighters, naval vessels, sleek yachts, and tiny sailboats
moved below them on the watery thoroughfare.

The sight caused Amy's conscience to gnaw at her. "Time to start thinking about my report on Washington."

"There's a manila envelope full of literature on it in my briefcase."

Amy unbuckled her seat belt and leaned over the back seat. Catching his knowing grin, she was reminded of that other day when, in the same precarious position, she had been thrown against Mark's shoulder with an electrifying jolt. Hurriedly, she retrieved the sleek black case and settled herself in her seat.

Still grinning, he apparently chose to ignore that earlier incident. "It took me by surprise to discover you were a beautiful young woman the day I picked you up at your grandfather's house . . . no longer little Amy."

"No longer *chubby* Amy, you mean," she amended.

They chatted easily about the past while she extracted the literature from the manila envelope and sorted through it. There were maps, guides to Washington— past and present, brochures on the Smithsonian, the White House, the Capitol, and more . . . far more than she had realized. "I don't see how I'll cover it all in a few days."

"We'll have tomorrow for an overview, but there won't be any work this weekend . . . we do have a wedding to attend. By the middle of next week, we should be able to wrap up the Washington report. Most of our tourists have only a day or two to spend in the city, and I've been there often enough to direct you to the highlights. So it shouldn't be a problem."

"Thank goodness!"

"Uh, while we're on the subject, could I coerce you into doing a report on Boston when I'm there?"

She laughed in astonishment. "Oh, I don't think it would take much coercion."

He cast a sidelong glance at her. "Good. I've been thinking about expanding a few of the tours to Canada too. But that wouldn't be until August or so. How does that strike you?"

"As if I'm going to wake up any moment! This seems

141

so incredible. I don't know what I've done to deserve it."

Mark smiled at her pleasure. "You've made me very happy—that's what you've done.'"

"And I thought it was my writing skills!"

He chuckled. "That, too."

"Then I'd better start learning all I can about Washington." She happily turned to peruse the literature in her lap.

Nearing Washington, Mark suggested, "Let's stop for dinner. I'm sure they've already eaten at Aunt Alicia's . . . besides, I'm not ready to share you with the others yet. There's an intimate little restaurant in Georgetown beside the canal—"

"Sounds wonderful. I accept with pleasure."

"You're right," he teased, "a fellow doesn't have to use much coercion on you."

"Well . . . I don't know about that! I'm usually not all that accommodating to fellows in general. The thing to keep in mind is that *this* fellow is you."

He caught her hand in his and held it against his cheek, sobering. "I'm glad you haven't been accommodating— very glad, Amy."

Their candlelit dinner was indeed wonderful, as was the leisurely nighttime drive into the center of the nation's capital. Despite the many pictures she had seen of Washington, Amy was unprepared for the tide of emotion she experienced at the sight arising from the darkness. Floodlights struck the grandeur of white marble: the Lincoln Memorial . . . Washington Monument . . . Jefferson Memorial . . . the White House . . . the Capitol. Old and familiar words suddenly gained new meaning: . . . *to the republic for which it stands . . . one nation, under God . . . with liberty and justice for all.* These splendid white monuments, silhouetted against the night sky, were part of a nation's dream—and that dream had come true. Sitting close to Mark, Amy dared hope that another lifelong dream might come true as well.

The next morning, in Aunt Alicia's stately Georgian house in Alexandria, Virginia, Amy was awakened by a persistent ray of sun beaming through the leaded glass windows. Valerie's twin bed was already made, which meant she was probably already busy downstairs with rehearsal dinner and wedding plans.

Last night when Amy and Mark had arrived, Val had eyed them curiously before mentioning that Rob and Glynia were already registered at nearby hotels, hoping to join them tonight for dinner.

"Fine," Mark had agreed. "The four of us can make an evening of it here in Alexandria, or try one of the new restaurants in Washington."

"Hey, how about Val and me?" Thom complained.

"Don't you two lovebirds want to be alone?" Aunt Alicia chided. The stylish platinum-blond widow with twinkling brown eyes was exactly as Catherine had portrayed her—a love.

Valerie laughingly slipped her arm through Thom's. "Oh, he's afraid he's going to be stuck with me all the way to the hereafter."

"Afraid!" Aunt Alicia responded with an incredulous smile. "I should think he'd be bursting with joy to have found himself such a lovely bride."

"I am . . . oh, I am!" Thom shook his head hopelessly. "I'm such an anomaly that I don't even have the sense to be a nervous bridegroom. Not a single sign of cold feet."

Catherine and James Marston led the laughter, and Amy's gaze wandered to Mark. Just as she had expected, he had not joined in the good-natured ribbing. He wasn't at all comfortable with the subject of marriage. Now a new thought troubled her. Though she had openly declared her love for Mark, he had only mentioned that he was falling in love with her. She had arrived at the final destination, but he was merely underway . . . possibly even hanging back to simplify a retreat. Why did she have to love the brother with cold feet!

Time to get up, Amy prompted herself. She slipped out of bed, determined to set aside last night's memory.

Outside, sunshine slanted across the grounds, and a

mockingbird sang from atop a brick wall laden with red roses. Arriving so late last night, she had scarcely noticed the charming garden, though she had taken note of the fine English antiques in her and Val's room. She noted now that her white crinkled cotton dress hung outside the closet for today's sightseeing. Fortunately it would not require pressing.

She hurried to the shower, mentally reviewing what she would be wearing for dinner tonight, tomorrow night's rehearsal dinner, and the wedding on Sunday. Everything seemed to be in order. A maid would be on hand later to press any wrinkles from the wedding finery. She knew, too, that Aunt Alicia had household and gardening help, and caterers would furnish the food.

Right after breakfast Amy planned to plunge into her report on Washington, D.C. Mark had scheduled an interview with a tour agency manager in the afternoon, but they would be able to spend a major portion of the day together.

Half an hour later, she took a final glance in the mirror mounted in a dark antique stand. Despite all of the rushing about, she seemed to be holding up rather well, she thought with satisfaction. Her white dress contrasted effectively with her hair, which she had twisted loosely at the crown of her head again. Looking more closely into the mirror, she noticed that her eyes were a deeper shade of turquoise than usual—anticipation, no doubt.

As she stepped into the long second-floor hallway, Mark was just starting down the stairs. "Good morning," he said, his eyes lighting up at the sight of her. "Fancy meeting you here."

"Well, good morning, yourself." Her heart must have been in her eyes because he stepped back up the stairs and strode toward her, catching her in his arms.

"Oh, Amy!" he whispered before his lips sought hers. Nothing about his actions gave any indication that he might be contemplating a retreat now, she thought before surrendering to his kiss.

"Ahem," Mark's brother interrupted, running his fingers self-consciously through his mop of auburn hair.

144

"Just call me Peeping Thom. Somehow I always manage to stumble in at just at the wrong moment—or maybe it's the right moment. Whatever, it looks just fine to me!"

Startled, Amy pulled away, feeling blood rush to her cheeks.

Mark laughed, though his tan face had darkened a shade too. "Your timing couldn't be worse. You might have done the gentlemanly thing and taken the window exit. It's only a one-story jump—"

"Now that's carrying brotherly love too far," Thom protested, giving Mark an affectionate jab in the ribs. "Besides, how would Valerie feel if her groom arrived at the altar with two broken legs? On the other hand, a silver-handled cane might add some dash to the wedding pictures."

They laughed at his running banter as the three of them made their way down the stairs. Catherine had often attributed Thom's facility with words to that same streak of Irish in their blood that had colored their hair such an unusual shade of auburn.

At the foot of the stairs Thom drew himself up. "My dear brother, it is my duty to point out that you are again wearing the lady's lipstick."

"Spoken like a true Southern diplomat," Mark responded with a grin as he reached for his handkerchief. "I predict you're destined for political greatness."

Amy might have blushed again if their further drolleries hadn't set them all laughing.

The rich aroma of freshly brewed coffee beckoned, and they continued to the dining room. Dr. Marston rose to greet them. "What's so hilarious already this morning?" he inquired.

Thom's eyes darted audaciously to Amy, then to Mark, who drew a threatening finger along his throat. Thinking better of betraying their kiss, Thom answered evasively, "I regret to say, sir, that it is highly classified information."

"I suppose we'll be hearing that line often now that you'll be working in Washington," Dr. Marston said with a chuckle, then nodded toward the buffet. "Breakfast is waiting. We're to help ourselves since the other ladies are plotting our course for the weekend."

The buffet offered orange juice, fresh strawberries and melons as well as silver-lidded dishes containing steaming scrambled eggs, sausages, hashed brown potatoes, and English muffins. Amy served herself, taking pleasure in Mark's presence just behind her and in the consciousness of being so lovingly accepted by his entire family.

Rob phoned during breakfast. "I thought you might like to explore Washington with me and my folks."

"Sorry," Amy replied, less than truthfully, "but I'll be working on a report. We'll be having dinner in Alexandria's Old Town tonight—that is, Val and Thom, and Mark and Glynia and I. You're joining us, aren't you?' "

"Sure, but I had hoped—" He could not quite conceal a trace of disappointment. "Where and when?"

Half an hour later, Amy and Mark drove through Alexandria and along the Potomac River into Arlington. To the west rose the green hills of Arlington National Cemetery crowned by the Custis-Lee Mansion. They turned onto the Arlington Memorial Bridge, which was flanked by great golden statues.

Mark's voice deepened with pride. "And here we are in Washington again."

Despite last night's wondrous sights, Amy's throat tightened to see the city by day—the great white monuments and buildings gleaming in the morning sun above the green grass and trees of Potomac Park. As Mark parked the car near the Lincoln Memorial, her anticipation and excitement grew. Cars, tour buses, a tourmobile, and throngs of tourists converged on the spot.

She grabbed her handbag and notebook, and quickly let herself out of the car to study the classical lines of the monument, so like a Greek temple. There was dignity and strength befitting a president like Abraham Lincoln.

Mark caught her hand in his. "Impressive?"

"Now that's an understatement! I really had no idea

that Washington would be such an . . . an emotional experience.''

Mark brought her hand to his lips and kissed her fingertips. "Then I'm definitely glad to be the first to show you the city. . . . The only problem is—'' Amy turned in alarm to catch the wicked gleam in his eye. ''—that all newcomers are required to climb to the top of every monument.''

"Good!" she laughed, darting just out of his reach. She almost danced across the green carpet to the base of the monument. "I need the exercise!"

Climbing the wide expanse of marble steps, Amy noted the reverent hush as a group of tourists neared the temple's platform and the formidable white statue of the martyred president. Above Lincoln's head, Amy read the words: *In this temple as in the hearts of the people for whom he saved the union the memory of Abraham Lincoln is enshrined forever*. Despite his homeliness, the bearded, lanky backwoodsman from Illinois had become a great luminary.

Lincoln's watchful gaze appeared to be directed across the shimmering ribbon of water of the Reflecting Pool toward the obelisk piercing the sky—the Washington Monument. And, after a few moments of quiet contemplation, they descended the steps to walk the grassy path to that famous shrine.

Fifty American flags surrounding the monument fluttered in the breeze, again bringing a catch to Amy's throat. At its base, a long line of anxious tourists awaited the elevator ride to the top.

"Do we have time to go up?" she asked.

"Absolutely. It's one of our most important stops— the perfect place to learn the layout of the city. When we traveled in Europe as kids, we always had to climb to the top of the highest building to get the lay of the land.''

"Poor Catherine. How did she put up with the two of you?''

"She loved it as much as we did," he returned.

"I guess she would." Shielding her eyes with her hand, Amy gazed upward in dismay. "Still, I'm glad we have an elevator!"

"You can walk down."

She shook her head. "No, thanks. I've an idea I'd better conserve my energy!"

The line to the elevator moved rapidly and before long they were at the top of the monument, overlooking the city. To the west, the Lincoln Memorial; to the east down the Mall, the Capitol Building; to the north, the serene beauty of the White House; and to the south across the Tidal Basin, the pristine Jefferson Memorial. The length of the Mall leading to the Capitol was lined by palatial buildings which Amy recognized from pictures she had seen, including the Smithsonian Institute and the National Gallery of Art. "I could stay up here all day," she said.

"Afraid you'll just have to capture it with your camera," Mark said, looking as pleased as she felt.

After she had snapped pictures, he slipped an arm around her shoulders. "And this is just the beginning."

She shivered, knowing that he referred to the sights of Washington, but wishing this were *just the beginning* of their love—that it would stretch on forever, like the great canopy of blue sky overarching the nation's capital.

With time at a premium, they chose the elevator for their descent from the top of the Washington Monument, too, then headed for the White House through a stand of trees and across Constitution Avenue. Ahead was the Ellipse, a park dotted with numerous small monuments, park benches, and trees. After a while, they joined the line of tourists waiting to purchase White House tour tickets. While they waited, a Dixieland band entertained them with its lively music.

"How will I ever keep it all straight?" Amy asked in consternation. "We've barely begun and, according to this map, around the corner are the State Department, National Academy of Science, Constitution Hall—"

"You'll do a fine job."

Mark's confidence was reassuring, but there was so much to cover. So far, with Mark squiring her around, it had been easy. But he had an appointment this afternoon. After he had purchased the tickets, she trailed behind him, jotting notes.

"Look," he said quietly, placing a hand on her shoulder.

There in the distance, through the high black wrought-iron fence, was the White House; it nestled serenely behind a sprawling lawn dotted with trees, fountains, and colorful flower beds. "How perfect it is," she commented, "grand and elegant, yet simple and private too. Precisely the kind of house for an American president."

"The architect was inspired by eighteenth-century French country houses."

"Country *houses?* It seems more like a mansion!"

"Executive mansion it is," he responded with a smile, obviously enjoying their tour as much as she. "We'll circle around for a better view."

On their way, they walked by the statue of Winged Victory poised upon a tall column, then turned northwest and passed the Old Executive Office Building, a gray Victorian megalith that filled an entire city block. Dark-suited dignitaries streamed in through security checkpoints.

"Just another day at the office?" Amy inquired dryly.

Amused, Mark replied with a laugh. "Just another day at the office."

Moments later, they were approaching Pennsylvania Avenue, then Lafayette Square, where statues of Revolutionary War heroes and old cannons stood among beds of flowers.

Later, as they stood in line with the colorful crowd near the White House, the air seemed to vibrate with anticipation, intensifying as they moved along to the North Portico. Once inside the impressive mansion, they moved through at a breathtaking pace. There were priceless remnants of the past: antique furniture, chandeliers, paintings. The Blue Room . . . the Red Room . . . the East Room . . . the Green Room—Amy could almost sense the presence of Adams and Lincoln, Roosevelt and Truman as she walked down the hallowed halls. So much to see and no time to take notes. It seemed only a few minutes before they were outside again.

The day flew as they investigated the Smithsonian

Institute, which she learned was comprised of buildings scattered about the city. They began in the Museum of American History with its intriguing collection of Americana: memorabilia of the presidents, Alexander Graham Bell's first telephone, Edison's light bulb, folk art, and a railroad hall with a huge green locomotive from the 1920s, an automotive hall with vintage cars and turn-of-the-century horseless buggies, and far, far more. Amy especially enjoyed an exhibit of the gowns worn by America's First Ladies.

"Your foreign female tourists will love seeing the gowns," she remarked.

"And the men," Mark added with a chuckle, "will be crazy about the Air and Space Museum."

Next door was the Museum of Natural History, featuring a huge African elephant in the rotunda, flanked by exhibit halls of dinosaurs, marine life, birds, and mammals. The Hall of Gems sparkled with stunning gems, including the astonishing Hope Diamond with over forty-five carats.

As they left Amy said wistfully, "It would take at least half a day in each museum to do them justice! Most of your foreign tourists will have only a fleeting glimpse."

"Unfortunately, that's all most American tourists have time for too."

After lunch in the National Gallery of Art's cavernous underground cafeteria, Mark dropped a kiss on her forehead. "I'll meet you in the sculpture garden at the Hirshhorn Museum at three-thirty. Sure you can find it?"

The location was circled on her detailed map. "Positive," she said, so radiant that he decided to kiss her again.

"I shall return," he vowed.

"Another great American made that statement, as I recall," she quipped. "I hope you're as reliable as he was."

Buoyed up by happiness, she hurried on, grateful that there would be time next week to inspect many more of the intriguing buildings and exhibits. Today she definitely had to view the Capitol, the most dominant and magnificent sight on the Mall.

Throngs of tourists—many of them in groups from abroad, chattering in their native tongues—climbed the steps of the Capitol with her, bringing to mind American Holidays, Inc. Mark's clients would want to know that the gleaming dome echoed those of Old World structures—St. Peter's Basilica in Rome and St. Paul's Cathedral in London. They would most likely be interested, too, in the fact that Constantino Brumidi, an Italian painter and muralist who had fled persecution in Italy, had made significant contributions throughout the Capitol building.

Inside, Amy joined a tour group and followed along through the series of grand chambers connected by a maze of passageways and corridors. When they reached the central Rotunda, she marveled with the others at Brumidi's masterwork, the decoration of the dome: a huge allegorical printing call the "Apotheosis," honoring George Washington. Below, eight historical paintings by early American artists depicted scenes from the lives of Columbus, Pocahontas, and the Pilgrims.

"Here in this Rotunda," the tour guide said, "American heroes have lain in flag-draped coffins . . . unknown solders and martyred leaders . . . Lincoln, Garfield, McKinley, and Kennedy."

Amy glanced at her fellow tourists; most seemed as awed as she to be here. Then it was time to move on again. Throughout the building there were statues of eminent Americans from Daniel Webster and Jefferson Davis to Will Rogers.

In the Senate corridors, they admired the elaborate murals by Brumidi. Congress was not in session, and the imposing chambers of the Senate and House of Congress were occupied only by tourists and their guides who spoke in English, French, German, Spanish, and Japanese. Amy picked up a smattering of information, enough to know that the guides were explaining the workings of the United States Government. Yes, most definitely, American Holidays' tourists must have time for a stop in these chambers. Even after her tour group disbanded, Amy wandered on through the Capitol, reluctant to leave.

When she glanced at her watch again, she realized that she would be late to meet Mark, and she rushed out to the Hirshhorn Museum. There would be no time to view the contemporary artwork inside today, though the outdoor sculpture garden with its many statues would surely intrigue modern art aficionados. She arrived out of breath, then saw to her relief that Mark was just arriving too.

"How did it go?" he asked.

"Too fast, but wonderfully."

He tucked her hand in the warm crook of his arm. "Even without me?"

"Well, of course, it would have been better with you."

He smiled with pleasure. "There's time to stop by the Jefferson Monument, and maybe Arlington Cemetery if we hurry."

Later, they admired the great white marble memorial to Thomas Jefferson, modeled after the Pantheon in Rome. According to the guidebooks, the low rounded dome and classical pediment leading to the interior resembled the architectural style of Jefferson's home, Monticello.

"Monticello is another place some of our tourists have said they would like to visit," Mark mentioned.

"On the extended tours, I hope!"

Before long, they were driving across Memorial Bridge and then into the gates of Arlington National Cemetery. Its historic Custis-Lee Mansion was lovely, and the Tomb of the Unknown Soldier and the Iwo Jima statue were impressive, but it was the rows upon rows of grave markers that touched Amy with their mute but heart-rending display. A sobering end to the day, she thought as they began their homeward drive to Alexandria.

"Tired?" Mark asked as he eased the car into traffic on the George Washington Parkway.

"A little," she admitted, "and sad, too, that so many have died for our country's freedom."

He shrugged. "Everyone has to die sometime . . . at least they died for a cause greater than themselves."

"I suppose that's more than most of us do, but it's still so sad. It reminds me . . ."

"Of your grandfather?" His tone was compassionate.

Her voice broke unexpectedly. "Yes . . . and my parents."

Mark studied the traffic thoughtfully. "My grandfather used to quote from the Book of Revelation: 'And God shall wipe all tears from their eyes; and there shall be no more death, neither sorrow, nor crying; neither shall there be any more pain: for the former things have passed away.' "

She gazed at him in surprise. "And you remember that after all these years?"

"I remember a lot of things he told me," Mark replied.

CHAPTER 10

At seven o'clock the family gathered in Aunt Alicia's parlor, as she called the elegant room in which the wedding would take place on Sunday. Mark and Thom had already rearranged the antique furniture to accommodate the string quintet. Although everyone was dressed for dining out, Catherine had coaxed the men into making further minor adjustments to the furniture arrangement.

"If you could just move the chair that way a trifle and the couch back a few inches—"

There was a general round of laughter.

As the doorbell rang Thom was teasing, "Let's practice the 'You-may-now-kiss-the-bride.'"

"Oh, you two!" his mother chided as she hurried to answer the door. The elder Marstons and Aunt Alicia would be dining out with relatives at the club where tomorrow night's rehearsal dinner was to take place. "Glynia! And here comes Rob too!"

Amy was wearing a favorite off-white linen dress, but felt she might disappear into the woodwork after one look at Glynia. Provocative was not a strong enough word for her smashing jade green silk dress with its halter neckline and side slits. Rob, on the other hand, was sedately dressed in a new tan suit.

154

"Hi, Amy," he said, his brown eyes shining with pleasure as he stepped into the room. She had forgotten how attractive he was.

Within minutes they were outside, heading for Aunt Alicia's silver Mercedes, which she had urged upon them. "I'll drive," Mark offered, "so you lovebirds can sit together."

With a flash of lovely slim legs, Glynia quickly slid in beside him while Amy looked on helplessly. Rob appeared as discomfited as she, but helped her in beside Glynia before joining Val and Thom in the back seat. It did not seem an auspicious beginning. Fortunately it was a short ride to the historic restaurant through the gracious tree-lined streets of Alexandria.

As they parked the car Thom, who had dined at Gadsby's Tavern before, expounded on its background. "In the 1700s," he began in exaggerated tour-guide style, "this was already a famous restaurant in which Washington, Jefferson, and Henry Clay dined. It was also the scene of a ball held in Washington's honor . . . and, from the steps of this restaurant, he reviewed infantry volunteers. As one might suppose, many a heated debate took place here between loyalists and patriots."

Thom's pompous delivery brought a round of applause, and, as Rob helped her out of the car, Amy devoutly hoped that the historic building would not be the setting for any heated debates tonight. She felt more and more uncomfortable, particularly with Rob at her side and Mark uneasily gravitating toward Glynia. But what else could Mark do? Amy reminded herself with a wistful glance at the striking couple.

Inside, a maître d' in early American garb greeted them, checked their reservations, and led them through the pale green colonial rooms to their table.

Rob seated Amy, who was enthusiastic over the old restaurant. "To use a cliché," she said, "it's as if we've stepped into the pages of history."

"It's so different for Californians," Rob mused as he settled into the chair beside her. "We're more accustomed to Spanish land grants and mission history. Here,

155

there's more of a feeling of national history. You should see where we're staying in Washington—"

As he enthused over their accommodations, Amy took note of the seating arrangement. Mark was seated to her right at the head of the table, Glynia on the other side of him, flanked by Thom and then Valerie at the other end. From the way Glynia was holding Mark's attention with something about a new modeling assignment in Egypt, onlookers would assume they were together . . . and that Amy was with Rob.

A waiter in colonial attire handed her the menu with a flourish. "Good evening, milady."

"Good evening, sir." She would enjoy herself no matter how difficult the evening might be, she decided.

After she ordered prime rib, Rob launched into an animated travelogue, detailing the sights they had encountered on his family's first cross-country trip. He made it so interesting that Amy almost wished she had been with them. Perhaps she was making a mistake, she thought, making a quick assessment of Mark.

As if reading her mind, Mark turned a questioning look on her, holding her gaze so warmly that she might have been in his arms. No—she had made no mistake. Mark was the man she loved. And he had said he was falling in love with her, even if he hadn't quite been willing to pronounce the more definitive *I love you*.

Yet, as the evening progressed, Glynia's presence made the time increasingly unpleasant. Not only was her interest in Mark obvious, but her beauty was breathtaking, drawing the attention of other diners in the room. How could Mark resist her wiles? Her coy chatter was directed exclusively to him. And when he attempted to draw Amy into the conversation, Glynia pouted.

By the time coffee and dessert were served, the woman finally deigned to address Amy. "Is this your first visit to the East Coast?"

"Yes, it is," Amy replied, then to fill the awkward silence added, "It's fascinating, isn't it?"

Glynia directed an incredulous look at Mark, only to receive a frown. Undaunted, she smiled smugly at Amy.

"I suppose so, though none of this is new to me. I attended boarding school in New England for several years, you know."

Amy did know, of course. Everyone knew. She looked to Mark for help, but he was deep in conversation with Thom.

Rob came to her rescue. "Why did you choose New England?"

Glynia paused before smiling engagingly. "The schools, of course, are outstanding here—the best in the country. I wouldn't have settled for less."

Amy concentrated on the hurricane lamp with its flickering candle. It was common knowledge that Glynia had been hustled off to boarding school during her mother's second divorce and that Glynia was by no means a scholar. . . . Before Amy was tempted to utter a cutting remark, she made a stab at her pecan pie.

When she looked up at Mark over a forkful of the luscious dessert, she was astonished to see his grateful expression. So he hadn't missed their interchange after all. While Glynia was concentrating on Rob, who was politely questioning her about her experiences, Mark took the opportunity to mouth a confidential, "Thanks."

Thanks—for what? Why was he concerned about Glynia? Did some dire problem lurk beneath that sophisticated veneer?

After dinner they roamed the picturesque cobblestone streets of Alexandria, admiring the shops and restaurants, finally wandering to Market Square. Here a young surveyor by the name of Washington had helped to plan the city streets. Later, as the owner of Mount Vernon, he had sent produce from the fields to be sold here on the Square.

"It seems that, wherever we go, we can't escape George Washington," Amy said with a wry laugh to Mark. But he was preoccupied with Glynia, who had twisted her ankle on the brick paving and was leaning on his shoulder for support as he examined her high-heeled sandal.

"We've run into Washington everywhere ourselves,"

Rob commented, and proceeded to tell about his family's first sight of the capital city, floodlighted in the darkness.

"I saw it for the first time last night too," Amy responded, her spirits lifting at the memory. When Rob gave her a curious look, she hurried on, "I started my research for the Washington report today. Tell me everything you think I should see."

Rob appeared pleased to be asked and lost no time in outlining an itinerary, though Amy had covered many of the sites already.

They continued to stroll through the delightful old town on their way down to the Potomac River. Lovely as the evening was, Amy felt relieved when Mark suggested they return to Aunt Alicia's. Rob would pick up his car there and drop Glynia off at the hotel where she was staying with her parents.

Later, when the couple drove away, Mark took Amy's hand and started up the brick sidewalk. "I'm sorry about the way things turned out. Glynia's going through a rough time." He unlocked the front door. "I hope you understand."

Amy dredged up a smile. "I know. You and Glynia go back a long way." She only wished that the memory of Glynia's green nightgown hanging on his bathroom door hadn't returned to haunt her again.

"I can't say that seeing you and Rob together makes me terribly happy either."

"Mark, you know he's only a friend—"

He looked only slightly relieved, then shot a sidelong look at Valerie and Thom behind them. "Let's find a more private place—the dining room. Come on."

Breathless, she willingly allowed him to lead her, only vaguely aware of Val and Thom slipping into the parlor across the hallway.

A dim stream of light filtered in through the half-opened double doors, illuminating the barely restrained passion on Mark's face. "Amy—," he whispered as his arms drew her to him and his mouth tilted down to hers. "What am I going to do about you?"

Her heart went out to him and her fingers found the

thick hair at the nape of his neck. *Love me, just love me,* she pled wordlessly.

Minutes later the front door opened, and the stairway light snapped on. "Where is everyone?" It was Aunt Alicia, peering about, followed by a laughing Catherine and Dr. Marston.

Thom chuckled. "Caught again!"

Aunt Alicia rallied. "Don't let us stop you! I'm glad to see that this old parlor is still good for courting! Excuse us—we're on our way upstairs."

Amy felt like giggling. On the other hand, it was one thing for Val and Thom to be caught in a passionate clinch, but quite another for herself and Mark, as matters now stood. Fortunately the footsteps moved on upstairs. After they were gone, Mark whispered with amusement, "I feel like a little boy with my hand in the cookie jar."

A bubble of laughter escaped her. "And am I a cookie?"

"Even more delicious."

"Oh, my!" she responded, and, remembering his partiality to cookies, decided it was time to wrest herself from his arms.

Saturday morning passed in such a flurry of activity that there was scarcely time for brunch before the wedding rehearsal with Aunt Alicia's minister, Dr. Rumsfeld.

At first Amy felt uneasy around the minister, never having been in such close proximity to a man of the cloth for any great length of time. But the middle-aged Dr. Rumsfeld looked very human in his slacks and open-necked shirt; in fact, he was quite down-to-earth, not spouting holy platitudes as she had expected. Thom had met him months ago while arranging for the wedding with Aunt Alicia, and he and Val had been counseled by Dr. Rumsfeld earlier this week. They seemed very fond of him.

"Is this where we'll have the string quintet?" Dr. Rumsfeld asked as they prepared for the rehearsal.

"Yes," Catherine replied. "They'll be playing while Alicia and I greet guests at the front door."

"The chairs for guests will be set up through the middle of the room," Dr. Marston explained, "leaving space for us to pass around on this side."

The chairs were to be delivered in a few hours. Plans had been made for every detail of the wedding. At precisely two o'clock Amy was to start down the impressive staircase; Mark would await her below, then escort her into the parlor, where the ceremony would take place. Then they would wait with Thom, the minister, and the assembled guests while Valerie and her father made their way down the staircase and into the parlor.

After the run-through, Valerie sighed. "Why can't we get it right?"

Aunt Alicia laughed unconcernedly. "This old parlor has known only perfect weddings, including your mother's and father's. But it seems a tradition to run through at least three rehearsals. Now let's take it again from the top!"

Even though they were dressed casually in slacks, Amy and Valerie had donned their high-heeled wedding shoes for their practice walks down the stairway. As Amy made her way slowly down the steps the second time, she felt more certain of her footing and glanced at Mark. He was smiling up at her as though unaware there was anyone else in the world. At the bottom of the stairs, he took her arm and ushered her into the parlor where the minister waited.

After the third run-through Aunt Alicia said with a twinkle in her brown eyes. "I do believe that's the best rehearsal this old parlor has ever seen."

"I prayed hard enough," Valerie said.

"Good for you, dear," Catherine smiled. "And don't forget tomorrow."

Valerie promised, "Believe me, that's one time I won't forget!"

Despite their light-hearted banter, Amy again sensed that Val's newfound faith was real.

That night at the rehearsal dinner in a stately Georgian club, Mark was more attentive than ever. Even though the two of them were surrounded with aunts, uncles, and cousins—since Val and Thom had dispensed with the tradition of confining the evening to the principals of the wedding—Mark continued to bestow adoring glances upon her.

When one of the elderly aunts asked Amy, "Is there another wedding in the offing?" Amy felt her cheeks redden.

The aunt patted her hand. "I shouldn't have asked, dear, but when you get to be my age, it seems more important to know things in advance. I have a feeling that there will be!"

Amy attempted a noncommittal smile. Surely Mark would make his intentions known soon. Still, it wouldn't be right to detract in any way from Valerie's and Thom's own special time. No doubt that was what was holding back Mark's total declaration of love.

When they returned to Aunt Alicia's house after the dinner, Mark hung back with her, allowing the others to enter first, then lingering behind in the warm June air. As he kissed her in the moonlight, she felt certain that it was no longer a matter of his falling in love with her, but that he, too, had arrived at that breathtaking destination. But when, if ever, would he say those wonderful words of commitment?

When Amy and Val awakened the next morning, it seemed impossible that the day of the wedding had actually dawned. Sunshine beamed through their windows, gilding everything in its path—a promise of the joy to come.

The morning hours flew and, just before two o'clock, Amy found herself fastening the diminutive white-covered buttons on the back of her sister's wedding gown.

"You must be the most beautiful bride who's ever walked the earth," Amy observed. "Just wait till Thom sees you! You've never looked lovelier."

Val's white gown, an old-fashioned confection with

ruffles and ribbons, suited her and the historic house perfectly. She wore her honey-blond hair in a soft pageboy, emphasizing her natural beauty.

The full-length mirror mounted on the antique stand reflected Valerie's smile. "Thanks, Amy. It's happiness."

"No-o-o, I don't think so. At least, not just happiness alone. There's something about you and Thom and the wedding that's so right." Amy tried to find the words. "It's not just you two . . . or the ribbons and ruffles on your gown. It's that everything seems so—*intended*."

"I believe it was," she replied with utter confidence. "I hope you'll feel the same way someday and want to wear this gown." She gave an almost self-conscious laugh. "I left an ample hem in it with that in mind."

"Oh, Val, I'd love to wear it someday—and I love you for thinking of it!" How she wished she were wearing it today as she took Mark's arm at the foot of the stairs.

Val only smiled as she placed the simple white circlet and veil on her head.

Catching a last glimpse of herself in the mirror, Amy hoped that Mark would approve of her beruffled and beribboned turquoise gown, patterned after Val's. It was charmingly old-fashioned, as was the beautiful French twist that Val had created of her hair. Coaxing wisps to curl around her face with her fingertips, Amy nearly jumped when the quiet tapping sounded at their bedroom door.

"Time to go, ladies," Dr. Marston called in a low voice from the hallway. "The fellows are starting down the back stairs."

"Coming!" Val returned quickly.

Feeling a new twinge of anxiety, Amy took up her bouquet, an asymmetrical cascade of pink rosebuds, white jasmine, and small green ivy with an abundance of trailing turquoise ribbons the shade of her dress. The pink roses brought to mind those that Mark had given her that wonderful afternoon in San Francisco.

"Ready, Val?" she asked and was surprised to see Val's head bowed in prayer.

Val opened her eyes. "Ready." Smiling serenely, she accepted her bridal bouquet—a cascade like Amy's, except for the white roses among the jasmine and ivy, and white trailing ribbons matching the ribbons of her white gown.

In the hallway Dr. Marston, looking distinguished in his black tuxedo, waited to escort Valerie downstairs. Below, the string quintet could be heard playing *Oh, Promise Me*, signaling that Mark and Thom should be in their places downstairs.

"Hurry!" Dr. Marston urged.

Amy blinked away the dewiness at her lashes, then stood with Val just to the side of the stairwell, listening to the final strains of the melody.

After a pause, the string quintet began the resounding opening chords of Wagner's "The Bridal March" from *Lohengrin*. The powerful fortissimo chords vibrated through the stairwell. At her musical cue Amy cast a hopeful glance at Val and, remembering to smile, started her slow journey down the stairs, the bouquet in her hands shaking slightly, giving off the fragrance of jasmine and roses.

Mark was waiting at the foot of the stairs, resplendent in his black tuxedo. As she moved down the steps to the majestic strains of the music, his unwavering gaze lent her assurance, then he was reaching out to take her hand, drawing it through his arm, and together they turned toward the guests in the parlor. It seemed an eternity as they moved in step with the music through the room and toward the improvised altar flanked by pink roses and ivy.

Then at last there was Dr. Rumsfeld—and Thom, looking achingly solemn. Mark ushered Amy to her designated place, then moved on to stand behind his brother.

Seven triumphal notes heralded the bride's entrance, and everyone turned to watch Valerie's descent down the stairway. At first there was only the sight of her white gown with its ruffles and ribbons, then the beautiful white bouquet with its trailing ivy, and then, on Dr.

163

Marston's arm, Val smiling so beatifically that she might have been an angel. Her hazel eyes turned to Thom, and their gaze held with such love that tears welled in Amy's eyes. If only their own father and mother might be here, she reflected as Val took her place next to Thom.

Dr. Rumsfeld began the service. "Dearly beloved, we are gathered together here in the sight of God and in the presence of these witnesses to join together this man and this woman in holy matrimony, which is an honorable estate, signifying unto us the mystical union which exists between Christ and His church—"

Calmer, Amy's gaze rested on the candelabra arrangement on the mantel as she listened. ". . . the union of husband and wife in heart, body, and mind is intended by God for their mutual joy, for the help and comfort given one another in prosperity and adversity—" Strange, Amy didn't recall ever having heard those vows before. Did God really intend marriage for the mutual joy of husband and wife? For their comfort in all circumstances?

"Love is always patient and kind, never jealous nor boastful; never arrogant nor rude. Love does not insist upon its own way; it is not irritable nor resentful; it does not rejoice at wrong, but rejoices in right. Love withstands all things, believes all things, hopes all things; love perseveres—" Then the minister was saying to Dr. Marston, "Who giveth this woman to be married to this man?"

Dr. Marston said firmly, "In the names of her departed mother and father, I do."

Was it possible that somehow their mother and dad knew of this wedding? Amy wondered with misty eyes. Were they looking down from heaven now? Bringing her thoughts back to the ceremony, she readied Thom's gold wedding band as the vows began.

"I, Thomas, take thee, Valerie, to be my wedded wife, to have and to hold, from this day forward, for better, for worse, for richer, for poorer, in sickness and in health, to love and to cherish, as long as we both shall live."

Then Val was repeating: ". . . to be my wedded

164

husband, to have and to hold, to love and to cherish, as long as we both shall live.''

Amy felt Mark's gaze resting on her and she looked down at her quivering bouquet, reminding herself that the exchange of the rings was upon them.

Moments later, the minister blessed the bridal couple, and Thom was saying, ''In token and pledge of our constant faith and abiding love, with this ring I thee wed.''

Val's voice was soft, full of love as she repeated the vow, and then the minister pronounced the final words: ''Forasmuch as Thomas and Valerie have consented together in holy wedlock, and have witnessed the same before God and this company, and hereto have pledged their faith each to the other, and have declared the same by joining hands and by giving and receiving rings; I pronounce them man and wife. Those whom God hath joined together, let not man put asunder.''

The final prayer ended, ''Grant that their wills may be so knit together in your will, and their spirits in your spirit, that they may grow in love and peace with you and one another all the days of their life. Give them such fulfillment of their mutual affection that they may reach out in love and concern for others. Amen.'' Dr. Rumsfeld turned to Thom. ''You may now kiss the bride.''

Holding Val's bouquet, Amy fought back tears as they kissed almost reverently, aware that Mark's eyes were on her. When Val turned for her bouquet, the quintet began to play the recessional. Mark offered his arm to Amy, his eyes shining, and they followed the newlyweds through the smiling guests.

Outside in the balmy air of the beautiful garden, Amy kissed Val and Thom. ''You two look so happy that I'm afraid you're going to float away!''

''We just might!'' they agreed. ''But not before we greet all the people who came to wish us well.''

The Marstons were behind them, kissing and embracing the bridal pair, then Mark and Amy. The very air around them was charged with joy. Mark laughingly caught Amy in his arms, dropping a kiss on her cheek before the guests flooded out into the sunshine, and everyone was swept up in congratulatory embraces. There were hugs from beaming cousins, aunts, and uncles from her mother's and father's families and handshakes from the Marston relatives, but it was the kiss and embrace from Mark that Amy held in her memory, even while others passed through the reception line.

Following the relatives, Glynia arrived in a cloud of pale green silk. She stepped past Amy after a cool handshake and turned her face to receive Mark's kiss. "Nice wedding."

"Yes," Mark said, "yes, it is."

"Though I favor a fast one in Las Vegas if one *must* tie the proverbial knot," Glynia laughed as she moved on down the reception line.

Amy forced a smile as she greeted Glynia's parents, the Benningtons. Just behind them were Thom's university friends and Rob, handsome in a dark blue suit, and his delighted parents lavishing compliments on her.

The string quintet moved to the spacious terrace where caterers served elegant canapés and punch from damask-covered tables. When the guests had all passed through the reception line, there were pictures to be taken, with the well-manicured grounds as a backdrop and toasts on the tree-shaded terrace.

It seemed only a short time later that Valerie was downstairs in a cream raw silk outfit, Thom in a dark suit, ready to leave for their three-day honeymoon in Boston.

"Time to throw the bouquet!" someone called out. "All eligible ladies onto the terrace."

Feeling rather foolish, Amy stepped forward hesitantly, then realized that she was not alone. Several others had joined her, including Glynia. Amy hoped Mark would not get the wrong idea—the last thing he needed was to feel trapped. At just that moment Val smiled at her, then took a precise bead on her position before turning her back to toss the bouquet over her shoulder.

As it sailed unerringly toward her, Amy reached out. But at the last moment, Glynia shoved her aside and snatched the bouquet away, scattering white rose petals across the terrace.

For a second Amy lost her balance, but a relative moved forward to stop her fall. Incensed at Glynia's rude behavior, Amy opened her mouth to protest, but there was no time. The newlyweds were making their departure in a shower of rice.

"Have a wonderful honeymoon!" she called after them, quickly forgetting her embarrassment and Glynia's ugly scene in her happiness for her sister and new brother-in-law.

Within minutes, they had sped away in Thom's car.

The long-awaited wedding was actually over and, delighted as she was for Val and Thom, Amy could not stem the sudden wash of emotion that flooded her. Now she was most certainly on her own.

She attempted to set the thought aside, looking about for Mark, but he was nowhere in sight. He was undoubtedly seeing Thom and Val to the airport. No, the arrangements had been changed. Several guests made tentative moves to leave, but Aunt Alicia encouraged everyone to stay and visit, and many lingered.

The quintet began the romantic strains of *Lara's Song*, and Rob came to her side with an adoring gaze in his brown eyes. "Would you like to take a walk around the grounds?"

She glanced frantically about for Mark, but he was still missing, and Rob awaited her answer. "That would be nice, Rob. It's so beautiful here—"

As they wandered around the far end of the house, admiring the grounds and the blue sky with its puffy white clouds, he suddenly slipped an arm around her waist and pulled her to him, his breath warm against her hair. "I hope you realize how much I care about you, Amy."

She fumbled for words. What could she possibly say in reply? She cared for only one man.

After a moment Rob seemed to understand her unspoken reaction and added a low, "I can wait."

"I'm sorry, Rob." Quivering, she bit her lower lip as they returned to the others. Where was Mark? And, for that matter, where was Glynia? The Benningtons were seated at a table near Aunt Alicia, so Glynia was no doubt still around too.

A horrifying premonition overcame her and, as they reached the terrace, she apologized, "If you'll excuse me, Rob, I have something to do in the house."

The caterers were still bustling about the kitchen, and she hurried on to the parlor, but there was no sign of Mark or Glynia anywhere. She was about to leave, when she heard the sound of a chair scraping a bare floor. Trembling, she continued across the hallway to the dining room, where the double doors were slightly ajar. Hesitating, she summoned her courage and pushed the door open.

The scene before her was as unreal as if she had stepped onto a stage: Glynia with her arms encircling Mark's neck, her lips tilting up toward his.

It was a moment before the reality of the situation penetrated her brain and she gasped, "Mark—!"

His blue eyes widened, turning to her as he pulled away from Glynia.

"How could you?!" she cried out, aware that her words sounded as theatrical as the scene being played out before her. "How could you, Mark?" she flared again from the depths of her anguish. She would have slapped his incredulous face with the phrase again if one of the caterer's assistants hadn't peered out from the kitchen at that moment, taking it all in.

Turning, she ran wildly down the hallway, composing herself only slightly at the door. Nearly obscured by her heartbreak and indignation, the crowd of guests across the lawn on the side terrace blurred so that they might have been subjects in a French Impressionist painting. She hurried out to join them.

Seeing her, Rob rose from his chair on the terrace, an expression of confusion crossing his face. "What's wrong, Amy?" he asked solicitously.

"It's just that—that I wanted to sit with you," she said

breathlessly and knew from the frown on his brow that he didn't quite believe her.

He pulled out a chair for her, and a speculative glimmer filled his brown eyes. "Mark and Glynia?"

She nodded, tears threatening, then spilling down her cheeks. She had managed to control her emotions throughout the wedding ceremony, but there was no stopping them now.

"I knew he'd hurt you," Rob muttered angrily as he handed over his handkerchief. "I knew he would! And I've never wanted to do anything more than give him the beating of a lifetime right now!"

"No—please. Let's don't do anything to spoil Val's wedding!"

He inhaled deeply, fists clenched, but he sat down again. Reaching for her hand, he patted it clumsily, then drew it to his lips.

"Please, Rob—" Amy felt her gaze drawn toward the house. Mark stood just outside the parlor door. He turned and spoke to Glynia, who was observing from within. Amy remembered the jade nightgown and decided there was no longer any question as to why Mark had been so reluctant to commit himself to her. Glynia was the one he had wanted all along!

Rob squeezed her hand reassuringly, his eyes filling with hope.

Oh, Rob, I'm just going to hurt you too! Even through her pain, she felt a stirring of compassion for him. Comforting as Rob's presence might be, she couldn't give him the kind of false hope that Mark had held out to her for so long. She would have to tell him as kindly as possible that there could never be anything but friendship between them.

Taking a deep breath, she began to explain—

CHAPTER 11

EARLY THE NEXT MORNING Amy's plane lifted off the
runway at National Airport, and she glanced disconso-
lately out the window, catching final glimpses of the
Washington Monument, the White House, and the
Pentagon before they flew along the Potomac River.

She had so looked forward to completing her research
on the city and then going on to Boston with Mark. But
any woman would be thrilled to work for Mark Marston.
Perhaps he had already found a replacement employee—
as easily as he had found someone to fill the void in his
heart.

Her note to him had been caustic enough: *Normally I
don't back out when I've given my word, but I'm sure
you won't have any trouble finding someone to finish the
research. I'll send the Philadelphia report to your office.
Amy Curtis.* She had added her last name with a flash of
venom, as though he might confuse her with countless
other Amys.

No one had been awake when she'd left, and she had
dashed off thank-you notes to the Marstons and Aunt
Alicia. If necessary, they would have to consider her an
unmannered ingrate before she would divulge yesterday's scene between Mark and Glynia. It had been

especially shattering that Mark had chosen the same setting for his—his dalliance with Glynia . . . the dining room where he had kissed Amy so fervently Friday night after their dinner in Alexandria. But then he probably always checked out the discreet corners when he was with women. And Glynia herself was no novice. Their mutual interest had endured for years.

It was impossible to force the heartbreaking image from her mind. Last night after the guests had departed, only her fury had enabled her to pack, change her flight reservations, and order a taxi for this morning. She hadn't slept more than two hours. She didn't even want to think about how Val and Thom would construe her sudden departure.

The flight attendant stopped by with a breakfast tray, but Amy waved it away. "No, thank you, I'm going to try to sleep instead."

And, to her amazement, she slept . . . and slept.

When the plane finally landed in Los Angeles, she felt drugged from sleep and disturbed dreams, but managed to collect her luggage and catch the airport bus to Santa Rosita, then a taxi to the Marstons' house, where she picked up Gramp's old Chevy. With the three-hour time change, it was only midafternoon as she parked in front of her apartment building, but she wanted nothing more than to go straight to bed.

Rhea Smithers, the apartment manager, was delighted to find her at the door, yet a trifle surprised too. "How can you possibly move in tonight, honey?" she asked. "Your furniture isn't here. You've no bed—"

"Believe me, I'm tired enough to sleep on the carpeting," Amy assured her. "I feel as if I could sleep for days."

But the woman insisted on loaning her an old sleeping bag and some linens.

"Are you sure you're not sick?" Mrs. Smithers persisted as she followed Amy up the stairs, her arms laden with blankets, towels, the sleeping bag and a pillow. "You look terrible. I hope it's not that young man—"

"Young man?" Amy's mind flashed to Mark.

"The one who brought you here last week."

"No, Rob's only a friend." At least she hoped that was still true. He had been hurt too.

Finally she was in the small studio apartment, dropping the heavy suitcases on the new carpeting, then rubbing her sore shoulders while Rhea deposited the sleeping bag and linens on the breakfast bar. The apartment smelled of carpeting and paint, fresh and clean.

"Isn't it lovely?" Rhea asked, admiring the rooms.

"Yes, it is. Far more attractive than I imagined it might be." Despite its small size, the high slanted ceiling and the crisp white walls imparted an airy effect, while the dark wooden cabinets and terra cotta tones of the carpeting lent warmth.

"I asked the workmen to finish your apartment first. I had a feeling you might need it early."

"Oh?"

Rhea started for the door, her brown eyes radiating the same kindly concern that Catherine Marston often turned on her. "Just stop by if you need anything else . . . and feel free to use my phone till yours is in."

The woman's kindness touched a lonely chord in Amy's heart, and she found herself saying, "Thank you for everything . . . thank you for caring."

"Isn't that what God wants us to do here on earth?" Rhea remarked before she closed the door behind her.

What God wants us to do here on earth? Amy's mind repeated groggily. She wasn't so sure about Him. She had prayed that He would work everything out, and look what had happened! True, the wedding had come off without a hitch. But, immediately afterward, there had been the horrible scene with Mark and Glynia. Why hadn't He worked that out too? She had prayed specifically that He would take care of matters between her and Mark. Was this the answer? Catherine had once said that God had three answers: yes, no, and later. Apparently His answer concerning her relationship with Mark was a resounding *No!*

When she lay down on top of the sleeping bag, Amy continued to ponder the subject, and she arrived at a conclusion: For some reason known only to Him, God didn't want them together here on earth. Most likely it was for her own good. All this time she had been trying to give God orders, if and when she thought of Him.

From now on, Lord, I leave everything in Your hands, she half-thought, half-prayed.

Be still. Be calm, an inner voice seemed to say.

Amy awakened the next morning with a peculiar sense of assurance that all would be well, much as she had experienced the day she and Mark had swum out beyond the ocean's breakers.

After dressing in a turquoise T-shirt and bermudas, she felt ready to begin to move her things in. She searched her wallet for the card of a neighborhood trucker, then hurried downstairs to use the manager's phone. The trucker would have to bring the things from the mini-warehouse: Gramp's brown hide-a-bed, oak end tables, lamps, a coffee table, occasional chairs, and, of course, the cartons of household supplies. Fortunately, he could deliver this afternoon. Within the next hour, she had made arrangements for utilities and a phone, although the latter would not be installed until Friday.

Rhea seemed delighted with her company, and set out coffee and sliced date nut bread for Amy to enjoy between the phone calls. "How much better you're looking this morning," she commented. "It's going to be fun having such a beautiful neighbor."

Amy set her coffee cup down. "Beautiful?" she inquired ruefully. If she were beautiful, Mark hadn't seemed to notice!

Rhea's gaze moved up over her steaming coffee and rested on Amy's eyes. "You don't even realize that you're attractive, do you?"

She recalled that Mark had once said almost the same thing. "No, I'm afraid I don't really see myself that way. So much of my life I've been overweight."

"Then you've probably acquired a better sense of

values than if you'd looked like this all your life. It seems that many beautiful women think being decorative is all that's required of them." She smiled reassuringly. "I'm sure we're going to have streams of young men wearing out your doorbell as soon as they know you're here."

"I doubt it. I don't seem to have much success with men," Amy confessed. "In fact, I've just been hurt— very badly. That's why I arrived early."

"Oh, dear . . . I'm so sorry to have brought up the subject."

"I suppose I should have kept it to myself, but just telling someone else seems to help."

"I'm here anytime you need someone to listen. I know a little about pain myself. The good news is that it can be overcome."

Amy stood to leave, preferring not to hear any bromides about time healing all wounds or hope springing eternally. "Thanks, Mrs. Smithers."

"Please call me Rhea."

Amy nodded. "Thanks, Rhea." She felt grateful to find a new friend, even though the woman was probably old enough to be her mother. "Time for me to get busy. I have an empty refrigerator and cabinets to fill."

"I'm going to a church luncheon for a few hours," Rhea said. "Take my extra key with you in case you want to use the phone."

"I couldn't. I appreciate your trust, but you scarcely know me."

Rhea placed the key in her hand and folded her fingers over it. "I know you well enough. You remind me of myself when I was your age." She had already wrapped three slices of the homemade date nut bread in plastic. "Here, take them with you. I insist. You'll save me from working off even more calories."

By Friday afternoon Amy was well established in her apartment, although the telephone, mounted over the kitchen counter, had yet to ring. Her happiness, she decided, was dependent upon staying very busy, and she had managed that easily this week. Niggling thoughts that Rhea might intrude too much had proven groundless, since the woman had an extremely busy life of her own in addition to managing the ten apartments in the building.

Saturday morning, after washing Gramp's car in the apartment building's carport area, Amy purchased plants and repotted them in new terra cotta containers outside on her small balcony. She hung the Boston fern near the kitchen window, placed the ficus benjamina and red geraniums on the balcony, and the tiny palm on the dark oak coffee table. Finally it was all done and she stood back to admire her accomplishments. Only now there was nothing left to do for another week until her summer classes began. She could read or write poetry, but she was not in the mood, and Gramp's old television set was out for repairs. A sense of despair slowly descended over her.

Worse, she could no longer hold her thoughts of Mark at bay. What if she could never forget him? She recalled how stunned she'd been the day he picked her up and helped her move from Gramp's house. "You certainly look surprised," he had said with that hint of amusement around his lips. He'd slid his dark glasses up into his hair in that characteristic gesture of his. And that night his voice had caressed her name in the billowing fog when he urged her to go to San Francisco. How she had fled upstairs to her room! Even then she must have subconsciously foreseen this day.

And then there had been the mix-up about the hotel room in San Francisco, when they had ended up sharing a suite—and that devastating first kiss. Her mind rushed past the unfortunate dinner with Tony and his pick-up to the day she and Mark had made up—when she'd tripped into his arms in the tower at Princeton. *I think I love you.* he had said, and, tentative though his words were, at that moment they had been enough. Strange, she had prayed at the Valley Forge chapel and not too much later, Mark had pulled off the road, and they had made up again. *I've been falling in love with you,* he had said. And there had been that breathtaking kiss in Aunt Alicia's dining

175

room—but no definite *I love you*. Then Glynia had come upon the scene.

Fool! Amy chided herself. What a fool she had been! A sob tore through her, then another and another until she dissolved in a torrent of hot tears. *Why, God? Oh, why?* she asked as sobs wracked her body. *Why couldn't things have gone right?*

It was a long time before she blew her nose and washed the tears from her face. She would have to do something to avoid this depression, she decided, and for some reason, it occurred to her to look for the religion page in the morning paper. Perhaps she would go to church tomorrow morning. It couldn't hurt—could it? At least going to church would give her something to do.

Scanning the list of churches in the city, she discovered that the one nearest her apartment was the church Mark's grandfather had pastored. She clipped out the information and started determinedly for her closet. She now had a reason to select something to wear, a reason to set her alarm clock, a reason for going on. Perhaps that was what was really important in life—purpose.

The next morning was warm and sunny, and Amy drove Gramp's old blue car to the church, not wanting to walk so far in her high-heeled sandals. Just around the corner from the old Spanish-style church, she found a parking space.

"Amy—is that you?"

To her surprise she saw Rhea Smithers just arriving too, hurrying along the sidewalk. Amy climbed out of the car, closing the door behind her.

Rhea extended her hand, smiling delightedly. "I'm so happy to see you."

"Is this your church?"

"It certainly is. I've been attending for the past ten years—ever since I became a Christian."

"Oh, really?" What a curious thing to say—*ever since I became a Christian*, she thought, but the church bells pealing out their welcome distracted her. A throng of people funneled to the entrance, and she and Rhea followed along.

As they climbed a short flight of stairs, Rhea said, "I'd ask you to join me, but I'm serving during the coffee hour, so I have to sit near the back door."

"Oh, I don't mind," Amy replied with a twinge of nervousness as Rhea guided her to an elderly couple greeting people at the door.

She found herself swept along with the worshipers. Suddenly she was in the sanctuary, feeling the swirl of organ music compelling her forward. Amy felt a moment's panic. It had been so many years since her Sunday school days; she had rarely been inside the walls of a church, except recently as a tourist. As a matter of fact, she had visited three churches—Grace Cathedral in San Francisco, the Valley Forge Chapel, and Christ Church in Philadelphia—all quite different in architecture, but sharing a common bond—the love and adoration of God. Was God trying to get through to her?

She and Rhea were no sooner settled in the second to the last pew than the organ began an anthem, one she had heard Catherine sing. She found the page in the hymnal as music flooded the church like a brilliant sunrise. "Joyful, joyful, we adore thee, God of glory, Lord of love . . ."

Amy joined in softly, her voice quavering, ". . . hearts unfold like flowers before Thee, opening to the sun above . . ." *Hearts unfold . . . ?* Yes, she thought, her heart had been unfolding to God since that first visit to Grace Cathedral, from her prayer at Valley Forge and the reverence she had felt so deeply at Christ Church. She sang on, a surge of hope in her spirit. ". . . Melt the clouds of sin and sadness, drive the dark of doubt away, giver of immortal gladness, fill us with the light of day . . ." By the third verse, the words had become her own prayer of exultation: "Thou art giving and forgiving, Ever blessing, ever blest, Well-spring of the joy of living . . ."

A gray-haired minister stood in the pulpit greeting the congregation, an enormous dark wooden cross on the white wall behind him. As the service proceeded, Amy settled back to listen. The sermon dealt with God dwelling in one's heart by faith, not by works . . . that faith was a gift of God.

At the end of the sermon the minister said, "God, through Christ, will not only forgive us of our sins, but will cast them into the deepest sea. He removes them from Himself and from us as far as the East is from the West. If you feel an emptiness, a loneliness, a longing for completion in your spirit, God is the one you are searching for. He is the one who will make you feel whole. And if you would like to dedicate or rededicate your life to the Lord, please repeat this prayer."

Amy bowed her head with a sense of expectation.

"Dear Heavenly Father, I need You," the minister began.

"Dear Heavenly Father," she repeated softly but with certainty, "I need You." She was scarcely aware that many others in the congregation were praying too as she followed the minister's words with growing conviction. "I acknowledge that I've been directing my own life and, that as a result, I've sinned against You. As I confess my sins, I realize that Christ promised immediate and complete forgiveness through His death on the cross. I invite Christ to be on the throne of my life. Fill me with the Holy Spirit as You commanded me to be filled and as You promised in Your Word if I prayed in faith. I pray this in the name of Jesus Christ . . . and thank You. Amen."

Tears clung to her lashes, but Amy's heart soared with gratitude and she felt wonderfully cleansed. She understood for the first time that Christ was the bridge to God, the way to experience His love. She silently prayed, "Make me the kind of person You want me to be."

A joyous serenity filled her, and she knew that this was what she had been seeking. She needed God in her life, just as He had been the center of her parents' life, and the Marstons' and Valerie's. If Mark was not a part of God's plan for her, then . . . that would have to be all right too . . . though the minister had added that God loved everyone so much He would never demand anything that would not be the very best for that person . . . that He had a wonderful plan for each life.

They stood as the service drew to a close, and Amy joined in singing *Amazing Grace*. She realized she had a lifetime of learning ahead to become the kind of person God wanted her to be, but now she had time . . . forever . . . eternity! It seemed as if the secrets of the universe had begun to open to her little by little, as if her own understanding was rearranging itself in her head around His truth, His wisdom.

"See you," Rhea whispered mid-hymn and quietly left to ready things for the coffee hour.

Amy turned slightly to watch her leave. To her astonishment she saw Mark in the row behind her, singing the words of the hymn with a wondrous light in his blue eyes as they met hers.

He stepped around to take Rhea's place in the pew, still singing in his rich baritone: "When we've been there ten thousand years, bright shining as the sun, we've no less days to sing God's praise than when we first begun."

Such a thrill rushed through Amy that there was no thought of protest when he took her hand in his. Together they bowed for the benediction.

When the service ended, Mark asked, "Did you know this was my grandfather's church?"

"Yes, I did. But I surely didn't expect to see you here!" she replied. "And, you—did you know I was here?"

"Not until I parked behind your Gramp's car. I knew then that something wonderful was in store for us because—" He looked around at the church building. "Because this is the church where God called that little six-year-old boy to be a minister . . . and because, after you left Alexandria, I realized my foolishness. I began to see how pointless my life was becoming . . . that it seemed to be leading nowhere. And finally . . . after years of running from Him, I rededicated my life to the Lord."

Her voice was hushed. "You've rededicated your life to Him?"

"Yes."

It seemed impossible, entirely too much to accept. She

reflected upon what people called God's mysterious ways, the astonishing circumstances so often termed coincidence. "You may not believe this," she began, "but I've committed my life to Him too . . . this morning . . . here. . . ."

Mark looked as incredulous as she felt. "Talk about timing . . ." He hesitated, then said, "Amy, I love you . . . I want to marry you."

"Mark . . . are you sure? You're not just reacting to your grandfather's church or to your new commitment?"

His eyes sparkled. "Amy, didn't you hear me? I said I love you."

"Oh, Mark!" she cried. "I love you too! I've always loved you!" Then to her own stupefaction, she heard herself asking, "But what about Glynia?"

"She's only a childhood friend." His expression grew somber. "She's always been so unhappy and—and unstable that I've felt compelled to try to help her. She's so much like . . ."

"Like Erika?"

"Yes, like Erika, who I've finally forgiven. I guess I've always thought that if I didn't please Glynia, she'd take that—that same rash road, which I now see was half-witted thinking on my part. Glynia doesn't need me. She needs God." He added in an embarrassed but forthright tone, "I know what you must think about finding us like that in the dining room. I didn't kiss her. I wouldn't be surprised if she saw you coming and maneuvered us into that pose."

"I wouldn't be surprised, either," Amy agreed thoughtfully. Glynia had managed to wreak more havoc than snatching the bridal bouquet from her that day—she had accomplished her purpose. Still, Amy was not entirely convinced. "But Glynia's nightgown in your bathroom—"

He reddened. "The apartment actually belongs to *her* friends, and she stays there when she has an assignment in L.A. That's *all* there is to it. You'll just have to believe me, Amy. You're the only woman I've ever loved, and it somehow seems fitting that you were God's instrument to bring me back where I belong. . . .." There was a long pause. "You *will* marry me, won't you?"

Suddenly there was no doubt what God had planned for them. The answer was in her eyes as she said without hesitation, "Oh, Mark . . . yes!" At his look of joy, she asked wryly, "That didn't take much coaxing, did it?"

He caught her in his arms. "Don't think I wasn't prepared to coax, no matter how long it took!"

"Mark . . ." she sighed, nestling into the curve of his shoulder, "do you think we could be married right here in your grandfather's church?"

"Nothing would make me happier!" He glanced around the sanctuary. "Do you think it would be irreverent for me to kiss you right here?"

Noting that everyone except the organist had moved on into the vestibule, Amy shook her head. As his lips trembled against hers, then tenderly held, it was as if she had never been kissed before, as if God were giving them His benediction. Their lingering kiss was the promise of a lifetime of love and commitment and growing together.

Moments later, the organist hit a final chord and called out an amused and enthusiastic, "Amen!"

They moved apart, blushing happily.

At the church door the minister shook their hands, his eyes twinkling as if reading on their faces the momentous event that had just taken place. "You're Mark Marston's grandson, aren't you?"

"Yes, yes, I am. And this is my bride-to-be . . . as of a few moments ago."

The minister beamed. "I can't imagine what in my sermon prompted that response, but it looks like an exceedingly fine idea to me."

As they started down the steps, Mark called back, "I'll be phoning for an appointment. I need to talk with you about . . . about another matter."

Amy pondered the idea that someday Mark might want to follow in his grandfather's footsteps after all. Overwhelming as the thought seemed, she felt sure that, no matter what happened, God would see them through.

Waving good-by to the minister, Mark hurried her out

to his car. "I have some things for you in the trunk. I was going to give them to you at your apartment after church, but here you are instead!"

"Presents in the trunk?" It didn't sound as if it were the most likely place for a ring—

"They're not from me." He smiled at her perplexity. "To add to the suspense, there are actually two presents—one from Mom and one from Valerie."

"What on earth could they be?" she asked as he opened the trunk. He reached in and held out an oddly familiar white box. Puzzled, she lifted off the lid, only to find a neat layer of white tissue. Suddenly she suspected what it was and stripped back the paper. "It's Val's wedding gown!"

He grinned. "She thought you might like it to have it."

Her eyes filled with tears of happiness. "Oh, yes!"

"No tears!" he admonished, dropping a kiss on her forehead. "Besides, there's another gift." He reached into the trunk again and turned around what appeared to be a framed picture.

"The sampler—the sampler your grandmother made!"

"Mom wants to keep it in the family, and she hoped that you—that we might like to have it. I think she meant it as a kind of engagement present for both of us."

"Oh, Mark, I love it!" Realizing the implication of the gift, Amy slanted a shy look at him. "Then you must have told your parents that you were planning to propose."

"Once the Lord got the course He wanted me to take through my thick skull, I couldn't bear to keep it to myself. And, judging by their reaction to the news, I wouldn't be surprised if they hadn't prayed for just that for years."

"You mean—they don't mind losing another son? They want me too?"

Cradling her closer in his arms, Mark said, "Of course they want you! You're already like one of the family. What is that old saying? 'They're not losing a son, they're gaining a daughter.' "

Sighing happily, she tore her eyes from him to gaze at the words embroidered on the old linen sampler:

Earth's crammed with Heaven
And every common bush afire with God;
But only he who sees takes off his shoes,
The rest sit round it and pluck blackberries.
                    Elizabeth Barrett Browning

At last she understood. When people allow God into their lives, they are given spiritual sight to recognize Him in the commonplace, for wherever He is, that is holy ground.

"I feel so very strongly that God intended us for each other, darling," he was saying.

"And I do too." How clearly now she could see God's loving hand in their relationship—bringing them together again after all the years apart, drawing them gently until they made their separate ways to Him, then granting them a love based on Christ as the center of the home that would soon be theirs. Even Glynia had played a part—reminding Mark of a chapter in his life that would now forever be closed because it had been forgiven.

Amy looked up into his shining eyes, and it seemed that they were caught again in a transcendent moment . . . in a golden burst of happiness. Its source, she understood now, was the wondrous and eternal song of joy God had placed in her heart.

ABOUT THE AUTHOR

Elaine L. Schulte has published short stories, articles, and novels worldwide. One of her novels often appears on television.

Her first inspirational novel for Zondervan was *On Wings of Love,* which is set on a Caribbean cruise; her second contemporary novel for the Serenade line, *Echoes of Love,* takes place in the Yucatan in Mexico.

Her two historicals in the Saga line are *Westward, My Love* and *Dreams of Gold.* Set in the mid-1800s, they chronicle the stories of two roommates who are caught up in the era of westward expansion to California. One travels across the United States, in part by covered wagon; the other travels by clipper ship around Cape Horn into the beginnings of the gold rush. Schulte is currently working on the third novel in this series.

Schulte and her husband make their home in Southern California and have two grown sons.

A Letter to Our Readers

Dear Reader:

Welcome to Serenade Books—a series designed to bring you beautiful love stories in the world of inspirational romance. They will uplift you, encourage you, and provide hours of wholesome entertainment, so thousands of readers have testified. That we might better contribute to your reading enjoyment, we would appreciate your taking a few minutes to respond to the following questions and return to:

> Lois Taylor
> Serenade Books
> The Zondervan Publishing House
> 1415 Lake Drive, S.E.
> Grand Rapids, Michigan 49506

1. Did you enjoy reading *Song of Joy?*

   ☐ Very much. I would like to see more books by this author!
   ☐ Moderately
   ☐ I would have enjoyed it more if _____

2. Where did you purchase this book? _____

3. What influenced your decision to purchase this book?

   ☐ Cover   ☐ Back cover copy
   ☐ Title   ☐ Friends
   ☐ Publicity   ☐ Other _____

4. Please rate the following elements from 1 (poor) to 10 (superior).

- ☐ Heroine
- ☐ Hero
- ☐ Setting

- ☐ Plot
- ☐ Inspirational theme
- ☐ Secondary characters

5. What are some inspirational themes you would like to see treated in future books?

_____

_____

6. Please indicate your age range:

- ☐ Under 18
- ☐ 18–24
- ☐ 25–34
- ☐ 35–45
- ☐ 46–55
- ☐ Over 55

Serenade / Saga books are inspirational romances in historical settings, designed to bring you a joyful, heart-lifting reading experience.

Serenade / Saga books available in your local bookstore:

- #1 *Summer Snow*, Sandy Dengler
- #2 *Call Her Blessed*, Jeanette Gilge
- #3 *Ina*, Karen Baker Kletzing
- #4 *Juliana of Clover Hill*, Brenda Knight Graham
- #5 *Song of the Nereids*, Sandy Dengler
- #6 *Anna's Rocking Chair*, Elaine Watson
- #7 *In Love's Own Time*, Susan C. Feldhake
- #8 *Yankee Bride*, Jane Peart
- #9 *Light of My Heart*, Kathleen Karr
- #10 *Love Beyond Surrender*, Susan C. Feldhake
- #11 *All the Days After Sunday*, Jeanette Gilge
- #12 *Winterspring*, Sandy Dengler
- #13 *Hand Me Down the Dawn*, Mary Harwell Sayler
- #14 *Rebel Bride*, Jane Peart
- #15 *Speak Softly, Love*, Kathleen Yapp
- #16 *From This Day Forward*, Kathleen Karr
- #17 *The River Between*, Jacquelyn Cook
- #18 *Valiant Bride*, Jane Peart
- #19 *Wait for the Sun*, Maryn Langer
- #20 *Kincaid of Cripple Creek*, Peggy Darty
- #21 *Love's Gentle Journey*, Kay Cornelius
- #22 *Applegate Landing*, Jean Conrad
- #23 *Beyond the Smoky Curtain*, Mary Harwell Sayler
- #24 *To Dwell in the Land*, Elaine Watson
- #25 *Moon for a Candle*, Maryn Langer
- #26 *The Conviction of Charlotte Grey*, Jeanne Cheyney
- #27 *Opal Fire*, Sandy Dengler
- #28 *Divide the Joy*, Maryn Langer
- #29 *Cimarron Sunset*, Peggy Darty
- #30 *This Rolling Land*, Sandy Dengler
- #31 *The Wind Along the River*, Jacquelyn Cook

Serenade / Serenata books are inspirational romances in contemporary settings, designed to bring you a joyful, heart-lifting reading experience.

Serenade / Serenata books available in your local bookstore:

189

Watch for other books in both the *Serenade/Saga* (historical) and *Serenade/Serenata* (contemporary) series, coming soon.